KING

CLASS AND RELIGION IN THE
LATE VICTORIAN CITY

CROOM HELM SOCIAL HISTORY SERIES

General Editors:
Professor J.F.C. Harrison and Stephen Yeo,
University of Sussex

CHRISTIAN SOCIALISM AND CO–OPERATION IN VICTORIAN ENGLAND
Philip N. Backstrom

THE INDUSTRIAL MUSE
Martha Vicinus

CLASS AND RELIGION IN THE LATE VICTORIAN CITY

Hugh McLeod

CROOM HELM LONDON

© 1974 by Hugh McLeod

Croom Helm Ltd
2-10 St. John's Road, London SW11

ISBN 0–85664–090–5

Printed by Biddles of Guildford

CONTENTS

ABBREVIATIONS
  COS   Charity Organisation Society
  ILP   Independent Labour Party
  LCC   London County Council
   PP   Parliamentary Papers
  PSA   Pleasant Sunday Afternoon
   RC   Royal Commission
   SC   Select Committee
  SDF   Social Democratic Federation

ACKNOWLEDGEMENTS

My greatest debt is to Dr Kitson Clark, who supervised my research at Cambridge. I am grateful to Dr Susan Budd for comments on two chapters and to Dr Geoffrey Rowell for advice on the subject of nineteenth-century attitudes to hell. I also have long-standing debts to Dr Sheridan Gilley, Mr Stuart Mews, Dr James Obelkevich and Mr Anthony Watkinson, and to the social historians at Birmingham University, who will have heard much of this many times before. No part of my research was more pleasant than the afternoons spent listening to Fr Ralph Gardner's memories of London at the beginning of this century: I wish he were able to receive my thanks.

I would like to thank Dr Lynn Lees for lending me a copy of her thesis, Mr Clive Field for lending me an unpublished paper, and Dr John Kent for allowing me to quote from an unpublished paper. I am also very grateful to Dr Peter Cominos for permission to see his doctoral thesis, and to Dr Susan Budd, Dr Bruce Coleman and Dr Sheridan Gilley for permission to refer to information obtained from their thesis, to Dr Susan Budd, Dr Bruce Coleman and Dr Sheridan me to refer to passages in their forthcoming books.

I wish to acknowledge the permission of the Librarian of the British Library of Political and Economic Science to quote from manuscripts in the Booth and Harrison Collections; of the Archbishop of Canterbury and the Trustees of the Lambeth Palace Library to quote from manuscripts in the Fulham Collection; and of the London Congregational Union Incorporated, the Ecclesiastical Commissioners, the Bishop of Southwark's Registrar and the Head Archivist to quote from manuscripts in the Greater London Record Office. My thanks are equally due to the Registrar General for allowing me to look at marriage registers in local offices, and to the Superintendent Registrars of Bethnal Green and Bow, Hampstead, Lewisham and St Marylebone for their help while I was doing this.

I have been helped by a number of librarians and archivists. I am especially indebted to the staff of the Greater London Record Office and, in particular, to Mrs Joan Kenealy. Several people have generously allowed me to see documents in their possession. I would like to thank the Rev E. Clipsham and the Rev E. Payne for allowing me to see an unpublished essay by Dr Payne; Mr F. Bacon, Mr and Mrs C. Bradby, Mr G. Canning, the Rev A. Davidson, the Rev M. Foizey, the Rev E. Roberts, the Rev C. Roe, Miss M.K. Sabin, Mr I. Smith, the Rev G. Taylor, the Rev J. Walsh.

In particular, I would like to thank Miss Cheryl Jones for typing all that follows, and David and Pamela Taylor, both for their hospitality on my visits to London, and for very kindly checking the proofs.

To

EILEEN

PREFACE

In the sixteenth century, attendance at church was a test of loyalty to the state, and most forms of religious Dissent were punishable by law. In the mid-twentieth century, the denominations born in sixteenth, seventeenth and eighteenth-century England compete with the religions of Ireland, North America, Asia and the Caribbean. Though the head of state is still crowned by the principal bishop of the State Church, religious education has long been interdenominational and promises soon to be inter-faith; while everyone is legally free to choose the religion he wishes, the force of social pressures is, at most levels, against him choosing any at all.

In was in the nineteenth century that the essential features of the modern situation appeared. The seventeenth century had maintained the association between orthodoxy and citizenship, but it had given freedom of conscience to the Dissenters. In the eighteenth century, Unitarians and Roman Catholics obtained the same freedom, and the opponents of Christianity itself came into the open after more than a thousand years. In the nineteenth the Church of England monopoly survived only in the closed village. In most of the country, church life took the form of competition between free and increasingly equal denominations for the favour of a largely unsympathetic population, with a small but usually growing Catholic minority existing in religious isolation. In the new industrial towns most of the population ceased to attend church except for the rites of passage but there remained a substantial minority of church-goers, and a multitude of religious bodies sprang up, representing every shade of theological and social distinction. As in contemporary America, the old association between religion and citizenship survived, though supported by social rather than by legal controls, through the belief that the patriotism as well as the respectability of the non-church-goer was open to question.

By the 1880s, the substantial separation from the churches of the urban working-class had for long been an accomplished fact. Now the association between religion and civic duty was beginning to weaken. The churches were slowly returning towards a sectarian position.

This study is focussed on London, and the period I have chosen — from about 1880 to 1914 — makes it possible to study both the

x

'Victorian' religious pattern and its fading away. My special concern is with the religious attitudes prevailing at each social level, and the degree to which particular kinds of religious allegiance integrated the individual into his environment or separated him from it; the varying nature and force of the social pressures limiting his freedom of action; the reasons why certain views of the world made sense to those within a given milieu.

The evidence is at three levels. At the most general level, church attendance statistics have been used because they indicate with a degree of precision that would otherwise be impossible differences between one part of London and another. These statistics confirm the central importance of class and social status as differentiating factors, and suggest that the distribution of immigrants from particular areas may also have some bearing on church attendance patterns. Collective conceptions of religion and attitudes to religious organisations have been studied at a London-wide level, mainly through autobiographies. The religious censuses do not suggest that distinctive patterns of church attendance were associated with particular industries or with the prevalence of large- or small-scale production, though it may be that more intensive studies will show that I have missed important local nuances. I have used a smaller scale for studies of the churches in two metropolitan boroughs, where newspapers and church records provide a fair amount of evidence about the local character of religious institutions, but evidence concerning individual or group attitudes is sparse.

The earlier chapters will be concerned with the 'Victorian' religious pattern, which survived in modified form in 1914, while Chapter VIII is about the ways in which that pattern was changing during this period. I have not regarded 1880 or 1914 as exclusive limits: around 1880 is a significant turning-point in the history of middle- and upper-class attitudes, because it is about then that the 'Victorian' facade of religious consensus began to crumble; in many areas of working-class life there seems to me a greater continuity of values and assumptions, and I have thus used autobiographies of those brought up both in the 1920s and in the 1860s and '70s. In Chapter VIII, where my concern is with long-term changes in English religion — especially that of the middle and upper classes — evidence has sometimes been drawn from outside London in support of my version of this change; otherwise, my evidence has been drawn, with one exception,[1] entirely from within the Greater London area (and mainly from within the County of London), though I have occasionally drawn comparisons with other areas.

The great majority of Londoners were nominally Christians, and defined their religious position in terms of, or in opposition to, some conception of Christianity. There was, however, a major exception: the Jews, who formed about three per cent of those living in the County of London at the beginning of this century.[2] Although London in the early twentieth century would be a very interesting time and place for the study of Jewish religious history, I have decided to leave the subject to someone better qualified than myself to do it full justice, and to limit my own work to the nominally Christian population.

Notes

1. The exception is Robert Tressell's *The Ragged Trousered Philanthropists*, which is about Hastings building workers, but which I have occasionally quoted for its pithy expression of certain types of working-class attitude which seem to me as characteristic of London as of Hastings.
2. L. P. Gartner, *The Jewish Immigrant in England, 1870-1914*, Allen & Unwin, London, 1960, p.197, estimates the 26,360 worshippers counted in Inner London on the first day of Passover in 1903 as a quarter of London Jewry. In the same year Jewish weddings comprised 3.4 per cent of those in the County of London.

CHAPTER I CLASSES AND PLACES

The colours of London are grey and brown – the grey of sky and river, the brown of the brick. The river gives London much of its character – wide enough to act as a formidable physical and psychological barrier, dividing South London from the rest, though not wide enough to separate the two Londons as decisively as the Mersey separates Liverpool from Birkenhead. But it is the bricks, brown sometimes with flashes of yellow, bricks found in every part of pre-1914 London, except for a white-stucco corner of the West End, that emphasise London's role as capital not only of international capitalism and of the British Empire, but of south-east England. The brown bricks are as characteristic of and exclusive to London and its hinterland as bright red brick is distinctive of the West Midlands or white brick of the Eastern Counties. On the eve of the First World War, 50 per cent of those living in London and born elsewhere were short-distance migrants[1], as against 25 per cent born in other parts of England, 9.9 per cent born in other parts of the British Isles and 15.1 per cent born abroad or in the colonies. In 1881, when the Irish-born proportion was higher, and the proportion of foreign immigrants substantially lower, 52.3 per cent of immigrants were short-distance as against 28.6 per cent from other parts of England.

Thus, if London was the most heterogeneous of English cities, it still drew a large part of its population from a relatively small area of the country.[2] While a substantial proportion of Londoners belonged to one of the long-established Irish colonies, the newer colonies of Italians or of Russian Jews, or the more anonymous Scottish-born population, most immigrants from England came from the agricultural counties of South and East, counties with few large towns and little industry and with a large rural proletariat, counties in political terms Conservative and in religious terms predominantly Anglican.[3] The religious and political peculiarities that distinguished London from most northern cities in the late nineteenth century were characteristics shared with its own hinterland.

If some came to London looking for work and lodgings and not knowing where they would find them, many others came to lodge with or near relatives or natives of their own village already established in the

1

capital. Thus Llewellyn Smith found 'one village sending the flower of its youth to Finsbury, another to Hornsey, a third to a big establishment in Cheapside. So, if an employer is Welsh, we may find a Welsh colony near his works; if from Devon, a colony of Devonshire men'.[4] And he gave the example of one village in the Eastern Counties from which a man had gone to Shoreditch at the beginning of the nineteenth century to work as a cabinet-maker: first his four brothers came to join him in Shoreditch; then a cousin tramped to London, sleeping in out-houses on the way, and after a few days search found the colony in Shoreditch, and lodged with one of his relatives; he in turn went on to become a foreman at a railway depot-in Poplar where he used his position to find jobs for new migrants from his native village, for whom his home had become the first call on arrival in London.[5]

Status Groups

'The reserve, the indifference and the blasé outlook which urbanites manifest in their relationships'[6] were not typical of Londoners in general. Those who came to lodge with friends and relatives immediately entered communities with their established mores and status hierarchy, their common attitudes to outsiders. Those initially isolated in the city soon found themselves, whether they liked it or not, members of one of three generally recognised status-groups – working class, middle class and gentry – each with some degree of common identity and limited mobility from one to another. Within the limits set by their income and the availability of work, they moved into streets or into neighbourhoods where the prevailing style of life accorded with their own. This form of selection reached furthest among the gentry, who could afford to be particular, and among whom every address in West London had its distinctive sound. But other people were equally conscious of the local tone, and ready to move if they did not like it:[7] if the basic status-divisions were inescapable, most people were also aware of more narrowly defined sub-divisions, and of their own position in relation to them. While social mobility was limited by inequalities of opportunity, the rigidity of the system was re-inforced by the development of value-systems characteristic of the three main status-groups – together with refinements peculiar to the sub-groups – a prime function of these systems being self-justification, and the definition of an identity distinct from that of other status-groups.

One consequence of this was the fact that spouses were chosen within a fairly limited social range. This can be seen from a study of inter-marriage rates between occupational groups in Lewisham and Bethnal Green between 1896 and 1903.[8] (See Tables 2 and 3.)

Bethnal Green, where 88 per cent of the sample came from the families of manual workers, seems to have been a fairly homogeneous district without clearly marked divisions. There is a significant tendency to inter-marriage within the unskilled group, but the largest group, children of skilled workers, appear to marry members of all other groups with equal frequency.

In Lewisham, however, where the social range was much greater, a clear pattern of stratification appears. Here 58 per cent of the sample came from manual working families, skilled workers and owners and managers of businesses being the largest categories. There is a clear divide between manual and non-manual workers and a well-defined hierarchy within the two groups. In each of the four working-class categories there is a significant tendency to marry into another working-class family; in each of the four non-manual groups there is the reverse tendency. At the top of the manual hierarchy were skilled workers, with semi-skilled and service workers in the middle, and unskilled workers at the bottom: the probability of the child of a skilled manual worker marrying into a non-manual family was three times greater than that of the child of an unskilled worker doing the same. On the non-manual side the pattern was similar, with professional families at the top, business and clerical families in the middle and retailers at the bottom: the proportion of retailers' children marrying into working-class families was nearly four times greater than the proportion of those from professional families. At the frontier between working class and middle class the lines were blurred, for there was a high rate of inter-marriage between retail and skilled manual families. But the mixing stopped at that point, the former preferring clerks to carmen, and the latter labourers to master builders.[9]

Social Geography

These divisions of status were further reflected in the social segregation of London. Large areas of the city were developed with an eye to a particular market — the more socially exalted the market the greater was the potential profit, but the greater, too, was the element of risk, so that the builder or ground landlord had to assess the general attractiveness of the neighbourhood to the intended tenants.[10] But large tracts gradually assumed a fairly uniform social tone, regardless of the builder's original intentions, as a given social or national group established its dominance and pushed the others out.[11] There was an analogy between the economics of house-building and of the transport facilities on which the letting of new houses substantially depended. Such was the difference in income between the average manual worker or clerk and the average business or professional man, that the latter was able to pay for an exclusive service with consequent neglect of those who could not pay. But if the area or the service lost this exclusive character, its attractiveness to the wealthy would disappear so rapidly that the company or landlord would be obliged to adapt the product with a completeness that would drive away any remaining old customers. At Clapham in 1857, wealthy residents had protested against the proposed railway, which was expected to attract the lower middle class, and when it came they moved to a distance at which season tickets were prohibitively expensive.[12] Local pressure groups opposed the introduction of trams, which attracted working-class passengers with moderate fares, while omnibuses protected property values by making their tickets expensive.[13]

The case was strikingly stated by William Birt, General Manager of the Great Eastern Railway, in his evidence to the Royal Commission on the Housing of the Working Classes in the early eighties. The GER had been obliged by Act of Parliament to run workmen's trains for the use of those displaced during the building of their Liverpool Street terminus in the sixties. As a result, large numbers of working men were attracted to the Lea Valley, from where they could travel to their places of work in the City or East End, and the GER was eventually running more cheap trains than it was obliged by law to do. The reason, as Birt stated with considerable frankness, was that all their first class passengers had moved to other districts, because they objected to sharing facilities with the holders of workmen's tickets, who 'were such a constant source of annoyance by expectorating all over the station and smoking very much with short black pipes'.[14] Tottenham and Stamford Hill had been 'a very nice district indeed':

> but very soon after [the GER began to issue workmen's tickets], speculative builders went down into the neighbourhood and, as a consequence, each good house was one after another pulled down, and the district is given up entirely I may say now to the working

man. I lived down there myself, and I waited until most of my neighbours had gone, and then at last I was obliged to go too.[15]

As result of many similar processes extended over many years, the social geography of London by about 1900 could be seen in terms of four rings round the largely depopulated City.[16] The first ring was marked by the most severe overcrowding and extensive poverty to be found in London, except to the West, where it was an area of extreme wealth; the second ring was slightly less wealthy to the West, and slightly less crowded and less impoverished elsewhere; the third ring was favoured by the short distance commuter, mainly belonging to the lower middle class, and prepared to spend time and money on rail travel in return for lower rents and surroundings that were healthier and more genteel; while the fourth ring belonged to the wealthy commuter. This overall pattern was disturbed by local factors, such as the siting of industry and the lie of the land. Houses on low-lying land usually, and by rivers and canals almost invariably, were of poor quality and deteriorated rapidly. In such places the drainage was bad,[17] and the proximity of water, whether as a sewer or as a means of communication, attracted industry. Thus, except in some parts of Westminster, Chelsea and Hammersmith, the Thames was lined with working-class and often with slum housing. The valleys of the Wandle, the Lea and the Ravensbourne were disfigured by gas-works, a form of industry that drove away anyone who could afford to live elsewhere, and so attracted building of the cheapest type.[18] The Grand Surrey and Regent's Canals had a similar effect.[19] On the other hand, areas next to parks, as at Clapham or South Hackney, tended to keep their social status longer than those surrounding.[20]

The process of social segregation continued apace. As the poor of Central London were pushed out to make way for offices, 'improvements' and grandiose flats in such areas as Chelsea, they moved into surrounding working-class areas, thus driving up rents,[21] and encouraging the 'respectable' to move out to the middle-class suburbs or to the estates built by the LCC or the philanthropic trusts. 'Southwark is moving to Walworth, Walworth to North Brixton and Stockwell, while the servant-keepers of Outer London go to Croydon and other places,'[22] or, as in Charles Masterman's more melodramatic conception, the South London suburbs were retreating before the remorseless advance of the 'abyss'.[23] At some points the 'abyss' leap-frogged areas of comparative respectability to establish itself in islands of 'roughness' and extreme poverty at Bell Green or Summers

Town, at Hackney Wick or Notting Dale, and the struggle between mutually exclusive status-groups and styles of life would resume on a new front. Suburban railways enabled the 'respectable' to remain a step or two ahead of the encroaching 'abyss'. Its advance was hindered by the continuing concentration of industry on Central London and the expensiveness of transport.[24] The central area and the East End remained the site of such major employers of unskilled labour as the docks, markets and railway termini, as well as many gas works; of the 'sweated trades' of tailoring, boot-making and furniture-making; and of the more specialised trades with surviving systems of apprenticeship, such as printing, bookbinding and coopering.[25] Those employed in the latter trades might have been in a position to travel to work. But casual workers were not: for even if they were able to pay the fares, they still needed to be within walking distance of a number of potential employers, and ready to start looking for work at 6 a.m. or earlier, and their wives were likely to work in the putting-out industries, located precisely in the areas where there was a demand for casual labour by men.[26] On the other hand, London's large-scale industry, except for breweries and gas-works, was concentrated on the periphery where land was cheap, and thus formed the basis for independent communities largely outside the County of London. If the casual labourer, the garret-master, and the artisan were characteristic of inner London, it was only in such areas as Woolwich, Beckton, Stratford or Enfield that there were communities dominated by a single large factory.[27] (See Table 24.)

Regions, Districts, Neighbourhoods

Hobsbawm has divided nineteenth-century London into three 'regions' (South, West and East) defined as the area within which building workers moved in search of work[28] — the river and the central area forming psychological barriers limiting the scope of such migration — and subdivided 'regions' into 'districts', these being the areas on which trade union branches were based (corresponding in many cases to the area of the metropolitan boroughs that came into existence in 1900).[29] Lynn Lees, who has used census data to chart the movements within London of Irish immigrants during the 1850s, has confirmed the validity of the 'regional' concept by showing that the Irish moved within rather than between West, South and East London, and that they tended to follow certain well-trodden paths of movement from the centre, such as those from Southwark to Camberwell, or from St Giles to Notting Dale and Kensal New Town.[30] But, as Hobsbawm implies, the 'London' of the casual labourer may have been even more narrowly defined: his chances of getting work fairly regularly appeared to depend on informal contacts within a small area, and there was thus a strong inducement to remain within this area, and to cultivate such contacts.[31] This 'neighbourhood' would be rather narrower than the areas defined by Hobsbawm and would form the most localised, and probably the most typical basis for the individual's conception of the community to which he belonged. Slightly less localised would be the 'district'-based conception, in terms of which the ancient parish or the metropolitan borough was a relevant unit. Here the central area, perhaps as a place of work, but in any case as the site of railway termini, places of entertainment and certain well-known national monuments, might be recognised as a distant extension of the area of detailed personal knowledge, but it also formed a barrier beyond which such knowledge largely disappeared, and migration was still likely to be regionalised. This regionalisation was only transcended in the small section of metropolitan society in which commitment to place was very small, commitment to an exclusive upper class and its way of life essential, and the individual's conception of his own community could be termed 'national and international'. Each of these conceptions could be seen as representative of three distinctive patterns of life, each with its basis in a different career pattern.

One indication of the boundaries of a community is the area within which marriage partners are found. From one point of view, the social life of a district was epitomised in the ways in which future partners met: at one level such relationships would begin quite informally, often in the street itself or through brothers and sisters; at another they would meet through institutions, such as choirs or amateur dramatics clubs; at another, through formal social occasions, in which clearly defined rules of etiquette existed. From another point of view the kind of choice a man or woman made considerably affected the opportunities open to them and the area within which their future life would be lived: the choice of a spouse from the opposite end of the country enlarged and extended their lives, just as the choice of someone from the next street strengthened attachment to neighbourhood.

An examination of the marriage registers in four London parishes in the years 1896–1905 shows three patterns. The parishes chosen were St Clement's, Notting Hill, where unskilled manual workers were a majority; St Andrew's, Bethnal Green, where skilled manual workers were the largest element; St Mary's, Lewisham, a middle-class district; and the wealthy district of St John's, Paddington.[32] In Bethnal Green and Notting Hill, the majority of men marry a woman from their own 'neighbourhood', defined as an area of less than half a mile square, and not crossed by a railway, waterway or main road, or broken up by a park or a belt of factories. In Lewisham, cases where both partners lived within such 'neighbourhoods' were much fewer, but in 42 per cent of weddings the partners lived within half a mile of one another, and in a further 43 per cent they both lived in London. In Paddington, local weddings were less frequent, and in a substantial minority of cases (35 per cent) either bride or groom lived outside London. (See Tables 4 and 5).

More surprisingly, an occupational breakdown shows parallels between different groups within the same parish. For instance, a manual worker in Paddington was more likely to marry outside London than a member of the professional/managerial group elsewhere, and retailers in Bethnal Green were more likely to marry within the 'neighbourhood' than were manual workers in Lewisham or Paddington. In some cases this may reflect deliberate choice, as with the 'respectable' working man who moved to the suburbs because the prevailing style of life coincided with his own. On the other hand, the difference between parishes and the relatively consistent pattern within them suggests that the dominant group may have placed its own limitations on the life of the area and that, for instance, the way of life of a Bethnal Greener transplanted to Lewisham might change in important respects.

These different marriage patterns represent three patterns of life, products of differences in income, career structure, the experience of power and the enjoyment of social status. The three patterns of life might be termed 'neighbourhood-centred', 'district-centred' and 'national and international', involving as they did different conceptions of the community to which the individual belonged, as well as distinctive patterns of family life and the organisation of leisure.

The 'neighbourhood-centred' pattern of life was most fully exemplified in the unskilled working class, tied to a narrowly defined area by poverty, insecurity and ignorance of any wider world. This small community provided not only personal contacts with potential employers or foremen, but concentrations of friends, kin who could help in times of need, credit-giving landlords and retailers, sympathetic pawnbrokers. Lack of means further required that unskilled workers lived near to their place of work and that, except on special occasions such as Bank Holidays, they seldom left it,[33] The result was extreme parochialism. The mother of one East End memoirist was upset when one of her family moved to Dagenham, which she regarded as stuck up: 'Once away from Waterloo Row and The [Whitechapel] Road, physically or mentally, Mum was no longer sure of herself'.[34] John Holloway has given a similar description of his own perhaps more socially isolated family at about the same time (the 1920s): his father was a hospital stoker, working in Hackney, but living in Norwood, from where he cycled fourteen miles to work each day. He sometimes considered moving, but he liked being near the country and did not know that there was as much country to the north-east of London; he did not have a map of London, would not have known where to start looking for somewhere in Hackney to live, and would not have known how to organise a move over such a distance.

My mother could screw herself up to almost anything if it really had to be done; but that is another thing. My father would have become unsure, nervous and therefore aggressive, if he had so much as gone into the enquiry office of a firm big enough to move across London in those days. In a minute or so he would have found some excuse to bluster his way out again.

He would not look for work in Norwood as he would then lose all the advantages of being known, and thus protected against dismissal, and when he was offered a job in Littlehampton, which would have suited his health better, he turned the chance down, as his close friends were all workmates at Hackney.[35]

Thus, in spite of the steady long-term movement away from the centre of London, and the fact that many unskilled workers moved with some frequency from one house to another, many factors combined to tie them to a fairly small area. Lynn Lees found Irish families who moved backwards and forwards across the Southwark/Bermondsey border several times in the 1850s, but 'their residences at all times were within the radius of one half-mile at most'.[36] A similar picture is produced in A. S. Jasper's *A Hoxton Childhood*. The Jasper family were continually flitting to avoid paying the rent — 'I have never heard of a family who moved more than we did' — but their moves all took place within a fairly small area between Essex Road and Hackney Road, and they were never more than half a mile from Hoxton Street, where they sometimes kept a market stall, until in 1919 they were offered lodgings in Walthamstow, and being unable to find any alternative, reluctantly moved. The high point of their travels was a return to Bridport Place near the Regent's Canal:

> We were now back where my story first started. We has to get a horse and van to move with. Mary had the ground floor, Jo' the first floor, we had the top floor and the old man had his favourite pub, the Bridport Arms, I knew the area well and we knew most of the people around.[37]

From the other side of the social fence, J. M. Thompson foreshadowed the preoccupation of more recent investigators with the street 'or 'turning' in this account of Poplar anthropology made in 1902 when he was working in a College Mission:

> Funeral of Mrs. Spooner this afternoon — a patriarchal old lady who lived in Willis Street, which is (apparently) chiefly inhabited by her 34 grandchildren and 42 great-grandchildren. One extraordinary and rather horrid feature of the case was that the relations had insisted on keeping the body in the house a whole fortnight, in spite of all the expostulations of Vaillant and others. Nothing could be done without offending the whole of Willis Street. But the precaution was taken of burning a lot of incense in the church before the service.[38]

At the other end of the social scale was what Beatrice Webb, speaking as one of its members, called 'the class that gives orders',[39] oscillating between one or more country home, a town house sometimes merely rented for 'the Season', and country house weekends at all points in the country, not to mention Paris, Biarritz, German spas and alpine villages, according to personal taste. Beatrice Webb's own family, whose wealth came from railways and timber yards and who lived on the fringes of county society in Gloucestershire where Beatrice's father had his timber yards, had homes in reserve in Herefordshire and Westmorland, took a furnished house each year for the London 'Season' and spent their holidays in Germany, Italy or Switzerland; the daughters also accompanied their father on business trips to the United States.[40] If the Potter family was unusually rootless because of its parvenu status and the wide range of Richard Potter's business interests, the looseness of local ties was common to many of those in 'Society'. Take, for instance, the diaries of Lady Monkswell,[41] married to a Liberal politician, whose father had entered the peerage through success in law and politics: they lived in Monkswell House on Chelsea Embankment, but the life she describes is that of a 'set' in Society — a life lived sometimes in country houses, sometimes at dinner in Belgrave Square, at Royal Balls, or (more privately) on holiday in Switzerland or Scotland (for all of August and September, and for two weeks at Whitsun). The one place that is very seldom mentioned (except if they were holding dinner parties at Monkswell House) is Chelsea. Where strong local attachments existed they would be based on family estates, the county bench and so on. London was merely the place where the 'Upper Ten Thousand' happened to assemble in spring and early summer. Those members of the gentry whose only home was in London still found their point of reference in a class, distributed across the length of the British Isles, rather than in a local community. Similarly the range of situations in which they were accustomed to wielding authority was equally wide. As Beatrice Webb put it, she grew up with the consciousness not of 'superior riches' but of 'superior power':

> As life unfolded itself I became aware that I belonged to a class of persons who habitually gave orders, but who seldom, if ever, executed the orders of other people. My mother sat in her boudoir and gave orders — orders that brooked neither delay nor evasion. My father, by temperament the least autocratic and most accommodating of men, spent his whole life giving orders. He ordered his stockbroker to buy and sell shares, his solicitor to prepare contracts and undertake legal proceedings, [etc.] . . . And when one after another my sisters' husbands joined the family group, they also were giving orders: the country gentlemen on their estates and at sessions; the manufacturer in his mill; the shipowner to his fleet of ships on the high seas; the city financier in the money market floating or refusing to float foreign government loans; the Member of Parliament as Financial Secretary of the Treasury; the surgeon and the barrister well on the way to leadership in their respective professions . . . Reared in the atmosphere of giving orders it was not altogether surprising that I apparently acquired the marks of the caste.[42]

Between these social extremes lay a large and very heterogeneous section of the London population. What I have termed the 'district-centred' pattern of life was characteristic of the suburbs, and especially of the middle class. The artisan, on the other hand, although his circumstances were comparable in some respects to those of the lower middle class, tended to adopt an informal style of life and to marry a woman living very near to his home. The distinguishing features

of the 'district-centred' pattern were local ties looser than those of most
of the working class, but still far more concentrated than those of the
upper class; the focus of social life on the nuclear family and on formal
associations; and life in 'residential streets', often at a considerable
distance from the main places of work. One determinant of this style of
life was intermediate income: enough to travel to work, to occupy a
whole house, to employ some sort of domestic servant, to pay school
fees and to take a summer holiday. A second was a clearly defined
career structure: usually beginning with a period of what was in effect
apprenticeship in which a young man would be quite likely to live in
lodgings at some distance from the parental home;[43] followed by a
period in which he would be looking for promotion, either by securing
the approval of his present employer or by moving, perhaps some
distance, to take a more promising position; and by the achievement of
maximum income relatively late in life. In terms of status and power,
there were very wide differences within this section of society, though
in this, as with income, its position was clearly intermediate.

Much of this would be equally true of the 'labour aristocracy', that
section of the working class which was organised in friendly societies
and trade unions, and which had gone through a period of
apprenticeship. They enjoyed an income similar to that of most clerks,
travellers and teachers;[44] they could afford to travel to work;[45]
because of their more specialised skills, they were not dependent for
work on the local contacts that the labourer had to cultivate, and so
they tended to be more mobile.[46]

Nonetheless, skilled craftsmen tended to be proud of the proletarian
identity that most of the lower middle class shunned; they lived in
more crowded conditions,[47] and took their children from school
earlier;[48] ritual drinking established the working-class character of the
workshop as surely as black coats defined the middle-class atmosphere
of the office; and 'from top to bottom clerks associate with clerks and
artisans with artisans'.[49] Part of this difference in identity — as decisive
as the difference, higher up the social scale between those who were
gentlemen and those who were not — arose from the greater security of
the clerk, traveller or teacher, and the possibility of dramatic
promotion.[50] But most of the differences in work situation were in
intangibles: the difference in identity produced by clean work in
'respectable' clothes, starting later, and requiring not the 'working-class'
skills of strength and dexterity, but the 'middle-class' skills of literacy
and memory.[51] And, if the working class gave itself dignity by exalting
strength, masculinity and craft skill, the lower middle class did likewise,

by stressing the differences in dress, speech and manner that were a necessary part of their occupations.[52]

Respectability

But behind all of this there was the feeling that manual work, however skilled or highly paid, was not really respectable. 'A very respectable sort of working man' had an air of the patronising, whereas 'a very respectable sort of clerk' had an air of the ironical. In a society acutely conscious of the more minute, as well as the all too blatant, distinctions of status, the most struggling member of the lower middle class was aware of being different from anyone who worked with his hands.

Respectability, in eighteenth-century usage, referred to social position, and denoted a person of established standing, enjoying a certain amount of property. Its increasing use during the nineteenth century as a term denoting moral worth, regardless of position, was thus one aspect of the democratisation of English society:[53] it was a part of the bourgeois concept of a free, competitive and mobile society, with a hierarchy based on achievement rather than birth. Respectability in the old sense of the term, as used, for instance, ironically by Wolfe Tone in his address to 'that large and respectable class — the owners of no property', involved a recognition of the traditional social order. Used in the newer sense it implied a challenge. It offered the individual, if he adopt its precepts, the chance of prosperity and status. It challenged both aristocratic dominance and the characteristic aristocratic life-style.[54] It equally challenged the life-style of large sections of the poor. It promised improvement for all through a combination of education and increased moral effort, and it frequently challenged existing conceptions of religion — usually on behalf of Evangelical Protestantism, though sometimes from a utilitarian or rationalist point of view.

But if much of the appearance of respectability was merely superficial, the theory was also delusive. Admirably egalitarian in principle, since it assumed a society with equal opportunity for all who showed the necessary virtue and application, it existed in a society where opportunities as well as rewards were actually extremely unequal, in which the majority of those who started with few chances showed no wish to join the race for achievement, and some resorted to means of compensating for their weak position that looked to the successful like blatant cheating — whether it were crime, terrorisation of property owners,[55] or violent strikes. Moreover, however earnestly some ideologists of respectability preached the dignity of all honest work, a stigma still attached to the manual labour that was the lot of the great majority of the population. Thus the existence — not of the proletariat in the strict sense of the term, for clerks, shop assistants and teachers were granted the status of honorary bourgeois, with salaries, albeit very meagre, more acceptable hours of starting work, and less supervision while doing it — but of those who worked with their hands as a separate and, in the view of the dominant elements in society, inferior class, with a sense of separate identity. Although some of this class espoused the values of industry, self-discipline, self-education, etc., very wholeheartedly, and as ends in themselves, if, as Tholfsen asserts, 'a good deal of [the artisan's] behaviour was motivated by the desire to secure the approval of his superiors',[56] the artisan was wasting his time. The point was made brutally clear to George Howell, the embodiment of all the self-improving virtues when, in 1855, he arrived in London with nothing but a letter of introduction from Bristol YMCA, which he took to the Aldersgate branch, only to be told that men wearing corduroy trousers and describing themselves as brick layers could not become members.[57] Working men who were respectable in the moral sense were thus in an ambivalent position, for they could not be respectable in the social sense. The moral and the social meanings of respectability tended to merge, so that the moral non-respectability of large numbers of working men appeared to justify their inferior social status,[58] and the 'labouring masses' in general could be dismissed as a lesser branch of humanity. In spite of all the Holyoakes, the Lovetts and the Coopers, the concept of respectability, potentially a great social leveller, was more often an instrument of middle-class ideology, used to justify the advantages enjoyed by its adherents, and the disadvantages suffered by those who ignored or rejected it.

There remained one section of the London population sharing both working-class localism and the middle-class taste for organisations: the class of petty capitalists who, because of their stake in a particular area, were those most strongly tied to their own districts of London. Their definition of their community was perhaps less narrow than that of many of the working class as they tended to sit on vestries and borough councils, to act as guardians and churchwardens, to own local newspapers, the columns of which were filled with the 'rows' and 'scandals' that divided them. At one end this section of society merged into the working class, at the other end into the upper middle class, and consequently into life in a select suburb at a distance from their work. This community of petty capitalists consisted of retailers and small employers living above their shops or close to them — these being, in the case of retailers, in the main roads, rather than the back streets[59] — possessing some degree of solidarity, exhibited in the tradition by which shop-keepers made a public show of 'respect' on the day on which one of their number was to be buried,[60] and frequently active in the affairs of the district in which they paid their rates, whether because of an inherited sense of obligation, or from more interested motives.[61]

The petty capitalists thus formed something of a group on their own, distributed fairly evenly across the length of London, and often leading a rather self-contained existence in partial isolation from those of other classes. But most of the population identified themselves as members of communities distinguished by one of the three typical patterns of social relationships — 'neighbourhood-centred', 'suburban', or 'West End'. Each of these was marked by a distinctive pattern of religious activity, and this pattern was the product not merely of hundreds of thousands of individual wills but of the whole organisation of life in that section of society.

Notes

1. Defined by Stedman Jones as those born in what the census termed The South-Eastern counties (Surrey, Kent, Sussex, Hampshire, Berkshire), South Midland Counties (Middlesex, Hertfordshire, Buckinghamshire, Oxfordshire, Northamptonshire, Huntingdonshire, Bedfordshire, Cambridgeshire) and Eastern counties (Essex, Suffolk, Norfolk). See G. Stedman Jones, *Outcast London*, OUP, London, 1971, p.148.

2. In 1881, the counties of short-distance migration' in which 64.6% of English immigrants to London had been born contained only 26.6% of the extra-metropolitan population of England.

3. Of the sixteen counties that were the chief suppliers of immigrants to London, there were fourteen in which Anglican worshippers outnumbered Nonconformists in 1851. For the weakness of temperance societies in the south-east, see B. Harrison, *Drink and the Victorians*, Faber, London, 1971, pp.108-9, 148-9, and for the weakness of the Liberal Party the figures in H. Pelling, *The Social Geography of British Elections, 1885-1910*, Macmillan, London, 1967. Out of ninety-three parliamentary seats in the counties of 'short-distance migration', there were sixty in which the average Conservative and Unionist share of the two-party vote exceeded

the English national average of 50.8%, and a further five seats in which it was equal to this average. There was, however, a difference between the counties to the South of London, which were overwhelmingly Anglican and Conservative (and where rural church attendance was also below the national average), and those directly to the north, where there was more rural industry, and where Liberalism and Nonconformity were stronger.

4. C. Booth, *Life and Labour of the People in London*, Macmillan, London, 1902-3, I [1st Series], iii [3rd volume], p.134. Llewellyn Smith contributed chapters on immigration to East London.

5. Ibid., I, iii, pp.132-3.

6. L. Wirth, 'Urbanism as a Way of Life', *American Journal of Sociology*, July 1938, reprinted in A. J. Reiss, jr. (ed.), *On Cities and Social Life*, Chicago UP, Chicago, 1964, p.71.

7. Thus the Jasper family were continually on the move within a small area of East London. When Mrs. Jasper decided their house had a curse on it, she found a new one in Scawfell Street: 'This wasn't far from Loanda Street. It certainly looked a road with some life in it, which was what we were used to. Loanda Street was a drab place of flat-fronted houses where everyone closed their door. There wasn't the friendliness'. A. S. Jasper, *A Hoxton Childhood*, Barrie and Rockliff, London, 1969, p.61.

8. Bride and groom have been assigned to the occupational groups of their fathers, as recorded in the marriage register. This method of measuring social distance has been used by C. Tilly, *The Vendée*, Edward Arnold, London, 1964, and by J. O. Foster, 'Capitalism and Class Consciousness in 19th Century Oldham', Univ. of Cambridge Ph.D. thesis, 1967.

9. The problem in such tests is to have sufficient numbers in each category without the categories becoming too broad to be meaningful. In this case, the numbers in the professional and service categories are too small, while the business category is too broad — at the one end, large employers would go with professional men, and, at the other, jobbing builders would go with retailers. However, the main point remains: the importance of the distinction between manual and non-manual workers, and the gradation of status within these broad groups.

10 In Liverpool the supply of new working-class houses almost ceased after 1846 when the imposition by the corporation of stricter building regulations made the provision of low rental houses unprofitable. J. H. Treble, 'Liverpool Working Class Housing, 1801-1851', S. D. Chapman (ed.), *The History of Working Class Housing*, David and Charles, Newton Abbott, 1971, pp.194-5. The over-provision of middle-class housing in late Victorian Camberwell is noted by H. J. Dyos, *Victorian Suburb*, Leicester UP, Leicester, 1961, pp.81-2, and failed middle-class speculation as sites for West End slums by D. A. Reeder, 'A Theatre of Suburbs: Some Patterns of Development in West London, 1801-1911', H. J. Dyos (ed.), *The Study of Urban History*, Arnold, London, 1967, p.265, and

Booth, op.cit., III, iii, pp.141, 152.

11. A religious worker interviewed by Booth (op.cit., III, i. pp.139-40) described the process by which Campbell Road had become the nucleus of a poor area south-west of Finsbury Park: 'About twenty-five years ago I resided in Lennox Road. The houses were cheap and the neighbourhood was very respectable, occupied by well-to-do families of the middle class, clerks and artizans, but there was one dark spot, and that was half of Campbell Road . . . . . inhabited by navvies and builders' labourers with large families living in tenements of one or two rooms. . . . Later the three best houses in the better part of the road were let to families living each in one room, and a large house at the corner of Paddington Street was turned into a lodging-house. From that time the respectable people began to leave. Houses were let in one or two room tenements and overcrowded. I have known as many as thirty-three persons living in one house. Campbell Road got such a bad name that no one would live in it except persons that had large families and could not live anywhere else. The place became a pest, and the parish cleared out some of the overcrowded houses. Two of them bought cheap were turned into lodging-houses. This proved profitable; others embarked on the same business, and the results are loafing, immorality and crime.'

12. J. R. Kellett, *The Impact of Railways on Victorian Cities,* Routledge, London, 1969, p.412.

13. H. Pollins, 'Transport Lines and Social Divisions', R. Glass (ed.), *London, Aspects of Change,* Macgibbon and Kee, London, 1964, pp.41-4.

14. *P.P.* 1884-5, XXX, Q. 10, 279.

15. Ibid., Q. 10, 217.

16. These descriptions are based on the social maps of London in 1900 in Booth, op.cit., 3rd Series.

17. See Dyos, op.cit., pp.84, 97, where he contrasts the risks of speculating in middle-class houses on low-lying ground with the assured status of Champion Hill, where the ground landlord was able to impose strict conditions in the leases.

18. 'Poverty and gasworks lie cheek by jowl in all parts of London' — Booth's comment (op.cit., I, i, p.247) on the Wandsworth Bridge Road.

19. On the Lock Bridge district of Paddington, Booth commented (op.cit., I, i. p.245): 'The group of streets included in this district, lying in the hollow of a bend in the canal, shade off from purple to dark blue [i.e., according to Booth's categories, from "mixed poverty and comfort" to "extreme poverty"], the greatest poverty being, as usual, next to the canal.'

20. Booth's social map of London in 1900 showed to the north of Victoria Park an area of 'red' (middle class) streets, surrounded on three sides by areas of poverty coloured 'blue'. Beside Clapham Common, surrounded by working-class and lower middle-class housing, were large detached houses marked 'yellow' (wealthy).

21. See Stedman Jones, op.cit., pp.215-7. Artisans liked to maintain 'a rent differential, normally in the form of an extra room'. By the mid-80s, in the inner East End, they could only do this by spending 25-30% of their income on rent.
22. Booth, op.cit., III, iv, p.166.
23. [C. F. G. Masterman], *From the Abyss*, Johnson, London, 1902, p.48.
24. A. S. Wohl, 'The Housing of the Working Classes in London, 1815-1914', Chapman (ed.), op.cit., pp.16-17, 29-33.
25. The few trades where entry was still strictly controlled are listed in Booth, op.cit., II, v, pp.126-7.
26. There is an excellent discussion of the reasons for the concentration of casual labourers in the central area and their unwillingness to move very far even within its confines in Stedman Jones, op.cit., pp.81-8. He notes that employers of unskilled female labour were concentrated in such areas as Southwark and Stepney because the irregularity of adult male earnings meant that at certain points in the year there would be large numbers of wives desperate for some form of work no matter how unpleasant and how badly paid.
27. Woolwich and Stratford had the only large co-operative societies in London in the 1890s, and Woolwich together with West Ham, was the first metropolitan stronghead of independent Labour. P. Thompson, *Socialists, Liberals and Labour*, Routledge, London, 1967, pp.38-40, 250-63.
28. He cites the examples of a bricklayer who moved from his birthplace in Kent to Croydon and from there to Woolwich, and of a carpenter born in Harrow who moved from Notting Hill to Ealing to Hammersmith. E.J. Hobsbawm, 'The Nineteenth Century London Labour Market', Glass (ed.), op.cit., pp.8-9.
29. For instance, Chelsea, Poplar, Greenwich, etc. Ibid., pp.19-20.
30. L. Lees, 'Social Change and Social Stability among the London Irish, 1830-70' (Harvard University, Ph.D. thesis, 1969), pp.60-4, 95-103. In this context, West London seems to have included most of North London. Irishmen moved between St. Giles or Kensington and 'every northern district west of Hackney' (ibid., p.62), but they seldom moved from St. Giles to South or East London.
31 Glass (ed.), op.cit., p.8. Cf. Stedman Jones, op.cit., pp.81-8; W. Beveridge, *Unemployment*, Longman, London, (2nd edition) 1930, pp.246-8.
32. All cases where both bride and groom give the same address have been excluded from this analysis. These are significantly more numerous in Notting Hill than in Bethnal Green and in Bethnal Green than in the other two parishes. This may arise because both are lodgers in the same house, in which case it would be a 'neighbourhood' marriage, because they were co-habiting at the time of marriage, in which case it would be impossible to classify, or because one partner was giving the address of the other as an address of convenience.

33. For some important exceptions to this tendency, see R. Samuel, 'Comers and Goers', H. J. Dyos and M. Wolff (eds.), *The Victorian City*, 2 vols., Routledge, London, 1973, I, pp.123-60. He notes the sizeable summer exodus from London to work in brickfields, to harvest, to pick fruit or hops, and includes among the migrants those such as gas stokers, whose work was highly seasonal, and dovetailed conveniently with another equally seasonal occupation, and those such as white-lead workers, whose work was particularly unpleasant. But he argues that there were few 'without a springboard, a haven or regular ports of call': he cites from George Acorn's memoirs of Bethnal Green in the 1890s the example of a cobbler who always spent the winter working in the same shop in Bethnal Green and the summer on the tramp; similarly, he mentions a Kent village that always took its hoppers from Poplar, another that took them from Shadwell, and so on.

34. E. Flint, *Kipper Stew*, Museum Press, London, 1964, p.43.

35. J. Holloway, *A London Childhood*, Routledge, London, 1966, pp.6-12.

36. Lees, op.cit., p.66. Compare this with Llewellyn Smith's well-known description (Booth, op.cit., I, iii, p.81) of the largely Irish residents of a block of model dwellings in Wapping: 'It is a roving population not easy to deal with, often flitting to escape rent, often to escape School Board officer. But this migration rarely proceeds outside the little charmed circle of alleys where the "old pals" reside: it is rather of the nature of a circular movement, so that at the end of ten years a man is as near his birthplace as at the beginning, having perhaps lived in each of the neighbouring streets in the meantime.'

37. Jasper, op.cit., p.98. This was about 1918. The author was aged thirteen and still lived with his parents; Mary and Jo' were his elder sisters, Mary living with her husband and their child, while Jo' lived with her child, her husband being in the merchant navy.

38. J. M. Thompson, *Diary*, 25 October 1902.

39. B. Webb, *My Apprenticeship*, Longman, London, 1926, p.43.

40. Ibid., pp.39-42.

41. E. C. F. Collier, (ed.), *A Victorian Diarist, 1873-1895*, Murray, London, 1944, and *A Victorian Diarist, 1895-1909*, Murray, London, 1946. About ten or fifteen entries a year are included in the published version. No indication is given by the editor as to how far the selections are representative of the whole.

42. Webb, op.cit., pp.43-4.

43. Young middle-class men in lodgings were numerous in Kennington and in Camden Town. The fact that middle-class occupations drew disproportionately from those born outside London can be seen from Booth, op.cit., II, v, p.29. In 1891, 50% of heads of households in London had been born outside the metropolis. The proportion of clerks and of those employed in the law was marginally higher, while those of merchants, architects, and of those employed in art and amusement, literature and science,

education, and medicine were below this average.
44. Surveys of 1906 and 1909 showed that whereas a minority of
    clerks (relatively numerous in banking and insurance) had a
    securely middle-class income, 90% of railway clerks and 75% of
    commercial clerks earned less than £160 p.a. and averaged £80 p.a.
    (The average annual income of adult males in manual work was
    about £72). D. Lockwood, *The Black-Coated Worker*, Allen and
    Unwin, London, 1958, pp.41-4. Booth found that in the early
    '90s, 70% of male teachers employed by the London School Board
    were earning between £105 and £165 p.a., while 15% earned less —
    this would have made them richer than most artisans, but not by
    much. Booth, op.cit., II, iv, p.169. A survey of 1887 in Battersea,
    Hackney, Deptford and St George's had shown that clerks and
    travellers living in those districts enjoyed a typical artisan income.
    'Conditions of the Working Classes', *P.P.* 1887, LXXI.
45. Booth, op.cit., II, v, p.29, showed that the majority of workers in
    such 'aristocratic' but centralised occupations as printing,
    watch-making and instrument-making lived outside the 'inner
    circle' in 1891 — though the proportion of clerks doing so was still
    much higher.
46. The Board of Trade enquiry quoted above (*P.P.* 1887, LXXI)
    found that 99% of manual workers, clerks and shopkeepers
    interviewed claimed to have lived in London for more than a year
    and 93% in the same neighbourhood. The latter proportion fell
    below 90% only in the case of printers and engine-makers. W. H.
    Beveridge stated (op.cit., pp.239-45) that some skilled men learnt
    about vacancies through newspaper advertisements or through their
    unions. For two examples of highly mobile young engineers, see T.
    Mann, *Memoirs*, Labour Publishing Co., London, 1923, and G. N.
    Barnes, *From Workshop to War Cabinet*, Jenkins, London, 1924.
    Both had come to London around 1880 after doing
    apprenticeships in the provinces. Barnes began in Clerkenwell, to
    which he had a special attachment, but before long he 'knew every
    workshop from Chiswick to Erith', and had worked in Shoreditch,
    the Isle of Dogs, Silvertown and Bromley. He eventually settled in
    Fulham, where he married. Tom Mann also worked in Clerkenwell
    for some time, but also changed employers frequently, and took
    jobs as far West as Chiswick, as far East as Tilbury, and as far South
    as Peckham.
47. In 1891 (Booth, op.cit., II, v, p.29) only 10½% of commercial
    clerks in Inner London lived in 'crowded' conditions, as against
    21½% of watch-makers, the least 'crowded' working-class group.
48. Booth, op.cit., I, iii, p.271. Lockwood (op.cit., p.129) quotes a
    survey of 1953, by when the economic position of clerical workers
    had deteriorated, which showed that their children were more than
    twice as likely as those of skilled workers to go to grammar school.
49. Booth, op.cit., II, iii, pp.277-8.
50. Though most observers considered this possibility to be faint. Ibid.,
    II, iii, pp.274-5; Lockwood, op.cit., pp.24-7.

51. Lockwood (ibid., pp.34-5) enumerates those aspects of 'the world of the counting-house' conducive to the 'estrangement from the mass of working men' and 'identification with the entrepreneurial and professional classes' of the clerk.

52. Lockwood (ibid., pp.100-5) cites various expressions of working-class contempt for clerks as not doing 'real work' and of dislike by clerks for manual workers, especially trade unionists, between 1909 and 1956.

53. The *Shorter Oxford English Dictionary* gives as one definition of 'respectable': 'Of good or fair social standing and having the moral qualities appropriate to this. Hence, in later use, honest and decent in character or conduct, without reference to social position, or in spite of being in humble circumstances'. The examples given of its use between about 1750 and 1900 reflect this widening of its meaning, and also its increasing use in the second half of the nineteenth century as a term of derision.

54. This was the doctrine of Samuel Smiles, an anti-aristocratic advocate of the middle class-working class alliance. See A. Tyrrell, 'Class Consciousness in Early Victorian Britain: Samuel Smiles, Leeds Politics and the Self-Help Creed', *Journal of British Studies,* vol.IX, no.2, May 1970.

55. In the discussion of his paper at the Urban History Group conference in 1966, John Foster stated that Oldham working-class politicians controlled the local government of the town in the 1820s and '30s 'through the downright intimidation of shopkeepers who "didn't toe the line on the Police Commission", by methods that ranged from black-listing shops to acid attacks'. Dyos (ed.), op.cit., pp.341-2.

56. T. R. Tholfsen, 'The Artisan and the Culture of Early Victorian Birmingham', *University of Birmingham Historical Journal*, vol.IV, no.2, December 1954, p.147.

57. F. M. Leventhal, *Respectable Radical,* Routledge, London, 1971, pp.17-18.

58. An extreme example of the linking of poverty with moral failings was the doubt expressed by a Church of Scotland parish missionary in 1849 as to the reality of the conversion of those working-class members who had failed to prosper after joining the congregation. A. A. Maclaren, 'Religion and Social Class in Mid-Nineteenth Century Aberdeen', University of Aberdeen, Ph.D. thesis, 1971, pp.181-2.

59. Thus, the incumbent of St Mary Whitechapel made (London Visitation, 1842) this essentially social distinction as to the varying degree to which Sunday was observed by the shutting of shops in his parish: 'In the *larger* Streets it is outwardly observed by all but Tobacconists and in the early part of the Day Butchers — in the *back streets and lanes* it is not observed generally.'

60. *East London Observer,* 13 October 1906, reported a general display of tokens of mourning by Bethnal Green shopkeepers to mark the funeral of the wife of a Green Street greengrocer.

61. Clerkenwell Vestry was said to be in the 1880s a particularly
    notorious example of the domination of local authorities by those
    with special interests to defend — in this case, slum landlords. P.
    Thompson, op.cit., pp.78-9.

CHAPTER II WHO WENT TO CHURCH?

One way of studying the religion of nineteenth-century London is through statistics. Church attendances on a single Sunday were counted in the national census of 1851 and in two newspaper censuses, those organised by the *British Weekly* in 1886-7, and the *Daily News* in 1902-3.[1] Throughout the century the various branches of Methodism published in their minutes of conference extensive statistics of membership.[2] From the 1860s such statistics were also published by the Baptists, and they were joined by the Anglicans – who had no such category as 'membership' but provided numbers of baptisms, confirmations and communicants in each diocese – in the 1880s, and by the Congregationalists in 1899. There are also unpublished sources of such information: for instance, bishops of Anglican dioceses frequently asked incumbents at Visitation time how many people attended their services, and 'If the numbers do not bear a fair proportion to the population to what do you attribute the deficiency?' Catholic bishops were only concerned with the 'Catholic population', but they were not interested in a 'fair proportion': at Visitation time priests might be asked to give numbers not only of those attending Mass, but of those 'neglecting Mass', 'out of the Church' or apostasising.[3] Marriage and burial registers indicate the occupational composition of the population associated with the various denominations. Many churches include in their records lists of the addresses, sometimes with occupations, of their members.

Some of these records, such as marriage registers, can be used by the historian as statistical sources, although they were intended to serve quite different purposes. But most of them were part of an attempt by governments, newspapers, and the religious bodies themselves to assess the effectiveness of the churches' work. The motives for such enquiries might be primarily pastoral or evangelistic, they might be sectarian, they might arise from a general interest in social statistics, of which religious statistics were a part,[4] or they might be mainly political and concerned with the loss of control by the possessing class over the 'masses'. For those whose main concerns were pastoral and evangelistic, the use of attendance at Sunday services as the main index of church attachment was in some ways appropriate: all churches made Sunday

worship the chief focus of their activity. For Roman Catholics, every
Sunday was a 'feast of obligation', and those who failed to attend Mass
were in mortal sin; for High Anglicans, weekly Communion was *de
rigueur;* for Evangelical Protestants, church attendance, preferably
twice, was part of the proper observance of the Lord's Day; liberal
Protestants, though they had no rules of this sort, would still have felt
pretty uncomfortable if they did not attend some sort of service; and
for respectable people generally church-going was simply among the
'recognised proprieties of life'.[5] Non-attendance at church in
nineteenth-century London was thus an act certain to shock a great
many people, and it can legitimately be seen as a form of social protest.
But the object of the protest cannot be so easily assumed. Nor should
the importance attached by so many nineteenth-century churchmen to
weekly attendance simply be taken for granted.

The choice of attendance on Sunday as the supreme index of
religious commitment was most appropriate to those whose main
interest was in social control: compulsory church attendance from
1559 until 1687 had been an instrument of state authority, supported
by civil as well as ecclesiastical penalties;[6] the efforts of the Council of
Trent to ensure that every Catholic went to Mass on Sundays and holy
days had been part of a larger code of universally required observances
designed to 'divert all streams of popular religion into a single parochial
channel', the parish being 'a passive recipient of hierarchically conveyed
instructions'.[7] In nineteenth-century England a monopolistic state
church was no longer possible, but attendance at some sort of church
service still satisfied a desire on the part of the dominant class for
public, formal and national displays of religion (on the same day and, if
possible, at the same time), for the equation of Christianity alike with
patriotism and with good taste.[8] Sunday in general was dedicated to
the demonstration of the essential religiousness of the English people,
and above all Sunday mornings from 11 o'clock to 12.45 was sacred to
the cause of national respectability.[9] For the last seventy years it has
gradually been losing this function, and throughout this time the
decline in church attendances has been among the stock in trade of
preachers and journalists. The moral usually drawn – that a decreasing
number of Englishmen are professing some sort of Christianity – is
justified in this context. But the reasons for the significance possessed
by weekly attendance from the sixteenth century to the twentieth were
mainly political, and it would be wrong to assume that the act has any
intrinsic religious value. To take attendance at public worship once on
Sunday as a chief test of an individual's or a community's religious

commitment is to accept the assumptions of those who regarded religion chiefly as an instrument of social control or as defined by formal acts prescribed and checked by ecclesiastical authority.[10]

The church attendance censuses remain a useful index of attachment to the churches, as long as the special political and social significance of such attendance in nineteenth-century England is recognised, and no conclusions in terms of religious belief are drawn.

Church Attendance Censuses

A detailed picture of the church-going population at a single point in time can be built up by using the *Daily News* religious census, which was taken between November 1902 and November 1903. This was probably the fullest and the most accurate census of church attendance ever taken in Britain. Comparison of the results with those of the *British Weekly* census taken in 1886-7 shows that both the average attendance rate for London, and the differential between the areas with the highest and lowest rates had fallen; but on many points the earlier census provides insufficient detail for comparison. The exact figures produced by the *Daily News* do not mean much, as they were subject to rapid change, but the contrasts they reveal between the habits of different sections of society hold good for a wider period, stretching backwards at least to the 1851 religious census and forward to the present day.

The *Daily News* counted 1,003,109 attendances in the course of the census, a number approximately equal to 22 per cent of the population of Inner London.[11] Of these, a certain proportion represented the same individual attending more than one service on the same day. By using the *Daily News* count of 'twicers' in sixty-nine churches it is possible to estimate that the proportion of individual church-goers to population was 19 per cent.[12]

The proportion of church-goers in some boroughs was considerably more than this 19 per cent, and in other boroughs much less. If smaller units were chosen, the range would be greater. The level of Anglican attendance in an area can be predicted with a high degree of confidence on the basis of its social composition. Nonconformist attendance rates are less predictable, and Roman Catholic rates not at all predictable on these lines. But the distribution of the church-going population as a whole followed in modified form the pattern set by the Church of England.

The twenty-eight metropolitan boroughs and twenty-three Outer London districts have been graded on the basis of the number of female domestic indoor servants per 100 families and of the percentage of the population counted in tenements of eight or more rooms.[13] Hampstead is ranked no.1 and Bethnal Green no.51. The Social Index thus formed correlates positively at the 0.1% level of significance with the ranking order of adult attendances per cent of population in 1902-3. That is, the probability of such a relationship arising by chance is less than 1 in 1000. The relationship between social status and Anglican attendances is even more clear cut. Although the figures are slightly lower than expected in the wealthiest *Inner* London districts, the association within the Inner and Outer areas is very close indeed. (See Tables 6 to 8).

The level of Nonconformist attendances was less uniformly determined by social status; but the rate was significantly related to the percentage of the population living in tenements of six or seven rooms at the time of the 1911 census — meaning usually those with a house of their own but a fairly small house. The number of Nonconformist worshippers generally increased as the number of those around the middle of the social hierarchy increased. (See Table 9).

The association between Anglican church-going and wealth, between Nonconformity and modest prosperity was common knowledge. A more precise idea of the level of church-going at each social level can be got from a comparison of adult attendance rates in eighty-one areas, each composed of three or four Anglican parishes, and each with an adult population of around 15,000. The eighty-one areas have been divided into seven groups according to their colouring on Booth's social map of London: poor, working class, upper working class, lower middle class, middle class, wealthy-suburban, wealthy-West End. From each group the median percentage of attendances to population has been taken. It must be emphasised that these percentages do not represent the level of attendances in a given social stratum, but merely the level of attendances in areas where that stratum is the dominant element: no area is socially uniform, and in every area some groups will be over-represented in congregations. Moreover, individual results can only be regarded as approximations, since they depend on estimates of the number of adults in an estimated population, the general character of which has been estimated, and not, as would now be possible, classified according to the return of occupations for the relevant ward at the census.

The results can be seen in Diagram 1. Taking the median percentage for each group, total adult attendance rises slowly from poor to lower middle-class areas. It is 11.7 per cent of the adult population in the poor areas, 13.2 per cent in the working-class, 16.1 per cent in the upper working-class, 18.2 per cent in the lower middle-class districts. There is then a steeper rise to 22.7 per cent in the middle-class districts, and an even steeper rise to 36.8 per cent in the wealthy-suburban districts, followed by a drop to 33.8 per cent in the West End. The figures for individual areas range from 6.0 per cent in Bethnal Green South to 43.4 per cent in Blackheath and Lee.

The pattern is established by the Anglicans, the number of whose worshippers rises at first gradually and then steeply with each step up the social ladder, ranging from 1.6 per cent in Somers Town to 34.5 per cent in South Kensington, the group medians ranging from 4.0 per cent to 22.1 per cent. Nonconformist percentages varied more widely within each group because of the concentration of their support on popular chapels. But their strength evidently lay in the upper working-class and in the middle-class suburbs: they were weak at either extreme of the social hierarchy. The figures confirm what was generally believed – that chapel-goers were slightly more numerous in the working and lower middle classes, while church-goers were the majority in the servant-keeping classes. (See Tables 10 to 12.)

Jews and Roman Catholics have not been considered separately in the present analysis, since the chief factor determining the location of their places of worship was not the social composition of the neighbourhood but the proportion of various types of immigrant and their descendants. Most of the districts included here did not have their own Catholic church, and Jewish worshippers were concentrated even more heavily on the City of London and the borough of Stepney. The smaller Protestant denominations, such as the Brethren and the Salvation Army, were also unrepresented in many areas. In wealthy and fashionable districts, churches of this type were scarcely to be found at all. Elsewhere, the gospel halls of the Brethren were distributed fairly evenly, while the barracks of the Salvation Army were found chiefly in working-class districts. The former seem to have been strongest in lower middle-class areas – though their chief concentration was regional rather than social, being in South-East London – and the latter in upper working-class areas.[14] However, in view of the claims made for the Salvation Army both by its admirers and by many of its members it is worth noting that most of the working-class districts considered here had no barracks or slum post at all, and that only in one of them (Deptford) did the most popular place of worship belong to the

Army.[15]

The most interesting result of this analysis of church attendance rates in seven types of area is the difference between the middle class and the wealthy. The difference that preoccupied contemporaries was that between the working class and the middle class. These figures suggest that the difference between the middle class and the wealthy was as great or greater.

The poorest districts thus tended to have the lowest rates of attendance, those with large upper middle class and upper class populations the highest. But this class pattern is slightly disturbed by a regional factor: Bethnal Green and Shoreditch do indeed have very low rates, but the lowest figures of all were returned in the more mixed West London borough of Fulham. These might be attributed to the fact that it rained heavily on the day the *Daily News* enumerators reached Fulham, but Fulham was not alone: nearly every district in West and South-West London returned figures lower than those for socially similar areas elsewhere. On the other hand, districts in north-east London returned higher figures than expected, with Nonconformity especially strong. Lower middle-class districts such as Ilford and Wood Green and a mixed district such as Enfield all have rates of over 30 per cent, while Walthamstow and West Ham, with rates of around 20 per cent, are placed rather higher than other strongly working-class districts. The reason seems to lie in the localisation within London of immigrants from different regions. The western and south-western suburbs of London contained in disproportionate numbers immigrants from Surrey, Sussex and West Middlesex, areas of low rural church-going, with fewer Nonconformists than any other part of England, while the north-eastern suburbs attracted immigrants from the Nonconformist strongholds of Eastern England, where rural church attendance was above the national average. Thus, the adult attendance rate was 19.6 per cent in West Ham, but 15.4 per cent in the socially similar area of Battersea, and 40.6 per cent in Hornsey but 32.8 per cent in Wimbledon. At the beginning of the twentieth century the localisation of culture was sufficiently marked even within London to produce not a single class-determined pattern, but a series of similar but still far from identical patterns of formal religion.[16] After allowance has been made for the fact that a disproportionate number of migrants were middle-class, it does not appear, however, that migrants as such were more or less likely than Londoners to attend church. (See Tables 22 – 23.)

Taking therefore as representative of three sections of society at the beginning of the twentieth century a Hampstead barrister, a Lewisham clerk and a Bethnal Green costermonger: the first would be likely to spend some part of an average week attending church services, probably Anglican; in the case of the second, it would be harder to predict, but if he did attend church it would probably be Nonconformist; in the case of the third it would be most unlikely that he would attend any sort of church. It would be wrong to conclude from this that the first was 'more religious' than the others. But whatever the reason for the different custom the fact of it necessarily had some effect on the feel of life at these various social levels.

It was in the matter of church attendance by adults that the class differential was widest. Except among Irish Roman Catholics, only a small proportion of working-class adults attended the main Sunday church services. On the other hand, most of them would have attended church regularly as children and would ensure that their children did the same. A higher proportion of children than of adults attended church on census Sunday, and many more must have attended Sunday School.[17] Children needed an elementary moral education and a bit of discipline, while their parents needed a rest on Sunday.[18] Sunday School appeared to fill both functions, as well as providing occasional treats.[19] In working-class districts Sunday School classes of varying degrees of roughness multiplied, and the main church services might be attended by more children than adults.[20] The churches' functions were strictly delimited. Working-class Londoners regarded church as a necessary part of childhood; but as soon as a man or woman began to earn a living the compulsion was dropped, and you only went to church because you had a reason for doing so.

Such special reasons might include membership of a sect or unusually strong convictions of a more orthodox kind, like those of Joseph Williamson, a Poplar sailor's son, and later a well-known East End vicar. As a choir-boy at St Saviour's, Poplar, around 1910, he fell under the influence of Fr. Dawson, and formed a secret ambition to become a priest: 'Whereas the majority of boys left the church at fourteen when they left the choir, it did not happen to me. Religion had become a very vital part of my life'.[21] On the other hand, most people were agreed that the great occasions of life needed a church, whether it was because priests and church buildings possessed some magical power, because of the dignity and sense of ritual that they provided, or simply because church services were fun, as long as you did not experience them too frequently. Besides 'birth, and copulation, and death', Christmas, Easter, Harvest Festival and Watch Night ranked as

great days, possibly demanding the dignity of a church service. Thus, in
Frederick Willis' lower middle-class family about the 1890s:

> The Church was the Church of England – all others were im-
> posters and ought to be put down. We were regular church-goers, for
> did not we go twice a year, at Harvest Thanksgiving and Christmas?
> I did hear vague rumours from time to time that we were to go
> in the long intervals, but nothing ever came of it.[22]

For working-class Londoners the great church festival of the year was
Watch Night. Thus the Rector of Bethnal Green in 1900 referred to 'the
long established habit of the people to refrain from church going
except on New Years Eve',[23] and Ernest Aves described Watch Night,
1898, in a crowded Somers Town chapel, when he stood near to a
'muscular, full-blooded ruffian of 35 or so' who 'accompanied the
preacher's remarks with a running commentary of his own, not very
complimentary or choice in phrasing', and his wife who 'was conscious
of the occasion' and 'during his little outbursts was half angry and half
fearful lest he should be turned out'.[24]

Just as many people felt that church attendance was appropriate on
certain occasions, but not on others, so there were many who felt that
the wife was the proper representative of the household at church
services. Thus, a Hackney clergyman complained of husbands who
called their wives when they knocked at the door.[25] This was not
necessarily anti-clericalism – merely a case of rather rigidly defined sex
roles. In every borough but Stepney (where the synagogues were largely
attended by men) the proportion of women attending church was
higher than the proportion of men. The differential was slightly greater
in working-class boroughs than others, and greater in Anglican and
Roman Catholic congregations than in Nonconformist chapels, perhaps
because Nonconformist families were those that made a definite
profession of religion, and had no time for any such division of roles.
(See Table 13).

The interesting point, however, is not that congregations were
predominantly female, but that the predominance was so slight.
Attendances by men were equal to 18.1 per cent of males aged 15 and
over; the equivalent figure for women was 24.0 per cent. This might be
compared to the diocese of Orléans in 1878, where the proportion of
women attending Mass was five and a half times greater than the
proportion of men.[26] The custom of women attending church but not
men is part of the double standard syndrome. It is characteristic of the
middle and upper classes of societies in which deep religious feeling is

rare, but the church is an important conservative institution, and a certain minimum of religious observance by its women a test of a family's · respectability. In nineteenth-century London there was certainly greater pressure on women than on men to attend church, and a certain proportion of church-goers, most of them in Anglican congregations, were there primarily as guarantors of family respectability. But the pressure on women to act in this way seems to have been weaker and the pressure on men greater than in the diocese of Orléans, where the very high proportion of girls doing their Easter duties was a further example of the application of strictly defined sex- and age-roles to religious custom. Meanwhile, there were relatively large devout sub-cultures, predominantly Nonconformist, in nineteenth-century London, in which the idea of the family was central and there was a minimum of separation between the male and female worlds.

Nonconformists

The size of the church-going population can thus be stated with a fair degree of accuracy, and its approximate social composition can be deduced. More precise information about the composition of particular religious groups can be obtained from the scattered evidence of marriage registers and church membership lists.

The occupations of men marrying in Nonconformist chapels in Lewisham and Bethnal Green have been used to determine the social location of the various branches of Dissent in these two boroughs, the one suburban with a large middle-class population, the other predominantly working-class. Unfortunately, it is impossible to say how representative the chapel-marrying population is of the population in membership or worshipping there. In Bethnal Green, there is at least strong evidence that few of those marrying in chapel were outsiders;[27] but it is possible that some sections of Nonconformity preferred church weddings.[28]

Whether or not the registers accurately represent the relative proportions of the various occupational groups within the Nonconformist population, they undoubtedly show a bias in favour of some groups and against others. The most obvious example is the relative absence of manual workers. Table 1 compares the proportion of manual workers in two Nonconformist samples with the proportions in samples of those marrying in registry offices and Anglican churches.

The working-class majority was not completely absent from the chapels, but it was certainly not represented in proportion to its numbers. Even in Bethnal Green, the most working-class of all metropolitan boroughs, no more than half of those marrying in chapel were manual workers.

Yet the simple division into working class and not working class masks important distinctions on either side of the divide. In each case skilled workers appear in the registers much more frequently than unskilled, and clerical workers more often than business and professional men. It is in fact these two groups that form the majority of those marrying in chapel in Bethnal Green, 1880-1901, and again in Lewisham, 1899-1914. No matter how other groups might be over-represented, they would be outnumbered by those on the borderline between the working and the middle class.

In Bethnal Green, for instance, the borough that finished last or second to last in every table of health, wealth or comfort, just over half those marrying in chapel came from the non-manual minority. Yet there is a division within the manual working population almost as great as that between working men and the others. Skilled workers appear in large numbers in the chapel registers, and semi-skilled workers are also fairly represented; but unskilled workers, porters, carmen, labourers are almost completely absent. At one end of the scale, clerks, employers, professional men are heavily over-represented; at the other, labourers are scarcely represented at all. In the middle, skilled and semi-skilled workers and retailers appear in about the 'expected' proportions. In the Anglican sample there are 155 unskilled workers and one professional man; in the Nonconformist sample, fourteen unskilled workers and thirteen professional men. Yet the large 'skilled' category also masked differences. Taking four of the largest local trades: cabinet-makers are fairly numerous, and printers, the labour aristocrats of London, appear more often than any occupation other than clerks or salesmen; but workers in the building or the boot trade are much less well represented. Those marrying in chapel remained a small minority even of skilled workers. These figures probably reflect not any sharp division between the skilled and unskilled populations of Bethnal Green as a whole, but the existence of a distinctive minority culture within the working class, its members heavily concentrated on skilled occupations, and many of them Nonconformists. (See Table 14.)

In Lewisham, vast estates for the lower middle class were being built at the end of the nineteenth century, but an older population existed of working men in the Ravensbourne valley and of the wealthy on the heights of Blackheath and Sydenham. While the new-comers were the largest element in the chapels, the chapel-marrying population was closer to the church-marrying population than it had been in Bethnal Green. Manual workers are again less numerous in the chapels, but of the occupational sub-divisions, only clerical workers on the one side and the unskilled on the other are significantly over-represented. (See Table 15.)

The three Nonconformist denominations that have been treated as a single unit were not interchangeable. But their social as well as their theological differences were matters of detail. Congregationalists, if caught off their guard, were capable of being superior about the intellectual attainments of the average Baptist. There were Baptists who held that a B. A. was no adequate substitute for a saving gospel. But both denominations drew the bulk of their support from the same sections of the population: the lower middle class and the 'respectable' artisan. In Bethnal Green, 55.3 per cent of Baptist husbands were manual workers, as against 52.1 per cent of Wesleyans and 38.9 per cent of Congregationalists; on the otherhand, 34.6 per cont of Congregationalist husbands were clerical workers, as against 24.0 per cent of Baptists. In Lewisham, the social differences between the main branches of Nonconformity were even narrower, but the Congregationalists had a significantly higher proportion of professional men than the other denominations.

Some of the smaller Nonconformist denominations might show different occupational distributions: for instance, the Quakers and Unitarians might show very high proportions of professional men, or the Methodist sects might show a large working-class population. A small sample of Methodist sectarians from Lewisham shows an occupational composition very similar to that of the main branches of Dissent. On the other hand, a Quaker sample, taken from the whole of Inner London, does show a significantly different pattern, with a very small proportion of manual workers, and a high proportion of employers. (See Table 16.)

When these figures are compared with those taken from the church attendances censuses there is one discrepancy: while the marriage registers confirm the general belief that Nonconformists were most frequently drawn from the lower middle class, the *Daily News* census suggested that chapel attendance reached the highest level in wealthy suburbs. The probable explanation lies in the concentration on the wealthier suburbs of some of the more prestigious Nonconformist chapels, with prominent ministers, a wealthy leadership, and a large and more socially varied membership.[29]

Roman Catholics

The distribution of Roman Catholic worshippers was almost exactly the reverse of the distribution of Nonconformists.

In the suburbs they seldom exceeded 1 per cent of the population; they exceeded 2.5 per cent in several parts of West London and in the riverside boroughs of Stepney, Bermondsey and Woolwich, and reached a maximum of 8.4 per cent in Holborn, home of the most famous of Irish ghettos, as well as of 2,000 natives of Italy. Some of the strength of the Catholic Church in West London must have been due to the conversion of wealthy Anglicans,[30] as well as to the location there of several thousand Frenchmen and Germans;[31] but all those boroughs with large numbers of Catholic worshippers had been favoured by Irish immigrants.[32] The relationship that this worshipping population bears to Catholic London as a whole is much harder to determine. Booth, basing himself on the number of baptisms, estimated that there were 200,000 Catholics in Inner London.[33] If this is accurate, the 74,000 who went to Mass during the *Daily News* census, formed rather more than a third of the Catholic population. Charles Russell, on the other hand, lecturing to a Catholic society in 1907, used statistics of children in Catholic schools and of Catholic children in LCC schools to produce an estimated population of 352,000. On this estimate, the proportion of Catholics attending Mass would be scarcely any higher than the proportion of Protestants going to church:

> To say that only one non-Catholic out of six or seven goes to church may not surprise some, but to say that only one Catholic out of four goes to church without fail every Sunday in the year will astound many. It is said to have made the late Cardinal Vaughan weep.[34]

In fact, Russell was probably over-optimistic: while the proportion of 20-30 per cent of Catholics attending Mass in any given week seems to be fairly well supported, the proportion going 'without fail every Sunday in the year' must have been lower.[35] What is clear is that there were many gradations of Catholic allegiance, extending from the relatively small number of those whose lives centred round their church, through those who went to Mass regularly and those who sent their children to the Catholic school,[36] to those who lived quite happily without a priest but would not die without one, and others who were Catholics only in the sense of not being Protestants.

There were similar gradations within the Protestant population, although the less devout Protestant had none of the strong sense of religious identity that made many who never went to Mass still very conscious of being Catholics.[37] The Catholic Church, however, was unique among the larger religious bodies by the fact that so many of the most devout were drawn from the working class and even from the poor. This was often remarked upon at the end of the century by such observers as Charles Booth and Charles Masterman.[38] Statistical support for these observations is provided by the only occupational list I have seen of the members of a Catholic confraternity. It is a list of men joining the Confraternity of the Holy Family at St Anne's, Spitalfields, between 1858 and 1860, stating among other things, their year and place of birth, address and occupation.[39] In a sample of a hundred, eighty-seven had been born in Ireland, as against two Germans, the rest having been born in England, and their dates of birth ranged from 1788 to 1844. The occupational distribution was very similar to that of the Irish population of London as a whole. Sixty-one of the one hundred were unskilled workers, as against 68 per cent of Irish-born heads of household in occupations in a sample drawn by Lynn Lees from the 1861 census.[40] The proportion of non-manual workers was even lower — two, as against 9 per cent, but the proportion of skilled workers was rather higher, a large proportion of them falling into such characteristic categories as shoemaker (eleven) and tailor (five).[41] These figures are in sharp contrast to the Bethnal Green marriage registers, which showed that even in such a thoroughly working-class district a very large proportion of Nonconformists came from the middle class.

It is evident from the figures presented in this chapter that formal religion existed within at least three sharply differentiated contexts — those of the working class, of the middle class and of the gentry — and that even within these basic status-groups there were further significant differences between the suburban and the West End gentry, between the unskilled working class and a section of the skilled, and between Protestant and Catholic working men. To understand the different religious assumptions imbibed in these largely separate worlds, assumptions of which the difference in formal religious practice was only one relatively trivial expression, it is necessary to look at other types of evidence — the findings of social surveys, newspaper reports, novels, and above all, the autobiographies of those brought up within each of these different environments.

Notes

1. For which see 'Religious Worship (England and Wales)', *P.P.*, 1852-3, LXXIX, *British Weekly* 5 November, 1886–17 December 1886 and 13–20 January 1888. R. Mudie-Smith (ed.), *The Religious Life of London*, Hodder and Stoughton, London, 1904.

2. 'Methodism, fascinated by statistics, and aware of itself as a very recent and dynamic phenomenon in English Christianity expressed its arrivism in a cult of size. Methodists contemplated their membership returns with the pleasure a successful business might derive from his sales graph'. R. Currie, *Methodism Divided*, Faber, London, 1968, pp.178-9. There is a valuable discussion of Methodist statistics in Chapter 3 of his book. Some of the conclusions he draws are less convincing: while justifiably scornful (pp.178-85) of the Methodist passion for size, Currie is himself prepared with a minimum of argument to equate (p.85) falling membership totals with 'the decline of Christianity'.

3. Visitation returns for the Archdiocese of Liverpool can be seen at Lancashire County Record Office. Unfortunately those for Westminster have not survived, and I have not obtained access to the records of the diocese of Southwark.

4. For an Anglican pioneer of the statistical investigation of religious affiliation, combining a pastoral and sectarian interest with a passion for the accumulation of figures, see W. S. F. Pickering, 'Abraham Hume (1814-1884), A Forgotten Pioneer of Religious Sociology', in *Archives de Sociologie des Religions*, no.33, janvier-juin 1972.

5. According to Horace Mann's definition of the attitude prevailing in the upper class. See 'Religious Worship (England and Wales)'. *P.P.* 1852-3, LXXXIX, clviii..

6. G. V. Bennett attributes high proportions of Easter communicants in the reign of Charles II to the fact that those failing to attend church or communicate at Easter were frequently called before the church courts and that if excommunicated they were liable to various civil disabilities and possible imprisonment. See his article in G. Holmes (ed.), *Britain after the Glorious Revolution*, Macmillan, London, 1969, p.157.

7. J. Bossy, 'The Counter-Reformation and the People of Catholic Europe', *Past and Present*, no.47, May 1970, pp.54, 60.

8. Thus Comte Goblet d'Alviella, referring in 1875 to 'l'idée essentiellement anglaise – le préjugé si l'on veut – qu' il n'est pas "respectable" de ne pas assister le dimanche à un office religieux', added that 'l'opinion ne s'inquiète pas si cet office est anglican, catholique, dissident ou même rationaliste, pourvu qu'il soit célébré devant une "congregation" par un "ministre" d'un dénomination quelconque.' See his article, 'Une Visite aux Eglises Rationalists de Londres', *Revue des Deux Mondes*, septembre-octobre 1875, p.193.

9. Melmotte, the parvenu financier (A. Trollope, *The Way We Live*

Now, OUP, London, 1941, I, pp.375-83, (first published 1874-5) demonstrates his outsider status by making appointments for Sunday morning. It was presumably because they felt out of place at such a celebration that most working-class and lower middle-class church-goers preferred the evening service (though also for the reason that they were more in need of Sunday morning sleep). Le Play, who was impressed by the irreligiosity of English artisans (this group apparently being distinguished for their piety in most Protestant countries), and shocked by the blatancy of class distinction in Anglican churches, asserted that 'l'usage veut que l'église ne soit fréquentée le matin que par les classes supérieures de la société' while 'les classes ouvrières ne se rendent ordinairement a l'église qu'a 6 heures du soir.' F. Le Play, *Les Ouvriers Européens* 2nd ed., Tours, 1877, III, pp.275-6. (first published, 1855).

10. For an example of the common tendency of clergymen, especially Roman Catholics and High Anglicans, to attach intrinsic value to formal acts performed at regular intervals, see A. F. Winnington-Ingram, *A Charge Delivered to the Clergy and Churchwardens of the Diocese of London*, Wells Gardner, London, 1905, p.36, in which he described the 40,000 men and women in the diocese who communicated weekly as 'the rock upon which we must build the Church'.

11. The *Daily News* enumerators visited each borough on a different Sunday, the direction of their next visit not being announced in advance, and the results were published on the following Tuesday, after which they were open to challenge, and recounts could be made at a later date. In the cases of Fulham and Hammersmith, thick fog on the Sunday chosen led to a general recount later in the year.

12. Although the method used by the *Daily News* to estimate the proportion of 'twicers' was probably as good as any, the results were presented in a misleading way, and the number of people attending church twice on the same day has accordingly sometimes been exaggerated. For an explanation of the methods used see Mudie-Smith, op.cit., p.6, and for a fuller consideration of the count of 'twicers', my Cambridge Ph.D. thesis, 'Membership and Influence of the Churches in Metropolitan London, 1885-1914', 1971, pp.89-90.

13. These are taken as social status indicators. Because of the inadequacy of the occupational data in the census no completely satisfactory indicator can be found.

14. R. Robertson, 'The Salvation Army: The Persistence of Sectarianism', in B. R. Wilson (ed.), *Patterns of Sectarianism*, Heinemann, London, 1967, pp.98-100, takes it as given that from about the 1900s onwards the membership of the Salvation Army was largely lower middle-class, apart from certain ' "non-communal" occupational groups', such as transport workers. Whether or not this is true, he provides no evidence beyond a priori reasoning.

15. Even at the time of the *British Weekly* census, when the reputation of the Army, then emerging from its period of persecution, was close to its highest point, attendance at Salvationist meetings in London was lower than was generally believed. When it was discovered that only 53,591 had attended Salvationist services at the mission hall census of 1887, Robertson Nicoll, the editor of the *British Weekly,* poured scorn on the Army's grand claims. Yet something had gone wrong with the Army's geography and the *British Weekly's* arithmetic: the total which Nicoll derided had still been substantially inflated by the inclusion of returns from such places as Hounslow and Canning Town and by a failure to add the figures correctly. The number attending Salvationist services in Inner London should have been 42,205 or 29,581 if, as in 1902-3, afternoon services were excluded.

16. This point is developed further in McLeod, 'Churches in Metropolitan London', pp.105-10 and in my article, 'Class, Community and Region: The Religious Geography of nineteenth-century England', in M. Hill (ed.), *A Sociological Yearbook of Religion in Britain, 6,* SCM Press, London, 1973.

17. Attendances at church by those aged 14 and under were equal to 23.8% of those in this age-group, as against 21.3% for those aged 15 and over. The differential would be rather greater if the very young were excluded. At Chelsea, the only borough where Sunday Scholars were counted, as many as 30% of the child population was enumerated at church and a slightly greater proportion at Sunday Schools and Children's Services.

18. Booth Collection, B287, pp.49-51; T. Willis, *Whatever Happened to Tom Mix?*, Cassell, London, 1970, pp.40-1. According to one East London priest (Booth Collection, B180, p.47), 'Even Protestants who have been brought up Protestants are quite content that their children should be brought up Catholics. Religion is good, they say because it makes the children more obedient and better to live with at home.'

19. The belief that Sunday Schools helped to keep children in order was probably a sign of failing memory on the part of parents. For the contrary view, see F. Willis, *101 Jubilee Road,* Phoenix, London, 1949, p.79: 'It was the Sunday Schools that specialised in Treats and Teas, and it was for these material joys rather than for the spiritual ones that most children went to Sunday School, I am afraid. They were conducted by earnest young men and women who had little ability to maintain discipline, and children found conditions there a welcome relief from the stern realism of the Board School'.

20. A 'ragged Sunday School' in Poplar, held at 5.45 on Sunday evening, is described in J. M. Thompson, Diary, 2.11.1902; and the assiduity with which parents in the Mint, Southwark, who seldom sent their children to Day School sent them to Sunday School was mentioned by a School Board Visitor in evidence to the Royal Commission on the Working of the Elementary Education Acts,

P.P. 1887, XXX, QQ. 52918-20.

21. J. Williamson, *Father Joe*, Hodder, London, 1963, p.50.
22. F. Willis, *Peace and Dripping Toast*, Phoenix, London, 1950 p.29.
23. London Visitation, 1900.
24. Booth Collection, B386, pp.87-9. Later the 'ruffian' shook Aves by the hand and promised to return on Sunday evening, 'my Bible under my arm and my hymn-book in my pocket'.
25. Ibid., B185, p.173.
26. 5.5% of adult men and 30% of adult women communicated at Easter. C. Marcilhacy, *Le Diocèse d'Orléans sous l'Episcopat de Mgr Dupanloup*, Plon, Paris, 1962, p.556. A recent study of Mass attendance in French cities in the 1950s shows much narrower sex differentials: about 2:1 or slightly less, Lyon, where 19% of women and 10% of men went to Mass being typical. F. Boulard and J. Rémy, *Pratique Religieuse Urbaine et Régions Culturelles*, Editions Ouvrières, Paris, 1968, Tableau A.
27. In the '80s a high proportion of the Bethnal Green population was still illiterate. Taking all Nonconformist and civil weddings in the district in the period 1880-1891 and a sample of 400 Anglican weddings from two parish churches, the following were the numbers of men and women signing with marks, the number of weddings being given in brackets. Nonconformist (304) m.0, f.3; Civil (296) m.7, f.19; C of E (400) m.25, f.48. The difference between proportions of illiterates among those marrying in chapel and in registry office is statistically highly significant, between those marrying in chapel and in church evidently much more so. The population marrying in chapel is clearly highly selected.
28. In 1903, 4.9% of those marrying in London chose Nonconformist ceremonies *(London Statistics, 1904–5,* p.xvi) whereas the percentage of the population attending Nonconformist services during the *Daily News* census was rather greater – about 7.5.
29. I have found one piece of evidence on this subject: the Manual of Lyndhurst Road Congregational Church for 1903. This showed that church members lived in the middle class, rather than in the wealthiest areas of Hampstead. In a sample of 100, 22 lived in streets marked yellow ('wealthy') on Booth's map of London, as against 53 in streets marked red (middle-class), 13 living in streets marked in red and pink (mixed middle-class and working-class), and 12 living in mainly working-class streets. Out of 23 elders whose addresses I have identified, 7 lived in streets marked yellow. It might be argued that this example discredits the whole procedure of identifying the social character of congregations with that of the neighbourhood in which they existed. In fact, the wealthiest Baptist and Congregational churches were the only examples of a kind of church concentrated in only two kinds of area, but drawing its members much more widely. The two types of area were depopulated central districts and outer suburbs favoured by the Nonconformist patron class. The reason for this

concentration lay in the autonomy of the local church and the consequent extreme inequality in church finances, and thus in buildings and ministerial salaries. The most attractive preachers, and thus the largest congregations, were generally to be found either in historic buildings in the older parts of London or else close to the homes of the patron class on whose munificence they depended for their large salaries and buildings capable of holding all those who wanted to hear them. (The Lyndhurst Road Church Manual for 1884 detailed the contributions made by the deacons to the building fund: while one could only manage £45, all the others gave over £100, and one gave £2,000).

30. Wealthy converts were sufficiently numerous, as well as interesting to Catholics, to form the subject of a biographical dictionary, running through several editions, W.G. Gorman, *Converts to Rome*.

31. Though Arthur Sherwell, referring to Soho with its French restaurant workers, claimed that 'this foreign element is largely and avowedly irreligious'. Mudie-Smith, op.cit., p.94.

32. In 1851, when 4.6% of the London population were natives of Ireland, the proportion exceeded 10% in St. Giles, Whitechapel and St. Olave, Southwark. By 1911, the proportion for London had dropped to 1.1% and exceeded 2% only in Woolwich and in the West London boroughs.

33. Booth, op.cit., III, vii, p.250.

34. C. Russell, *The Catholics of London and Public Life*, London, 1907, p.9. The chief purpose of the lecture was to show how badly, in relation to their numbers, Catholic Londoners were represented in public life.

35 When Charles Booth's team was interviewing Catholic priests in the late '90s, they were asked to state the numbers of their parishioners and average attendance at Mass. Attendances of around 30 per cent were reported in Rotherhithe, Southwark, Walworth, Woolwich, Fulham, Somers Town and Bow, with rather higher figures at Manchester Square and Little Albany Street and lower figures (around 20%) in Marylebone Road, the Isle of Dogs, Bermondsey, Vauxhall and another Fulham parish. The level of Mass attendance seems to have been similar in 1851, when a higher proportion of Catholics were first-generation immigrants, but the provision of Catholic churches for them to worship in was rather worse. Thus McDonnell estimates that 22% of Catholics in Stepney went to Mass on Census Sunday, and Gilley suggests a London average of 25 per cent. S. Gilley, 'Evangelical and Catholic Missions to the Irish in London, 1830-70', Cambridge University Ph.D. thesis, 1971, pp.12-13; K.G.T. McDonnell, 'Roman Catholicism in London, 1850-65', in A.E.J. Hollander and W. Kellaway (eds.), *Studies in London History*, Hodder, London, 1969, p.431.

36. According to priests interviewed by Booth, about 30% of Catholics went to Mass in Walworth but 80% of the children went to Catholic schools; in Rotherhithe, 30% and 95%. A priest

in Fulham distinguished between the 'respectable poor' who 'attend well to their religious duties' and the 'rough poor' (mostly costers), who did not go to Mass but sent their children to the Catholic school. Booth Collection, B277, p.7; B265, pp.131-3.

37. The Annual Report of St. Patrick's, Soho, 1870, reported a Jesuit mission, in which the missioners had tried to visit every Catholic household in the parish. They were disturbed to find how many Catholic adults never went to Mass and how many children never went to school, but they were cheered by the fact that 'with few exceptions our Catholics still cling to the faith, and in their hearty welcome to the visit of the priest pay homage in his person to the teaching of their church.'

38. Masterman, who at that time lived in a block dwelling in Camberwell, claimed to have seen 'the poor in bulk' at only two churches in South London — the Wesleyan Central Hall in Bermondsey and the Southwark Roman Catholic cathedral. Booth described the Catholic poor as 'a class apart, being as a rule devout and willing to contribute something from their earnings towards the support of their schools and the maintenance of their religion.' Mudie-Smith, op.cit., p.196; Booth, op.cit., III, vii, p.401.

39. This list is in a cupboard containing nineteenth-century records at St Anne's Presbytery. There is no indication on the list of what its purpose is, and this I have had to deduce by comparing it with other papers in the same collection. The significance of confraternities in the eyes of some of the Catholic clergy and thus the value of knowing which sections of the Catholic population belonged to them, can be seen from the Annual Report of St. Patrick's Soho, 1870: 'Again, knowing as we do the immense importance of Confraternities, whether we consider general or individual sanctification it is really afflicting to our hearts to see so few joining our Confraternities, whose rules are so easy and simple, and even after all the force of the Mission scarcely a new candidate has appeared.'

40. Lees, op.cit., p.172.

41. Cf. ibid., p.166.

CHAPTER III WORKING-CLASS LONDON

Stedman Jones places 8 per cent of occupied males in Inner London in 1891 in his Class I of large employers, property owners and members of the liberal professions; Booth in the late '80s had estimated that 12 per cent of the total population belonged to the upper middle and upper classes.[1] This, then, was the top of the social pyramid. At the bottom were the three million or more of manual workers (70 per cent of occupied males aged ten and over, according to Stedman Jones) and their families. In between, their social status less clearly defined, were retailers, small employers, clerks, shop assistants, teachers — rather over 20 per cent of occupied males in Stedman Jones' calculations, in which they form Class II, but most of them included by Booth in the working class. 'Working-class London' includes all of East London (except for parts of Hackney) and of the inner South and North, together with the numerous, but more scattered areas of the periphery in which wage-earners formed an overwhelming majority of the working population. Besides the working-class majority, such areas also included a small but influential class of retailers and small employers, a smaller number of clerks and salesmen, and a negligible proportion of the wealthy. Such areas were marked out by the intermixture of houses with large or small-scale industry; by the large number of public houses, small shops and street markets, of music-halls and board schools; by the relative strength of the Liberal Party[2] and the relatively small attendance at places of worship.

In spite of divisions of status, and differences of race, religion and party, the majority of those living in working-class London shared a body of attitudes that I shall term 'secularism and parochialism'. The first part of this chapter will be concerned with this majority, and I shall subsequently look at those who rejected - the prevailing assumptions at one point or another.

'Secularism and Parochialism'

The chief principle of this 'secularism and parochialism' was the concentration of knowledge, responsibility and personal ties within a small area, and lack of interest in events outside; its corollaries included indifference to questions of abstract principle, a low valuation of education, and non-participation in organisations. The features of working-class London that gave rise to this body of attitudes were the poverty of many, the insecurity of most, and, in relation to the social system as a whole, the lack of status and power that was universal. Working-class parochialism was imposed by the exigencies of the struggle to scrape together a living; it was a form of physical self-defence against the threat of destitution and the workhouse; it was a form of escape from obligations that the gentry inherited together with their social position; above all, it was a form of psychic self-defence — the demarcation of a limited area within which those at the lower end of a highly stratified society could secure for themselves a degree of status and recognition.

As was argued in Chapter I, economic pressures inhibited the mobility of a large part of the working class, and even those who were not tied in this way showed a strong tendency to marry someone living near to their home. From another point of view, working-class parochialism was an escape from responsibilities that members of the possessing classes could be coerced by the threat of a loss of status into accepting. In a relatively unstratified society, community sanctions may be powerful because everyone is born with status that can be lost through deviant behaviour.[3] In nineteenth-century London, on the other hand, the majority of the population was born with a stigma on them. In the 1850s, referring to recent improvements in the moral and material conditions of the 'industrious classes', Bracebridge Hemyng wrote that: 'The upper ten thousand and the middle-class as a rule have to combat innumerable prejudices, and are obliged to reject the traditions of their infancy before they thoroughly comprehend the actual condition of that race of people, which they are taught by immemorial prescription to regard as immensely inferior if not altogether barbarous'.[4] Thirty or forty years later these prejudices were little diminished. The evidence of William Birt, quoted in Chapter I, is a classic statement of the view of working men, as a class, as generally tending towards the 'altogether barbarous'.[5] Moreover, all had been brought up to dependence and subordination, although this subordination was less pronounced among the skilled working class generally, and especially among those in trades where a long apprenticeship was obligatory and the closed shop was enforced. It is not surprising, therefore, that few of the working class grew up with the sense of obligation to 'society' embodied in an ethos of service that impelled members of the gentry to perform duties and recognise conventions even when they had little desire to do so.

There were gradations of status and power within the working class, but even the most highly placed ranked very low on the overall social scale. Even so, differing ideas of respectability were a powerful source of tensions. Those at the upper end of the class felt an obligation, analogous to the impersonal social pressures to which the gentry were subjected, to send their children to school, to make them learn a trade, to obey the law, to occupy as many rooms as they could possibly afford. Up to a certain point this could be interpreted by neighbours as legitimate pride, but after that it became 'stand-offishness'. At the other end of the spectrum, informality could degenerate into what appeared to neighbours to be 'rough' and thus objectionable. Ability to gain acceptance within a working-class neighbourhood depended on the ability to adjust to the standards applied locally.[6]

A. S. Jasper's account of his Hoxton childhood circa 1914 illustrates the process by which the 'solid working class' met the 'rough working class' in the same street or even in the same family. Jasper senior — with his rackets and his beer, to which he was said to have devoted his life — or his son-in-law Gerry, who was arrested the day after his wedding, and escaped with a relatively light sentence because of the pleas of his obviously pregnant wife, would have been at home with one of Mayhew's costermongers. On the other hand, Jasper himself would seem to have the attitudes of a Labour Aristocrat, while his mother provided a bridge between the two — not over-attached to legality as such, but conscious of the shame of detected illegality.[7] Some streets were entirely given up to the 'rough' working class, while in many others the 'solid' or 'respectable' lived side by side with the 'rough'.[8] Only the very prosperous working class could afford to be fussy about its neighbours. Within most streets, therefore, there were families tending towards the labour aristocratic life-style, with its stress on family and home, on self-improvement and education and its 'respectable' habits; and families approximating to the navvy life-style — and many gradations between. Those at different points on the spectrum did not welcome this proximity.

The chief positive function of working-class parochialism was the demarcation of a limited community within which everyone who did not exclude himself by objectionable behaviour was recognised and had some sort of claim on the friendship of his neighbours, and in which the individual could find a meaning to his life in the responsibilities and rituals of the family, or the conviviality of established friends in the public house. Since status was accorded to all who accepted the mores of the community and treated other members as equals, it was essential that self-improvers of any sort should be ostracised. They were attempting to seize the prizes in a race where the great majority were bound to be also-rans — and were thus defying the essential principle that the prizes were worthless and that the winners were those who did not attempt to compete for them. But this intolerance could be extended to include any form of freak. Up to a point, a certain amount of eccentricity could be taken as a sign that the person concerned was a character: if he accepted ridicule with good humour, and was in other respects a tolerable person, he might establish himself as a local institution, teased interminably, but respected as a man of integrity, rather as the two Socialists were in *The Ragged Trousered Philanthropists*.[9] Beyond that point, eccentricity would be taken as stand-offishness, as a sign that he wished to set himself off from his fellows. Thus, a Mozart-loving lighterman, ridiculed by his workmates for his musical tastes, remembers that even greater scorn had been poured on another lighterman, 'one of the real old school of Labour men', who was known as 'Honest Tom because he never pilfered, never fiddled on over-time or expenses, and always believed in doing a fair day's work. ...He earned nothing but derision from his fellow-workers; he was far too honest to be their hero.'[10]

Middle-class observers, used to an ethical system that was both more legalistic and inclined to attach a general value to such qualities as self-discipline and heroic non-conformity, found it a strange sort of morality. It required some effort of the imagination to find order in the apparent chaos, human values in a seeming morass of amorality. Stephen Reynolds made the effort, and concluded that the values of the poor were vastly superior to those of the rich.[11] A contemporary whom Reynolds quoted with approval is interesting because she clearly found the effort of understanding more difficult. She was a District Nurse, who wrote several garrulous, but occasionally perceptive books on 'the poor'. 'When', she wrote:

> one gets to know the poor intimately, visiting the same houses time after time and throughout periods of as long as eight or ten years, one becomes gradually convinced that in the real essentials of morality they are, as a whole, far more advanced than is generally believed, but the range of human virtue is of a different order from that commonly adopted by the more educated classes. Generosity ranks far above justice, sympathy before truth, love before chastity,

a pliant and obliging disposition before a rigidly honest one.[12]

In terms of this value-system, the thief and the drunkard were not admired, but the good companion was better respected than the tee-totaller, and the man who pilfered in moderation was preferred to the one who remained righteously aloof. Betrayal was the worst sin of all.

In a suburban environment neighbours could gossip, but each family fashioned its own private life: in the working class neither buildings nor style of life allowed much room for privacy.[13] And while the inhabitants of this or that villa were brought together by associations of musicians or actors, the only working-class equivalents were the trade unions and friendly societies that flourished chiefly at the upper end of the class, together with the working men's clubs. The working class were like the aristocracy in preferring clubs to associations, and gatherings only on the basis of being neighbours and of similar social status to those brought together by a specific common interest. Even in sport there was a difference between suburban and working-class tastes: cricket, the favoured recreation of the middle and upper classes being among the most complex and formalised of games, whereas football and sports involving animals were generally preferred by working men.[14] Charles Booth's description of Belle Isle catches the flavour of the poorer streets:

> A group of rough hobbledehoys are at horse-play in one street, varying this amusement by making uncomplimentary remarks regarding any decently dressed pedestrian, while women with unkempt heads and generally a dirty-faced baby in arms peer out from windows or look on from open doorways. The corner houses are doing a thriving business, and outside one a couple of besotted individuals are indulging in a 'friendly spar' giving and receiving blows with half-imbecile good humour. In another street a group of young men have a cage of rats, and are letting them out one at a time for the sport of themselves and a couple of terriers, who make short work of the rodents.[15]

The informality of working-class life was fostered by financial necessity. But budgets — above the level of starvation — were a matter of priorities. Forced to choose between the food, clothing and fuel essential to 'physical efficiency'; the pleasures and companionship of the pub; or subscriptions to a school, a trade union or a church, most people preferred the first or the second. But some, like the poor immigrant Jews, gave precedence to their children's religious and secular education;[16] others, like the Irish Roman Catholics might spend on the pub and the church, and save on clothes.[17] If the native poor preferred their pigeon loft, their fishing rod and their pint pot, this was because organisations, religious, political, cultural, ranked low on their list of priorities.[18]

It was not only organisations as such that were suspect, but also the assumptions of most of those who belonged to them. This can be illustrated by looking at characteristic working-class attitudes in the broad areas of education, politics and religion. While opinions differed, underlying assumptions varied much less.

Those with a passion for books could be attacked from two sides: they could be branded as egotistic self-improvers or as hopelessly unpractical. Either way there was widespread agreement that books were a waste of time and money, and the standard admonishment for those who insisted on reading them was *'That'll* never bring you bread and cheese'.[19] Schools were subject to the same sort of criticism. Just as the upper class liked to define itself as the 'educated class', with an implied justification of its own power, working men shored up their own self-esteem by exalting strength and craft-skill and decrying book-learning and those such as clerks who had to some degree benefitted from it.[20] Educational and financial considerations could be in direct competition when families needed the pennies their children could raise by 'hopping the wag' to go running errands or foraging for saleable metal. But even families that were not in severe need tended to take their children from school at the earliest opportunity.[21] The relative importance of the various reasons for non-attendance at school is less easily determined.[22] It is undoubtedly true that child labour was essential to many household economies, and probably equally true that many parents believed that school, as well as being an expense, was a waste of time. But parents who held such views were seldom in a position to give them public expression, while those who were in such a position generally had an axe to grind. The question of the reasons for non-attendance at school was put to many of the witnesses to the Cross Commission on Elementary Education, since one of its prime tasks was to consider the abolition of fees. Those who favoured fees as a matter of principle naturally minimised the significance of poverty as an obstacle to attendance. An Inspector of Schools in Greenwich was particularly unequivocal:

So far as I can make out, there is very little real poverty in the

district in which I am employed, but the parents are indifferent, and
the children are indifferent. Children now-a-days take the law into
their own hands very much.[23]

But even enthusiasts for free, compulsory, secular education, such as
the representative of the London Trades Council, granted that too
many parents did not care what or whether their children were
learning.[24] Of these parents, an appreciable, though rapidly diminishing
proportion was illiterate.[25] And among the majority who could read
and write and who had received some form of elementary education
there was little enthusiasm for extending it: in the later years of the
nineteenth century and the early years of the twentieth a number of
social settlements and bodies such as the WEA and the University of
London were attempting to provide for an assumed need of lectures
and classes on the part of the working population; many found that
working-class students were hard to attract, and that a large part of
their support came either from clerks and shopkeepers or from Jewish
immigrants.[26] The working-class demand for intellectual stimulus was
largely met by public debate; thus the popularity of park oratory, of
the contests between Christians and Secularists that were a main
attraction at Bradlaugh's Hall of Science,[27] and of the Sunday
afternoon discussions, which proved more attractive than extension
lectures at Toynbee Hall, and where the audience was said to be 'male,
large, uncouth, inclined to be irreverent'.[28] Most London working men
were indifferent to knowledge as an end in itself and uninclined to the
discipline of the self-improver, the abstract and the speculative entered
their lives in the form of public contest.

Preoccupation with keeping afloat in a cruel environment produced
an indifference to questions about the meaning of the world and a good
deal of scepticism about most schemes for changing it. Such concerns
were at best a waste of time and could be a positive nuisance to
neighbours intent on the real business of life. The classic accounts of
this philosophy are in two books written around 1910, the one about
Devon fishermen and the other about Hastings building workers. The
religious attitude of the former was described as follows: ' "Us can't
'spect to know nort about it," says Tony, 'Taint no business o' our's.
May be as they says; may be not. It don't matter that I sees. 'Twill be
all the same in a hundred years time when we'm a grinning up at the
daisy roots." '[29] The latter book, Tressell's novel, *The Ragged
Trousered Philanthropists*, is written from the point of view of a
Socialist decorator, equally scornful of the callousness of his employers

and of the stupidity of his less enlightened workmates:

> 'There's so much the matter with the present system that it's no use tinkering at it. Everything about it is wrong and there's nothing about it that's right. There's only one thing to be done with it and that is to smash it up and have a different system altogether. We must get out ot it.'
>
> 'It seems to me that that's just what you're trying to do', remanded Harlow sarcastically. 'You seem to be trying to get out of the question what Easton asked you.'
>
> 'Yes!' cried Cross fiercely. 'Why don't you answer the bloody question? Wot's the cause of poverty?'
>
> 'What the hell's the matter with the present system?' demanded Sawkins.
>
> ''Ow's it goin' to be altered', asked Newman.
>
> 'Wot the bloody hell system do you think we ought to 'ave', shouted the man behind the moat.
>
> 'It can't never be altered', said Philpot. 'Human nature's human nature and you can't get away from it.'
>
> 'Never mind about human nature', shouted Cross. 'Stick to the point. Wot's the cause of poverty?'
>
> 'Oh, bugger the cause of poverty!' said one of the new hands. 'I've 'ad enough of this bloody row.' And he stood up and prepared to go out of the room.[30]

Parents who knew that an accident at work, a reputation for being a slow worker or a brush with the boss might mean the workhouse for the family instilled in their children suspicion of the dreamer, the thinker or the agitator. This is sometimes termed 'deference'; in fact, it was not an acceptance of the moral validity of the employer's claims, but merely a recognition, however unheroic, of reality.[31] Thus in the 1930s, Ted Willis' father, himself a Labour voter, was infuriated by the irresponsibility of his son's political enthusiasm: a man's first duty was to himself and his family, and to be known as an agitator was to be on the high road to the slums.[32]

The prevailing conception of religion in the working class was that of the Stratford people whose indifference to their own salvation a City Missionary deplored: 'Have found the people here so careless', he wrote:

> These people's idea of Christianity is 'Doing the best you can and doing nobody any harm.' They appear to think that if they don't get

to heaven, there was little chance for anybody.[33]

The views of many otherwise obscure working men and women are recorded in the diaries of the missionaries who came to convert them to their own form of Christianity.[34] Most of the missionaries were preaching Evangelical religion: the Bible, conversion to God, the Sabbath. They found the religion of those to whom they preached perplexing. Thorough-going scepticism was the exception, but the Christianity prevalent among those whom they visited was scarcely one that the missionaries could recognise. For the people of Stratford and Islington, the meaning of life was to be found in the everyday round; to look outside was futile and irrelevant — as well as being anti-social, because it caused embarrassment to neighbours. Within this everyday round there was room for achievement, in merely keeping afloat, and avoiding the humiliation of charity; for virtue, in bringing children up well; for goodness, in generosity to neighbours and workmates; there was also plenty of room for failure, especially for those who wasted their time with less relevant considerations. In this category were included all questions of doctrine, together with the sabbatarianism that mattered so much to the missionaries:

> 22 Popham Road. Had conversation with person here upon subject of closing business on Sundays. She did not see her way clear to do so she said. Sundays they did more than other days and she thought there was no harm in trying to put by a little for the future. I spoke of the realm of the soul and how unwise to neglect for the sake of earthly gain.[35]

Similarly with church attendance. As Ted Willis' mother said in about 1930:

> 'You don't have to go to church, do you? I mean you can live a decent life without all that rigmarole, can't you? Strikes me that half the people who go to church are humbugs anyway, Sunday Christians.' She smiled. 'No, I don't think that He'll hold it against me. When I get to the pearly gates He won't hold it against me, I'm sure of that. And if he does, I'll tell him straight. I was too busy on Sundays getting dinner and tea for you bloody lot to have time to sit on my arse in church!'[36]

Others put 'religion' in general into this category. Thus, at 28 Peabody Square, the missionary met Mrs. Driver, a widow, who 'works hard for her living, but seems to regard religious matters with indifference. Says she has so many things to think about that she could not give her mind to it.'[37]

If such issues as the Trinity or biblical inspiration were simply ignored, hard doctrine, such as hell, was vehemently repudiated. The idea of God was associated with the idea of justice, with which eternal punishment seemed to be incompatible. There were many people who regarded the universe as a conspiracy, but the usual corollary of this was denial of God, or at least the distinction between an unknown God who embodied the principles of beneficence and fair play, and an all too evident cruel God who embodied the reverse.[38] Thus at 55 Popham Road:

> Mrs. Hooker. Had conversation upon spiritual matters. Is rather sceptical: sometimes she thinks there is a heaven, and sometimes she thinks there is not, but she certainly did not believe there is a hell. She does not attend place of worship; they generally had some music at home, which she thinks is as good as going to church.[39]

This repudiation of the obligation, implied or stated by the missionaries, to attend church was common. Church-goers were suspected of thinking they were better than they were, of a sense of superiority to their neighbours, and were thus apt to be mercilessly taunted for any act that fell short of these standards of perfection. Any sort of religion that set a man apart from his neighbours in any way or gave him distinctive habits was suspect for this reason.

In so far as religion *was* useful, it consisted of a primary obligation towards family and a secondary obligation towards friends, together with various basic moral principles embodied in the Golden Rule, which should be taught to children and as far as possible, and as unobtrusively as possible, observed. The fact that children needed some teaching of this sort was generally agreed, and though Secularists claimed that these were just 'the principles of morality' most people, hazy as their ideas of God were, thought they had some form of supernatural sanction. As Mr. Low of Islington said, when invited by the missionary to a Bible class: 'He thought religion was good for children, but he did not see what men wanted to go to Bible classes for'.[40]

There are numerous parallels between the views expressed in the late '90s in the middle-working-class districts of Islington and Stratford, and those of the Hastings building workers, described a dozen years later by Robert Tressell, or of the destitute population of St Giles, visited thirty-five years earlier by James Oppenheimer, a missionary attached to the parish church. The woman who was too busy to think about religion was echoed by the painter's labourer who told his workmates:

> 'Religion is a thing that don't trouble me much; and as for what happens to you after death, it's a thing I believes in leaving till you comes to it — there's no sense in meeting trouble 'arfway. All the things they tells us may be true or they may not, but it takes me all my time to look after *this* world.'[41]

Similar views were frequently expressed in St Giles, though there the poverty of some of those visited was so extreme that they could scarcely achieve the defiant insouciance of the 'philanthropists'. Thus, 'an old woman, named Collins', living in the back room on the second floor at 17 Dudley Street, 'complained very much of poverty, so much so that I found it extremely difficult to avert the subject from things temporal to things spiritual'.[42]

The disbelief in hell of Mrs. Hooker was shared by all the decorators except for the 'converted' Slyme and by most of the St Giles people who mentioned the subject. For instance, in the front room on the first floor at 48 Dudley Street, the missionary met 'old blind Mr. Law', who was 'very well versed in scripture', but indifferent to what the missionary regarded as 'the one thing needful':

> 'I know all about it, you can't tell me anything which I do not know, but I think we shall be all right at last; "do to others as you would be done by", if we do that we need not fear; God made us what we are and he won't require what we can't do.'

The missionary's exposition of Evangelical religion 'did not seem to have the least impression upon him'.[43]

The Stratford people's idea of religion was very close to that of Old Joe Philpot:

> 'I don't see as it matters a damn wot a person believes as long as you don't do no 'arm to nobody. If you see a poor bugger wot's down on 'is luck, give 'im a 'elping 'and. Even if you ain't got no money you can say a kind word. If a man does 'is work and looks arter 'is 'ome and 'is young 'uns, and does a good turn to 'is fellow creature when 'e can, I reckon 'e stands as much chance of getting into 'eaven — if there is such a place — as some of these 'ere Bible-busters, whether 'e ever goes to church or chapel or not.'[44]

Some of the same phrases recur in the remarks of Mrs. Terry at 28 Dudley St., whom the missionary found to be 'very indifferent to things that are made for peace':

'poor people can't do what they ought, my husband and I work hard and don't have a drop of drink from one week's end to another and we try our best to bring our children up well, they are all going to school; I know all this won't save us, but there are plenty of people who go to church and all that, but who are much worse than we are, we don't like to profess what we are not.[45],

And Mr. Low of Islington, would have met with the general agreement of the men of Mugsborough: 'It seemed to be the almost unanimous opinion, that, whether it were true or not, "religion" was a nice thing to teach children.'[46]

It might be assumed that Secularist ideas would be more widespread in London that in Hastings, but few of them seem to have entered the conversations reported by the missionaries; in Mugsborough, the decorators, apart from the atheist Owen, combined a nominal Christianity with an extreme dislike of parsons and vigorous mockery of the only religious man among their workmates. Among the Londoners, only one or two seemed to have a second-hand and one a first-hand knowledge of Secularist or deist arguments. In the first category was the man at 18 Pickering Street, Islington, who 'professes not to believe in the Scriptures. Says one part contradicts another, but he could not name the parts. He declined to continue the conversation, saying that religion was all rubbish.'[47] Perhaps also Mr. Duncan at 34 Pickering Street, who is 'really an infidel and ridicules many of the truths of the Bible such as the Fall of Adam and Eve and the Resurrection of Christ and called it all "a beautiful hallucination".'[48] In the second category was the shopkeeper who asked Oppenheimer:

'Now do you think that God punishes all who don't believe in what you call the gospel and if there is a hell do you think they will all go to hell; well you tell me you are sure of that because your Bible tells you so but I tell you then that God must be very cruel and would act like a tyrant to send to hell more than half the human race. What did he send them in the world for if it were only for to damn them?'[49]

This man seems to have been, apart from one or two Jews and Roman Catholics, the most articulate of the people interviewed by Oppenheimer. The others knew their own mind, and often expressed it vigorously, but their views were seldom the result of prolonged thought, and when the missionaries tried to refute their 'awful delusions' by quotation from Scripture, they certainly could not reply

in kind.[50] Their philosophy was usually a fairly simple one, formed by
private reflection or by the occasional discussion in the home or the
workshop, in the course of which they had come across maxims that
made sense to them, and were not easily shaken. While Tressell's book
is no evidence of the popular beliefs prevailing in London, the close
parallels, extending almost to identical phrases, between the London
missionary diaries of the 1860s and '90s and Tressell's conversations
written about 1910 suggests the existence of a stock of beliefs and
clichés widely diffused among the less intellectual sections of the
working class in south-eastern England at this time. These were typical
of the first stage of proletarian independent consciousness, described by
Engels in the 1840s, in which a frequent 'trace of Deism too
undeveloped to amount to more than mere words'[51] was combined
with ignorance of religious doctrine, a this-worldly outlook, communal
solidarity and vehement anti-clericalism,[52] but the second stage
predicted by Engels,[53] in which Socialism would be combined with
conscious and consistent irreligion, had been reached only by a few.

Those who escaped at one point or another from the prevailing
indifference to religious (or anti-religious) doctrine and organisation
were mainly drawn from the most prosperous sections of the working
class. If extreme poverty provoked any religious response at all, it seems
most frequently to have been a hatred of the Creator, like that of the
Irish woman in St. Giles visited by James Oppenheimer:

> 19, Dudley St., Top Front. An Irish family extremely poor, no
> Scriptures, attend occasionally St Patrick's chapel. Their children
> five in number, are not going to school at all for they are all but
> naked, two of them were running about with nothing on them but
> rags in the shape of a shirt. 'I wish we were all dead', said the
> mother, 'I don't care, we could not be worse off than they are now.
> I don't believe there is a God at all. If there is He don't care much
> for us I know. Maybe we have not tried Him, but I don't think it will
> be any use. I wish He would send us a loaf of Bread now.'[54]

Nor did those who believed the world to be dominated by a cruel fate
expect otherworldly compensations. The missionary diaries suggest that
while many believed in an after-life, many, especially the most
disadvantaged, did not.[55] More often the attitude was 'wait and see',
and God was pushed, together with a great deal else, into the area of
that which had little bearing on the day-to-day business of earning a
living and snatching such pleasure and companionship as life had to

offer. Those who were attracted to systems were drawn not from those who needed to compensate for the miseries of their existence, but from those whose existence was relatively secure and who wished to find a meaning in life beyond the daily round. The charge that dogmatic religion acted as an 'opiate' was peculiarly wide of the mark. In fact, those critics of organised Christianity who directed their attack at individuals, instead of making such grand general assertions, made the reverse criticism: that 'religious men' tended to be excessively pushing. Thus, Alf Slyme, Robert Tressell's savage caricature of an Evangelical building worker, goes to the Post Office to put some of his wages in the bank, while his workmates go off for a drink – 'Like most other "Christians" he believed in taking thought for the morrow'.[56] Belief in any sort of systematic doctrine tended both to arise from, and to reinforce, a self-reliant individualism, and to make its adherent an outsider.

If working-class religion was severely practical, Secularist doctrine was as effectively by-passed as Christian doctrine, and Robert Tressell was as dissatisfied with the results as the City Missionaries were.[57] Consistency was pedantry, and for each role that a man found himself in he might have a different religious stance. In a workshop debate or in a park crowd an aggressive and tough-minded approach would be called for, and the most outspoken would be most successful in making himself heard. In the pub, he would be feeling rather more mellow, and attitudes of 'fair play' would tend to prevail, with a hearing for all views, however eccentric. At home he might turn from the role of lower class rebel to that of head of the household and voice of authority, and the tone might become one of 'moderation' and 'responsibility'. Which part of a rather ill-defined complex of attitudes came to the fore at a given moment might depend upon where a man was. The differences seem to have been reflected in the experiences of the missionaries. In the workshops, and especially at the docks, they might receive rather rough treatment; in the bar they might expect a good-natured argument, in which the drinkers would take the Secularist side; in the home they were usually politely received (except by Irishmen) – their religious message would be heard with varying degrees of interest (often pretty small), but they might be enlisted to solve a family problem.[58]

It was among communities of men, where there was no 'home' situation, and where the 'crowd' situation was normal that a defiant irreligion, more blasphemy than Secularism, was usual and the marginality of religious institutions was greatest: among sailors, railway navvies, brickmakers, residents of common lodging-houses. Such communities were usually located in partial isolation from society at large — in barracks, on board ships, in shanty towns around the periphery of the city or deep in the open countryside — though a very similar style of life was found in the 'roughest' sections of the settled working class of the capital. The virtue most admired in these male societies was strength, and it was proved by physical prowess at work, in a fight, or at the beer-shop; family ties were ephemeral, short-term co-habitation or prostitution was common, and legal marriage, in any case, the exception.[59] These were violent communities, in which the sense of solidarity with comrades in need might be very strong, but where fights between individuals or between factions were also frequent, and often fatal; anyone who showed a sign of weakness could expect to be picked upon — an aggressive demeanour might be a requirement of self-defence; any form of religion (except, perhaps, Roman Catholicism, which could be seen merely as a harmless form of Irish eccentricity) was seen as such a sign of weakness, and qualified its professor both for bullying and for general suspicion.[60] The Evangelical sectarianism (as well, probably, as the political radicalism) commonly associated with dangerous occupations in more settled communities was much rarer.[61] If, in all classes, it was the mother who tended to pass on the family religion to the children it would seem that fathers too were more likely to respond to evangelism where they were linked by permanent ties with wives, children, parents, neighbours, than where their only permanent ties were to a gang of young men, ready to jump on anyone who gave a chance. When incumbents in the dioceses of London and Rochester replying to episcopal visitation queries, singled out particular occupational groups for criticism they were generally occupations of this kind. After Sunday traders,[62] navvies were mentioned more often than any other occupation, with brick makers and workers in market gardens running second.[63] All of these, by the last twenty years of the century, had retreated to the fringes of London, leaving such famous slums as Agar Town and Notting Dale behind them. They might have provided apt examples of the 'wandering tribes', the member of which according to Mayhew, was distinguished 'by his delight in warfare and all perilous sports — his desire for vengeance — by the looseness of his notions as to property — by the absence of chastity among his women, and his disregard of female honour — and lastly by his vague sense of religion — his rude idea of a Creator, and utter absence of all appreciation of the mercy of the Divine Spirit.'[64] The costermongers, whom he took as most representative of this section of the London population, exhibited some of the same characteristics in less extreme forms. Since they lived in the 'coster districts' of the metropolis — the courts and alleys surrounding the major street markets — with wives to whom, although not legally married, they remained, apparently, permanently attached,[65] they are hardly 'wanderers' in the same sense as sailors or navvies. But the culture described by Mayhew was similar, and typical of the 'rough' working class. A basic feature was the relative unimportance of the home — frequently, in any case, bare and unattractive in the extreme. Men found their amusements with men, women such amusement as they got in gossip with other women; marital relations might be affectionate, but were generally violent.[66] Dog-fights, rat-killing and pigeon-shooting were among the favourite amusements; and among men physical strength and daring were the qualities most admired, and the heroes were pugilists and men imprisoned for assaulting policemen.[67] They had little knowledge of the Bible (or of any other book) and when a coster boy was presented with quotations from it, he said: 'I'd precious soon see a henemy of mine shot afore I'd forgive him.'[68] (Nor was he very sympathetic when Mayhew suggested that 'the gals the lads goes and lives with' might object to being beaten.) Costers did not steal from other costers, but most other people were fair game, and successful thieves were admired; there was no respect at all for the law as such.[69]

This was the most extreme form of the secularism and parochialism that pervaded working-class London. It was a typical proletarian response to a world in which most decisions were made by other people, in which the environment, however unattractive, appeared to be unchangeable, and in which only the most intent parochialism could save the individual and those who depended on him from disaster. If life is a matter of priorities, most people will give precedence to concerns in which they have reasonable chances of achieving their aims, and in which they will enjoy the approval of their social equals. For reasons already suggested, little neighbourly encouragement was likely to be offered to those who concerned themselves with matters of abstract principle or world-interpretation. Practical considerations limited attempts at world-changing to those who regarded such attempts as a duty and to small circles of those who had made them their one central interest in life. As long as the social and political system had an air of solidity, efforts to change it promised only a lot of rather tedious work with little result — it was far easier to concentrate attention on those areas of life where the individual clearly could exercise some influence upon his fate, and to dispose of any supposed obligation to be concerned with more general questions by declaring the system itself to be a given. In politics, the result was an ad hoc approach, consisting of the use of direct action to remove particular grievances, together with the lack of any long-term commitment.[70] The complex of attitudes that formed the typical working-class Londoner's view of the world closely resembles that found in other times and places among those in a similar social situation. Few descriptions of the religious views of working-class Londoners at the end of the nineteenth century could be more apt than this account of the views held by the 'ouvrier type de Paris' in the third quarter of the century:

> On sait que l'un des traits saillants de notre caractère au point de vue économique, c'est l'imprévoyance personnelle. Au point de vue religieux cette éspèce d'imprévoyance est encore plus prénoncée; elle est presque absolue. Rien ne préoccupe moins l'ouvrier type de Paris que le salut de son âme dans l'autre monde. Quoique, dans sa jeunesse, il ait reçu l'enseignement catholique, et que cet enseignement soit assez habilement fait pour laisser aux jeunes âmes une empreinte profonde et durable, surtout en ce qui touche les peines de l'enfer, il se comporte exactement comme s'il n'y avait pour lui, au delà de ce monde, ni enfer ni ciel; ou du moins, comme si l'Eglise ne pouvait rien pour lui.[71]

Corbon, the Republican journalist who made this assessment, believed that this 'imprévoyance' was not duplicated in the political sphere — that at least half the Parisian workers were 'accessible à la passion politique et capable de vertus civiques' in normal times, and at least 70 per cent in periods of 'crises sociales', such as 1848-51.[72] In fact, he saw this 'imprévoyance' as evidence of a superior sort of religion, liberated from the Catholic preoccupation with individual salvation. Others have described systems of more thorough-going parochialism. The most famous of these is Oscar Lewis' 'Culture of Poverty', which he has identified in Mexico City, Puerto Rico and New York, and which he believes to characterise a significant minority of the great city poor throughout the capitalist world. People belonging to this culture 'do not', to quote Lewis, 'belong to labour unions, are not members of political parties ... make very little use of banks, hospitals, department stores, museums or art galleries. They have a critical attitude towards some of the basic institutions of the dominant classes, hatred of the police, mistrust of government and those in high position, and a cynicism which extends even to the church.' He also notes 'poor housing conditions, crowding, gregariousness' and 'above all a minimum of organisation beyond the level of the nuclear and extended family'.[73] Lewis' 'Culture' would seem to describe in a considerably exaggerated form the conditions normal in working-class London in the nineteenth century. The demoralisation and the total alienation from the laws and dominant institutions of the land would be typical only of a minority, but the basic attitudes would be similar.

These attitudes could be undermined when the foundations of everyday life were threatened, and questions that had seemed to be the preserve of a few fanatics became everybody's business. In such a crisis the revolutionary and millenarian could emerge from the shadows, and reality might for a time assume a new dimension. Saviours, revolutions, earthly and heavenly paradises might for a time seem plausible and relevant, though most people would probably remain unconvinced and, as in 1794, 'le billard et la femme auront en général le dernier mot'.[74] There are three such millennial epochs in English history: the middle decades of the seventeenth century, the first half of the nineteenth century, and the second decade of the twentieth. In one of the most interesting accounts of the rise and fall of a revolutionary challenge to the social order, John Foster has argued that the crucial factor was the vulnerability of the system: between about 1812 and 1847, class-conscious working-class politicians controlled Oldham; the mill-owners were partly at their mercy; the central government had lost command and would reassert its position only if the Oldham radicals went 'too far'; briefly the Oldham proletarian enjoyed a measure of power. After 1847, with the imposition of the New Poor Law and the arrival of the police and the military, the authority of the central government was re-established; capitalism was once again undubitably 'the system' and 'working'; the working class divided into three mutually hostile status-groups (the Irish, the Tory-beerhouse culture, and the chapel-temperance-new model unionist syndrome) and fundamental criticism of the system again became eccentric and 'irrelevant'. Brilliant and largely convincing as Foster's argument is, the missing link is still the Oldham proletarian; various of the leaders are identified; his attitudes are deduced from marriage certificates, census schedules and diocesan visitation returns. But the proletarian's beliefs and view of the world can only be assumed; we cannot hear the man himself speak. This is not Foster's fault, as the evidence probably does not exist. But it is a constant problem when the extent of and reasons for involvement in popular movements are being gauged.[75] In the sphere of millenarian religion, John Kent has drawn a similar contrast between the apocalyptic Primitive Methodism of the coal-fields in the 1830s and 1840s and the routinised, respectable Nonconformity of the following decades when the hope of supernatural deliverance faded away.[76]

London remained relatively untouched by the religious revivals that swept across Britain between about 1790 and 1850. The only important exceptions were the Catholic missions of the mid-nineteenth century, which won back many Irish immigrants, temporarily estranged from the Church, but still susceptible to the mass conversion achieved by Protestant preachers in Wales and Cornwall, but not in London. All forms of Methodism remained relatively weak in the metropolis until the last two decades of the century, when the new mission halls won adherents to Wesleyanism at a time of Nonconformist decline. In the 1860s London produced its own sect, the Salvation Army, but General Booth's greatest successes seem to have been won in other towns.[77] If London had its moment of mass conversion it was in the years immediately following the First World War, when the Labour Party and the Communist Party won the allegiance of the great majority of the city's working class.

Artisans and Petty Capitalists

Those inhabitants of working-class London who were interested in understanding or in changing the world even when such concerns were 'unpractical' or 'irrelevant' generally belonged to the artisans, shopkeepers, or workshop owners: those who read books and newspapers, who attended political meetings and took an interest in the activities of the local vestry or borough council, and who had some conscious position (whether of allegiance, hostility or detachment) in relation to the various religious sects. There is no reason to think that such habits were characteristic even of the majority of printers, but it was in such trades that these habits could mostly be learnt and into such trades that parents with such habits put their sons. The fact that retailers and skilled workers were far more likely than unskilled workers to marry in a Nonconformist chapel was noted in Chapter II; a large proportion of active Secularists also came from these groups;[78] Stedman Jones distinguishes between the 'distinctive and self-conscious', albeit declining 'political tradition' of the London artisan and the 'traditionalism punctuated by brute expressions of hunger and desperation' of the 'ignorant, inarticulate and unorganised' casual poor.[79] Those who adopted such interests were often conscious of being somewhat eccentric. For instance, Thomas Okey, whose family owned a basket-making workshop in Spitalfields, wondered how he could have acquired his love of books and fascination with language: 'No bookseller's shop existed in the East London I knew. I was repelled, at home, rather than encouraged to read, and I never remember to have seen a book in my elder's hands. Literature was limited to the *Daily Telegraph.* '[80] Later, as an apprentice basket-maker in the City, he found his workmates articulate chiefly only on the subject of sex, though the foreman initiated him into the views of Tom Paine and Robert Owen.[81] Nonetheless, those like Okey or the foreman made up a large and influential minority of the artisans and petty capitalists. Among the former, they tended to be distinguished by a strong working-class consciousness combined with a style of life unlike that of most of their neighbours, and a consequent sense of social isolation. One example of this working-class elite is given in the autobiography of the Communist, Thomas Jackson. His father was a Clerkenwell compositor, proud of descent from a watchmaker, a whitesmith and a blacksmith, and an expert on Dickens, the history of Clerkenwell, Fenianism and the crimes of blacklegs – 'a first-class comp. highly respected as such in the trade'.[82] Jackson himself, born in 1879, was soon reading the Bible, the history of England, Darwin and '100 Best Books'.[83] A contemporary and near-neighbour of Jackson's, George Isaacs, the future Labour cabinet minister, exemplified similar values, though in his case Nonconformity and temperance seem to have been important components. Isaacs' family, like many that had come from Cornwall were Wesleyans, but unlike most Cornishmen,[84] they had also been Chartists and trade unionists. His father, although his earnings as a printer's reader were far from 'aristocratic' saved his spare pennies to send George to a Wesleyan day school, and, as a fanatical tee-totaller, he encouraged him to join the Band of Hope, and subsequently the Sons of Phoenix and the Boys' Brigade. In his teens, Isaacs was spending days of unemployment in the public library, and before long he was attending WEA classes, moving out to Dalston (on marrying) and then to Leyton, and becoming General Secretary of his printing union.[85]

It was in the petty capitalist class that individualists, sometimes with hints of the crank, best flourished – anti-rate fanatics, no-popery extremists, political anti-clericals. One rich specimen seems to have been F. W. Soutter, with his circle of artisans and small masters in Southwark and Bermondsey, intensely concerned with local grievances and prepared to settle them by unconventional means, but conscious of an international context of the struggle of 'small nationalities' and 'subject races'.[86] A rather similar figure was John Kensit, the Protestant bookseller from Shoreditch, who resorted to direct action to provoke the intervention of a Protestant state in the affairs of an apostate church. Kensit claimed in Powellesque fashion to speak for the 'ordinary people' betrayed by those in power, and was despised by respectable opinion generally, regarded as a fanatic even by many of those who sympathised, but listened to and reported everywhere he went.[87]

Among the few inhabitants of working-class London who *did* regard religious doctrines and institutions as important, were four main groups. One of these, the Irish Roman Catholics, included many of the poor; but the others were predominantly drawn from the more properous sections of the population: ultra-Evangelicals, Secularists, and those whom I have termed 'unitarians'.

One other group might seem to deviate from the general working-class pattern: the traditionalists, women for the most part, who attended church *because* it was a social duty and deferred to clergymen *because* of their social position,[88] though respect for the established church was perhaps a less important part of this body of attitudes than patriotism, fascination with royalty and hostility to working-class radicals. But this tradionalism was no more than a slight variant on the more characteristic working-class indifferentism, with respect, instead of resentment, towards the upholders of an order that was seen as unchangeable, and a similar lack of interest in questions of abstract principle.

'Unitarians'

Those whom I have defined as 'unitarians' were closest to the rest of the working class in their thinking; they were seldom Unitarians in the denominational sense — nor, for the most part did they belong to any religious denomination — but their religion was closer to that of the Unitarians than it was either to Secularism or to 'orthodox' Christianity. They represented one of the two main streams of thought in the working-class intelligentsia. It was the religion adopted by the kind of working man who preferred the ILP to the SDF and by those working-class leaders, such as Hardie, Mann and Tillett who gave their Socialism a distinctively ethical colouring, and it was in the spirit of this religion that Keir Hardie wanted to 'rescue Christ from the hands of those who did not understand him and restore him to the common people',[89] and that Tom Mann preached to a Presbyterian church in Hackney on the texts 'I hate, I despise your feast-days' and 'Shew me thy faith apart from thy works', compared the modern church to the Jewish Church as seen by Amos and demanded that modern Christians 'grapple with the industrial problem' as their religious duty.[90] The exponents of this creed rejected what was termed 'dogma', such as miracles and the infallibility of the Bible, as well as more abstruse doctrines,[91] as irrelevant, but accepted Christian ethical teaching and argued that churches should be 'agents of moral progress'. The existence of God was taken to be a reasonable assumption; the Sermon on the Mount to be a credible summary of his message to mankind; Brotherhood to be the end for which Man was created; and a heaven on earth, the product of science, reason and comradeship, to be the ultimate form of human existence. If the churches hastened the coming of this ideal world, all well and good. But any preoccupation with sin, personal salvation or sacraments smacked of morbid introspection or anti-social egotism, and was an affront to human dignity. Among men of this sort, their estimate of the social role of the churches was, so to speak, the crucial variable. Doctrinal positions deemed consistent with agnosticism might differ only slightly from those deemed consistent with a Christian allegiance.

This form of religion was probably strongest in the ILP strongholds of Scotland and the North of England. It found typical expression in the Labour Churches.[92] But similar ideas were common enough in London. It is notable, for instance, how many metropolitan working-class Socialists and trade union leaders of around the end of the nineteenth century did *not* emerge from the Secularist tradition that, in Hobsbawm's well-known phrase, provides 'the ideological thread that binds London labour history together'.[93] One reason for this is simply that so many of them spent their formative years far from Old Street. For instance, the leading Socialists in the Amalgamated Society of Engineers, Mann and Barnes, came from Birmingham and Dundee respectively, and whether or not Mann's claim that he had considered becoming an Anglican ordinand is to be taken seriously, the leading influences on his religious thinking were clearly not Secularist. Will Thorne of the Gas Workers also came from Birmingham, Ben Tillett from Bristol, Harry Quelch from Berkshire, while others, like Jack Jones, the Canning Town docker, came from Ireland. Of these, Quelch was an ardent Secularist, and Thorne, although his *Reminiscences* might suggest that he was a deist, belongs to

Hobsbawm's 'great tradition',[94] but this would scarcely·apply to the others.[95] A passage in Ben Tillett's autobiography throws some light on the nature of the Secularist appeal to many working-class Socialists and radicals who did not regard themselves as adherents: when Tillett was eighteen (1878) he had started reading, and soon turned to the Science versus Religion debates; he decided that the agnostics had the better of it, and became an admirer of Bradlaugh and Besant.

> But there was an inherent strain of mysticism in my nature that was too much a heritage of the centuries for me to accept negation. I felt the force of their realism, their intellectual courage, their passionate devotion to truth, but I was never their convert, though I revere their memories, as I am grateful for their help.[96]

As a Socialist his place was on the rebels' side. But the Secularist heroes were icons, rather than influences on his thinking — or even on his language, which was fairly close to the 'chapel rhetoric' for which London Socialists are generally expected to show an 'unconcealed distaste'.[97]

Even among those leading Socialists and trade unionists who were born in London, there would seem to have been a good many who were little influenced by the Secularist tradition. Secularist branches might have provided as natural a training ground for future Socialist activities as chapels in Wales or Yorkshire. John Burns followed just such an evolution and claimed never to have had any interest in religion.[98] On the other hand, it is hard to think of many leading working-class politicians who had been brought up in an atmosphere of Secularism in the way that so many of those in the provinces had been brought up in an atmosphere of Nonconformist radicalism.[99] In a few cases, the formative influences· seem to have been Christian, as with George Lansbury,[100] who was an active member of the Church of England all his life, except for a few years as an ethicist, or with Will Crooks, the cooper from Poplar, or Charles Ammon, the postmen's leader from Camberwell, who were both associated with the Brotherhood movement. Other working-class politicians brought up in the same London upper working-class milieu, and who subsequently became atheists, had, like Thomas Jackson or Guy Aldred, to learn their own atheism without any assistance from parents or relatives, and, in Aldred's case, only after a period as an active Christian.[101] Important, therefore, as the Secularist tradition was in London, it was still far from exercising an exclusive hold over the politically aware working class.

When George Haw, a journalist specialising in subjects with

'religious' and 'social reform' components published a volume on 'Christianity and the Working Classes', the three working-class contributors (a North-Easterner, Henderson, and two Londoners, Crooks and Lansbury)[102] made it their business to attack, Lansbury with most and Crooks with least vigour, the record of the churches. Comradeship, solidarity, good fellowship were the aspects of Christianity which they stressed; involvement in movements of social reform they saw as the churches' first duty. Sacramentalism and sacerdotalism, matters of church order and of doctrine, did not enter their consideration at all. Formal Christianity was at a discount.[103] Crooks' idea of what the church should be doing can be deduced from his account of the Sunday afternoon lectures at Poplar Town Hall that he organised in conjunction with the rector, Chandler:

> The gatherings are not religious in any orthodox sense, nor is any attempt made to teach religion, but I venture to say that they have as much influence for good on the workpeople of Poplar as many of the Churches. We nearly always begin with music, by singers or players who give their services and then we have a 'talk', generally by a public man, on social questions, on education, on books and authors and citizenship. Some of our speakers take Biblical subjects. ... Without pretending to be this, that or the other, our gatherings have made for the love of one's neighbour, and thus for the cause of Christ.[104]

If the Labour Churches might be regarded as an extension of the Ethical Movement, the equivalent on the Christian (generally Nonconformist) side of the fence was the PSA and Brotherhood Movement, which provided an institutional expression of working-class social idealism and indifference to theology, and a form of worship adapted to the informality of working-class life. In its heyday, between about 1890 and 1914, it was the most representative, and one of the largest bodies of working-class Christians in London.[105] At the turn of the century the words 'PSA' symbolised all that was original and fresh in Nonconformity. R. B. Suthers, for instance, chose them as representative of the minority of the clergy of whom he approved.[106] Silvester Horne, one of the leading ministerial figures in the movement, called it 'A New Protestantism', a continuation of the Reformation, the revolt of 'a miner's lad' against the 'priest and theologian'. There had been opposition to the movement because of 'our free-and-easy methods', 'our perverse habits of interesting ourselves in modern times and modern sins' (notably those of brewers, capitalists, landlords and militarists), 'our tendency to call a spade by its proper name even in church', and 'our simplicity in prayer, our brevity in devotion, our naturalness in expressing our feelings'. 'What we are witnessing,' he said, 'is a New Protestantism. It is a return to what is primitive and fundamental. It is an impressive challenge to all those complexities of doctrine and ritual that have obscured the divine ends for which Christianity exists, and would have destroyed the essential power of Christianity itself were it not indestructible.'[107] In many chapels, the PSA had its separate hierarchy, its distinctive (more proletarian) membership, and its different (less churchy) style. There would be a certain amount of overlap, and the style of the PSA necessarily bore some relationship to that of the chapel on which it depended,[108] but it largely existed for a population that was in some degree repelled by certain features of most chapels. The distinction was partly political: the members of the PSA were both more likely to prefer political and social subjects and more unequivocally to the Left in their political standpoint.[109] But even in the most Evangelical Brotherhoods there seems to have been a social divide between Sunday morning and Sunday afternoon, and, no doubt, a difference, if not in doctrine, in the manner in which it was preached. Thus, at F. B. Meyer's Christ Church Westminster Bridge Road, where politics were barred at the PSA and salvation was preached, the 700 members were said to be 'mostly of the roughest class of working man' and to live within walking distance of the chapel, whereas the church members were only one third working class, and came from all over South London: moreover, this new focus of chapel life had been regarded with a great deal of initial suspicion by the older members, and by the old hierarchy, represented by the deacons.[110]

Secularists

Those who adopted the 'brotherhood' style of religion resembled the mass of the working class in their this-worldliness, in their attachment to a religion of solidarity, and their insistence that it had nothing to do with deans or dogmas. They differed in their moral rigour, in their utopianism and in definite hints of puritanism.

The other main current of thought in the working-class intelligentsia was the 'tough-minded' Secularist-SDF element. If a certain ethical rigour set a George Lansbury apart from the practical, sceptical, common-sensical, easy-going men who supported him, a Robert Tressell was set apart by a certain mental hardness, a contempt for the illogical, emotional, inconsistent, theoretically incorrect views of others. Yet the Secularists enjoyed an influence in London out of proportion to their numbers. Between the '60s and the '80s there was no working-class politician more popular in the metropolis than Bradlaugh; Secularist ideas were — as Republicanism was, and subsequently Socialism — part of the workshop culture of London, and many were in some measure influenced by them who never joined the Secularist movement. If the various forms of Christianity could be learnt at Sunday School, at church or at mother's knee,[111] and if 'unconscious Secularism'[112] could be unconsciously absorbed, Secularism might be learnt in the park or from a workmate.[113] Secularist ideas might thus be known at second-hand to many who had not undergone the period of prolonged soul-searching that was the training ground of the Securalist militant.[114] Thus, while most of the Islington working men and women interviewed by the Scripture Reader from St Barnabas' church made excuses for not going to church, there were a few, like the man at 18 Pickering Street, who were able to announce that they did not go because the Bible contradicted itself.[115] For such people, knowledge, however vague, of Secularist arguments made it possible to articulate objections to the churches conceived on quite other grounds. William Rossiter, a Maurician Anglican, who wrote two articles on 'Artisan Atheism' in 1887, distinguished between the 'few earnest men' who provided the leadership at Secular Clubs, and the many who liked an evening of 'Bible, beer, and "bacca",' who approved of science chiefly because it proved the clergy to be liars, and whose knowledge of the Bible was largely limited to what could be learnt from the *Freethinker*. But if the hostility to religion of the latter was more political and social than intellectual, it was nonetheless deep-rooted, and Rossiter believed that 'the great body of artisans' was characterised by 'a very deep and very bitter antipathy to teachers and professors of religion'.[116]

As the Brotherhood was to the Baptist chapel, so was the Working Men's Club to the Secular Society — the basic allegiance was the same, but Secularist ideas circulated in a cosier, less obsessive and less intellectually demanding manner. Bradlaugh was one member of a pantheon that included Garibaldi and Mazzini, Marx and Bronterre O'Brien, Huxley and J. S. Mill.[117] Hostility to the Established Church was as much a matter of course as hostility to Crown and Aristocracy, but Nonconformists also had the wrong style — the clubmen tended to see themselves in the role of 'the Atheistical Socialists' versus 'the Rev. William Stiggins of Little Bethel'.[118] This is not to say that most working men were atheists. As has already been suggested, their position was seldom so well-defined or consistent. But in a crowd in the park, in a workshop argument or at the club, the Secularist could make himself heard much more easily than the believer.[119]

The best account I have met of a Secularist *family* comes from Manchester.[120] But Secularism was primarily a faith of individuals and of individual *men*. Isolated by a sense of the hatred of the rich and powerful and the ignorance and indifference of their own class, they found support in the companionship of an enlightened minority, oppressed by the knowledge that even their own children were liable to indoctrination in the beliefs that they loathed.[121] While most working-class critics of religious institutions admitted to an approval of Jesus and the Sermon on the Mount, the Secularist was committed to the view that the whole lot was rotten. Middle- and upper-class atheists tended to argue this from a Nietzschean or Darwinian point of view, but working-class atheists, in spite of their reverence for science, were usually unwilling to do this. Instead, (without sacrificing any of the moral indignation heaped by ethical Socialists on the possessing classes) they adopted a determinist theory of the world, which made the Sermon on the Mount beautiful but irrelevant, and got rid of the spell cast over so many egalitarians and reformers by the personality of Jesus, by deciding that he never existed.[122]

Ultra-Evangelicals

When Charles Booth went to Southgate Road, Hackney, to discuss Christian Socialism with Bruce Wallace, he found the co-operator and Garden Cities enthusiast dejected:

> ... he admits that he has not yet had much success and takes a gloomy view because of the lack of any moral ideals among the mass of the people – they are steeped in low ideas from youth upwards and cannot rise out of them – partly due to competition and the struggle with poverty ...
>
> Here, as everywhere, we find the little band of hearty adherents and workers – about a score he said – they are the organisers and managers of the guilds and to them he turns for consultation and suggestion and assistance.

In Wallace's view, his Brotherhood Church had not found its way to 'the religious feelings of the people', though he thought that the

Baptists, the Salvation Army and the Roman Catholics had each in some measure succeeded in doing this.[123] The reason for this measure of success was not that their doctrines were more widely believed than those of Wallace's church, for they were probably less widely believed, but that those who accepted the teaching of these denominations were encouraged to worship together both by the nature of what they believed and by the very fact that they were in a 'cognitive minority'. Wallace's problem, however, was that of many of the Labour Church Pioneers: there were many people who accepted in principle the ideals which they taught, but most of them were embarrassed at the idea of celebrating them in a church or of engaging in the introspection that most churches encouraged. Most of those working men, however, who made a sufficiently radical break from the life of their workmates to make them wish to join a church adopted highly evangelical beliefs, in which the blood of Jesus was more prominent than the Sermon on the Mount, and in which great symbolic significance was attached to abstinence from drink, oaths and sometimes tobacco. They regarded Anglicanism as a sham religion with no room for 'converted Christians';[124] they dismissed political parsons such as R. J. Campbell, saying that they wanted not attacks on landlords but the saving gospel of 'Christ and Him crucified'. The humanitarian optimism of those like Campbell did not appeal to men who had cut themselves off from the life of their neighbours and were daily butts of workshop wits, but only to the more tender-minded of the middle class. For, as the Drury Lane milliner is supposed to have said on hearing of F.D. Maurice's views on hell: 'Oh, but Mr. Headlam, if that is true, where is the reward of the righteous?'[125]

The Brethren, the Salvation Army and the numerous tiny churches of the 'railway arch mission' type were all attractive to men of this sort; but the largest number of 'converted working men' was probably to be found among the Baptists, who had a large lower middle-class membership and a few distinctly wealthy chapels, but also a considerable working-class element in most of their chapels. Though a few of the leading Baptists, such as John Clifford, were distinctly liberal Evangelicals, the 'orthodoxy' of the denomination as a whole was proverbial: thus Charles Masterman, in a catalogue of suburban personalities drawn up in 1909 referred to 'the Baptist Chapel, where the minister maintains the old doctrines of hell and heaven, and wrestles with the sinner for his immortal soul', and Charles Booth, saying much the same thing in less urbane language, reported that a sermon by Charles Spurgeon junior 'was filled with all the usual crudities of the Baptist views'.[126]

From the point of view of the working-class convert, the 'usual crudities' were 'the gospel', with no milk and water modern modifications, and the Baptist chapel provided the comradeship of men like himself who proudly proclaimed the 'old old story of Jesus and His love', while middle-class neologists flinched and workshop bullies sneered. His hero might be Archibald Brown who preached to congregations of 2000 at the East London Tabernacle in Bow Road, or D. H. Moore, a former sailor who, on becoming a 'Christian man' had bought his discharge and worked as a fireman, before becoming a City Missionary, and then minister of a chapel near King's Cross. If Brown might seem slightly aloof, Moore was an approachable and unpretentious man.[127] The communities to which they ministered were of the same type: fellowships of the converted conscious of their good fortune in having been saved, and anxious to share their experience through testimonies, and to pass the message on by distributing tracts and by open-air preaching. Moore's church had a cricket club and a 'Christian Cycling Association'; but conversion came first. He referred, in his interview with A. L. Baxter, to one member of his chapel who had been a 'hopeless drunkard', living in a brothel, until he had one day stumbled out of the pub and into an open air meeting, unsuccessfully invited the preacher for a drink, and stayed to be converted.[128] This was just the stuff for a testimony: Moore liked his prayer-meetings to include a few of these, and he was 'not too particular as to their speaking the Queen's English'.[129] Indeed, the Queen's English tended positively to diminish the interest taken in such testimonies.[130] Moore was contemptuous of the local Congregationalists, with their PSAs and other 'unspiritual' methods, and a neighbouring Baptist minister, a painter from Scotland, thought that churches should be more exclusive: the Baptists in Scotland were too ready to expel people, but they erred in the right direction.[131]

It was not surprising that Moore chose as his 'typical member' a reformed drunkard, for drink, together with the violence, the lack of order and restraint, the profanity and the gambling that accompanied it, was at the centre of the ultra-Evangelical perception of the world.[132] If, as satirical observers usually claimed, most ultra-Evangelicals probably led blameless lives before their conversion (indeed, came from families in which conversion at an early age was expected) it is also likely that any Baptist church or Salvationist barracks would have one or two members with a past and, indeed, that only the more melodramatic Evangelical preaching, combining the

promise of complete forgiveness, with a special status for the more
obviously sensational convert and unambiguous threats concerning the
future fate of those who did not respond, could achieve such
conversions.[133] If Secularists had a conception of Christian beliefs that
seemed to many Christians very distorted this was partly because, as
Susan Budd suggests,[134] many of them had become Secularists after
being badly treated by Christians, and the sort of Christianity with
which they came most often into contact, for instance on Christian
Evidence platforms, was often of a crude and rather intolerant kind.[135]
Similarly, if the ultra-Evangelical view of average human nature was
often rather lurid, and if hell and the devil both played an unusually
large part in their religion, this was because of the kind of people they
preached to, their own experience of persecution and their own
experience, in some cases, of a clearly marked hiatus within their own
lives. The biographer of Watts-Ditchfield who was vicar of St. James the
Less, Bethnal Green, from 1894-1914, gives an example of the sort of
persecution that working-class Evangelicals could face:

> One young fellow who was confirmed was much ridiculed the
> following day in the workshop where he was employed. Some of his
> fellow-workers made a wooden cross; one of their number put an old
> shirt over his clothes in imitation of a surplice, and as the converted
> young man sat eating his dinner in the works, the others formed a
> procession with the cross at their head, and walking round and
> round sang him blasphemous songs. The young man, however, was
> true to his colours, with the results that one of his assailants yielded
> to Christ; the mother and sister were converted and became regular
> attendants at the services, while father, who was a drunkard of long
> standing, became a moderate drinker, so that he might not bring
> shame on his lad of whom he was justly proud.[136]

Among the attractions of ultra-Evangelicalism to the working-class
Christian was the fact that it could explain persecution in terms of
original sin, wilful unbelief and the effects of drink — much as members
of ultra-radical political groups could dismiss the objections of their
critics by branding them either as moved by class selfishness or as dupes
of those who were. Such means of automatic rejection of criticism
made an important contribution to the survival of eccentric minorities.
Combined with this instrument of self-defence were certain symbols of
separation from their hostile neighbours. Abstinence from many of the
popular pleasures made it possible to save, and the money saved tended
to go on a black coat, and possibly a house a little further out in a

'nicer' district. Inevitably working-class Evangelicals could be accused of being on the make, and inevitably it was among those already in some measure dissatisfied with their environment that Evangelical chapels won many of their recruits.

Roman Catholics

The only form of religion that integrated its adherents into a working-class environment, instead of making them stand out from their neighbours, was Roman Catholicism. The large Roman Catholic minority in the working class was to a considerable degree concentrated within distinctive sub-communities. Saffron Hill was proverbially Italian; the German sugar-bakers lived in Whitechapel, where they had their own church of St Boniface; but most of these communities were Irish. There were said to be Irishmen in St Giles in the reign of Queen Elizabeth; from the 1790s migration was continuous, and by 1840 there were about 120,000 Catholics in London.[137] During the next decade the Catholic population of the metropolis increased by about 50,000. Irish immigration to London continued at a lower level in the following decades, and by 1961, after further extensive immigration not only from Ireland, but from Poland, Malta, Italy, and Trinidad, the Catholic population of Inner London was estimated as 23 per cent.[138]

The Irish tended to live in houses where everyone was Irish, to live in streets or courts where several other families were Irish, and to live in distinctively 'Catholic' districts. They also went to Catholic schools, they usually married a Catholic and they often took a job in which a large proportion of their workmates were Irish. The tendency has been documented statistically for 1851 and 1861 by Lynn Lees. She found the Irish population mainly concentrated on three areas — St Giles—Strand, Poplar—Stepney and Southwark—Rotherhithe, but with a tendency to migrate to new Irish colonies a little further out; Irish families were large not because they had more children, but because they tended to include relatives and lodgers; very few of the Irish lived alone, and very few lived in a household headed by an Englishman; about three heads of household in five were unskilled workers.[139] The more subjective evidence collected by Charles Booth at the end of the century presented many of the same features. Although there were now Catholic churches in nearly every part of the metropolitan area, most priests claimed to have distinctive Irish colonies within their parishes, and the largest of these were still in the classic Irish districts, such as Rotherhithe and Wapping.[140] The Catholic-worshipping population was still less evenly distributed than that of any religious group but the Jews.[141]

Catholics could, like Evangelicals, still be subject to violence though it usually took different forms. It was directed against the Catholic community rather than against individuals; it was perhaps directed more against their persons than their beliefs; and it was invariably reciprocated. By the end of the nineteenth century in London such violence seems to have assumed a ritualised character, being limited in scope and in the type of situation where it occurred.[142] These occasions seem typically to have been 'Protestant' lectures, at which provocative remarks would be made causing Catholics present to attack the speaker, after which a free-for-all would ensue. The London press gives some examples. In November 1893, a Protestant Alliance Lecture in Victoria Park was broken up by 300 young Catholics, said to be members of the same guild.[143] In 1898 a series of Catholic lectures were given in Bow and Bromley Institute these being followed on the night after by Protestant lectures, delivered by such a specialist in the baiting of Catholics and ritualists as Walter Walsh, in the course of whose address, directed against the Catholic practice of burning Bibles and Protestants, there were many fights.[144] In 1905, a lecture by John Kensit junior was the occasion for a fight between Protestants and Catholics within the Woolwich Tabernacle. At the first mention of auricular confession, a large body of Catholics charged the rostrum, and although some were ejected and others arrested on the arrival of the police it was thereafter impossible to hear more than a few consecutive sentences. The meeting ended with the chairman calling for the Doxology, and the Catholics countering with 'Faith of our Fathers'.[145] If the Catholics sometimes appeared to be the aggressors, it should be remembered that a 'Protestant' lecture meant an attack on Catholic doctrine and practice of a type calculated to infuriate any Catholic present and to inflame the animosities of the more bigoted Protestant. In fact, these sectarian battles amounted to pre-arranged brawls, in which doctrinal differences were little more than a pretext for a fairly harmless fight. They served, however, to emphasise the pariah character of the Catholic population, and to reinforce the type of Catholicism that had little time for conventional Catholic obligation, but liked providing bodyguards for priests or placing sentries outside churches.

The Charles Booth Collection at LSE records interviews with priests from nearly every Inner London parish. The first impression

given by these reports is the great variety both in the personalities and
views of the priests and in the parochial situation that they described.
This might be stating the obvious. But, if religious denominations lend
themselves especially to stereotyping – the 'grim' Puritan, the
'conventional' Anglican, the 'dry' Unitarian – this is especially true of
the Catholic clergy. Two stereotypes are most common: one of the
petty tyrant, crazed with power, jangling the keys of hell at everyone
without the guts to resist, and driving his ragged flock into craven
submission or intransigent rebellion; and the other of the 'Father
Murphy', celebrated in Irish patriotic songs, never too busy to pull out
the whiskey bottle and exchange stories of '98 and '67, ready at any
hour to jump from his bed and visit the sick and dying, or to put on
gloves and exchange blows with the lads from the Guild of St Patrick.
The Catholic poor lent themselves equally to stereotyping, whether
sympathetic or satirical. All the stereotypes found flesh and blood in
one or other of the parishes visited by Booth and his team.
Fr. Whelahan of Woolwich was characterised as a 'benevolent
tyrant',[146] and the tyranny, benevolent or otherwise, of the priest
within his parish was a constant theme. Fr. Whelahan would denounce
wrong-doers in the pulpit or face to face in the street, and such was his
authority within the Catholic community that public opinion would
bring most of them to heel, he named 'loafers' and those who neglected
their children as special targets for his wrath.[147] Fr. Lawless in Poplar
and Fr. Thompson at Bow Common would march into pubs to break
up fights,[148] and several priests threatened terrible things if anyone
were to seek to proselytise one of their flock. Aves reported the views
of Fr. Carey of Holloway thus:

> Their own people come under no other religious influence. If it
> were known in any case, it would not be allowed for 24 hours, for
> (with emphasis) 'dogmatically we suffer no toleration. It is
> impossible – any more than it would be for the teacher to allow his
> pupils to be taught that 2+2=5.'[149]

And a look at a leaflet by Fr. Reaks of Woolwich advertising his Lent
addresses led Aves to reflect:

> No wonder that over certain minds the authority of the church is
> maintained when such terrors can still be threatened, and when she
> is believed to hold the most certain means of escape from them.
> There is something Mediaeval in the tone of this little leaflet dated
> 'Lent 1900' and issued AD MAJOREM DEI GLORIAM.[150]

But threats of hell are not sufficient in themselves to explain the hold
of priests over people, for large numbers of Irish Catholics lapsed and
many remained very loosely connected with the Church, and among
those who did remain in some sense Catholics there were signs of the
sort of rapport between priest and people that Mayhew had described
fifty years earlier.[151] The priest's view was recorded by Ernest Aves.
As his account of Fr. Reaks suggests, he was, like Booth's ·other
collaborators, far from being a Roman Catholic himself. But he seems
to have enjoyed few of his interviews for the Religious Influences series
more than the afternoon that he spent smoking and drinking tea with
the 'fathers' at Holy Trinity, Bermondsey. Their leader had 'the
eloquent Irishmen's tongue', and the others were 'a languid saint', 'a
blustering intellect' and one of 'the rougher type of Irish priest'. In this
parish, only 1200, out of an estimated Catholic population of 10,000
came to Mass on an average Sunday.[152] 'While therefore,' he wrote,

> there are many whose connection with Mother Church is very
> slight, all thought there was very little falling away so far as ultimate
> sympathy and loyalty were concerned. All emphasised and were
> proud of the generosity of their people, poor and struggling and still
> paying some £200 each year to the Schools, and some £600 for
> other Mission purposes – enough to make it self-supporting. In this
> respect all sang the praises of their people. ... They described the
> readiness of the people to pay their coppers; the incidents when
> some person had been passed over in the house to house collection,
> as for the schools, running out with a contributory mite. ... They
> appeared to think that the rougher and more neglectful of his
> religious duties a man was, the more stalwart a defender he would
> prove in case of real or imagined need. Let the Church or a priest be
> insulted in the bar of the public house, in a club, on the wharf and
> fisticuffs would soon be flying about. And Fr. Mostyn gave an
> amusing instance of what happened to him lately. Owing to a
> complete misunderstanding a man was supposed to have insulted
> him. The next day going down Tooley Street he was met by one of
> the flock: 'Mornin', F'thurr, I've been waiting for you. Two of us
> 'ave got 'im down there by the river all right, the chap who insulted
> you, and we want to know wot we shall do to 'im.'[153]

And Charles Booth reporting on the congregation at the same church
found a degree of involvement in the services that was far from
universal:

Holy Trinity (RC) was crowded to the doors. I just managed to squeeze in and knelt among a lot of children and others while a great sacred procession passed round the church. I know not what the cause was but the show was a delight to churchfull of poor people and children - especially children. Perhaps it answers to the Protestant Sunday School Anniversary. In the procession were a large number, 70 or 80, girls covered in white muslin veils — girls of all ages. Some quite little things who walked backwards and strewed flowers in front of the priest under the canopy who covered the host — the canopy being supported by four rough looking men.'[154]

Equally varied were the political allegiances of the clergy interviewed by Booth's team, and they were perhaps less predictable than those of the Anglicans and Nonconformists. There was often an implication that priests were less radical than people: at Holy Trinity, Bermondsey, for instance, three priests out of five were pro-Boer, but all the adult Irish were said to oppose the British government on this issue.[155] There were few, if any, Socialists in the Catholic priesthood at this time,[156] but there were representatives both of High Toryism and of 'agin the government' radicalism, mixed with Irish nationalism.[157]

Relations with their people were certainly closer than in most Anglican parishes, though more strained than some of the cosier accounts of Catholic life might suggest. A few of the Catholic clergy were as dejected as their Protestant counterparts. The priest on the Isle of Dogs told Booth's representative that the local Irish were 'a bad lot', that there was no response to his efforts, and that they made the excuse of having no good clothes for not going to Mass.[158] And the more energetic Fr. Lawless was prepared to dismiss that part of his flock living in Orchard House, an area surrounded on three sides by the river Lea, as 'incarnate mushrooms'.[159] In West London where one priest compared the local Catholics unfavourably with those in the East End,[160] Fr. Brenan of Marylebone Road claimed that his parishioners were drunken and generally 'very indifferent Catholics':

Speaking of the lapse of many Irish RCs in London, Father B. found that it was almost inevitable: even newcomers from Ireland, mixing with general London life, soon lose their fervour: there is little or no Catholic sentiment, and the second generation soon lose their respect for the priest, and even their fear of him is much 'watered down'.[161]

On the other hand, the sort of self-identification with their parishioners that some Anglo-Catholic clergy were trying to make at this time came more easily to many of their Roman brethren.[162]

The praise for their people of the five priests at Bermondsey has already been quoted; similarly, in tones less ecstatic but still rather different from those that most Anglicans would have adopted, Fr. Buckley of Southwark said: 'our people are noisy, but there's not much else the matter with them'.[163]

Various groups were mentioned by priests as being 'difficult': adolescent boys (as in other denominations), and (as elsewhere) clubs for cricket, boxing, etc., were used as a means of keeping them within the church's sphere of influence;[164] European (i.e. non-Irish) Catholics;[165] and the very poor.[166] Many of these kept a strong sense of 'being Catholic'. This excluded participation in the life of the church as a community, with its common worship, its confraternities and so on. It included on the other hand a sense of having a Catholic identity, and thus of being a different sort of person from a Protestant or an atheist;[167] a belief in the church as a source of magic; a respect for the priesthood; and an (admittedly highly selective) form of Catholic morality. Thus Fr. Buckley claimed that the third of his flock whom he identified as never going to Mass were 'all convinced RCs at heart', and so far as sending for the priest was concerned 'the worst of all: just as you have got warm between the blankets some fellow who has got bellyache and thinks he's dying gets you out of bed to go and see him' — it would often be the first the priest knew that the man was a Catholic, though a few would be brought permanently back into the fold as a result of such incidents.[168] Similarly, Billy Hill, a London gangster of the 1930s and '40s brought up with twenty Irish brothers and sisters in Camden Town 'thought religion was all right' and had a sister who 'did often try to be a good Catholic', the Catholic chaplain at Holloway prison being the only person who had been known to be able to influence her. Hill's form of Catholicism was perhaps embodied in his firmly asserted moral notions, including pride in his Robin Hood role as benefactor of struggling Irish neighbours, immense indignation at the Home Office's refusal to let him out of prison to pay his last respects to his father (which he had, in the event, to limit to the saying of a few prayers in his cell), condemnation of illegitimate forms of crime — including any 'unnecessary' violence.[169]

Most Catholic priests would have regarded any kind of Catholicism as better than none at all, but they would not have rated Hill's kind very highly. The Church tried to dominate the whole non-working life of its members,[170] providing clubs for every distinctive group within the parish; personal advice on all subjects – from the pulpit, if necessary; schools for the children; loans at low rates of interest for financially precarious adults; and, of course, the sacraments, that few Catholics, however insouciant during their life-time, dared to die without. There was a tendency to cultural imperialism among its priests – a resentment of any rival influence, neutral or even benevolent, over their parishioners. Several were disturbed by the sway of the Dockers' Union;[171] Board Schools were hated, although, as a Southwark priest said, they had 'introduced a new sense of discipline and decency in manner and dress',[172] harmless organisations for Irish conviviality could meet with clerical opposition, simply because the Church was the only proper place for such gatherings.[173] Consequently, the Catholic was tied to his church, whether by love or by hatred, in a way seldom found among Protestant Englishmen.[174]

Since the Catholic wing of the Church of England was trying to do much the same with rather less success, a consideration of some of the differences might throw some light on the distinctive features of Roman Catholicism in London. First it is necessary to emphasise the missionary character of both. If the Anglican church like most established churches of Europe, was slow to adapt to nineteenth-century urbanisation,[175] this was no less true of the Roman Church in England. Until the 1840s, little attempt was made to build churches for the London Irish, and by then 'the so-called Irish leakage from the faith' was, as Sheridan Gilley puts it, 'through sheer want of chapels hopelessly beyond control'.[176] Of the 100,000 or more London Catholics who missed Mass on Census Sunday, 1851, many remained permanently estranged from the Church, but a considerable number were won back by missions, street preaching and house-to-house visiting. In the '40s, '50s and '60s new churches were being built in long-established Irish settlements; in old churches, symbols or instruments of class exclusiveness, such as galleries, appropriated seats and door money were being removed.[177] The diaries of the Scripture Reader in St Giles provide vivid descriptions of Irish 'spiritual destitution':

> 8 Dudley St. First Back. Another Irish family in a most miserable condition on account as they said of having no army work to do, but everything looked as if both were given to drink. 'No we have got no Bible', said the woman, 'we never trouble any church or chapel; we used to send those two girls to St Patrick's school, but they have got no clothes now, so they may as well stay at home'. Spoke to them of the one thing needful, but I might have as well spoken to the stones.

They said 'yes' and 'no' to everything I said.[178]

Some of these may have been among the 'nearly 700 "out of the church" ' who 'made their peace with heaven' when the Jesuits held a mission at St Patrick's Soho in 1870.[179] Blood-curdling hell-fire sermons were employed to bring thousands back to the church,[180] and special inducements were sometimes offered, such as indulgences for kissing a ten foot high cross.[181] Anglo-Catholics were seldom able to offer their parishioners ten foot high crosses, let alone indulgences for those who kissed them; nor were they so liberal in the threats of hell which the Roman missionaries used to such effect. Even if they had wished to engage in such preaching, which most of them did not, it is unlikely that their parishioners would have responded.

The first and most crucial difference between Roman Catholicism and Anglicanism was that, in the middle decades of the century at least, large sections of the Catholic population, although they did not practise their religion, accepted that it was very probably true, and had certainly adopted no alternative system of belief. Their position was analogous to that of the West Indian migrants to Britain, described by Malcolm Calley: among these migrants 'there is no cultural or ideological barrier' between those who do and those who do not belong to Pentecostal sects: the non-member remains aloof not because he denies the truth of Evangelical Christian doctrine, but because he is unwilling to accept the prohibitions that sectarian morality imposes, and a successful rally will be attended by large numbers of those who seldom go to religious meetings at other times.[182] This is the atmosphere within which conversionist religions flourish, for it needs only a sudden crisis to turn a sinner into a saint. Observers of both groups of immigrants – in the 1840s and in the 1960s – noted their readiness to listen intently to religious propagandists when the English would gather round to jeer.[183] Both groups came from countries where Christian ideas, in the one case Catholic and in the other sectarian Protestant, were diffused among all sections of the population, and where no alternative system had deep roots. On the other hand, the migrant from the English countryside often came from an area where church was remote from people; and 'religion' the province of zealous minorities;[184] where financial resentment of the parson was as great as it was in Ireland, but the political and social ties between the Irish priest and his people were completely lacking;[185] where the moral norms were in large measure independent of those of the Church, and did not have the strongly Catholic colouring that they had in Ireland.[186] Furthermore, atheist or

deist views could be heard in any park in London, and some knowledge
of non-Christian views of the world was fairly widespread; on the other
hand, political conflict, a source of friction between working-class
Englishmen and the religious denominations, and the chief means of
'liberation' from the Church for the Catholic poor in Europe, ranged
the Irishman and his priests on the same side, albeit with different ideas
of how the battle should be pursued. In time, the mass reconversions of
London Irish achieved in the '50s and '60s would be no longer possible.
New parishes created at the end of the century in areas previously
somewhat neglected were said to include unusually high proportions of
the totally lapsed,[187] and an article written in 1901 noted the difficulty
the Church had in retaining the loyalty of second and third generation
immigrants.[188]

The Anglo-Catholic priest was trying to build the automatic
relationship with each member of his flock that the Roman priest had
with his. The devoted work of men like Wainright of London Docks,
Stanton of Holborn and Dolling of Poplar won many individual
converts; but their impact on the community as a whole was very
limited. They were respected as individuals rather than as priests, and
there was no social pressure to support their churches. The London
pattern of life had grown up in independence of the Church, and when
the church tried to recreate a traditionalist church-centred organisation
of life, this sort of community was irrevocably a thing of the past. 'Les
réussites chrétiennes'[189] in Britain were sectarian *réussites*. The sort of
community the Anglo-Catholic was trying to recreate did not exist in
the English countryside, let alone in the metropolis. The areas of
Britain in which large numbers of the poor were converted to forms of
Christianity in eighteenth- and nineteenth-century Britain were areas of
small farms, fishing and mining, in which the established church was,
and remained, weak: Cornwall with its Methodism,[190] Wales[191] and
the Scottish Highlands with their Calvinist sectarianism.

Notes

1. Stedman Jones, op.cit., p.387; Booth, op.cit., I, ii,pp.21-2.
2. By the end of the nineteenth century, the Liberals were weaker in
   London than in most other cities, but their strength was greatest in
   working-class areas. In general elections between 1885 and 1910
   the average Conservative and Unionist share of the vote exceeded
   50% in all of eighteen middle-class constituences and in
   thirteen out of fifteen mixed constituencies but only in nine out of

twenty-four that were mainly working-class. H. Pelling, op.cit.,pp.30-43.

3. This is well-illustrated by H. Miner, *St Denis: A French Canadian Parish*, Chicago UP, Chicago, 1939. St Denis was a community of small farmers with little social differentiation where nearly everyone was a practising Catholic, where tradition defined correct behaviour in wide areas of work and leisure, and where there was very little crime. On the other hand, there was a small class of landless labourers, and they were 'more individualistic, less under paternal dominance, and tend to be less faithful Catholics' as well as providing some of the farmers' sons with prostitutes (ibid.,pp.88, 210).

4. In his contribution on 'Sailors' Women' to H. Mayhew, *London Labour and the London Poor*, London, 1861-2, IV, p.226. The identity of 'that race of people' is not absolutely clear, but it appears to be 'the industrious classes' as a whole.

5. 'I should be very sorry indeed', the General Manager of the Great Eastern Railway told the Royal Commission on the Housing of the Working Classes, 'to allow any respectable female connected with my household to travel third class upon the Great Eastern Railway during those hours of the day in which the workmen are travelling', and he concluded that 'There is no doubt that the conveyance of workmen by railway causes the general public a very large amount of inconvenience and annoyance'. *P.P.*, 1884-5, XXX, QQ. 10170, 10209.

6. For an example of such sanctions being applied in both directions see E. Flint, *Hot Bread and Chips,* which describes the author's childhood in Whitechapel c. 1914. Her father, who made his living by buying produce in one vegetable market and selling it elsewhere, was fairly easy-going and prepared to take his neighbours as he found them. On the other hand, her mother ostracises one fanatically clean neighbour for thinking herself 'too good for the likes of us around here', and is equally hostile to another who is regarded as disreputable, and whose son is thought to be involved in crime.

7. Jasper, op.cit.,pp.61-3.

8. This is noticeable in the Oppenheimer diaries, covering the very poor area of St Giles: in Dudley St., although few families had more than one room, incomes and life styles seemed to vary a good deal; on the other hand, Marmautte Court contained several houses of prostitutes or thieves and several with the 'rougher' Irish, and after completing his visitation on 6 February, 1862, the author, a City Missionary, wrote of 'that court, where proverty and misery, sin and profligacy are predominant; there is not one christian family to be found [there were in fact one or two practising Catholics;] and more than half the population change every month so that I very seldom meet the same people again.' James Oppenheimer, Diary.

9. Tressell, op.cit., p.18, Frank Owen 'was generally regarded as a bit

of a crank: for it was felt that there must be something wrong about a man who took no interest in racing or football and was always talking a lot of rot about religion and politics. If it had not been for the fact that he was generally admitted to be an exceptionally good workman, they would have had little hesitation about thinking that he was mad.'

10. D. Fagan and E. Burgess, *Men of the Tideway*, Hale, London, 1966, pp.138, 155. Dick Fagan was born around 1905 into a Bermondsey 'river family' and apprenticed at 15. 'Honest Tom', a revolutionary and an atheist, 'got to despair of the working class' and found a rare kindred soul in the vicar, whom he could engage in prolonged argument.

11. See, for instance, Reynolds' comparison between the conversation of the Devon fishermen and that in a nearby hotel: the people in the hotel talked of 'the things that don't matter', and the fishermen of 'the things that do matter'. S. Reynolds, *A Poor Man's House*, Macmillan, London, 1928, pp.23-4, (first published 1908).

12. M. Loane, *From their Point of View*, Edward Arnold, London, 1908, p.92.

13. A certain claustrophobia is conveyed in Flint, op.cit. With seven people in a four-room house her family would not have contributed to the overcrowding statistics. But tap and lavatories were common to all those in Waterloo Row, and users of both were visible to everyone.

14. The role of animals in the leisure of the London working class was a feature of the *Daily Telegraph* enquiry of 1905 into the British Sunday. Among the forms of amusement noted were rabbit coursing on Hounslow Heath, whippet racing and bird-catching on Hackney Marshes, fishing in the Lea, and in Bermondsey repairing rabbit hutches and chicken runs. *Daily Telegraph*, 6-13 October 1905.

15. Booth, op.cit., I, i, pp.249-50.

16. According to Willy Goldman, brought up in St Georges in the East in the 1920s, 'We Jewish children acknowledged the superiority of the Gentile's method in one field: religion. He was practically exempt from it. With us the Rabbis dominated one part of our life as the school-teacher dominated the other'. Four days a week between tea and supper was spent at the Kheder. However, he thought that most of what they learnt had been forgotten within a week of the Barmitzvah. Goldman, pp.22-6. See also T. Okey, *A Basketful of Memories*, Dent, London, 1930, pp.100-1.

17. Thus Booth, describing a procession at a Catholic church in Bermondsey where four 'rough looking men' had marched at the side of the priest, concluded: 'I waited to see the congregation come out — the people seemed to be there by families and were of all classes (Bermondsey) but especially the poor — they looked well fed — better fed than dressed — and this I think is characteristic of the RC (Irish) population.' Booth Collection, A 46.3, 98, record

of a day in Bermondsey, 13 May 1900. The willingness of many very poor Catholics to contribute to the support of their church and schools was frequently noted, e.g. in the 1850s, when some Catholic parishes were dependent on a few wealthy patrons, St Patrick's, Wapping, remained self-sufficient and supported five priests and five schools through a vast apparatus of penny-collectors. S. W. Gilley, 'Evangelical and Roman Catholic Missions to the Irish in London, 1830-70', Cambridge Ph.D. thesis, 1971, pp.170-83.

18. Stephen Yeo, in the course of a valuable analysis of working-class incomes in Reading at the beginning of the twentieth century argues that lack of means excluded a large part of the town's population from active membership of any sort of organisation. It might be fairer to say that it limited membership to those among the poor who had very strong reasons for joining. The Irish Catholics who were the most devout section of the English working class were certainly drawn disproportionately from the poor (though among them it was the poorest who were least likely to practise their religion). As far as church membership is concerned, it is also worth noting that it might be a good investment as Robert Tressell frequently hints. At the least it could put a person in touch with potential employers; but churches also tended to provide financial help for those of their members who were in difficulties. (E.g. gifts or loans to members, worshippers and their relatives are fairly often recorded in the Deacons' Minute Book of Greville Place Congregational Church, Kilburn. 28 March 1865., 13 November 1870., 29 November 1904., 1 October 1907., etc..) Self-interest might have prompted more of the poor to join churches. The remarkable fact, therefore, is that working-class church members were so largely drawn from those who were least in need of financial assistance. See S. Yeo, 'Religion in Society: a View from a Provincial Town in the late nineteenth and early twentieth Centuries', Sussex Ph.d. thesis, 1971, pp.397-409.

19. These were the words with which Thomas Okey's grandfather an East End work-shop owner reproached him when he found him reading a cheap Shakespeare (Okey, op.cit., p.18), and Mayhew (op.cit., I, p.43) claimed that coster girls never got any schooling because, as their parents said 'What's the use of it *that* won't yarn a gal a living.' Seventy years later when Dick Fagan left school (Fagan and Burgess, op.cit., pp.13-14) his lighterman father feared that he would not be tough enough for life on the river and wanted him to 'stop all this reading nonsense': 'Bermondsey was then a solid working-class district, poor and proud, yet more concerned with the size of the wage packet than with anything else, because the size of the wage packet wasn't big; in many cases it was non-existent. In other words, life was a struggle. When you left school at fourteen, you were expected to get hold of the best job that was going, always assuming you could find any sort of job at all to go to. You were certainly considered a bit on the queer

side if you found time to do a lot of reading as I did.'

20. 'You may not perhaps have realised', the President of the National Union of Clerks told the annual conference of his union in 1910, 'that clerical work is very generally looked upon as "unskilled" work, not only by employers, but by the skilled artisan as well'. Quoted in Lockwood, op.cit., p.101.

21. Okey, whose parents were on the border between the upper working and the lower middle classes, notes that they could have afforded to keep him on at school, but they took him away to serve an apprenticeship when he was 12. Okey, op.cit., p.24.

22. Rubinstein, *School Attendance in London, 1870-1904*, University of Hull, Hull, 1969, stresses financial obstacles to school attendance, and does not discuss parental attitudes to schooling as such, though he notes some of the more extreme expressions of hostility to teachers and to the 'kidcopper' or 'school board man' in such areas as Nichol St., Bethnal Green. He provides the following percentages of regular attendances in relation to the number of children on the roll of London elementary schools: 76.7% in 1872, 77.7% in 1892 (just after the abolition of fees), 88.2% in 1906 (a figure scarcely exceeded since). In 1891, the range was from 66.9% at Johanna St., Lambeth, to 88.2% at Dulwich Hamlet. Rubinstein, pp.40-4, 80-1, 112.

23. RC on Working of Elementary Education Acts, *PP* 1886, XXV, Q.2739.

24. Ibid., *PP* 1887, XXX, QQ. 52457-8.

25. In 1882, the last year in which the Registrar General's Annual Report published a district by district breakdown of the proportion of those marrying who signed the register with a mark, the proportion for men exceeded 15% in three districts and the proportion for women exceeded 20% in four — all in the East End. The highest level was in Bethnal Green, where 18.1% of men and 27.2% of women signed in this way.

26. At Toynbee Hall, in Whitechapel, only a quarter of those taking courses in 1905-8 were working men, while clerks and shop assistants preponderated and a quarter of all the students were Jews. At the Working Men's College the proportion of manual workers was 53% in 1893-4; after that it began to fall and in 1913-14, after the move from Holborn to St Pancras, it was 33.2%. J. A. R. Pimlott, *Toynbee Hall,* Dent, London, 1935, pp.92-3; J. F. C. Harrison, *A History of the Working Men's College,* Routledge, London, 1954, p.151.

27. The Rev. Brewin 'Boanerges' Grant gained a special reputation as a Christian champion on such occasions with a style of apologetics described by John Kent as 'coarse' and 'aggressive'. For an account of a six-night debate between Grant and Bradlaugh at South Place chapel in 1875, see J. Kent, *From Darwin to Blatchford,* Dr. Williams' Trust, London, 1966, pp.17-20.

28. H. Barnett, *Canon Barnett*, Murray, London, 1918, II, p.101.

29. Reynolds, op.cit., p.103. Reynolds, as a middle-class refugee from

the formality and the less 'natural' way of life of his own class, lapped all of this up eagerly. But he claimed to be very surprised by 'the thorough-going agnosticism that prevails here', referring 'not so much to immortality or the existence of a God, as to the religions, the nature of God, the divinity of Christ, and so on'.

30. Tressell, op.cit., pp.145-6.
31. An analogous attitude is well defined in J. Martinéz Alier, *Labourers and Landowners of Southern Spain*, Allen and Unwin, London, 1971, p.238: 'Not "to have ideas" — that is to say, to hide many of the common beliefs and attitudes, not to talk about them, to ignore the political theories that under-lie them or to refuse to make attempts to learn these theories — is approved as a mark of prudence, not condemned as a mark of cowardliness. Were it simply fear, they would admire the valiant ones who take risks. They do indeed admire them—but only half way. They also feel annoyed by their lack of common sense.' But, Martinez-Alier continues, if the government's capacity for repression were to decline, those who now are regarded as brave but foolish might suddenly find that they had a large following. Although the Andalusian labourer is clearly at once more class-conscious and more constrained in the expression of this consciousness than the working-class Londoner of the early twentieth century, Martinez-Alier's definition of the former's non-deferent political passivity seems equally applicable to the latter, especially in his reference to the need of the passive to defend their 'self-respect'.
32. T. Willis, op.cit., pp.3-5.
33. Booth Collection, B158, p.48. Diary of H. Gilks, City Missionary at Stratford, entry for 30 May 1896. All missionaries had to keep a record of their visits. Booth's representative was allowed to see some of the diaries and to copy extracts.
34. Booth Collection, B158, includes extracts from the diaries of City Missionaries in several parts of London. Booth Collection, B196, pp.41-51, consists of extracts from the diary of a Scripture Reader attached to St. Barnabas', Islington, in about 1898.
35. Ibid., B196, p.47.
36. T. Willis, op.cit., pp.140-1.
37. Ibid., B196, p.45.
38. To John Holloway's mother at Norwood in the 1920s (Holloway op.cit., p.49) Satan was more real than God, 'God, in our sector of the creation being self-evidently half-hearted or incompetent'. At about the same time Ted Willis' mother in Tottenham was distinguishing between the Christian God who 'sits up there, like Patience on a blessed monument', in whom she did not believe and a God in·whom she does believe, and whose presence she feels in nature (Willis, op.cit., pp.140-1). The family of a Bethnal Green autobiographer believed in an absent God: 'we felt sure that there was a God, but that He was no friend of our's, that it was of no use to depend on Him for anything, and that it behoved us to sharpen our wits and fight the world for what we could get' (G.

Acorn, *One of the Multitude*, Heinemann, London, 1911, p.51.

39. Booth Collection, B196, p.47.
40. Ibid., B196, pp.49-51.
41. Tressell., op.cit., p.142.
42. Oppenheimer, Diary, 1861-2.
43..Ibid.
44. Tressell, op.cit., p.142.
45. Oppenheimer, Diary.
46. Tressell, op.cit., p.142.
47. Booth Collection, B196, pp.43-5.
48. Ibid., p.51.
49. Oppenheimer, Diary. Mr. Viney, 61 Dudley Street.
50. An old man at 63 Dudley Street told Oppenheimer: 'I hope God will have mercy on me, he knows I have been trying to do the best I could. I have never been a drunken fellow. I worked hard and tried to keep a little home together; it is true I have not been what is called a religious sort of chap, but you see I had no time to spare to attend to it and I am not a scholar.' The missionary 'endeavoured to awake him from his awful delusion ... but am sorry to say he did not seem the least concerned about all I said and read'. A Jew at 34 Dudley Street did in fact try to refute the doctrine of the Trinity by quotation from the Old Testament, but soon found himself out-quoted.
51. Cf. George Lansbury interviewed by Ernest Aves in 1897: 'Of course people have a sort of belief: they believe in a God, but it doesn't mean anything in their lives.' Booth Collection, B178, p.113.
52. For examples of this, compare Easton's view that 'all this religious business' is 'just a money-making dodge. It's the parson's trade just the same as painting is ours, only there's no work attached to it and the pay's a bloody sight better than ours is' (Tressell, op.cit., p.141) with the views of an old woman visited by Oppenheimer at 1 Marmautte Court, who refused a tract because she could not read: 'I don't care for nobody and you need not trouble yourself about me. I am old enough to know all about it; its nothing to nobody else as I have a soul or not; what of that, I am not such a fool that I don't know I will have to die. Of course I must die and so must you. I never bother myself with heaven or hell, my old man when he was alive always said it was all parson's tricks and no more and I believe so too.'
53. F. Engels, *The Condition of the Working Class in England*, (English Translation), Panther, London, 1969, pp.155, 263-4 (first published, 1845).
54. Oppenheimer, Diary. Similarly at 72 Dudley Street, in the back room on the top floor, he found an old Irishwoman with a baby: 'I could wish I was dead if it was not for this little Baby and he would be much better off if he was dead too; don't know as I would be better off but I could not be much worse; well I heard a great deal about heaven and hell, but I am sure I have got my hell

here. I need not have another. I am sure if anyone ought to go to
heaven I ought.' And at 40 Dudley Street was 'a miserable looking
old Irishman, in extreme poverty and almost in a state of idiocy',
who said 'I don't want no religious talking, don't care a — farthing
for no religion at all.' On the other hand, at 18 Dudley Street, he
found 'an old and poor woman' who told him: 'I trust in Christ
and prays to Him every day of my life', and at 25 Dudley Street,
was a 'poor Mrs. Oldham', who said: 'It is very hard for me, but
God knows best what is for our good. I pray to him and he gives
me strength to bear any trial, etc.' But the poorest of those visited
by Oppenheimer tended to respond neither with hostility nor with
expressions of piety, but with listless apathy.

55. During Charles II's reign, the 4th Lord North had claimed that the
number of those believing in life after death 'especially among the
vulgar' was very small, and a poll taken in twelve European and
American countries in 1947 found that while the great majority of
those in the British sample claimed to believe in God, the
proportion claiming to believe in the immortality of the soul
(49%) was equal to the proportion in Sweden, and lower than in
any other country included. K. Thomas, *Religion and the Decline
of Magic,* Weidenfeld and Nicolson, London, 1971, p.172; S. S
Acquaviva, *L'Eclipse du Sacré dans la Civilisation Industrielle,*
French translation, Tours, 1967, p.140.

56. Tressell, op.cit., p.220. A similar point is made in less hostile
fashion by Guy Aldred in *No Traitor's Gate,* Strickland Press,
Glasgow, 1955-7, pp.45-6: when Aldred worked for a mission in
Clerkenwell around 1902, a typical colleague was a carter on a low
wage, who devoted most of his spare time to the mission and was a
total abstinence enthusiast, and had, in spite of his very small
income bought a house and let rooms to men earning more than
himself.

57. His contemptuous conclusion was: 'Although they laughed and
made fun of those things the reader must not think that they
really   doubted   the   truth   of   the   Christian   religion,
because — although they had all been brought up by "Christian"
parents and had been "educated" in "Christian" schools — none
of them knew enough about Christianity to really believe it or
disbelieve it . . . They believed that the Bible was the word of
God, but they didn't know where it came from, how long it had
been in existence, who wrote it, who translated it or how many
different versions there were. Most of them were almost totally
unacquainted with the contents of the book itself. But all the
same, they believed in it — after a fashion.' Tressell, op.cit.,
pp.143-4.

58. Booth Collection, B158, pp.25-9, 32, 38-9, 48.

59. Among railway navvies, who might move *en bloc* from one site to
another many miles away, or who might individually leave to go
on the tramp, temporary co-habitation in the shanty town seems
to have been the rule — sometimes solemnised by an improvised

ceremony in a beer-shop, but more commonly not at all; life in the armed forces or on board ship did not lend themselves to sexual relationships with even this degree of permanency (Mayhew argued that soldiers' pay was so low that their women were inevitably shared), and ports and barracks towns were thus the chief centres of prostitution. T. Coleman, *The Railway Navvies* (2nd ed.), Penguin, Harmondsworth, 1968, pp.192-6; H. Mayhew, op.cit. IV, pp.233-6, 226-33; H. R. E. Ware, 'The Recruitment, Regulation and Role of Prostitution in Britain from the Middle of the 19th century to the Present Day', University of London, Ph.D. thesis, 1969, p.329.

60. For solidarity among navvies, see Coleman, op.cit., pp.29-30; for prolonged fighting between Irish, Scottish and English factions in the 1840s, ibid., pp.93-103; for more casual violence, pp.105-107. Frank Bullen, *The Apostles of the South East,* Hodder, London, 1901, is a novel by a former sailor recording the struggles of a community of converted seamen, chimney sweeps and waitresses in Rotherhithe. The hero succeeds, by force of personality and the impression made by his physical prowess in converting the majority of a crew, that had previously associated Christianity with mental and physical feebleness, during a voyage to India. At first the going had been pretty hard, and Bullen observes that the population of Christian sailors is in perpetual danger of drying up, since those who are converted tend to seek jobs ashore.

61. J. G. Rule, 'The Labouring Miner in Cornwall, c. 1740-1870' University of Warwick, Ph.D. thesis, 1971, pp.240-60, has argued that the large role of chance in the lives of miners and fishermen inclined them to develop rituals intended to preclude and superstitious beliefs intended to explain wrecks, failure to catch fish, falls of rock, explosions, etc., and that in the early nineteenth century Methodism, with its special stress on providential interventions, was particularly suited to supplement and in some degree to replace the pre-Christian superstitions previously favoured.

62. 'The cries of costermongers during Afternoon Service are a most painful nuisance', Reply of the minister of St. Peter's Chapel, Buckingham Gate, London Visitation, 1862. Throughout the century Sabbath desecration by costermongers and by small traders generally is a constant complaint of London incumbents.

63. Navvies (usually referred to as 'railway labourers') are noted for their non-attendance at church, non-observance of Sunday and general bad influence in the Essex parishes of Stanway, Widford, West Bergholt, and Shenfield. (In view of Coleman's claim that the Anglican church largely ignored navvies until the 1870s (op.cit., pp.173-6) it is worth noting that the vicar of the latter parish was trying, without much success, to form them into reading classes). London Visitation, 1842. 'Depraved brickmakers' are mentioned at Thurrock (London, 1842), 'low brickmakers' at Enfield Highway (London, 1883) and 'the lowest of the

low — brick-makers and the dregs of other villages and towns' at Hoo, Kent (Rochester, 1889).

64. Mayhew, op.cit., I, p.2.
65. Ibid., I, pp.20-1, 47.
66. Ibid., I, p.21.
67. Ibid., I, pp.15-16.
68. Ibid., I, pp.24-39.
69. Ibid., I, pp.26, 46, 61, 101.
70. See Stedman Jones, op.cit., pp.341-6, where he identifies this style of politics with the 'casual poor', though it was probably also characteristic of many who were nominally skilled. He mentioned as examples of such ad hoc interventions, bread riots in the 1850s and '60s, the killing of Sunday trading legislation in 1855, Trafalgar Square riots in 1886.
71. A Corbon, *Le Secret du Peuple de Paris*, Paris, 1865, pp.305-6.
72. Ibid., p.21.
73. O. Lewis, *La Vida*, Secker and Warburg, London, 1967, xlii.
74. R. Cobb, *Terreur et Subsistances*, Clavreuil, Paris, 1965, p.52.
75. See J. Foster, 'Nineteenth-Century Towns — A Class Dimension' in Dyos (ed.), op.cit., pp.281-99, or, for a more fully developed version, Foster, 'Capitalism and Class Consciousness in Nineteenth-Century Oldham'.
76. A paper read by John Kent to a staff-graduate seminar at Birmingham University in November 1971.
77. The *British Weekly* census of mission halls in London (results published 13-20 January 1888) exaggerated the strength of the Salvation Army by including some services from outside the metropolitan area and by adding up the totals incorrectly. Even so, the editor was disappointed with the result, which suggested that the Salvation Army was a smaller force than was generally believed. If these mistakes are corrected, Salvationist attendances in London in 1887 are equal to 0.7% of the population, as against (in 1881), 11.1% in Scarborough, 7.4% in Hull, 6.8% in Barnsley, 5.3% in Bristol, 4.2% in Barrow, and 3.3% in Portsmouth.
78. In the 1850s about a quarter of the Secularist militants whose activities were reported in the movement's press were artisans, and about a third were newsagents, shopkeepers, innkeepers or managers of temperance hotels. E. Royle, *Victorian Infidels. The Origins of the British Secularist Movement*, 1791-1866, Manchester UP, 1974, pp.237-44, 304-5.
79. Stedman Jones, op.cit., pp.341, 346.
80. Okey, op.cit., p.18.
81. Ibid., pp.4, 32-5, 55.
82. T. Jackson, *Solo Trumpet*, Lawrence and Wishart, London, 1953, pp.26-7, 32-9.
83. Ibid., pp.15-21, 42, 48-9, 60.
84. The weakness of Chartism in Wesleyan Cornwall is discussed by John Rule and others in *Bulletin of the Society for the Study of Labour History*, no. 22, Spring 1971, pp.8-11.

85. G. G. Eastwood, *George Isaacs*, Odhams Press, London, n.d.

86. F. W. Soutter, *Recollections of a Labour Pioneer,* Fisher Unwin, London, 1923, pp.23, 61. In the 1870s, Soutter organised a campaign against the church rates that continued in Southwark and Bermondsey after general abolition. His methods included the breaking up of vestry meetings and throwing the churchwarden in effigy from Southwark Bridge.

87. J. C. Wilcox, *Contending for the Truth*, Protestant Truth Society, n.d., appears, unfortunately, to be the only biography of this very popular figure. In the late nineteenth and early twentieth century the *East London Observer* gave a lot of publicity to local anti-ritualist campaigns, such as that in the parish of St Michael, Bromley, led by a newsagent and Liberal councillor, for which see the issues of 15 June 1909, 20 May 1910, 17 June 1910.

88. For one example see Jackson, op.cit., pp.39-40. Tom Jackson's mother was an expert on royalty and a believer in 'real gentlefolks'. 'Naturally with her bias my mother drove me and my sisters regularly and punctually to day school, Sunday school and (with less rigour) to church. She was little concerned with what we learned — all that mattered to her was that it was the "right thing" for us to go. In any profound or mystical sense she was as incapable of religion as a barn door or a grasshopper. But she seized a chance to wangle me into the church choir, not because I could sing any better than a crow, but because it was "so nice and respectable" to see me in a surplice — or, more often, to know that she could so see me if she took the trouble to go.'

89. E. Hughes, *Keir Hardie*, 1956, p.202, as quoted by S. Mayor, *The Churches and the Labour Movement,* The Independent Press, London, 1967, p.311. The phrase comes from an address to the Dowlais Adult School.

90. Sermon at St Thomas' Sq., as reported in *Lewisham Gazette*, 13 October 1893, which devoted a whole page to the sermon. The minister of the church, J. H. Belcher was a Fabian, and later an ILPer. See P. Thompson, op.cit., p.24.

91. Rather similar views were expressed by two of the three 'representatives of the working classes' giving evidence to the Cross Commission on Elementary Education. One of these, Thomas Smyth, a Chelsea plasterer, appeared to be a Secularist, and urged that 'a teacher would be able to inculcate morality, and the higher morality, without the aid of religious teaching at all'. But the other, Thomas Powell, a Bermondsey bookbinder, and apparently a Nonconformist, argued for 'board school religion' with no 'abstruse dogmas' — 'there are a great many things presumed to belong to religion which are altogether unnecessary to religion; there are a great many dogmas welded on'. *P.P.* 1887, XXX, QQ 52308, 52905-7.

92. Similar ideas, according to H. U. Faulkner, were held by the Chartists, the majority of whom were 'decided believers in Christianity', but 'indifferent to all the churches' and anti pathetic

to creeds and ceremonies. *Chartism and the Churches,* Columbia University, New York, 1916, pp.18-23.

93. E. J. Hobsbawm, *Primitive Rebels,* Manchester UP, Manchester, 2nd ed., 1971, p.128.

94. Although Will Thorne's *My Life's Battles,* Newnes, London, 1925, makes no reference to Secularist or to Christian doctrine, he mentions his admiration for Bradlaugh and Besant and the fact that as a migrant to London in the '80s he was a frequent attender at the Hall of Science (ibid., p.55).

95. Although Paul Thompson (op.cit., pp.162, 209) cites Jack Jones as a typical SDF critic of Nonconformists and temperance advocates, his attacks were those not of a Secularist but of a Roman Catholic, and one who apparently approved of the Roman and Anglo-Catholic clergy as warmly as he approved of beer. See J. Jones, *My Lively Life,* Long, London, 1928, pp.30, 150-1, 220-1.

96. B. Tillett, *Memories and Reflections,* Long, London, 1931, pp.77-8. According to P. d'A Jones, *The Christian Socialist Revival, 1877-1914,* Princeton UP, Princeton, 1968, p.183, Tillett was a Congregationalist.

97. Hobsbawm, *Primitive Rebels,* p.128.

98. W. Kent, *John Burns: Labour's Lost Leader,* Williams and Norgate, London, 1950, p.298. For some examples of the way in which Secularism could act as 'a nursery of London Socialists', see S. Shipley, *Club Life and Socialism in Mid-Victorian London,* History Workshop Publication, Oxford, 1971, pp.40-1.

99. In reading the interviews with labour movement veterans that are published in the *Bulletin of the Society for the Study of Labour History,* it is noticeable how many of those interviewed had come from upper working-class families in which some form of Nonconformity, usually Methodist, had one or more active adherent. Although the interviewees, usually born about 1890, had in most cases reacted against the Nonconformity of their childhood and adolescence, it was a central feature of the culture within which the early members of the ILP and SDF had grown up.

100. Lansbury was born in Suffolk, but brought up in East London.

101. Aldred was brought up by his grandfather, a Clerkenwell bookbinder, who combined Broad Anglicanism with radical politics. Aldred, op.cit., pp.55-7.

102. George Lansbury might be categorised as petit bourgeois, but in relation to the other contributors (mostly clergymen or journalists) he would be seen as a working-class spokesman.

103. Thus Crooks claimed 'to have known the time when if I wanted some kind neighbourly action done the last person to come into mind would have been the regular attendant at church'. G. Haw, (ed.), *Christianity and the Working Classes,* Macmillan, London, 1906, p.74.

104. Ibid., p.83.

105. See K. S. Inglis, *Victorian Churches and the Working Classes,*

Routledge, London, 1963, pp.79-85; J. W. Tuffley, *Grain from Galilee*, Headley, London, 1935. The first PSA (Pleasant Sunday Afternoon) was established in West Bromwich in 1875 by a Congregationalist deacon who, believing that most religious meetings were 'so blessed dull', wanted something that would rival the attractions of cock-fighting for Black Country youth. Similar meetings were soon established in other parts of the Midlands, usually in association with a Nonconformist chapel, but sometimes under Anglican auspices or independently. The first London branch appeared in 1888 and a national organisation (against the opposition of the founder) in 1905. In 1913, the London Federation claimed 329 branches and 55,931 members. Tuffley, pp.2-28; *Brotherhood Journal*, May 1913.

106. R. B. Suthers in *Clarion*, 17 June 1904.

107. C. S. Horne, *The Brotherhood Movement, A New Protestantism*, London, 1913. (Presidential Address to the National Brotherhood Conference, Birmingham, 22 September 1913).

108. There were 'Salvation Army' types of Brotherhood linked with the more Evangelical churches, and 'labour church' types linked with such places as Browning Hall.

109. This was especially apparent in the early 1920s: while most Nonconformist ministers remained Liberals and many chapel-goers were beginning to vote Conservative, the most articulate members of Brotherhoods tended to be Socialists. Thus *Brotherhood Journal*, August 1919, carried a report by the chairman of the movement's Reconstruction Committee, who admitted the inevitability of the trend towards nationalisation, but could not commit the movement to the 'total nationalisation' that many branches were demanding.

110. H. G. Turner, Meyer's secretary, interviewed by A. L. Baxter, 19 July 1899. Turner thought, however, that although the membership of church and PSA remained largely distinct, Meyer had acted as a bridge between the two, that the animosity was gone, and that he had 'developed a spirit of camaraderie between rich and poor which before was unknown'. Booth Collection. B271, pp.79-99.

111. Maternal influences were prominent in the confessions made at a special testimony meeting during the National Brotherhood Conference in 1913. Typical was Bro. J. Leech, one of the biggest blackguards in Gateshead, the beginning of whose regeneration had been the pangs of remorse he felt after being drunk while burying his pious mother. *Brotherhood Journal*, October 1913.

112. Horace Mann's famous definition of working-class religion; 'Religious Worship (England and Wales)', *P.P.* 1852-3, LXXXIX, clviii.

113. E.g. Thomas Okey, educated at a church school in Bethnal Green in the 1850s and '60s and brought up in a home where, although his parents were non-church-goers, the Bible and Foxe's Martyrs were the only books, first heard of the existence of sceptics

through an article in a religious periodical about Tom Paine's death-bed; first met one in the person of the foreman in the basket workshop where he was apprenticed, who was 'as a boy working there soon informed me with hushed voice, . . . a man "what didn't believe in no God" ' (though he turned out to be a deist, and a follower of Paine and Owen); and was converted to Secularism after hearing some Bradlaughites refute a Christian Evidence lecturer in Shoreditch, and accordingly paying a visit 'almost trembling' to the Hall of Science. Okey, op.cit., pp.10-11, 18, 32, 35-6.

114. See S. Budd, 'The Loss of Faith: Reasons for Unbelief among Members of the Secular Movement in England, 1850-1950', *Past and Present*, no.36, April 1967, pp.108-10

115. See above, p.65.

116. W. Rossiter in *Nineteenth Century*, vol.XXI, pp.262-72, and vol.XXII, pp.111-26. Rossiter had been a portmanteau-maker, a student at the Working Men's College, and then a teacher there, and a Christian champion in public debates. See J. F. C. Harrison, op.cit., pp.54-5.

117. See Shipley, op.cit. Shipley notes the 'strong current of anti-clericalism' in most clubs, the tendency of ostensibly political or scientific lectures to provide occasions for attacks on the clergy, and the adoption by the clubs of patron saints noted for their anti-Christian views; also the anti-church implications of the fact that Sunday was *'the* club day' (Shipley, pp.30-3). Several of the Anglican clergy interviewed by Booth deplored the influence of the Working Men's Clubs in their neighbourhoods: e.g. B231, pp.57-9 (a violent attack by a Haggerston vicar on Hackney Working Men's Club); B231, p.99 (another Haggerston incumbent, noting the anti-clericalism of the clubs); B182, p.219 (a Bethnal Green vicar condemning a local radical club as 'worse than the Public-House'). The first attack mentioned 'socialistic rot' excessive consumption of beer, and 'songs full of beastly innuendo'.

118. The terms in which the *West London Advertiser* described the conflict within the Hammersmith Liberal Association in 1885. P. Thompson, op.cit., p.92.

119. An example of this was the final meeting of the 'Great Crusade' organised by the Church of England among Woolwich munitions workers in 1917: this was an address by the Archbishop of Canterbury in Beresford Square, which was constantly interrupted, and had to compete with a rival meeting organised by some Secularists. The interpretation of this incident was subsequently debated by religious journalists: on the one hand the *Church Times* reporter took it as a sign that 'this huge conglomerate of souls . . . regard the Church with undisguised hostility'; on the other hand, another observer was impressed by the smallness of the group trying to shout Davidson down. *Church Times*, 21 September 1917, 19 October 1917; for the latter view,

see also *Pioneer and Labour Journal*, 21 September 1917, and for
the former view S. P. Mews, 'The Effects of the First World War
on English Religious Life and Thought', University of Leeds
M.A. thesis, 1967, pp.242-7.

120. C. S. Davies, *North Country Bred*, Routledge, London, 1963,
Chapters 8-11. The Davies family had come to Ancoats from
Anglesey about 1840 and belonged to the upper working class,
most of them being engineers. All, apart from one Primitive
Methodist, were Secularists; their family faith was 'bred in' and
'cut-and-dried': 'They believed, and the experience of three
generations lent colour to their belief, that "though there are good
bosses and bad bosses, all are concerned in exploiting the working
class, and so the proper attitude to the bosses is hostility". They
held equally firmly that "religion is the opium of the
people" – propaganda to keep the workers docile and unresisting
in the expectation of a reward hereafter. They combined these
beliefs with sound ethical conduct . . . '

121. S. Budd, 'The British Humanist Movement, c.1860-1966',
University of Oxford, Ph.D. thesis, 1969, pp.153-64, notes that
Secularist extremism was conditioned by the experience of petty
persecution: the more durable and self-contained Secularist
societies, such as those at Failsworth and Leicester tended to be
the least militant. The division between the more intellectual
members of the Secular and Working Men's Clubs, often convinced
Secularists, and their 'beer and billiards' addicted fellow members,
of whom they tended to be very contemptuous, is noted by
Shipley, op.cit., p.26, and in the autobiography of a Leicester
Secularist, T. Barclay, *Memoirs and Medleys, the Autobiography
of a Bottle-Washer*, Backus, Leicester, 1934, pp.59, 64. For the
difficulty Secularists had in preserving their children from religious
education, see Tressell, op.cit., pp.133-4; *P.P.* 1887, Q 52645 (the
evidence of Thomas Smyth, a Chelsea plasterer, to the Cross
Commission concerning the hostile attitude of the teachers at his
son's school after he had been withdrawn from religious
instruction).

122. The chief expositions of this form of humanist Socialism were
Robert Blatchford's *God and my Neighbour*, Clarion Press,
London, 1904, and *Not Guilty*, Clarion Press, London, 1905. Both
played a part in a number of the Secularist conversions studied by
Susan Budd. In 150 Secularist obituaries of 1850-1965, *God and
My Neighbour* was named as a formative influence in five cases (a
number only exceeded by The Bible and *The Age of Reason*).
When in 1940-1 the *Literary Guide* published articles by fifty
Rationalists, naming the books that had influenced their beliefs,
six mentioned books by Blatchford. 'The Loss of Faith'.
pp.109-10; 'The British Humanist Movement', pp.279-82.
Tressell's Frank Owen refers to Blatchford's *Britain for the British*,
but not to his anti-religious books, but his views are similar:
disbelief in God, approval of the Carpenter of Nazareth, together

with hints that he never existed.

123. Booth Collection, B195, pp.24-6; B385, pp.161-7. Booth visited the church in 1897 and again in 1899. In spite of his own individualist politics he was eulogistic of Wallace. In a conversation on 'Mammon and Capital and profit and industrial relations' it is hard to see what the two could have had in common. But Booth was prepared to appreciate altruism wherever he found it, especially if it were expressed in a spirit of humility and willingness to learn.

124. A Baptist minister in Poplar told Booth's representative: 'If the people want pea soup they go to church; if they want the Gospel they come to chapel.' Booth Collection, B171, p.34.

125. F. G. Bettany, *Stewart Headlam*, Murray, London, 1926, p.31.

126. C. F. G. Masterman, *The Condition of England*, Methuen, London, 1909, p.75; Booth Collection, A49, pp.3, 12.

127. Baxter described him in very sympathetic terms. He wore a blue reefer jacket and black tie, and looked like a combination of Tom Mann and John Burns. Booth Collection, B237, pp.1-31.

128. For a less sympathetic description of a similar situation, see the story of the temporary conversion of a thief by a revivalist mission in Arthur Morrison, *Tales of Mean Streets,* Methuen, London, 1894, pp.255-69. Morrison who was born in Poplar and made his name and fortune through novels and short stories about the East End, usually stressing its quainter aspects, was well aware of the Evangelical presence, which he usually treated rather cynically. (The hero of his most famous book was an Anglo-Catholic priest.) Thus, in *Tales of Mean Streets*, pp.15-16, he described the streets on Sunday morning, empty except for 'one or two heads of households' 'in wonderfully black suits', their children running along beside with 'solemn little faces towelled to a polish' who 'fare grimly though the grim little streets to a grim little Bethel where are gathered together others in like garb and attendance and for two hours they endure the frantic menace of hell-fire.'

129. Booth Collection, B237, pp.25-7.

130. At the Wheatsheaf Mission in Lambeth to which William Kent belonged around 1900, the leading open-air preacher was Jack Jones, 'the converted Coster'. Kent commented that while 'converted Costers were always being advertised, you never seemed to meet Bill Smith 'The Converted Bank Clerk'. W. Kent, *Testament of a Victorian Youth*, Heath Cranton, London, 1938, p.104.

131. Booth Collection, B237, pp.41-3.

132. A preoccupation with drink, the all-embracing symbol of the unredeemed state, is a recurrent feature at the Brotherhood Conference testimony Meeting in 1913, which appeared to represent that wing of the movement that would have been at home in the Salvation Army. One of the speakers had been 'a respectable sinner' from Seven Kings, and managed nothing more exciting than Sunday gardening, but, besides Bro. J. Leech, who

has been mentioned before, there was 'Drunken Bill' from Hull and a pugilist from East Ham. *Brotherhood Journal*, October 1913.

133. In the Salvation Army the precociously sinful were definitely preferred. Elijah Cadman, the Rugby chimney-sweep who was a leading member, claimed to have been drunk at six. For a few examples of drunkards and other conspicuous sinners suddenly converted: Joseph Wailey, who ran a gang called the 'Forty Thieves' at Old Ford, and spent half his life in prison, but in later years was converted by Celestine Edwards, the black Evangelist from Antigua, in Victoria Park; a merchant captain who settled in Limehouse and became a leading member of a local chapel after being dismissed for drunken violence at sea; Bendigo, the champion prize-fighter of the '30s and '40s who ended his life as 'a mission preacher with a special vocation to London cabmen'. St. J. Ervine, *God's Soldier*, Heinemann, London, 1934, pp.344-6; obituary in *Bethnal Green News*, 28 September 1895; D. V. R. Titterton, *The World is so Full*, 1961, p.2 (the author's father); K. Chesney, *The Victorian Underworld*, Penguin, Harmondsworth, 1972, p.330.

134. 'British Humanist Movement', pp.156-8.

135. One of Booth's 'illustrations from his note-books' was an account of a hot Sunday afternoon in June 1901, on Peckham Rye. The ablest of the numerous speakers was a Secularist, but he 'lacked all reverence. It was a narrow Christianity that he attacked, and his criticisms of the Bible were of the old-fashioned type, for which the doctrine of literal inspiration alone affords any excuse. But round him on neighbouring platforms were plenty of speakers whose views are sure to be met in this way, one, for example, on the Unity platform, who, holding up the Bible said, "I believe every word in this book; I believe in the cover too, for it keeps the rest together".' Booth, op.cit., III, vi, pp.185-95.

136. E. N. Gowing, *John Edwin Watts-Ditchfield*, Hodder, London, n.d., pp.67-8.

137. Lees, op.cit., pp.304-5.

138. J. Gay, *The Geography of Religion in England*, Duckworth, London, 1971, p.225.

139. L. Lees, 'Irish Slum Communities in 19th Century London', S. Thernstrom and R. Sennett (eds.) *Nineteenth Century Cities*, Yale UP, New Haven, 1969, pp.365-83.

140. When the priests at Holy Trinity, Bermondsey, were shown Booth's map of the area, with 'dark blue' indicating streets where the majority of people lived in extreme poverty, one of them said: ' "Why! it might have been coloured dark blue to show our people; that's where they all are", and he rattled off the names of some of the patches of squalour: "In every one of them our people form the bulk of the occupants" and the others agreed that while in these places the RCs were always more or less congested, elsewhere they were only found scattered.' 80% of the Catholics, according to their priest, were in riverside occupations.

Interview with E. Aves 22 February 1900, Booth Collection, B280, pp.248, 3-4. The concentration of Catholics was also noted at Lambeth, where Hemans St., Pascal St., and the courts on either side of Vauxhall Walk were named; Southwark (no specific street mentioned); Fulham (Grove Avenue); Bow Common (Fenian Barracks in Devons Rd.). Booth Collection, B271, pp.167-71; B274, p.61; B265, pp.131-3; Booth, op.cit., III, i,p.47.

141. At the *Daily News* church attendance census in 1902-3, Catholic attendances equalled 8% of the population in Holborn and over 4% in Kensington, Westminster and St Marylebone, but only 0.5% in Lambeth, 0.6% in Bethnal Green and 0.8% in Stoke Newington.

142. See J. Hickey, *Urban Catholics*, Chapman, London, 1967, pp.128-9, for an account of the much more severe violence to which the Irish community in Cardiff was subjected in 1848. For the continuing strength of Protestant-Catholic antagonism in Liverpool, see the account of the riots in 1909 in E. Midwinter, *Old Liverpool*, David and Charles, Newton Abbott, 1970.

143. *East London Observer*, 18 November 1893.

144. Ibid., 2 May 1898.

145. *Borough of Lewisham Gazette*, 10 February 1905.

146. Booth Collection, B289, p.73.

147. Ibid., pp.53-7.

148. Ibid., B180, pp.29, 65. Though a few Anglican priests were also said to be able to do this: J. M. Thompson, noting the large crowd at Lawless' funeral, mentioned the ability both of Lawless and of Robert Dolling to stop fights. Thompson, Diary, 16 October 1902.

149. Booth Collection, B180, pp.229-31.

150. Ibid., B289, p.25.

151. Mayhew, op.cit., I, p.108. Among the Irish visited by the City Missionary, Oppenheimer, by no means all professed to practise their religion, but one old woman might have been the 'crone' who shouted 'You're a good father. Heaven comfort you', as the priest went by with Mayhew. She told him: 'I never goes to your people for nothing at all and I don't want to be visited I know all you can tell me. Father Kelley, bless his soul is my priest and I knows him and he knows me. He is as good a soul as ever breathed and I will never listen to nobody else. Yes he told me of Jesus blessed be his name and his blessed mother and here (taking a crucifix out of her pocket) he gave me that and told me never to part with it, which I never shall.' Oppenheimer Diary, 6, Marmautte Court.

152. Though the *Daily News* census reported 1,654 attending Mass at the church on a Sunday in 1903.

153. Booth Collection, B280, pp.248, 6-7.

154. Booth Collection, A46.3, pp.97-8. Service attended by C. Booth on evening of 13 May 1900.

155. Ibid., B280, 274, pp.12-13. But the priests thought that Irish *children* identified themselves with the British cause.

156. Mayor, op.cit., p.303, notes that the *Universe* was the most

anti-Socialist of all the religious papers in the period 1900-10, in spite of strong competition from the Low Anglican *Church Family Newspaper*.

157. Whelahan, the 'benevolent tyrant', had scenes from '98 and portraits of O'Connell and Irish MPs hanging on his wall. He remarked that all his flock were Home Rulers and Progressives, and that 'We will do anything within the Ten Commandments to help the old country to her own'. Fr. Buckley was a guardian at Southwark, who believed in generous out-relief, and 'would not touch the C.O.S. with a long pole'. Egglemeers, the despondent priest from the Isle of Dogs, remarked that his flock had no liking for Cardinal Vaughan as they were all radicals and they saw him as a Tory. (The common assumption that Catholics voted as their priests told them [see e.g. Pelling, op.cit., p.58] may exaggerate the authority of the priests in *political* matters). As for Fr. Thacker at Bow, he was 'proud of being a conservative Tory'. Booth Collection, B289, p.69; B274, p.67; B180, pp.45, 89.

158. Ibid., B180, pp.47, 51.

159. Ibid., B180, p.69.

160. Ibid., B265, p.215. A Lambeth priest thought that London Catholics in general went to Mass less than those of Glasgow or Liverpool. Ibid, B271, p.173.

161. Ibid., B251, pp.133-9.

162. S. Gilley, 'Vulgar Piety and the Brompton Oratory, 1850-60,' a paper read to the Ecclesiastical History Society, Cambridge, July 1972, identifies a common set of beliefs, prejudices and devotional practices uniting the Catholic poor with their priests, but morally or intellectually repellent to most Prostestants.

163. Booth Collection, B274, p.69.

164. Booth Collection, B280, p.7.

165. At Walworth there were quite a lot of Italians, who never came to Mass except on certain feast-days 'when there is a sudden irruption of Italians into our church'. Ibid., B277, p.41.

166. A priest at Hackney named the unemployed as a group seldom seen at Mass, and Canon Keatinge of Southwark Cathedral mentioned the 'really poor'. Ibid., B180, p.191; B278, p.5.

167. Pinkie in *Brighton Rock* was perhaps an example of this type of Catholic.

168. Booth Collection B274, pp.63-5.

169. B. Hill, *Boss of Britain's Underworld*, Naldrett, London, 1955, pp.15-22, 38, 46-7, 69-70.

170. For a very interesting discussion of this theme, see W. M. Walker, 'Irish Immigrants in Scotland: Their Priests, Politics and Parochial Life', in *Historical Journal*, vol. XV, no.4, December 1972. The weak point in his analysis seems to me to lie in his presentation of the Catholic clergy as a sinister conspiracy, the motives for which are assumed to be disreputable, but remain completely mysterious.

171. Booth Collection B180, pp.19, 63. It is perhaps significant that Fr. Lawless, who claimed to have supported the Dock Strike, deplored

the fact that it had 'destroyed the spirit of obedience'.

172. B274, p.69. Hatred of Board Schools, and fear of their possible influence on Catholic children was expressed by every priest who mentioned the subject. Anglican incumbents on the other hand, while critical of the Board Schools and of the form of religion they taught, were generally much more moderate in their attitude. See, for instance, the replies to questions on this subject in London Visitation, 1900.

173. For instance a Hibernian Club meeting at a pub in Spitalfields was closed as a result of pressure by the priest in 1884 after Manning had written condemning its tendency to keep men away from their families. Gilley, 'Evangelical and Roman Catholic Missions to the Irish', pp.245-7.

174. Tom Barclay, the ex-Catholic bottle-washer, claimed that having once been a Catholic he could not adopt another religion – it was Catholicism or nothing. Barclay, op.cit., pp.48-9.

175. Cf. F. Houtart, *L'Eglise et la Pastorale des Grandes Villes*, Bruxelles, 1955, pp.13-15.

176. S. Gilley, 'Papists, Protestants and the Irish in London', G. J. Cuming, and D. Baker, (eds.), *Popular Belief and Practice*, CUP, Cambridge, 1972, p.263.

177. Gilley, 'Evangelical and Roman Catholic Missions', pp.97, 229-37.

178. Oppenheimer, Diary.

179. Annual Report of St Patrick's, Soho, 1870 (Westminster Diocesan Archive).

180. Cf. Tom Barclay's account of a mission at Leicester in the '60s: 'If Love and Duty could not draw us nor the prospective delights of Heaven, what was there to do but threaten and frighten us? The new preacher, a Dominican, drew a lurid picture of the torments of the damned and their duration ... The entire congregation was moved; some were evidently disturbed: nothing could be heard but deep breathing and sighs: even the rows of boys on the front bench were less restive than usual. What fervent resolution did we not make on coming away, henceforth to lead different lives – with the help of God really to renounce the Devil and his works, the World with all its pomp and the Flesh with all its temptations. Some of us kept away from the public-house a whole fortnight, then we began to back-slide and slacken again.' Barclay, op.cit., pp.29-30.

181. Gilley, 'Evangelical and Roman Catholic Missions', p.218.

182. M. J. C. Calley, *God's People*, OUP, Oxford, 1965, p.96.

183. Ibid., loc.cit.; T. Bliss, (ed.), *Jane Welsh Carlyle, A New Selection of her Letters*, Gollancz, London, 1949, pp.128-30. In a letter to her husband, dated 9 August 1843, Jane Carlyle described a visit to Mile End, 'that hitherto for me unimaginable goal!' to see Fr. Mathew administering pledges on a patch of waste ground. She had gone for the purposes of 'Hero-Worship', Fr. Mathew being 'the very best man of modern times (*you* excepted)', but she also noted 'the thousands of people all hushed into awful silence, *not a*

single exception that I saw — the only religious meeting I ever saw in cockneyland. which had not plenty of scoffers hanging on its outskirts'.

184. E. P. Thompson has recently suggested that the rural population of eighteenth-century England was characterised by an 'at times almost pagan' popular culture, with its 'alternative system of beliefs and sanctions' to that of the Church.'Anthropology and the Discipline of Historical Context', *Midland History*, vol.I, no.3, Spring 1972, p.54. There are hints of what he is thinking of in his article ' "Rough Music": Le Charivari anglais', in *Annales*, vol.XXVII, no.2, mars-avril 1972, pp.285-312. This theme is fully developed in J. Obelkevich, 'Religion and Rural Society in South Lindsey, 1825-75', University of Columbia, Ph.D.thesis, 1971.

185. For rural anti-clericalism in early nineteenth-century Ireland, see E. Larkin, 'The Devotional Revolution in Ireland, 1850-75', *American Historical Review*, vol.7, no.3, June 1972, pp.627-34; and for England, W. R. Ward, 'The Tithe Question in Early 19th Century England', *Journal of Ecclesiastical History*, April 1965, pp.67-81.

186. See K. Connell, *Irish Peasant Society*, OUP, London, 1968.

187. E.g. at Walworth, Booth Collection, B277, pp.41-5.

188. Gilley, 'Catholic and Evangelical Missions', pp.360-8.

189. F. Boulard and J. Rémy in *Pratique Religieuse Urbaine et Régions Culturelles*, Editions Ouvrières, Paris, 1968, pp.18-19, an important contribution to the work of the Le Bras School of 'Religious sociology' invite the reader to consider 'les cas de "réussites" chrétiennes, les "pays de foi" dont la richesse est un peuple entièrement chrétien . . . Pays basque, Bretagne, Bocage vendéen, Flandres, Irlande, Canada français.'

190. For which see the excellent account in Rule, op.cit..

191. Also well served by E. T. Davies, *Religion in the Industrial Revolution in South Wales*, University of Wales Press, Cardiff, 1965, and D. Jenkins, *The Agricultural Community in South-West Wales at the beginning of the Twentieth Century*, University of Wales Press, Cardiff, 1971.

CHAPTER IV THE CHURCH IN THE EAST END: BETHNAL GREEN

Bethnal Green was one of the most uniform, as well as one of the smallest of metropolitan boroughs – a narrow strip, about two miles from west to east, and half to three-quarters of a mile from North to South, extending from Shoreditch High Street at the north-eastern corner of the City to Victoria Park, the chief open space of the East End, and covering some of the poorest areas of London. Formerly part of the parish of Stepney, it was given its own church in 1743, when the only concentration of population was at the south-west adjoining Spitalfields. By 1801 the population was about 40,000, and in the course of the nineteenth century houses – mostly two-storey cottages with small yards or patches of grass behind – covered the parish from west to east. The population reached 90,000 in 1851, 127,000 in 1881 and a maximum of 130,000 in 1901, after which it gradually declined. Already in 1851, 82 per cent of all those living in the registration district were native Londoners, far more than in any other district, and the proportion varied only slightly in the decades following. Very few Irish had settled in Bethnal Green, and until the 1890s the only immigrant community was of very long standing – the Huguenots. But then considerable numbers of Russian and Polish Jews moved into the district – chiefly into the south-western corner.[1]

In the early nineteenth century, Bethnal Green and Spitalfields had been the centre of silk-weaving in London. The industry went into decline in the late '20s and collapsed in the 1860s.[2] Its dominant position in the economy of the area was taken by boot-making and furniture-making, characteristic 'sweated trades', dominated by the wholesalers who were supplied by large numbers of small workshop-owners and out-workers. Both provided goods of low quality for the working-class consumer, and made their profits by minimising labour costs and overheads. In the boot trade the manufacturing process began on the wholesaler's own premises, and the following stages were generally sub-contracted to a series of owners of small work-shops and to women working at home, with the aid of a sewing machine. The work-shop masters tended to be skilled men specialising in a particular branch of the trade and employing a few less skilled assistants, several of whom would be laid off in the slack season.[3] In the furniture trade, the activity of the wholesalers of Curtain Road was very largely limited to distribution, and manufacture was concentrated on the small workshops, typically employing four to eight men, where it was estimated by Ernest Aves that 80 per cent of East End cabinet-makers worked.[4] The characteristics of the trade according to Aves, were the near-absence of apprenticeship, a low level of unionisation, the survival of 'pre-industrial' work rhythms, including a modified St Monday, and the excessive number of small and precarious units of production.[5]

Bethnal Green was overwhelmingly working class. In a sample of 506 Anglican weddings in the district in 1888, 82.1 per cent of the men marrying were in manual occupations, including 33 per cent skilled, 13.4 per cent semi-skilled and 30.6 per cent unskilled. The 'better' end was around Victoria Park, where one or two streets are marked with 'red' (middle-class) as well as 'pink' (upper working-class) in Booth's map of 1900.[6] Streets marked 'blue' (majority living in poverty) appear in every part, although the heaviest concentration was to the south west, where Bethnal Green merged by way of Brick Lane into Spitalfields, and by way of Arthur Morrison's 'Jago' (rebuilt by the LCC in the '90s) into Shoreditch. It was here too, that several streets were marked 'black' (the lowest class). In Booth's scale of poverty, drawn up in 1887-9, it ranked third of the 36 registration districts, with 44.6 per cent estimated to be living in poverty; and in 1891 49½ per cent of the population lived in households where the number of persons per room was two or more.[7]

It was a vulnerable population in which even the most prosperous family was heavily dependant on the physical strength of the chief bread-winner,[8] and many other families, in which the earnings of the chief bread-winner were inadequate, were forced to set each of their members to work in one way or another. A hand to mouth economy developed in which food was bought in minute quantities, older children were kept away from school to run errands or mind the baby, frequent appeals had to be made to neighbours and relatives for (often grudging) help, and mothers submitted to the even more humiliating ordeal of begging for food and blankets from Guardians and charitable agencies.[9] Some resolved their problems by stealing, and tensions developed in poor families and neighbourhoods between those who did and those who did not think this a legitimate solution.[10] These tensions were exacerbated by extreme overcrowding: where families of five, six or more were crowded into one or two rooms, at least two families lived in each house, and happenings in any one house were audible to those in each of the neighbouring houses, there could be no such thing as privacy. In some streets (or, more often, courts), 'rough' families established primacy, and drove the others out.[11] In other streets, families who were 'very respectable' and those who were 'low drinking people' lived in close proximity,[12] each resentful of the other. There were nonetheless, grades of 'respectability', and many who were disgusted by Acorn's 'Turkey Lane' or Arthur Morrison's 'Jago' felt forced by the threat of starvation or the workhouse to make some compromise of their principles. Standards of cleanliness created further problems in so cramped an environment: those whose standards were lax made life unpleasant for their neighbours, while those whose standards were strict were apt to be regarded as putting on airs. Nor were the latter encouraged by the external appearance of the neighbourhood: Booth gave a pathetic description of a winter's morning in the 'Jago' in the late '80s, the streets covered with scraps of paper and pieces of bread, frozen dirt filling the gutters, and a dead dog lying in one street, two dead cats in another, all flattened by the traffic, while the women queued with jugs, looking 'exceeding cold', outside a mission that was providing soup, and the children 'with much lagging were trooping into school'.[13]

The opportunities for and scope of recreation were limited by long hours of work, the responsibilities of bringing up large families and very limited means. George Acorn's parents were at one point reduced to spending the evening in a cold room while George read to them from *David Copperfield*.[14] James Oppenheimer, a City Missionary who attempted to evangelise the impoverished district of St Giles in 1861 had found more than one room where an adult sat with a group of naked or near naked children and not a stick of furniture.[15] Thus the importance of amusements that could be had for nothing: adolescents would spend the evening marching up and down the main thoroughfares, or fighting gangs drawn from other streets or other races;[16] while the Sunday dinner was being cooked, men might go to Petticoat Lane or Club Row, just to look around;[17] and throughout Sunday free entertainment was provided by the orators in Victoria Park.[18] Sunday was spent by others in pigeon-flying matches,[19] or fishing in the Lea.[20] For men, Sunday was also the most active day in the clubs,[21] while they kept the ubiquitous bookie's runners busy all the week;[22] but their wives might have to wait until Sunday night for the chance of a drink in the pub or a visit to the club,[23] or until Bank Holiday for a family trip to Hampstead Heath or Southend.[24]

The Church

The Church of England had been late in coming to Bethnal Green. St Matthew's had been built in 1745, after the parish had been detached from Stepney, and St John's, at the centre of the district, had been added in the 1820s as a chapel of ease. When, in 1837, Bishop Blomfield chose Bethnal Green to be a 'model parish' the population had reached 70,000. Ten churches were then built in as many years, all free from pew-rents. It was regarded as a testing-ground for the theory that if the parochial system were restored by the sub-division of large parishes and the provision of adequately staffed churches, with schools and charities, the people would come.[25] Yet, in 1846, Blomfield was already referring to Bethnal Green as 'the spot where it is said that we have sown our seed in vain,'[26] — though the 1851 religious census showed that Anglican church attendances were at least higher than in most other East End districts.[27]

The Church of England in Bethnal Green was a missionary church, its ministers isolated by the suspicion of the natives and by the differences in language and custom that made the life of the local population repugnant to them. 'My position', wrote one incumbent at the 1858 Visitation, 'is productive of what I might venture to call mental torture. I can only pray for grace and strength to do what lies within the compass of my ability.'[28] Sometimes, the reactions of the clergy could be seen as those of members of a threatened ruling class in a polarised society. Thus, in 1862, the rector of the parish claimed that 'the greater part of the population consists of Radicals, Infidels, and of persons who are to all good works reprobate'.[29] But it was usually the mores rather than the politics of the people or a conspicuous portion of them that moved the clergy to expressions of horror. Thus the same rector's comment on Sunday observance: 'shops ever open, Streets and Road crowded with Blackguards on Sabbath, profanation lamentable and awful'.[30] And in 1857 his predecessor had given the following account of his parishioners to a Select Committee of the House of Lords:

519. What is the general moral character of your population — Very low indeed.

520. Could you mention any vice as more prevalent than any other — I am afraid that fornication prevails to an enormous degree.

521. Does drunkenness prevail — We have several gin palaces

and a great deal of gin-drinking.

522. Have you any reason to know whether there is much infidelity in your parish — Not much.

523. Can you say whether there has been any change in the moral condition of your parish since you have been there — During the three-and-a-half years that I have been there it has been in great degree the same; but people who have been there longer say that the whole aspect of the parish is altered and improved; you can walk the streets with safety and comfort at any hour of the night.

524. Yet you stated, did you not, that you would not like yourself or your family to reside in the neighbourhood of the church, on account of the fair-like appearance of the streets on a Sunday — Yes.[31]

The clergy were pained by the overt and public existence of much that in the 'respectable' classes was pushed into a private 'man's' world, where gambling, heavy drinking, improper language and recourse to prostitutes were accepted and regarded as normal as long as they were limited to this private world; they were disturbed by the loss of that 'influence' over the lower classes that many of them, in the 1850s, still regarded as normal, and fearful of the effects of this loss of 'influence'.[32] In so far as they mentioned any reason for the material misery of the population they tended to find it in the rapacity of landlords, though they did not suggest any remedy.[33]

In the 1880s Bethnal Green incumbents less often spoke of their parishioners in such hysterical terms, but many of them were quite demoralised. C. E. T. Roberts, the vigorous priest-in-charge at St Peter's, Hackney Road, when asked to name 'anything that specially impedes' his ministry, mentioned 'the deadness of the Church in so many parishes round, owing in a great measure to the incumbents being broken down', and he recommended 'more frequent change of incumbents'.[34] His own parish was the most notorious example: the Vicar, Bishop Beckles of Sierra Leone, lived in Eastbourne.[35] Another incumbent, who was at least resident, when asked if he had any recommendations, suggested: 'A good county living for the Vicar and a goodly staff of earnest young clerical workers for the parish.'[36] There were many reasons for this demoralisation: the size of most East End parishes, daunting to those who still thought that a country parish in the South-East approached the optimum size, and that even the relatively small parishes in the West End were too large;[37] the great inequality of incomes between incumbents of wealthy and of poor parishes, and the constant drain of charity and schools on the limited incomes of the latter;[38] the defiance by most of those around them of much that they held as sacred; the indifference to their efforts of most and the sneers of some. If some incumbents lapsed into inactivity,[39] others suffered nervous breakdowns.[40] It was usually held that there was 'almost no actual antagonism', but 'the great indifference of the vast majority of people'[41] was inescapable, and it was depressing enough; moreover, the lack of 'actual antagonism' could conceal a cynical suspicion of the parson's motives. Londoners showed none of the Spanish passion for church burning; nor is it likely that an English revolution would have shot any bishops. But A. L. Baxter held that the prevailing view among the working class was 'we don't want nothing to do with no bloody parsons', a feeling that he attributed to 'a dislike for the restraint which a religious life involves' and resentment of the efforts of the Clergy 'to get hold of the people', though the position of the clergy as 'almoners' protected them from the underlying hostility of those whom they visited.[42] In any case, there were always a few East Enders who regarded parsons as fair game for any insult they could devise,[43] while their comical appearance and the fact that they were expected to turn the other cheek made them promising material for practical jokes.[44] The East End clergy were thus apt to feel unloved, though, by the end of the century there was a widespread feeling that the worst was past, and that the Church was enjoying something of a revival.

The Chapel

Nonconformity, on the other hand, was indigenous to the East End, and by 1900 the talk was largely of lost glories. The Independent chapel in Bethnal Green Road dated from 1662, and since then several large Baptist and Congregational chapels had been added, with the help of such local magnates as James Link, a wholesaler dealer in sausage meat, who was said to have given at one time or another £5,000 to Approach Road Congregational Church,[45] or James Branch, a member of the same church, who was a boot manufacturer, a Liberal County Councillor, and a supporter of peace, temperance and trade union uses. These belonged to the aristocracy of East End Dissent, the ron class. Most of the leaders of local chapels, to judge from Booth's rviews with senior deacons, and from the obituaries in the local press seem to have come from a slightly lower social stratum — that of small traders and clerks. Among the officials of East End religious organisations interviewed by Booth were a lithographer (Ragged Schools, Spitalfields), a greengrocer (Little Alie Street Strict Baptist) — 'a rough, frank middle-aged son of the people'[46] — a chemist (Bow Congregational), a corn merchant (Poplar Wesleyan Circuit), a postmaster (Bow Baptist), a master printer (Approach Road Congregational).

Some leaders of Bethnal Green Nonconformity lived in South Hackney — an island of relative gentility on the other side of Victoria Park. Many others lived above the shops that lined the main thoroughfares of the borough. Beyond a few streets near the Park, Bethnal Green had nothing to compare with the area round Tredegar Square in Bow, favoured by East End employers. But such a middle class as the borough had was rapidly deserting it for the Essex suburbs. In the '80s and '90s the *East London Observer* frequently published obituaries of employers who had been mainstays of local chapels and leaders of Liberalism, before retiring to Woodford in their last years.[47]

Their children, with no local ties to hold them back, would probably have preceded them. The chapels they had built were closing, or were, like those of their Anglican neighbours, assuming a missionary character, and coming to depend on funds from outside. The sharpest changes were in Stepney, which had the pockets of wealth that Bethnal Green lacked, as well as a number of historic churches and chapels.[48] But Bethnal Green, too, had its 1662 chapel which had attracted 1300 to its services on census Sunday in 1851, as well as Approach Road chapel, built to seat 2,000, and several other large buildings put up around the middle of the century, generally to the north and north-east of the borough. The situation at the end of the century can be seen from the minutes of the London Congregational Union. Out of five Congregational chapels in Bethnal Green in 1886, one was sold in 1900 and one in 1909,[49] while Bethnal Green Road church surrendered its independence in 1910, and went under the direct control of the Union.[50] The case of Cambridge Heath Congregational church was that of many. Its predicament was described in a letter to the Secretary of the LCU in in 1904, 'a fine building in a prominent position', erected only forty years ago at a time when Hackney was a 'flourishing Nonconformist district', but now shrunken in membership and finance in an area overstocked with churches. The only solution appeared to be 'amalgamation' and 'the adoption of a more popular form of public ministry'.[51]

The medium-sized Nonconformist church which had been characteristic of the East End was dying out. It depended on the presence of a certain number of church-going families rather than on ministers with special talents. Those churches that survived were either very small – like the Brunswick Gospel Mission in South Hackney, which was run by two working men, and claimed 30 or 40 members[52] – or very big – like the new Wesleyan missions in Shoreditch and Poplar, or the vast preaching centres focussed on the personalities of F. N. Charrington and Dr. Barnardo.

The very small churches only accounted for a small proportion of the worshipping population – though some may have been overlooked by the censuses. In 1903, 86 per cent of those counted at services in Bethnal Green on census Sunday were attending churches of the five major denominations; of the others, Brethren and Quakers were most numerous, and two distinctively working-class denominations – Salvation Army and Primitive Methodists – attracted only a hundred worshippers each. As in some other parts of the East End, the decline of Old Dissent – previously the largest body of worshippers – was partly counter-balanced by the expansion of some Wesleyan and Anglican churches. (See Table 17).

Old Dissent was indigenous to the East End, and declined with the migration to the suburbs of a large section of its following. The Anglicans and Wesleyans were enjoying something of a revival as missionary churches, dependent on outside funds. It may be that the older Baptist and Congregational churches, with their well-established elites, repelled outsiders, who were more likely to be attracted to a new or previously empty church. The Wesleyan revival was based on the Central Mission movement, launched by Hugh Price Hughes in 1885. Each mission was led by a single dominant personality, who would stay long enough to make himself known in the area as a preacher, and would be supported by ministerial assistants and a team of 'sisters' engaged in social work. The first of these missions was placed in Stepney, under the leadership of Peter Thompson, and though there was never one in Bethnal Green, others followed in Shoreditch, Clerkenwell, Poplar, Bermondsey and Deptford. All attracted very large congregations, notable according to the account of Booth's observers, for their predominantly working-class character.[53] In the East End the best known of these centres was the mission in Poplar of which W. H. Lax was superintendent from 1904 until his death in 1937, and which, he claimed, was known simply as 'Lax's'. His chief means of making contact with the local population were open-air preaching before the dock gates[54] and extensive visiting;[55] but he was also active in local politics, being Mayor of Poplar in 1918, and was a great founder of clubs. A. L. Baxter who attended evening service at Great Central Hall in Bermondsey, the most popular of all these missions, reported that the hall holding 2,000 was packed and that some were turned away. The congregation was almost entirely of the working class: 'a few top hats came in, but not many: the general impression was of solid working class comfort: obtrusive poverty was of course almost absent, though just in front of me were a male and female denizen of some neighbouring slum, the man collarless, the woman with the dowdiest of shawls thrown on a threadbare dress.' The service was 'half concert, half religious meeting', and the preacher 'attacked, assaulted and battered our feelings and emotions, appealing to our hopes and fears, especially our fears'.[56] At Lax's the style was probably fairly similar, but the emphasis, to judge from his autobiography, was on hope rather than fear. The tone is of a humane and rather sentimental man, caught up in the adventure of 'winning souls' and rather proud of the skill with which he did it.

How the Church Saw Bethnal Green

As a minister in Poplar, Lax had the advantage of working-class origins, albeit Lancashire, and emphatically respectable. In his account of Poplar, there is a continual stress on 'poverty', 'sordid conditions' and the prevalence of casual labour, with the implication that the residents belong to a lower social stratum than his own;[57] but there is not the feeling of being in a foreign country that accounts of East End life by Anglican clergymen tend to convey. The first task of the East End clergy was to find some common ground between themselves and their parishioners, and the task defeated many of them.

Bishop Winnington-Ingram claimed in 1909 that 'twenty years ago in Bethnal Green every church but two was empty. Now they were gathering in so many of the people that the nets were breaking.'[58] Both assertions were clearly exaggerated, but most of the bewilderment pitifully apparent in the Visitation Returns of 1858 and 1862 had been overcome.[59] Oxford House, the High Church Settlement established in Bethnal Green in 1884 was the prime embodiment of the new ideas. The basic principle was the clergyman as priest his first loyalty to 'the Church', rather than the clergyman as gentleman, and part of a cohesive ruling class. His aim was 'the well-worked parish': systematic visiting, the multiplication of clubs and guilds designed for each class of parishioner, a personal relationship between priest and people.[60] The latter was perhaps too readily assumed by some of the clergy: in 1898 the new rector of St Matthew's reported that he had just finished visiting every house in the parish and the reception had been friendly but 'many seem to have yet to learn that parochial visiting from house to house is one of the duties of the parish priest'.[61]

The young High Churchmen who were taking over vacant East End parishes in the '80s and '90s sought to establish this relationship by identifying themselves with the local community and giving each of its concerns a sacred significance. Thus, J. M. Thompson at the Christ Church mission in Poplar spent afternoons taking a team of boys from the parish to play football on Plaistow Marsh, and evenings at the Men's Club; Sundays with a variety of Sunday Schools, segregated by local custom by degrees of 'roughness'; the patronal festival was used to emphasise the links of the parish with its patron St. Frideswide, and a funeral was 'a great success' because 'the church was filled with the grandchildren and greatgrandchildren, and many others of a class that never goes to church on other occasions'.[62] Others expressed their solidarity with the local population by adopting the role of neighbourhood counsellor, like Father Wainright, by boxing, like Osborne Jay of the 'Jago', or by political involvement on the working-class side, as with W. A. Morris, the South Lambeth vicar who became a trustee of the Gas Workers' trade union.[63] Smoking could also acquire a symbolic importance as token of fraternity and informality.[64]

Behind these efforts at self-identification with the people of Bethnal Green was sometimes a fear of the informality of East End life, and a desire to impose patterns of discipline and regularity drawn from a different culture. This motive was particularly apparent in the work of Oxford House. One of the earliest Annual Reports defined the 'problem' of the East End as lying in the fact that the people had lost the sense both of the duties and of the privileges of citizenship:

> Among the privileges should be education, rational amusement, and social intercourse; and these can best be supplied by Local Clubs with their various guilds, classes and societies. Among the duties, on the other hand, which require to be revived, thrift and prudence stand pre-eminent and thrift and prudence can only be taught by men who will associate with the people and thus induce them to face the elementary laws of economy.[65]

In the same spirit of control was the tendency of Winnington-Ingram and others to make a fetish of attendance at ordinary church services,[66] as well as the more explicitly political motives of some of the House's supporters:

> Lord Selborne said that from a political point of view there could be no greater service to the State than that a colony of gentlemen should live down in the East End, should live among the working men, and let working men see what kind of men they, the gentry were, and learn by experience that, after all, they were God's creatures first, as they the working men themselves were.[67]

But the motives of those of the gentry who actually went to the East End as settlers or as clergymen were usually more complicated than this. Fear of those around them was much less conspicuous than it had been in the 1850s.[68] One point was common to most of those who went as parsons to Bethnal Green in the thirty years or so before the First World War: a desire to make the church the focal point of the local community through the attractions of 'Catholic' worship and a re-invigoration of the parochial system. Beyond this were the widest differences in attitudes to theology, politics and such powerful symbolic issues as drink and the Sabbath. To those like Stewart Headlam, who founded the Guild of St Matthew when he was curate at Bethnal Green parish church in the 1870s, life as an East End parson was a form of personal liberation, a means of asserting a counter-conception of church and 'priest' to that prescribed by convention. As Shaw put it, he belonged to 'a type of clergy peculiar to the latter half of the nineteenth century. ... They wanted the clergyman to be able to go to the theatre, to say damn if he wished to do so, to take a large interest in political and social questions, to have dancing in his house if he chose, and to affirm the joyousness and freedom and catholicity of the church at every turn.'[69] Headlam's years at Bethnal Green were said to be the happiest of his life; they enabled him to make contact with the Secularists, at whose meetings he was able to enjoy his favourite dual role of propagandist on behalf of the church of his own conception and of confounding all those, Christian or Secularist, whose conception was quite different.[70] To those, however, like Winnington-Ingram, who was also inclined to get sentimental about Bethnal Green, it was a place for making friends with working men, and extending the scope of their public-school values of discipline, rules and team-work.[71] If High Anglicanism attracted at once the most and least conventional, it also covered a wider

political spectrum than Broad or Low Church, extending as it did from
the neo-medievalism of Fr. Wainright,[72] via ardent supporters of the
COS,[73] to Socialists, such as J. G. Adderley, the latter category being
increasingly prominent among the East End clergy after about 1906.
All were inspired by a strong belief in 'the Church'. This could take the
form of clericalism − but the term could only be applied to one wing of
High Anglicanism.[74] What was common to all wings was the belief that
the highest of all priorities was to make the Church of England truly
national, and that this could only be done by asserting the church's
independence, emphasising its peculiar traditions and rites, effacing the
marks of class on clergy and on church buildings. Those at political and
theological poles also believed that Catholic ritual could provide the
focus for the life of a revived national church, that it gave colour to
drab lives, that 'to many' the parish church was 'their only quiet
retreat; all that they have to soothe them in the privations of a hard
life. It is their home'.[75]

How Bethnal Green Saw the Church

But those to whom these benefits were offered sometimes had quite a
different conception of the church's uses. In the hand to mouth
economy of large parts of the local population, the church was chiefly
seen as a source of material help. 'Why, Mrs Jones, you're out early',
the caretaker of a Bethnal Green school had said on meeting the mother
of one of the children on Sunday morning. 'Yes, sir. I'm going to
church.' 'Going to church' 'Yes, sir, I've lost my mangle.'[76] Canon
Barnett was perhaps least appreciated by his own Whitechapel
parishioners, who did not take kindly to being given lectures on Milton
instead of coal tickets.[77] An energetic new Bethnal Green incumbent,
mentioning the difficulties that he faced some twenty-five years later,
included: 'the identification by so many of religion with 'Relief' due in
great measure to the unscrupulous 'bribery' and indiscriminate giving by
well-meaning persons, mainly nonconformist and undenominational in
the neighbourhood and in times past by the Church'.[78] The large part
played by claims for relief in the clergyman's daily round can be seen
from the diary kept by the Rev. James Woodroffe, curate at St
Matthew's, Bethnal Green, between 1887 and 1892. It is a pathetic
document. Woodroffe was plagued by beggars, tramps, cranks and
parishioners in trouble, and he seems to have spent most of the day in
trying to determine whether applicants for hospital letters were

deserving cases, and whether seekers of advice or spiritual consolation were merely after his money. Some clergyman invested the East End with a murky romance,[79] but Woodroffe was certainly not among them. His period in Bethnal Green seems to have produced only bitterness and cynicism.

Relations could be uncomfortable between a priest who thought he was surrounded by shameless cadgers and a people who believed that the bottomless coffers of the church were equal to any claim. Thus, Mrs. Donald of 63 Hare Street asked Woodroffe for a little money 'if it were only eighteen pence so as to get food to the end of the week. — Told her I had no notion of giving her money out of my own pocket. She said it would go hard with the poor if all clergy were like me. I said the poor would be much better off as they would depend more on themselves. She went away saying it was very hard'.[80] And Mrs. Crump of 10 Church Row, when he refused to sign a document because he did not know her, called him a 'mean cur who was paid for doing nothing'.[81] As another parishioner said, the rector was 'a very hard man not to help to keep people out of the Workhouse'.[82]

Many of the clergymen who were most reluctant to satisfy the material demands of their parishioners accepted more eagerly a second requirement: that of assisting in the control of the district's children and adolescents and of supplementing the meagre facilities for the recreation of the population as a whole. Sunday school was an essential part of childhood, but when at twelve or thirteen the child began to earn a living, Sunday became a free day. The clergy could no longer depend on parental coercion to bring the children to them, but many adolescents voluntarily joined the clubs and brigades which were the means of retaining their loyalty.[83] Church also provided for the leisure of a wider population of adults than the relatively small numbers who attended services.[84] No doubt, the clergy hoped that this would be a means of winning converts, but they soon realised that such converts were likely to be few. They also saw it as a means of breaking down prejudice against the church, and thus, in the long term, assisting the task of conversion.[85] But such work was also seen as being good in itself. At the lowest level, it provided an alternative to the public house. More positively, it represented a conception of the role of church or chapel wider than that of simply a place of worship or 'soul-saving' agency: in Fr. Wainright's terms, the parish church as focus of the parochial 'family' and the place for confessions and processions, for dancing and for cricket, each at its due time;[86] in Dolling's terms, 'the chief centre for social righteousness to the whole district', providing for 'man – body, soul and spirit', 'treated as a whole';[87] in Headlam's terms, 'the best and the largest Secular Society'.[88]

The large membership attracted to the clubs at Oxford House suggests that there was a considerable demand for entertainments not provided by public houses and working men's clubs. The Oxford House Club, which attracted 'the upper grade of East End society' had 200 members by 1886, while the less superior University Club claimed 1,000 members three years later, and the Sunday afternoon Men's Services at which famous preachers were the chief attraction, drew average audiences of 500 in 1910.[89] But popular as the activities provided by these clubs were, they were not, from the point of view of their managers, altogether a 'success'. In the first place, their members saw them as supplements, rather than as alternatives to the public house;[90] furthermore, members tended to select from the range of activities offered by the clubs those that were least intellectually or physically demanding, and refused to reconstruct themselves along the lines suggested by the House,[91] and they either ignored the religious facilities or limited their interest to the Men's Services, which the settlers (not to mention local incumbents) saw as merely a preparation for higher things.[92] The movement to make the churches centres for the recreation of the local population was one aspect of the decline of Evangelicalism and the advance of a Liberalism that defined the Christian task in more 'secular' terms, and of a Catholicism that sought to resurrect the idea of the parish; the movement was bitterly attacked by conservative Evangelicals who saw it as a perversion of the Church's true function.[93] It was, however, killed not by opposition within the churches but by commercial competition: in the age of the wireless, the cinema and the dog track the clubs for boys continued to flourish, but those for men were no longer needed by their former supporters.[94]

The Church-going Minority

Thus the churches certainly had a significant place in the life of Bethnal Green, but it was not always the place that their ministers intended. There remained a minority of the population who identified themselves completely with the life of their church. Most of them were women, though the imbalance between the sexes was probably slighter than was generally believed.[95] A disproportionate number came from the class of shopkeepers and small employers who dominated local government, and most of the others came from the lower middle and skilled working class, rather than from the families of labourers and street sellers. Those among them who had begun fairly poor tended to 'improve themselves' and migrate to the suburbs.[96] Their special distinguishing mark was total abstinence. If sexual morality was probably the area in which devout men of the middle and upper classes diverged most obviously from those who merely fulfilled the demands of propriety, in the working class the great symbol was drink. In spite of the immense social significance of drink in working-class life many men were for financial or other reasons very moderate drinkers: but the religious man was expected to be a tee-totaller.[97] Many of the clergy were equally insistent: even a man as cosy and unfanatical as Winnington-Ingram thought that all East End parsons should be total abstainers,[98] and Fr. Dolling was persuaded by the fact that 'all the best' labour leaders were tee-totallers to follow their example.[99] Temperance could be a form of purely negative self-separation: Booth quoted a clergyman who told him that 'tee-totalism is apt to become a cult of its own of a rather narrow kind, and it is added that "those who yield to the seductions of temperance are too much bitten by the idea of saving".'[100] On the other hand, temperance could be the symbol of an alternative type of leisure, as it was with Oxford House: lectures, debates and sport in a 'healthy' atmosphere, as against the sort of amusements that went on in pubs. Or it could be a moral alternative, as it was for Frederick Charrington, who placed his Great Assembly Hall beside the family brewery in Mile End Road, and the story of whose conversion epitomised the side of East End life that temperance advocates believed themselves to be fighting against.[101] It was an alternative very attractive to some of those brought up in a more typical Bethnal Green environment. A. S. Jasper, some of whose family were distinctly 'rough', got friendly with a Welsh boy living at the other end of the street, whose family were 'very religious' and 'firm supporters of Lloyd George'. Jasper was amazed when the boy's father invited them into the back garden to play games, as he 'didn't know fathers played with their children'.[102] But perhaps the best self-portrait of the kind of malcontent to whom the churches of Bethnal Green offered an alluring alternative culture is George Acorn's *One of the Multitude*. Acorn was born in Bethnal Green about 1885. His parents were in intermittent poverty, and belonged to the middle working class, holding aloof both from the 'rough' and from those who 'put on airs'. George himself went into the furniture trade after leaving school at twelve and eventually became a journeyman cabinet-maker, having picked up the requisite skills as he worked. From an early stage in his life Acorn had 'a curious sense of isolation' and felt himself 'an Ishmael'. He liked reading, but his parents would take his book from him on the slightest pretext.[103] When he had spent a few weeks in the country with a group of boys from his school, he returned to reproach his parents for uncleanliness, and thus to gain a reputation for 'aping his betters'.[104] Most of all he desired the affection that his parents seemed unable to give either to him or to one another: he admired the stoical determination that enabled them to survive periods of illness and unemployment, but his childhood memories were chiefly of violence and arbitrary punishments, and of cold water poured on his enthusiasm.[105]

By the time he started work he was infuriating his father by tracing 'most of our misfortunes to over-indulgence in alcoholic liquors', and being told in reply that he was 'a stuck-up nincompoop, who was trying to be what I could never reach to, one who was not content with the honest "choker" or neckerchief of his father, but must needs to go to a sixpenny-halfpenny shirt-front and collar which by no means matched my corduroy trousers or place in life'.[106] Before long, in fact, he was abandoning his Saturday night at the music-hall to save up for a second-hand suit that enabled him to feel 'more content' with his 'outer person'.[107] At the workshop his favourite time was the conversation over tea, when he made religion and politics his special topics though some of his workmates preferred to talk about horses, sex, or a son in Mandalay. He gave up betting after one of them had lost a lot of money on the 'deadest of certs', and before long he had given up going into pubs even for a glass of lemonade, his view being that they were managed and largely patronised by rogues, chiefly interested in extorting money by whatever means from any honest person who entered them.[108]

Partial release was provided by a local chapel that a friend of his persuaded him to visit, though new anxieties now arose as the atmosphere of the chapel was so respectable that he felt his coming from a rough neighbourhood must be held against him.[109] But in one of the societies attached to the chapel – the emphasis is entirely on this sub-group, rather than on the chapel community as a whole – he found young men with similar intellectual interests to his own and girls who would go to concerts with him. The result was that he was shaped 'into the image of an ordinary sort of middle-class youth', that he married a girl from the chapel, and moved to practise his trade as a cabinet-maker in a different area, after breaking with his parents – though he insists that they rejected him and not he them.[110] Here the story ends, in terms rather closer to George Gissing than to Samuel Smiles. Like

Godwin Peak, Acorn was 'born in exile' and doomed to be a stranger in whatever environment he lived. The chapel had brought him for the first time friends with interests similar to his own, but it had also brought him new problems. It widened the gulf between him and his parents, and after he had broken with them his loneliness was made worse by a religious crisis in which he was left desperately searching for evidence that 'all was not chaos and chance'. He recovered some of his confidence in a period of serious illness, and came through to the period of relative happiness in which he wrote the book.[111]

Acorn was first persuaded to go to chapel by a friend who told him: 'They don't preach at you much, no shouting about Jesus, or telling you what a wicked sinner you are. I believe they live good first and influence you like that.' And although he became an enthusiastic adherent he condemned the bogus nature of many conversions and of the insistence on such an experience for admission to the inner circle.[112] But it was conversion-centred Evangelical Nonconformity that attracted the largest church congregations in the East End. In Stepney there was Dr. Barnardo at the Edinburgh Castle; at Whitechapel George Nokes at the Pavilion Theatre; in Mile End Road, F. N. Charrington's Great Assembly Hall; in Bow Road, Archibald Brown's East London Tabernacle. The equivalent in Bethnal Green was William Cuff's Baptist Shoreditch Tabernacle. At any of these a Sunday evening congregation around the end of the nineteenth century might have exceeded 2,000. Booth described the Great Assembly Hall as 'a great permanent expression of the revivalist spirit',[113] and all of these religious centres were in the same tradition as Moody and Sankey: the 'Good Old Gospel' preached with no modernistic frills.[114] Nokes, who was a leading figure in the Liberal and temperance worlds in Bethnal Green provided Sankey hymns and eloquent denunciation of such abominations as the Continental Sunday.[115] The *East London Observer* described him 'as some quaint conceit, illustrative of his material strikes him, inciting to a ripple of laughter' and 'before this has scarcely died away, moving his hearers to tears as he pictures the position of the irrevocably lost, or touches the feelings by an illusion to a bereavement, the memory of which is still present in all its acuteness with those before him'.[116] Brown and Cuff were perhaps more exclusively Evangelical in their interests, while Charrington gave the Great Assembly Hall a social crusading atmosphere with drink and prostitution the chief targets. The casual visitor would have found it easier to slip into a crowd of 2,000 than into one of the close-knit circles that made up many of the East End congregations. The regular supporter must have quickly accustomed himself to the atmosphere of permanent revival, so that the constant references to death and hell, to conversion and decision, to the monstrously evil and the perfectly good, became part of a performance that he could appreciate intellectually − and which he greatly enjoyed − but which had lost its power to shock.

The attitudes of some converts to their neighbours were simply expressed in migration to the suburbs. Others stayed in the East End and devoted their spare time to religious propaganda and philanthropic activity, like William George, a Congregationalist deacon interviewed by A. L. Baxter.[117]

Church and 'Labour'

Something of the attitude of ministers and active laymen to the poverty of so many of their neighbours and the demand of some of them for measures of redistribution can be seen from their response to the Labour-controlled Board of Guardians at Poplar. Under the Crooks-Lansbury regime the Poplar Guardians became nationally famous for their generosity, and Booth's team asked for opinions on the subject when they visited the area in 1897.

These opinions were predominantly critical, though extreme hostility was expressed only by two Anglican clergymen.[118] More typically, those questioned wanted a middle course between the COS, who were felt to have too little feeling for the poor, and the Labour men, who were thought to have too little feeling for the rate-payer.[119] Some answers were coloured by the feeling that the idle and feckless elements in society were placing excessive burdens on the thrifty,[120] but criticism could be tempered by praise for Lansbury and Crooks, who were certainly ideally suited to disarm opposition in religious circles.[121] No one expressed himself as an out-and-out supporter of the new regime, though there were a few who were even more anti-workhouse than they were pro-thrift.[122] Still very rare was the parson who accepted the inevitability of social conflict, and chose the working-class side.

At the time of Booth's research for the Religious Influences series in the late '90s there were a few such parsons scattered across London: Anglicans such as C. E. Escreet at Woolwich, W. A. Morris at South Lambeth, or J. Cartmel Robinson at Hoxton; the Unitarian Jenkins Jones in Woolwich; Congregationalists such as F. H. Stead at Walworth or Bruce Wallace at the Brotherhood Church in Hackney.[123] Most of these, though outspoken radicals by the standards of their church and class, would appear as moderates in periods of social crisis as from 1911 on, when far more strident voices made themselves generally heard.[124] But in the decade following Booth's enquiry, the Socialist parson was increasingly in evidence in London. The two main church-based Socialist organisations, the predominantly High Anglican Church Socialist League and R. J. Campbell's neological Progressive League, were formed in 1906 and 1908 respectively. In the East End Socialists were probably more numerous among the Anglican than the Nonconformist clergy, perhaps because bishops selected incumbents with some idea of the supposed desires of their parishioners in mind,[125] while Nonconformist ministers were, in most denominations, selected by their congregations, who might be less enthusiastic about progressive sermons than middle-class idealists in the suburbs.[126] A gesture typical of the new forms of self-identification by priests with their people was the declaration of support for the 1912 dock strike by sixteen Poplar clergymen, including the rector.[127]

Nonetheless, a Wesleyan minister at Old Ford announced his conversion to Socialism as a result of his East End experiences in 1908,[128] and in 1909 there was a public debate at Bromley Public Hall between the Rev. Wilfred Davis (Congregationalist), a 'red flag Socialist' who stood for justice, brotherhood, peace, equality and the uplifting of humanity, and the Rev. George Freeman (Baptist) who argued that Socialism killed private initiative and forced capital abroad.[129] On the Anglican side was George Lansbury, the leading Socialist in East London, who rejoined the Church of England in about 1901 after a period as an Ethicist, and who had three parsons on his platform when he stood as parliamentary candidate for Bow in January 1910.[130] Bethnal Green clergymen had not been very active in local politics. But when after 1918 East London rapidly fell under Labour control the new regime had a fair number of clerical supporters.[131] Anti-clericalism still flourished, but it was not fed by clerical opposition to working-class political aims.

Yet, at a time of social and political tension of an intensity unequalled since the 1840s, bridge-building institutions favouring moderate reform and agreed solutions were naturally attacked from both sides.[132] The Brotherhood Movement, which might be regarded as a religious equivalent of pre-war Progressivism, found itself an equally spent force in the '20s, divided between a Liberal leadership and a Socialist rank and file who were in no mood for half-measures.[133] And in Bethnal Green itself it was in the '20s that Oxford House suddenly became aware that the all-embracing apathy, so much deplored before the War, had given way to 'antagonism and distrust' stirred up by class-conscious 'street corner orators'.[134] Precisely those sections of the Bethnal Green population who, twenty years earlier, would have been the most probable recruits for church clubs and PSAs[135] were now likely to see the one overriding priority as the destruction of a social order of which the churches, in spite of the reforming enthusiasm of so many of their ministers, were seen as an essential part.

Notes

1. Those born outside the British Isles comprised 3.5% of the population in 1901 and 6.4% in 1911.
2. F. Sheppard, *London 1808-1870: Infernal Wen*, Secker and Warburg, London, 1971, pp.166-8.
3. P. G. Hall, 'The East London Footwear Industry: An Industrial Quarter in Decline', *East London Papers*, vol.V, no.1, April 1962, pp.13-17; Booth, op.cit., I, iv, p.122.
4. Ibid., I, iv, pp.172-5. There were also in the East End 'not more than three or four' large furniture factories, and about sixty medium-sized shops, with an average work-force of twenty.
5. Ibid., I, iv, pp.202, 213.
6. Booth, op.cit., III, i and ii.
7. Ibid., I, ii, Table III; Stedman Jones, op.cit., p.220.
8. For one example, see G. Haw, *From Work-House to Westminster: The Life Story of Will Crooks*, Cassell, London, 1907, pp.1-10. The Crooks family, living in Poplar, had been fairly well-off until the father, a ship's stoker, lost an arm. He could not find work, and they were soon forced into the workhouse.
9. A vivid description of such a regime is given in the autobiography of a Bethnal Green cabinet-maker, born about 1885. When his father was forced to spend several months in hospital, his mother kept herself and her children alive by making match-boxes, getting two loaves a day from the Guardians, a blanket from a Police Court missionary, and sixpences from relatives. They lived in terror of the Sanitary Inspector: 'To our minds at that time they were soulless inhuman "powers", mysterious inquisitors, whose one object was to get us all into the workhouse'. When his father returns from hospital he is helped by £9 collected in a lottery at a nearby public house. Acorn, op.cit. pp.74-80, 104-5.
10. Acorn quotes the example of a family living above their own, in which the woman had been shop-lifting clothes. When the police called, the landlady and Acorn's mother hid the clothes, but as soon as the woman returned she and her family were told to get

out. 'My mother and the landlady had of course, no complicity in the "hook-and-eye" business, as thieving is termed, but had acted from that feeling of uniting against the law which is so strong in such streets.' Ibid., p.85.

11. In Acorn's neighbourhood the rough court is 'Turkey Lane', Acorn's father terms its inhabitants 'them riff-raff' and Acorn resents the fact that they thrive on crime, while the 'respectable' poor of his own street die. Ibid., pp.168-9, 225-6.

12. Booth's house by house account of incomes and living conditions in Bethnal Green. Op.cit., I, ii, pp.172-213. In the large houses of west Bethnal Green, the ground and first floors were often socially superior to those above and below.

13. Booth, op.cit., I, ii, pp.94-5.

14. Acorn, op.cit., pp.34-5. George's parents did not approve of books, so this was a sign of desperation.

15. Oppenheimer, Diary, entries for 49 Dudley St., back attic. 86 Dudley St., 2nd floor back; 83 Dudley St., 2nd floor back.

16. Acorn, op.cit., pp.19-23; Goldman, op.cit., pp.15-17, Ch.10.

17. The weekly visit to Club Row and Petticoat Lane was one of the 'greatest relaxations' of Acorn's father, 'an important part of his life's ritual'. Op.cit., p.72.

18. Nearly every open space in London had its regular or occasional speakers. Finsbury Park, where Thomas Jackson made his debut as a Socialist in 1902 was still flourishing in the early '30s, when Ted Willis became known as 'Connie's lad' through his advocacy there of Confucianism. Booth, op.cit., III, vi; pp.185-95; Jackson, op.cit., pp.71-8; T. Willis, op.cit., pp.142-3.

19. Thomas Duke, a City Missionary in Bethnal Green, recorded in his diary for Sunday, 9 June 1895, 'To-day a large number of men and lads came into my district to witness a pigeon-flying match'; when he tried to speak to them 'some used very ribald language'. Booth Collection, B158, p.45.

20. *Daily Telegraph*, 7 October 1905, reporting on how Sunday was spent in London.

21. Shipley, op.cit., p.33.

22. According to a wide-ranging hostile survey of the various forms of gambling prevalent at the beginning of the twentieth century, betting on horses, although severely restricted by law, became a 'national foible' after the failure in 1874 of the prosecution of a bookmaker. There were now said to be 'thousands' of bookmakers each with a large team of runners, as well as of foremen, acting as agents within their workshops. B. S. Rowntree, *Betting and Gambling, A National Evil*, Macmillan, London, 1905, pp.26-9, 155. See also Acorn, op.cit., p.139.

23. Jasper, op.cit., p.7; *Daily Telegraph*, 7 October 1905.

24. Flint, op.cit., pp.54-66, describes August Bank Holiday on the Heath.

25. B. l. Coleman, 'Church Extension Movement in London, c.1800-1860', University of Cambridge, Ph.D. thesis, 1968, p.124.

26. Ibid., p.183.
27. Ibid., p.310. Anglican attendances, as a percentage of population, were lower than in Whitechapel, but higher than in Poplar, Stepney or Clerkenwell, and much higher than in Shoreditch.
28. London Visitation, 1858, reply of vicar of St Andrew's, Bethnal Green.
29. London Visitation 1862, reply of rector of St Matthew's, Bethnal Green.
30. Ibid.
31. Evidence of the Rev. J. Colbourne, rector of Bethnal Green, to the SC of the House of Lords on the Means of Divine Worship in Populous Districts, *P.P.* 1857-8, IX.
32. Thus the Rev. T. F. Stooks, Secretary of the London Diocesan Church Building Society, warned the Select Committee of the 'large masses of population congregated in the east of London, whose whole moral, social and political state is becoming year after year in a more unsatisfactory condition, and more formidable'. He included the Church, together with the 'controlling influence' of employers and landowners, 'personal intercourse between the employers and the employed', 'the charities of life' and 'the visiting of ladies', among the 'higher associations of social life' that could favourably influence the conduct of the 'working people'. Dangerous politics and revolting mores were different aspects of the same problem, though the political dangers were still largely latent. Ibid., QQ, pp.813-21.
33. Colbourne described the 'extreme poverty' of the weavers and the 'grasping' character of the landlords. Ibid., QQ, pp.479, 637. High rents were the social evil most often mentioned in Visitation Returns. E.g. rector of St Matthew's, London Visitation, 1883.
34. London Visitation, 1883.
35. He was still vicar, and still non-resident when Booth came some fifteen years later. Booth Collection, B228, pp.167-9.
36. London Visitation, 1883, reply of vicar of St Andrew's, Bethnal Green.
37. Stooks claimed that the maximum number of people per clergyman should be two thousand in socially mixed and one thousand five hundred in poor districts. *P.P.* 1857-8, IX, QQ.822-3.
38. Clergymen in wealthy areas might have a considerable income from pew-rents, whereas Anglican churches in poorer areas were often 'free and open', and if they did have pews not much could be raised by letting them. Thus in 1903-4 the average income of Anglican incumbents was £693 in Chelsea and £577 in Kensington, but £235 in Poplar and £300 in Stepney; in Bethnal Green the highest was £571, the lowest £200, the mean £340 and the median £299, four out of fifteen livings having parsonages attached (Statistical Returns for the Diocese of London, 1903-4). The latter incomes, though larger than those of the great majority of their parishioners, were far from princely – or of a sort to

attract upper middle-class men in search of an easy life.
39. The most famous example was E. F. Coke, vicar of St James the Great, the 'Red Church' in Bethnal Green Road from 1852 until 1898. Believing that the cost of the ceremony discouraged his parishioners from legal marriage, he appealed for a Bethnal Green marriages fund, which raised enough money to enable him to charge sevenpence for the banns and two shillings and sevenpence for the certificate, and thus to attract couples from all over the East End. By the 1880s, about four hundred marriages were being performed in a year, and these, together with a certain amount of relief, were Coke's only concern. He lived outside the parish, and left a curate to do such work as there was to be done. The Bishop of Bedford who regarded Coke as 'a very clever man' and 'one who has no principle' was continually searching for a pretext for his ejection. *East London Observer*, 16 July 1898; Bishop of Bedford Temple, 24 August 1894. Spitalfields Box, Temple Collection; Morrison, *A Child of The Jago*, pp.174-5.
40. *East London Observer*, 30 August 1896, reporting the resignation of Rev. J. H. Scott, vicar of Christ Church, Spitalfields, a large and substantially Jewish parish made notorious by Jack the Ripper, claimed that he had 'broken down' and that his predecessor had done the same. A parish with a similar record seems to have been St Mark's, Kennington, where Ernest Aves reporting an interview of 12 July 1899, (Booth Collection, B272, p.117), described the vicar as 'a very good fellow who should do well if he does not break down. In this he has two bad examples as his immediate predecessor is now a "wreck" and the man before him died of brain paralysis.'
41. London Visitation, 1900, reply of vicar of St Andrew's, Bethnal Green.
42. Booth Collection, A40.7, pp.41-2.
43. W. Lax, *Lax of Poplar*, Epworth Press, London, 1927, begins "Take orf that damned collar, yer blasted skunk!" The genial speaker was a sombre, lean, hungry-looking man of about thirty-five years of age. The person addressed was Lax of Poplar.' A minister whom I met in 1968 told me of a conversation beginning in a somewhat similar way on Mile End station, though, as in the book, it ended with parson and baiter good friends.
44. J. M. Thompson, the historian, worked at one time for an Anglo-Catholic mission in Poplar, and while he was there recorded the following experience of a clerical friend named Le Fanu. 'A man came up to him and said there was a woman taken suddenly ill in a public house close by, who wanted to see a clergyman, and would he come? Le Fanu, after suggesting various alternatives, yielded, and went. The man took him into a public house and along various corridors, and at last opened a door, and they were in the public bar, where several men were standing drinking. "Now convert us", said the man, and thought it a huge joke. Le Fanu made as dignified an exit as possible. He didn't think the man did

it for a bet, but "just for fun" – odd fun!' J. M. Thompson, Diary 3 November 1902.

45. *East London Observer*, 21 September 1889.

46. Booth Collection, B223, p.167.

47. E.g. (14 March 1896) death of Thomas Scrutton, a shipowner, a leading Congregationalist layman, and a member of Stepney Meeting, who had now retired to Blackheath, and had forsaken Liberalism because of the growth of 'mad Radicalism'.

48. See J. H. Taylor, 'London Congregational Churches since 1850', *Transactions of the Congregational Historical Society*, vol.XX, no.1, pp.22-42, which includes an account of the difficulties experienced in the chapels at Barnsbury and Wapping at this time.

49. LCU minutes, 12 November 1900, 15 November 1909. The latter, the Adelphi chapel in Hackney Road, built to seat 850, had suffered a rapid decline under the ministry of a Yorkshireman who pined for Leeds and ended with a nervous collapse. Booth Collection B229, p.39; LCU minutes, 9 July 1900, 17 March 1902.

50. LCU minutes, 21 February 1910.

51. F. Brown-A. Mearns, 19 April 1904, a letter in LCU records, as printed in *Transactions of the Congregational Historical Society*, vol.XX, no.12, October 1970, p.372.

52. Booth Collection, B190, pp.10-11.

53. For Shoreditch, Booth Collection, B230, pp.145-7; at Clerkenwell (Ibid., B237, pp.84-6) the congregation was formed chiefly of artisans, including a fair number of youths, 'some of these being almost rough in appearance, of the type that if unconverted one might expect to belong to the Clerkenwell gangs: but here as elsewhere the prevailing type was of the YMCA'. Robert Currie describes the new Wesleyan missions as places attended by 'superior Wesleyans who wished to sit under the great men of the denomination', where 'the poor are somewhat lost sight of', (op.cit., p.211). While this description might apply to Hughes' own West London Mission, it would scarcely fit the others in London.

54. 'To a speaker who loves his job there are few more delightful experiences than to stand in front of a thousand people in the open-air! Oh, the thrill of such a sight! There you have the waiting, plastic, raw material of humanity.' Lax, op.cit., p.83.

55. Ibid., pp.88-9.

56. Booth Collection, B387, pp.13-17. Report by A. L. Baxter of service attended 18 March 1901.

57. Lax, op.cit., pp.54-7.

58. *East London Observer*, 17 July 1909, reporting a sermon at St Peter's, Bayswater.

59. Ernest Aves, writing on Bethnal Green in about 1900, granted that 'here as in other parts of East London there is much more vitality in the work of the Church than there was ten years ago', but he felt that Winnington-Ingram exaggerated the extent of the revival.

Booth Collection, A39, Report on District 9, pp.5-6.

60. A writer in the *East London Church Chronicle* claimed that 'Twenty-Five years' experience in East London has strengthened our conviction that the regeneration of East London as far as the Church is concerned will be brought about by the parochial system, for nothing else can reach the people in the same way.' As quoted in *East London Observer*, 26 August 1911.

61. *East London Observer*, 5 November 1898.

62. J. M. Thompson, Diary, 17-19 October 1902, 25 October 1902, 2 November 1902.

63. For an eulogy of Morris, see Thorne, op.cit., pp.118, 127. Thorne asserts that 'for his courage and the expression of his love for humanity that shone through his writings he was unfrocked from the Church of England'. If this is true (and it seems pretty improbable), it is surprising that there is no reference to his 'unfrocking' in Morris' obituary written by P. Dearmer in *Commonwealth*, vol.IX, no.3, March 1904.

64. Rev. Tom Collings, a rather brash exponent of informal Christianity, who was sacked from his curacy at Spitalfields in 1896 and moved to a mission church at Upper Edmonton, liked to be known as 'the dossers' parson' or 'the smoking parson'. Ibid., 1 August 1896, 7 November 1896, 21 August 1897.

65. Annual Report of Oxford House, 1886.

66. When Winnington-Ingram, who had been Head of the House since 1888, also became rector of Bethnal Green, he stopped the House's popular mission services, and invited their supporters to attend the regular services at St Matthew's: 'the time had just arrived after seven or eight years' training in the Mission Service, for them to be able to join in the Church Service, and take their places eventually as full members of the Church.' He gave careful instruction during the services, so that 'the congregation of St Matthew's, many of whom have never been to church before, are able to follow intelligently throughout the service.' When a later Head decided to place more emphasis on the 'religious side' of the House's work, he defined this as compulsory church parades for boys' clubs members. Annual Reports, 1895, 1907.

67. *East London Observer*, 30 March 1896, reporting the annual meeting in support of Oxford House at Keble College, Oxford.

68. That 'fear' rather than 'empathy' was the chief characteristic of the 'Outcast London' literature produced by the 'social crisis' of 1883-7 has been powerfully argued by Stedman Jones (op.cit., p.285) who sees the settlement movement culminating in the establishment of Toynbee Hall in 1884, as representative of a 'new urban gentry', anxious to turn London into 'a gigantic village' under its own control (ibid., pp.261, 270). While the High Church-led Anglican revival of the late nineteenth century was in one of its aspects a part of this movement, empathy, revulsion, and puzzlement are all emotions more evident than fear in the reactions of the clergy to the East End.

69. Bettany, op.cit., p.125.
70. Ibid., pp.47-50, 55-6, 60-1.
71. S. C. Carpenter, *Winnington-Ingram*, Hodder, London, 1949, pp.30-1, 40-2, 54-5.
72. Wainright believed in lavish relief, church schools, completely under church control, as a means of ensuring that the children of his parish were brought up as 'Catholics', ritual of model correctness, and the role of the Church of England as 'the true representative of The Church Catholic in these realms'. St Peter's, London Docks, Parish Magazine, March 1887, May 1901, November 1901; L. Menzies, *Father Wainright*, Longman, London, 1947, pp.24-5.
73. E.g. Rev. Herbert Eck of St Andrew's, Bethnal Green, for whom see Booth Collection, B228.
74. Booth's assistants had a keen nose for priestcraft: thus A. L. Baxter described a Hackney vicar as a 'pale young curate type', 'clothed in a cassock and altogether priestly in appearance' who could see 'nothing beyond "The Church" ', and at St Columba's, Shoreditch, Aves found 'a vast amoung of ecclesiasticism – perhaps superstition' (Booth Collection, B186, pp.83, 107; B231, p.137).
75. Fr. Charles Lowder, as quoted in Menzies, op.cit., p.31.
76. Booth, op.cit., III, ii, p.242.
77. Barnett, op.cit., I, pp.83-97. Ṣtedman Jones (op.cit., p.274), says that Barnett's example was not widely followed because 'the provision of alms was often the only means of holding together a congregation in a working-class district'. In fact, it was precisely for this reason that Septimus Hansard, Headlam's superior at Bethnal Green, *stopped* giving alms. See Bettany, op.cit., p.36.
78. London Visitation, 1900, reply of the vicar of St Andrew's, Bethnal Green.
79. As a young don at Oxford, Scott Holland described a visit to a mission in Hoxton: 'I did enjoy my glimpse of rough London thoroughly – that thrilling sight of the black and brutal streets reeling with drunkards and ringing with foul words, and filthy with degradation – and the little sudden blaze of light and colour and warmth in the crowded shed, with its music and its flowers and its intense earnest faces – and its sense of sturdy, stirring work, quick and eager, and unceasing – God alive in it all.' S. Paget, *Henry Scott Holland*, Murray, London, 1921, p.88.
80. James Woodroffe, Diary, 15 April 1891. In fact, Woodroffe's objection was not to poor relief as such – though his ideas on the subject were probably fairly strict – but to providing the money from his own pocket. In an additional note he criticised the C.O.S. for not helping her.
81. Ibid., 1 January 1890.
82. Ibid., 20 January 1888.
83. George Acorn joined the cadet corps attached to the Webbe Institute at Oxford House – in spite of protests from his parents,

who 'considered that joining the army was as bad, and brought as much disgrace on a family, as becoming a burglar' and that 'social degradation' inevitably followed even from 'playing at "Saturday night soldiers".' After he left the cadets, he continued to spend much of his time in the Institute's library. Acorn, op.cit., pp.140-2, 155.

84. Some examples: the opening of a coffee-house in Commercial Road by the Anglo-Catholic Rev. Harry Wilson in 1899; Fr. Jay's boxing club made famous by a *Child of the Jago*, which attracted he said, a different, and distinctly less 'respectable' membership from that of his congregation; the numerous sporting activities associated with Oxford House; R. F. Horton's Saturday Evening Lectures for Working Men at Hampstead (later simply 'Saturday Evening Lectures', because, although they were well attended, most of the audience were not working men); and the light entertainments provided on Saturday evenings between 1888 and 1898 at Anerley Road Congregational Church. *East London Observer*, 3 June 1899; Booth Collection, B228, p.47; *The Oxford House in Bethnal Green*, 1948; *Hampstead and Highgate Express*, 9 July 1887; A. Peel and J. A. R. Marriott, *Robert Forman Horton*, Allen and Unwin, London, 1937, p.202; Anerley Road Congregational Church, 'Minutes of Saturday Nights for the People'.

85. According to the Annual Report for 1899, the aim of Oxford House had been 'to undertake social work which, by improving the condition of social life, by efforts to promote healthy recreation, by the endeavour to widen the intellectual interests of men and boys, by banding together in a common work all who desired the improvement of the district, might strengthen and organise the forces of opposition to irreligion and viciousness of life. The ultimate end in view has always been the promotion of religion by the creation of a more congenial atmosphere and a higher tone of morality. To build upon the foundations thus laid the edifice of a religious life must be the task of those to whom is committed the care of souls. The results of the efforts made will only become apparent as the years go on. The children of our club members will no longer hear religion laughed at and its practice discouraged. But the particular work of the settlement must remain only indirectly religious'. Quoted in *The Oxford House in Bethnal Green*, pp.35-6.

86. Menzies, op.cit., pp.24-9.

87. While at Poplar, Dolling ran boys' and girls' camps, a rowing club, men's club, and dancing club, and organised theatre trips. He saw visitation of parishioners as simply a part of his duties and thought it irrelevant whether any of them became active members of his church as a result. C. E. Osborne, *Life of Father Dolling*, Edward Arnold, London, 1903, pp.260, 268-72, 313-4.

88. M. Reckitt, (ed.), *For Christ and the People*, SPCK, London, 1968, p.64.

89. Annual Report of Oxford House, 1886; *The Oxford House in Bethnal Green*, pp.12-13; Annual Report, 1910.

90. The Annual Report for 1902 recorded an intervention by the Head of the House in the affairs of the University Club and the expulsion of 'an undesirable clique' with 'loose ideas on such obvious evils as gambling and the public-house'.

91. The Annual Report for 1897 declared: 'The fact has to be faced that as the years go on the Club does not become keener on educational and social subjects; does not develop manifold athletic activities, does not become increasingly "a power for righteousness" in Bethnal Green.' It was, in fact, 'far too largely given up to billiards'.

92. At St Frideswide's, Poplar, the tone of the Men's Club was 'non- or anti-religious'. J. M. Thompson, Diary, 17 October 1902. At Oxford House, where the simplified Men's Services, regarded by the Head as 'milk' for those unable to take the 'meat' of the Anglican liturgy, attracted several hundred each Sunday afternoon in winter, attendance fell in summer, when supporters presumably spent Sunday in Victoria Park or Epping Forest; only twenty-six were confirmed as a result of a Lent mission. 'If only we knew the men who come to our services better!' was the comment of the *Oxford House Magazine* when seven hundred came to hear Winnington-Ingram. *Oxford House Magazine* January 1909, April 1911.

93. Especially outspoken in condemnation of this movement was the Rev. Archibald Brown of the East London Tabernacle. A speaker at Brown's Sunday School anniversary 'declaimed against the tendency of certain churches and Sunday Schools of the present day to pander to amusement and recreation. Amusement was not devilish, but the Mission of Christ's Church was to instruct, inspire, regenerate, but not to amuse.' *East London Observer*, 30 May 1891.

94. In 1929, it was proposed to shut the men's clubs, though they remained open and revived slightly in the '30s. The Sunday afternoon meetings which were still doing quite well, with a politico-religious slant in the early '20s, were suspended in 1934. *The Oxford House in Bethnal Green*, pp.71-7. Sir Hubert Llewellyn Smith in *New Survey of London Life and Labour*, Macmillan, London, 1935, devoted special consideration to the 'revolution in popular entertainment' produced since Charles Booth's day by two inventions: the wireless and the cinema. He concluded (XI, p.9) that the time now spent at the cinema was then spent either at work or 'idly at the public-house, club or street-corner'.

95. According to the *Daily News*, attendances by women in Bethnal Green on census Sunday in 1903 equalled 16% of the adult female population, those by men 11% of adult males.

96. 'N. B. Many of our best, both youths and adults, leave the neighbourhood when improved in character and position.

Otherwise the church would be full'. London Visitation, 1883. Reply of vicar of St Paul's, Bethnal Green. The same claim had been made by the vicar of St Philip's in 1862, and forty years later, A. L. Baxter reported that typical church workers in Shoreditch were local people who had been converted, prospered, and moved out to Dalston. Booth Collection, A40.7. Report on districts 5 and 6, pp.45-7.

97. According to the vicar of St Andrew's, Bethnal Green, the working class 'took it for granted' that church-goers were tee-totallers. Booth Collection, B228, p.111.

98. Carpenter, op.cit., p.45.

99. Osborne, op.cit., p.135.

100. Booth, op.cit., Final Volume, p.75. He himself added: 'But carping such as this leaves untouched the great main fact to which we have endless testimony, that "christian people are nearly always temperate and thrifty", and the better in every way for being so.'

101. Charrington cut all connection with the family brewery in about 1873, when he was in his twenties. According to G. Thorne, *The Great Acceptance*, Hodder, London, 1912, pp.20-1, he made the decision after seeing a woman being brutally treated by her husband, who had been drinking in a Charrington's pub.

102. Jasper, op.cit., p.77. There is a rather similar scene in E. Flint, op.cit., pp.145-53. The author had a revelation of a new world, when invited to tea with one of her class-mates in Forest Gate.

103. Acorn. op.cit., pp.11, 46.

104. Ibid., pp.10-11.

105. Ibid., pp.1-8, 191, 227.

106. Ibid., p.117.

107. Ibid., pp.135, 140.

108. Ibid., pp.131-2, 139, 204-5.

109. Ibid., pp.168-70.

110. Ibid., pp.173-9, 265-9, 277, 288-91, 299-300.

111. Ibid., pp.288-300.

112. Ibid., pp.149-53.

113. Booth, op.cit., III, i, p.44.

114. Brown was particularly insistent on this point. A speaker at his Sunday School anniversary in 1891, after condemning most trends in the modern church called for 'the old story with which these walls were so familiar'. *East London Observer*, 30 May 1891.

115. *East London Observer*, 17 April 1886. The way in which Sankey's hymns had become part of the general culture of the working and lower middle classes is suggested by the scene in *The Ragged Trousered Philanthropists* where common ground between the 'religious' and 'irreligious' sections of the party on their return from the annual beano is found in the singing of the choruses of such hymns as 'Pull for the Shore' and 'Where is my Wandering Boy?' Tressell, op.cit., pp.454-5.

116. *East London Observer*, 12 February 1887.

117. Booth Collection, B183, pp.95-129.
118. One thought the Poor Law administration was 'abominable' and the other chose the phrase 'perfectly dreadful'. Booth Collection, B175, pp.41, 65.
119. No one presented exactly these alternatives, but some such balance of approval and disapproval of the new regime is implied in such comments as those of Chandler and Neil (C of E), Lawless (RC), Dean (Congregationalist deacon).
120. 'Christian men never have to be relieved. They keep their distress to themselves and usually make provision by joining clubs, etc.,' (W. Hayward, Baptist, Pastor of Berger Hall). Ibid., B176, p.47.
121. Though this was during Lansbury's non-Christian period.
122. Most notably the Roman Catholic Sisters of the Assumption at Bromley. But such an order of priorities was implicit in the championing of out-relief by Fr. Lawless and by David Roe (Wesleyan).
123. Booth's team also interviewed a fair number of otherwise unknown Nonconformist ministers who expressed themselves in radical terms, such as the Baptist Newton Vanstone in Catford, and the Congregationalists, J. Adams in Shepherds Bush and D. W. Vaughan in Kentish Town.
124. The Rev. Egerton Swann of the Church Socialist League was very unusual among Christian Socialists in his enthusiasm for the class war. See P. d'A. Jones, *The Christian Socialist Revival, 1877-1914*, Princeton UP, Princeton, 1968, pp.267-9.
125. Archbishop Benson chose W. A. Morris for the living of St Anne's, South Lambeth, because of his popularity with working men, noting in his diary that he was 'a fine, romantic, large-eyed Chartist-looking fellow'. Ibid., p.246.
126. In 1909 the nine Inner London branches of the Progressive League were at Hampstead, Stoke Newington, Islington, St Pancras, Norwood, Clapham, Lewisham, Blackheath and the City Temple. The movement's main centre seems to have been Wales. *Christian Commonwealth*, 10 February 1909.
127. *East London Observer*, 8 June 1912.
128. Rev. S. B. Cumberland reported in *East London Observer*, 4 April 1908.
129. Ibid., 9 October 1909.
130. Ibid., 15 January 1910.
131. For a biography of the best known of these, St John Groser, vicar of Christ Church, Watney Street, in Stepney, see K. Brill, *John Groser, East London Priest*, Mowbray, Oxford, 1971.
132. J. Oliver, *The Church and the Social Order*, Mowbray, Oxford, 1968, pp.83-95, describes the unsuccessful attempts of various church leaders to mediate in the General Strike. In this case the attacks seem to have come mainly from the side of the government, together with those clergymen, such as Henson and Inge, who were unconditionally committed to the government side.

133. The decline of the movement in the '20s is noted in Tuffley, op.cit., pp.132-40.

134. *The Oxford House in Bethnal Green*, pp.68-72.

135. For one example of such a person, see H. J. Hammerton, *This Turbulent Priest*, Lutterworth, London, 1952: the 'turbulent priest' was Charles Jenkinson (1887-1949), later famous as a slum-clearing Labour councillor in Leeds, much hated by landlords, who was a Poplar stonemason's son, organiser of a Church Socialist League branch at St James The Less, Bethnal Green, where he led successful agitation against pew-rents, and subsequently Conrad Noel's secretary at Thaxted. Another example might be W. J. Lewis, elected Mayor of Bethnal Green in 1913 (see *East London Observer*, 15 November 1913). Described by another councillor as 'one who had risen from the lowest rank', he had been born in 1868 in the Boundary St. area and left school at eleven to work in the boot trade. Coming under the influence of Oxford House, he had become a tee-totaller and Secretary of the University Club debating society, and began to devote his spare time to reading to enter the Anglican Ministry. Later he had abandoned this idea and had become a trade union organiser and Liberal election agent.

CHAPTER V THE SUBURBS

It was one aspect of working-class parochialism that snobbery went by streets, or even sides of streets. Most working men had to live near their work, and if Somers Town or Bethnal Green did not sound like a good address it could not be helped. But within such areas, each street or buildings had its slightly different status, and there was room at least for relative respectability.[1] In the fashionable West End, too, snobbery was highly local – simply because the area within which 'one' lived was so tiny. As Lady Bracknell pointed out, to live on the wrong side of Belgrave Square was as bad as not living in Belgrave Square at all. But, if Trollope, the novelist of Society, defined his characters by streets and squares, Gissing, the novelist of the middle class, defined his characters by their suburbs. In *New Grub Street*, the hero's wife leaves him after he tells her he has taken rooms at Islington. This was about as far as a consciously middle-class person could sink, and the wife protests that such a move would 'degrade' her. One step above this middle-class 'submerged tenth' was the hack writer, with his uneducated wife, whom he was ashamed to show to his fellow-practitioners, living in a street of 'small, decent houses' in Camden Town, while the ambitious young writer, who is prepared to live pretty cheaply while building his career, lives in the area of 'respectable' lodging houses for the less opulent middle class (later adopted by H. G. Wells and his runaway science student – until their marital status was discovered) to the east of Regent's Park.[2] For his established, but distinctly 'vulgar' middle class of *In the Year of the Jubilee*, Gissing moved south of the river to Camberwell. The French sisters, who represented 'sham education and mock refinement grafted onto a stock of robust vulgarity', and whose father had been a builder who left just enough money for 'elegant leisure', he placed in De Crespigny Park, where 'each house seems to remind its neighbour, with all the complacence expressible in buff brick, that in this locality lodgings are *not* to let'. A more established, but also more old-fashioned middle class, represented by a wholesale piano dealer and an insurance clerk, he put in the less pretentious main road villas of Grove Lane, which the younger generation regard as much too small. A third, and more unmistakably modern, type of vulgarity is represented by the flats in Brixton – 'flats' certainly, and even, to some

132

degree 'Brixton' reflecting a slightly unconventional style of life – to which one of the French sisters moves when she has established herself as a pushful, if not over-scrupulous, woman of business.[3] Its equivalent among the more refined would be the flat in Notting Hill, where the somewhat world-weary Christian Moxey lived with his earnestly *avant-garde* sister in *Born in Exile*.[4] For those with only moderately large incomes but social pretensions there was the Western hinterland: thus Amy Reardon's mother lived in Westbourne Park, dreaming of houses in South Kensington.[5] But the apex of Gissing's suburban society was the mansion on Champion Hill occupied by Mr. Vawdrey and his descendants, whom success in business had won the title and much of the way of life of 'gentlemen'.[6]

The suburbs were proverbially the home of the middle class but the suburban way of life was shared by some of the working class and some of the gentry. Intermixed with the suburbs proper were old working-class settlements around the 'village' centres, or by rivers and canals, and new districts for the working-class commuter – from the late '60s, the Lea Valley towns, depending on the GER services to Liverpool Street, and from the early twentieth century the electric tram based LCC estates at Southend and Totterdown. But when people referred to 'suburbanites', or more satirically, to 'villadom' or simply to 'Tooting', they referred to a ring around London, beginning three or four miles from the City, which had its own institutions, its own pattern of life and its distinctive tone, and within which the working-class settlements were – in point of area – rather small islands.

The Suburban Pattern of Life

The middle-class suburbs extended far in social range – from the wealth of Blackheath or Putney to the Battersea of Richard Church's parents with their artisan and lower middle-class neighbours, struggling to maintain a 'small margin of safety' between 'their respectable little home and the hungry ocean of violence whose thunder never left our ears',[7] by way of the literary and Jewish colonies of Hampstead, the *demi-monde* around Regent's Park, and the homes of the middle middle-class, who were struggling neither to escape the working class or to join the gentry. Those at different points on the scale had various points in common: travel to work, often five to ten miles; instead of working-class communal solidarity or the class solidarity of the gentry, a family-centred individualism; and a career pattern in which moves in search of promotion were quite common, at least in youth, and local roots were thus shallower than those of many working-class people. After marriage one focus of family life would be the family unit: the piano, games in the back garden, the annual decampment to the South Coast,[8] walks in the countryside with the children, the small dinner party with other married couples from the inner circle. A reason, perhaps, for this pattern was the special position of the suburban wife: where working-class women often had little energy for anything beyond housework and childminding and their husbands sought escape in the pub or working men's club from a cramped and uninviting home, and where the women of the upper class were freed by servants from all household cares, and able to devote all their energies to intercourse with adults of their own class, middle-class women passed on the most unpleasant household tasks to a maid, leaving themselves free to concentrate on bringing up the children and providing companionship for their husbands. It was perhaps in the lower middle class that parents most dominated the early consciousness of their children. The lower down the social scale you went, the greater the part played by the street in the child's upbringing: thus Mayhew described the costermonger's children as 'left to play away the day in the court or alley, and pick their morals out of the gutter'.[9] The higher up the scale you went the more parents came to be overshadowed by nurses and governesses, grooms and gardeners, so that Sir Osbert Sitwell grew up in the '90s in a home where:

> Parents were aware that the child would be a nuisance and a whole hedge of servants, in addition to the complex guardianship of nursery and schoolroom were necessary not so much to aid the infant as to screen him off from his father and mother, except on such occasions as he could be used by them as adjunct, toy or decoration. Thus, in a subtle way, children and servants often found themselves in league against grown-ups and employers.[10]

In contrast to this are such childhood memories as those of Richard Church, dominated by the three figures of his parents and brother, and by their special individual passions — saving in his mother's case, cycling in his father's, music in his brother's, and books in his own;[11] or those of Mary Vivian Hughes whose Canonbury childhood seemed, at least, in retrospect, to be a constant round of cricket and charades, story-time and trips to Epping Forest with four brothers and an ever good-humoured father.[12]

The second focus of social life was in the network of local clubs and associations, many of them linked with a place of worship. In the 'neighbourhood' type of culture, friends met in the street itself, in the general store or in the pub, of which most streets had one or two.[13] In the 'West End' type of culture, the basis of social intercourse was not proximity of residence or common interests, but the mutual recognition of equivalent status: a person's claim to an invitation was not that he was liked, but that in the absence of any obvious disqualifications it would be a breach of etiquette to exclude him. In the suburbs social status was more loosely defined and mere proximity of residence was no sufficient claim to friendship: 'Londoners', wrote Mrs. Vivian Hughes, whose family lived for fifteen years in the same house in Canonbury without gaining the slightest acquaintance with their 'semi-detached', 'have no neighbours'.[14] But neighbours came together in golf and cricket clubs, in miniature parliaments and amateur dramatics groups; lovers met in church or at a concert. Most of these, apart from cricket clubs, could provide for husband and wife simultaneously, and, even for sport, mixed parties could turn, at least among the wealthier middle class, to tennis and croquet. Thus the parents of one suburban autobiographer grew up in the 1890s in Burnt Ash Congregational Church, which provided them not only with sermons and with Sunday Schools where they taught, but with 'dances, socials, badminton tournaments, discussions, and amateur entertainments' — the badminton being part of a general local obsession with games, which the author thought absorbed as much of the energies of his parents' generation as had been absorbed by work in his grandparents' time.[15] Similarly, Basil Willey's father met his wife-to-be in Wesleyan circles in North-West London, largely as a result of a common interest in music.[16]

Another feature, associated with the relative autonomy of the family with its own traditions and rituals, was the diversity of the suburban pattern of life. The symbol was the little garden behind which the two or three storey villa hid, keeping itself to itself.[17] Neighbourly gossip was used to protect the respectability of the neighbourhood, but there was no 'good society' from which the deviant could be excluded. Through dinner parties and 'convivial evenings', clubs and outings to the theatre, each family formed its own circle of intimates which a neighbour entered only by sharing similar tastes. In the working class, social pressures tended to be applied overtly and often crudely. In the upper class they were applied more subtly but with more deadly effect: Society (and outside Society you were lost) would talk about an eccentric, a faddist or anyone who hinted at a lack of breeding — it would expel a cad. Moreover, a good deal of upper-class discipline was self-imposed, for the gentleman was conscious of the need to set an example, though he was allowed far more latitude in private than in public. The organisation of middle-class life was looser; the individual was more likely to belong to several circles and to be the only link between them. There were church circles and chapel circles, sporting groups and slightly bohemian groups coexisting in the same neighbourhood, and every such circle has a set of associations providing for its needs. One reflection of this was in the churches of the suburbs: although the number of people attending services was (except in the wealthiest) considerably smaller than in the West End, the proliferation of back-street chapels and minor denominations gave the religious life of these areas a colour that was lacking in Earl's Court and South Kensington. These were also the areas where volumes of the Thinker's Library were snapped up, where Ethical Societies were formed, and where many of the strongest branches were found of the ILP.[18]

There was a sense, therefore, in which the suburbanite, freed from the exigencies of extreme poverty and also from those of life in Society, had more freedom to live his life as he chose than those above or below him in the social scale. But the use of this freedom was limited by the idea of respectability. Most people were conscious of 'standards' to be maintained and of a status in society to be lost by indecorous behaviour or a lack of propriety. Some might be haunted by Charles Masterman's vision of 'a loud-mouthed, independent, arrogant figure, with a thirst for drink, and imperfect standards of decency, and a determination to be supported at someone else's expense'.[19] Others, with less pressing a sense of being under attack, were still imbued with a sense of respectability both positive and negative: negative in so far as it consisted of a mere observance of certain conventions, defiance of which might entail a certain loss of caste; positive, in so far as it was expressed in a scheme of values, that might be defined as 'respectable', such qualities as industry, sobriety and self-restraint being highly prized and pursued as desirable in themselves.[20] Common to adherents of both kinds of respectability was a sense of upholding a morality that was being defied by those below them and perhaps (especially from the point of view of Nonconformists) by those above them in the social scale. But the contents of this morality varied widely in extent and rigour, and there was always a raffish middle class, indifferent alike to the principles of positive respectability and to the maintenance of their middle-class dignity. In its milder forms this raffish class was represented by the hack writers and journalists who maintained a bohemian life style on a sub-bohemian income,[21] and in its more extreme forms by those whose style of life was only publicised when they appeared in a court of law — like the Staunton brothers, whose macabre expedients for improving the family fortune almost resulted in them, together with their wife and mistress, being hanged.[22]

New ideas spread more easily in the suburbs than in working-class districts, and intellectual debate played a greater part in daily life. Most people, probably, were as parochial and practical in their interests, as unconceptualised in their modes of thought as any ragged trousered philanthropist, but even they were at least superficially affected by the fact that they probably spent a few more years at school and might be 'expected' to contribute to discussions on issues of the day, books of the moment, etc.[23] On the other hand, sermons (if you chose the right preacher), newspapers and books kept those who were interested in touch with new ideas in a wide range of fields, and a characteristic institution of the suburbs was the literary and debating society formed, without reference to any sect or party, for the exchange of ideas. The ideas themselves might be merely modish, like those of the debating society where Samuel Bennett Barmby was a leading light, in which the views expressed were always 'advanced' and their knowledge of the authors from which they were drawn were always second hand.[24] But this same sensitivity to the vagaries of fashion meant that a large number of people had some knowledge of new intellectual developments, and views on general subjects were constantly changing.[25] Sermons were one of the more accessible sources of new ideas, though clearly limited by the particular interests and theological position of the preacher chosen. The Unitarians were most uninhibited about using the pulpit to convey information about 'great thinkers', comparative religion, etc. But Congregationalists also expected their ministers to be 'abreast of modern culture',[26] and the same was true of Presbyterians and of some Anglican and Methodist congregations. A favourite subject for such sermons was the 'book of the day'. This may partly have been because of the large number of leisured middle-class women in congregations. But the books that made a splash were short, pithy, polemical, by well-known authors. People liked pundits on their book shelves as well as in their pulpits. Eric Gill's autobiography provides examples from both sides of the religious fence at the end of the nineteenth century. His father, a Broad Churchman, who was first a Nonconformist minister and later an Anglican clergyman, revered the names of Tennyson, Carlyle, Maurice, Robertson, Farrar, MacDonald, Kingsley and liked giving dramatic renderings of his favourite poetry to

the embarrassment of his wife and children.[27] This was a classic Liberal
Christian list of heroes. When Gill moved to an architect's office in
London, about 1899, and his Anglican beliefs collapsed under the
attack of his rationalist colleagues, he adopted a new set of rationalist
oracles:

> H. G. Wells was the rising god. Omar Khayam, a herald of the
> dawn — a sort of cheerful, cynical but kindly prison-warder, who
> took pleasure in letting out the prisoners. Stevenson — not
> anti-Christian, but not a buttress to Anglicanism either. Thomas
> Carlyle . . . I took to reading the sixpenny booklets of the
> Rationalist Press Association and Fabian Tracts and of course I read
> Ruskin (especially *The Seven Lamps* of which I had a first edition),
> and William Morris.[28]

Whether or not, then, people read books they certainly talked about
them. Samuel Bennett Barmby, for instance, 'posed as a broadminded
Anglican, and having read somewhere that Tennyson's *In Memoriam*
represented this attitude, he spoke of the poem as "one of the books
that have made me what I am".'[29] In the late '70s F. W. Farrar's
Eternal Hope, in which he adopted an agnostic viewpoint with regard to
the length of future punishment, was debated equally hotly by the
religious public. Farrar received a large correspondence, most of it
enthusiastic and most of it from non-theologians.[30] In 1902 there
appeared one of the RPA favourites, *The Riddle of the Universe* by
Haeckel, and this set off a controversy in the leading Socialist weekly,
Clarion, that ended in Blatchford's *God and My Neighbour*, the most
popular attack on Christianity since *The Age of Reason*. Although
Blatchford's articles and subsequent book probably attracted the
maximum interest in Socialist circles, and especially in areas where
working-class Nonconformity was strong, the *Clarion* quoted, and
sometimes printed in full, sermons from a wide range of sources.
Sermons were quoted by the Rev. Ambrose Pope (Congregationalist) in
Derbyshire, the Rev. T. Rhondda Williams (Congregationalist) in
Bradford, Rev. C. F. Aked (Baptist) in Liverpool, Archdeacon Wilson
(Anglican) in Rochdale; at R. F. Horton's church in Hampstead a
Saturday evening lecture was devoted to the articles, and three hundred
men and women stayed on to pray for Blatchford; artides criticising
Blatchford appeared in the *Daily News* (by G. K. Chesterton) and the
British Weekly (by Rev. Frank Ballard); Rev. Arthur Baker of the
Brotherhood Church, Hackney, who claimed to have a photograph of
Blatchford on the wall of his Sunday School, wrote one of many letters

of refutation; and the Christian Social Union announced its intention of replying with a series of lectures and pamphlets.[31]

The Middle-class Sunday

Even in London, where middle-class families were less conspicuous and less subject to social pressures than in the village or small town,[32] it was difficult for a middle-class child born in the second half of the nineteenth century to escape a fair amount of contact with some form of Christianity in his early years. The forms, and the intensity with which they were adhered to, varied greatly, but 'religion' was ubiquitous, and in relation to it everyone was obliged to adopt some sort of position. Almost the only exception I found in the autobiographies of those brought up in middle-class families in London between about 1870 and 1914 was David Garnett, and he clearly regarded his parents as outsiders.[33] When he was in his teens they went to live in East Heath Road, Hampstead, where they had many literary and artistic friends, so that David could attend University College School, where there was no religious teaching. But before that they had built a house in a Surrey wood, far from any 'existing community', to emphasise the fact that 'they did not belong, that they rejected and did not wish to fit into the Victorian social hierarchy'. But even there: 'It was when I was five years old that I was first made rudely aware that my parents were atheists' by a boy who came to do odd jobs and told David 'with relish' that 'my father and mother would burn in hell for ever because they did not go to church.'[34]

It is perhaps a mistake to describe 'religion' as 'ubiquitous', since many people contrived to limit it to Sunday. But the problem of Sunday was difficult for anyone to escape. Though the pietistic veneer imposed on most middle- and upper-class families during the first half of the nineteenth century was cracking in the '80s and '90s, Sunday (like the Anglican service) was still a ritual in which every gesture had a meaning that the informed observer would recognise. And, in this instance, the ritual – whether it were the week's nadir, or the day of intensest life – was one with which most members of the middle and upper classes had an intimate acquaintance. What kind of reading was permitted on the Sabbath, and what kind of amusements, if any? Should you travel? And how many times should you attend church? All of these were indices of theological standpoint, of puritanical rigour and of social conventionality. Even those who were totally indifferent to the question could not avoid the fact that their neighbours and relatives would read some significance into what they did or wore.[35] Thus, the organiser of the first Labour candidature in Southwark in 1869, not knowing where his supporters might be, began by circularising all the South London members of the National Sunday League, their support for Sunday concerts and excursions being taken as sufficient warrant of a generally progressive outlook.[36] In Scotland, where Sunday observance was proverbially more rigorous than in England,[37] even a walk anywhere except to church could be a matter for criticism around the mid-century.[38] In England, private observance of the day varied widely, but until about 1890, most people in the middle and upper classes maintained a show of decorum in public. Those who were unequivocally non-believers could not escape the distinctive Sunday atmosphere,[39] and the many who were religiously undecided were faced with the fact that since religious meetings were the only socially acceptable form of public activity, they might as well make the best of what was available.[40] Thus, the number of sermon tasters, the popularity of Sunday lectures by clergymen, and the non-Christian alternatives offered by South Place and the Ethical Societies.[41]

Of all this socially required Sunday activity, the item with the widest appeal was the sermon. It was a prime source of intellectual stimulus for many church-goers; it accorded with the prevailing conceptions of religion, pragmatic, moralistic, this-worldly; it was an art form. Mudie-Smith, who had an axe to grind, since the evangelistic-social crusading form of Nonconformity to which he adhered depended heavily on preaching, took it as a lesson of the *Daily News* census that 'the power of preaching is undiminished'.[42] Whatever this power was, it was true that preaching could still attract very big congregations. R. J. Campbell led the way, with more than three thousand attending both morning and evening services at the City Temple on census Sunday. He, like Spurgeon, who had attracted even bigger congregations on the day of the *British Weekly* count in 1886 was a metropolitan rather than a local figure. But preachers strongly associated with a particular locality, such as R. F. Horton in Hampstead or John Wilson in Woolwich could still attract a thousand or more to a single service (the evening service usually being more popular, in both senses of the word, among Nonconformists).

Another suburban preacher with a wider reputation was the Congregationalist, Campbell Morgan, though his church in Upper Holloway was perhaps far more exclusively a preaching centre than, say, Horton's in Hampstead, with its large apparatus of attached organisations. A. L. Baxter gave two accounts of services at New Court in the late '90s:

> The church to my mind more than 'looked full', it was practically full; I doubt if more than another hundred could have been crowded in. They were almost exclusively, as Mr. M. says, middle-class. I watched them streaming in for five to ten minutes, and only saw one who looked like a working man. There was a sprinkling of young people, but on the whole they were an elderly lot; and in no church have I seen so small a proportion of the congregation under eighteen; few of the parents seem to bring their elder children. The service lasted for eighty minutes of which forty-five were given up to the sermon; prayer and praise take a very subordinate place, and even at that led up to the culminating glory of the sermon, the hymns, lessons, etc., all being chosen with reference to it. The singing of the hymns and anthems was hearty and congregational, but there is no attraction in the music. One felt indeed all through that the people in the main had come not to worship, but to listen to a sermon. Mr. M. preached the first of a series of three sermons on Sin, taking as his text the sin of Achan. Though his whole point of view was completely different from my own I thought him a preacher of extraordinary eloquence, indeed after the late Archbishop of York the most eloquent preacher I have heard. He completely held his audience; and in spite of the damp and cold not a word was lost through coughing.[43]

Two months later, Baxter attended an afternoon service:

> I . . . made for New Court Chapel where Mr. Morgan was billed to address his 'Men's Own' on 'The Paralysis of Impurity'. Mr. M. begins his address at 3.15. I arrived at 4.15 and he was still speaking: almost as I came in he said 'I have been speaking for almost an hour and must stop' but here he was saluted by a tremendous burst of applause telling him to go on: he then spoke for about fifteen minutes with tremendous passion and eloquence. That for the time being at all events he profoundly moved his audience there can be no question. The whole body of the chapel was filled with men, I suppose about six hundred or seven hundred in all: a large number were young men of the upper artisan class.[44]

The sermon was the most characteristic feature of the Victorian Sunday. It could be a convention resented by preacher and

congregation and kept as short as possible, or it could be a
compensation for those who took little interest in the rest of the
service, or it could be excellent entertainment,[45] or it could be 'passion
and eloquence', completely absorbing all those present and forcing
them to see some part of life in a new light.[46] The pulpit also had a
further function, arising from the nineteenth-century association
between religion and civic duty and the status of official conscience
that the established church shared with the leading Nonconformist
denominations and, to some extent, with the Roman Catholic Church:
the function of public platform, on which preachers were expected to
pronounce on matters of public interest, in circumstances of assured
publicity. On such occasions as the death of Queen Victoria or
Gladstone, local papers devoted several columns to the references made
to the fact in local pulpits, and when prominent local figures died the
same happened on a smaller scale. Other major public events, especially
if 'moral issues' were apparently involved, were also expected to be the
subject of such references: Hugh Price Hughes could hardly have
avoided pronouncing in some way on the Parnell divorce case, though it
was by his own choice that he turned it into the principal political
question of the day. On such occasions the preacher fitted easily into
the role of public orator, expressing sentiments common to all;
everyone listening agreed in deploring the adultery of a party leader or
the death of a revered figure who had ceased to be a subject of
controversy. Wars, strikes, elections, atrocities, presented more difficult
problems. Since no consensus existed, the preacher could speak for all
only by pronouncing amiable platitudes. Perhaps the nearest thing to a
national consensus was the reaction to August 1914, and it was by
declaring the righteousness of the national cause that patriotic
clergymen then enjoyed a renewed authority. As one London local
paper put it:

> We have often criticised the local clergy for what seemed to us
> the futile and wrong-headed views many of them have held on the
> big social questions of the day and the way to deal with them, so
> that it is with the more pleasure now that we pay tribute to the fine
> lead they have given their countrymen on their duty at this time. It
> gives the rest of us some comfort to find that those who are
> pre-eminently men of peace believe that our cause is holy, righteous
> and just. . . . We are also glad to pay tribute to the many helpful
> suggestions that have been made by many of the local clergy as to
> preventing and relieving distress arising out of the war, although at

the same time we feel that the clergy are rather over-represented on the local distress committees.[47]

But, as the anti-clerical undertones of this editorial suggest, clergymen who pronounced on public affairs outside this area of the apparently uncontroversial would be accused of abusing the freedom of the pulpit. Naturally, any clergyman whose patriotism was less uncompromising than that of Bishop Winnington-Ingram would face such charges during the First World War.[48] At other times, when political passions were less extreme, ministers who were at all outspoken could still be subject to protests, perhaps to dismissal, at the hands of those who wanted to be preached at, as long as the matter preached were uncontroversial.

Those middle-class people who wanted to escape all aspects of Sunday could do so most easily at the lower end of the class where many of the strongest supporters of the Baptist and Wesleyan denominations were found and where many people were isolated from contact with non-believers, but where the sense of what one's position in society demanded was relatively weak. One reason for this was that they seldom had servants living in the house, and that those families who did tended to be coerced into observing the proprieties by the sense of living under the eyes of their inferiors. As long as public opinion in the upper and middle classes demanded an observance of some of the forms of religion, this was one of the chief means by which conformity was enforced.

'Black-coated Proletariat'

At this bottom end of the middle-class status hierarchy were the petty capitalists, who have already received some mention, in the chapter on working-class London, and also the fastest growing and most homogeneous section of the middle class, the 'black-coated proletariat' of clerks, shop assistants, commercial travellers and elementary school teachers concentrated around the northern and southern limits of the County of London, and in the newer suburbs outside. About 10 per cent of occupied males in the metropolitan area fell into this category 'at the end of the nineteenth century, and a slightly higher proportion of occupied females. Clerks, the largest group, were 6.4 per cent of occupied males aged 10 and above in 1901, rising from 2.1 per cent in Shoreditch and 2.7 per cent in Bethnal Green to 12.9 per cent in Lewisham and 13.1 per cent in Stoke Newington. They tended to live in the middle-class suburbs, where rather monotonous estates, focussed on the railway station, were built specifically for them.[49]

The black-coated workers were the outstanding example of a group whose cultural traditions produced a style of life incongruent with their economic status. If proletarian insouciance was related to proletarian impotence in every sphere but the most local, the clerk or teacher, no less impotent, saw 'culture', 'education', an interest in general questions, as being among the marks of his own section of society, separating him from his fellow proletarians. Moreover this stress on housing, schooling, dress, language, etc., superior to those with a similar income made him specially receptive to ideologies that emphasised individual moral effort. The hero of 'The Story of a London Clerk' resolves to make himself worthy of the woman he loves by a long programme of self-improvement, including Saturday afternoon visits to the National Gallery and the British Museum, daily reading of the Bible and prodigious saving.[50] If Robert Thorne was earnest enough to be a bit of a rarity,[51] he was far from being alone either in his self-improving interests or in his Nonconformity.

In the number of church-goers, districts with large populations of clerks and those in similar occupations fell about half-way between working-class districts and the wealthiest suburbs. In 1902-3, the ratio of adult attendances to population was, for instance, 18 per cent in Catford, 19 per cent in East Dulwich, 20 per cent in Upper Holloway, 23 per cent in Balham. About half of these were Nonconformists; in fact marriage registers from Hampstead, Lewisham and Bethnal Green all suggest that clerks and those in the same group were better represented than any other section of the population. Around the turn of the century, they made up 30 per cent of those married in chapel at Bethnal Green, 37.5 per cent at Lewisham and 42.1 per cent of a small sample at Hampstead. All of the main Nonconformist denominations had a large element of clerks, travellers, salesmen and teachers — in Lewisham the proportions only vary very slightly between one denomination and another. Presumably the Congregationalists drew more heavily from those whose interests were intellectual and political, the Baptists from those who were strictly Evangelical, while the Wesleyans drew to some extent from both sides. Some idea of the milieu can be got from the autobiography of William Kent, an LCC clerk, born in South Lambeth in 1884, whose first thirty years were lived in a world that centred round the chapel.[52] Wesleyanism was the family religion, Kent's grandparents being Wesleyans of a fairly easy-going sort, who were not tee-totallers or especially active in the affairs of their chapel; but his parents being convinced Evangelicals, thoroughly absorbed in matters of religion. Kent himself, who graduated from a disorderly Sunday School to a Junior Temperance Tent, was converted at about eleven, and joined a Congregational mission at fifteen, was a soul-searcher from the first; and introspection took him from Evangelical orthodoxy, via Liberal Protestantism to the South London Ethical Society where, apart from a spell as a Spiritualist, he remained. The account is often bitter – he resented having grown up knowing too much about religion and too little about sex – but the satire is sometimes softened by nostalgia (it seems that some of those whom he described had remained friends and did not know of his change of beliefs); it remains, however, a suggestive picture of the attractions of the chapel community, and of the contrasts and tensions within it. The special strength of the Wheatsheaf was the cohesiveness, if not of the church as a whole, at least of the cliques within it; it provided Kent, and others like him, with a circle of friends, and a complete range of leisure activities, besides those that were strictly religious in nature; most important of all, from this point of view, it provided a place where middle-class adolescents, who obviously could not be chaperoned, but who were still restricted by severe notions of propriety, could meet members of the opposite sex.[53] There were contrasts within the community described by Kent, to some extent in social status, and also in religious approach; the tensions were theological and to some extent political. In social status, most fell within the upper working/lower middle bracket, though there seems to have been a fair range of occupations within it, and it stretched at one end to a fairly high civil servant and, at the other, to Jack Jones, 'the converted coster', who liked shouting 'Praise the Lord' at open-air preachings, and condemned the tepidity of some of the brethren. In religious approach there was the contrast between the instinctive and unquestioning faith of those like Kent's parents who 'were kind, and meant well, but they lived mentally . . . in a deep valley over the sides of which they never saw', and the more intellectualised and restless belief of those like Kent, who was addicted to the keeping of diaries and the reading of Mark Rutherford, and who was continually restating his position in controversial articles. The tensions were between the aggressively Socialist views of many of the younger members and the more quietist older generation, and, perhaps more significantly, between the protagonists of the 'good old gospel', such as a preacher who liked repeating 'I believe in hell, I believe in hell', and those who were suspected of irregular views on the Atonement and other

Evangelical corner-stones — the battle being joined in the Bible Class and in the columns of *The Wheatsheaf*. Kent eventually joined the Liberal Protestant preaching centre of Brixton Independent, where the sermons had more to contribute to the resolution of his perplexities — but that was just for Sunday morning: he continued to play cricket with the Wheatsheafers and to argue with them at the Bible Class and the Literary Society.

The chapel thus comprehended a fairly wide range of attitudes; but in the context of lower middle-class life as a whole the chapel represented no more than a significant minority. Kent, who relished his position always one stage more 'advanced' than the rest of the 'brethren', was regarded by some of his fellow-clerks as excessively pious, and he had to put up with a good deal of chaff from them. Boozing and betting were the chief interests of the young men in Robert Thorne's office,[54] and Eric Gill, in an architect's office around 1900, found the atmosphere 'impious and lewd'.[55] It may be that the custom of sending young clerks to live in lodgings where they were relatively free from parental controls tended to produce a young male culture, in which piety was slightly suspect, and in which games mania was the dominant concern.[56] Within the more orderly and conventional world of married couples and families, it was the view of Anglican incumbents that the prevailing conception of religious 'duty' was less rigorous than in the upper middle class. Many people wished to attend the church, and it was regarded as the thing to do so: but there was less of the feeling that society has specific claims in the matter.[57] Equally, for every family, such as the Kents, whose life revolved round the chapel, there were probably several within whose lives their religion was much more marginal. There were some for whom it was merely a matter of social usage, but for many others it was a question of right and wrong, on which they might have quite strong views, without wanting to discuss the matter too much. Richard Church's family in Battersea, for instance — his father a post office official and his mother a board school teacher — exemplified many of the lower middle-class values with a Nonconformity that may have been deeply felt, but was not obtrusive. 'Social and moral quietism' was, in Church's view; the guiding principle of his parents and their circle, a quietism only modified by a fierce resentment of the aristocracy on the one hand, and on the other a fear of 'the violence of the streets, the crass mob, the ever-rising waters of the indifferent masses'.[58] The result of the latter was the motto 'keep yourself to yourself', 'a safe job, a respectable anonymity, a local esteem', preoccupation with a hobby (in this case, cycling), and unease when any subject outside this private world was mentioned. Beyond the obsession with saving to buy a house, and the acceptance of the Congregational chapel, with its Protestant services and eloquent preaching as a natural part of this small world, it was similar to that of many 'respectable' working-class families. Although the tone of Church's book is quite different, there is also a close resemblance to the Pooters, with their convivial evenings, glasses of port, bezique and games of 'Cutlets'. In such families, one side of lower middle-class culture was much in evidence — the stress on home and family, and on a regular, respectable and law-abiding existence — but there were few signs of the belief in knowledge as an end in itself, and of necessary involvement in politics, theology and social questions, exemplified by Kent's Wheatsheafers debating the Atonement and trade union rates, or by S. B. Barmby's parading of 'advanced' views at the young men's debating society. It was proletarian insouciance together with a middle-class style of life.

'Solid' Middle Class

The petty capitalist stratum merged at one end with the working class, but at the other it merged with the 'solid' middle class of established men of business — those who were unquestionably middle-class and of their own locality, without the education or style of gentlemen, but with a very comfortable income, and living at a certain distance from their work. This, probably, was the 'serious and steady middle class, with its bounded horizons', identified by Matthew Arnold as Moody and Sankey's audiences and 'the main body of lovers of our popular religion'.[59] It was represented by Gissing in the Lord and Barmby families, within which could be seen the transition predicted by Arnold from a 'Puritan middle class' preoccupied with making money and saving its soul[60] to a younger generation for whom such things were 'impossible'.[61] The old was represented by the Barmby sisters, who found their reading in 'certain religious and semi-religious periodicals' and who were 'in the strictest sense' 'provincial': 'nominally denizens of London, they dwelt as remote from anything metropolitan as though Camberwell were a village of the Midlands'; and an older world still, was represented by grandmother Lord, a Norfolk farmer's wife, and thus a member of the equivalent section of rural society, whose 'thoughts found abundant occupation in the cares and pleasures of home', who had known neither hardship nor luxury, and who stood for 'the old religion, the old views of sex and society'. The new was represented by Samuel Bennett Barmby and the younger Lords – more educated and with more 'accomplishments', less interested in making money and more interested in spending it, sceptical of their fathers' religion (or, like most Gissing characters, uninterested).[62] The provinciality was perhaps the distinguishing feature of this section of the middle class. Like the small master stratum, it was closely tied to a particular locality, where it had its shops, warehouses and factories, and it tended to take a leading part in the public affairs of that locality. It provided a large proportion of the mayors and guardians and of the leaders of church and chapel in each part of London. It was within this limited sphere that they possessed power and status and that they were news; their status outside was limited by the fact that their education (though at a 'middle-class school') was generally local and stopped somewhere in their teens, and that they seldom had the air of 'gentlemen'.

This group of medium-sized employers was more fully integrated into the middle class than the small masters. They usually lived in three-storey suburban villas rather than as odd men out among the model dwellings and working-class cottages; they were thus more susceptible to the pressures of neighbourly opinion – the more so because of their unusually strong local ties. It was here that the middle-class stereotype was most applicable: conformism; a belief in work; an intolerance of failures, loafers, eccentricity, frivolity; a respect for the 'practical man', defined as the astute and unsentimental man of business; 'deferment of gratification', together with a devotion to the interests of his own family as the supreme end. This frequently took the form of an Evangelical Protestantism in which 'hard work and strict adherence to principle'[63] was seen as the secret of success. There are hints of the type in Frederick Danzelman, a manager at the Commercial Gas Company in Stepney, a leading member of the East London Tabernacle and a board school manager, who retired to Woodford; he was an official of several building societies and took a special pride in their financial soundness. When he died he was said to be 'a man of great patience and self-control. Seemingly to some he may have appeared a little stern in manner; yet to those who knew him he was always kind and approachable'.[64] Again, there are hints of similar values in the speech with which Robert Kemp, one of a family of oven manufacturers at Stepney Green active in local politics on the Conservative side, presented 'a handsome silver-plated tea and coffee service' to their Primitive Methodist pastor:

He reminded his hearers that the task which had been undertaken by their pastor and his wife four years ago was by no means an easy one, but thanks chiefly to their indomitable pluck and perseverance, and a kindly consideration for their poorer brethren and sisters, the position of the church was financially and numerically far better at the present time than it had been for years past. (Cheers.) Their pastor possessed a business sense that many of them envied – (laughter) – and this combined with a profound reverence for Almighty God's blessing on all undertakings, had resulted in the achievement of glorious results. (Loud applause).[65]

And these cautious East End businessmen had a theology to match. As the secretary of a leading Bethnal Green chapel told an anniversary meeting:

While there was every temptation in these days for men of intellectual power and emotional nature to wander off into the scientifically speculative aspects of theology, which in some respects were pleasant, and to some minds profitable, yet such a congregation as they did not require such teaching.[66]

Arthur Baxter confirmed some features of the stereotype, but also humanised it when he interviewed William George, the senior deacon of the same church, and an official at Somerset House:

I had never before consciously met a Deacon in the flesh, but Mr. G. was almost to a button what I had pictured the typical deacon: medium height, grey hair and full but trimmed beard and whiskers, plain but not unpleasant face; inclined to be stout; dressed in a frockcoat of shiny black broad-cloth, with waist-coat opening rather low and showing two gilt studs; black boot-lace tie tied in a bow. He saw me at his home in Church Crescent, Hackney; everything very hideous and very philistinish: large portrait of Spurgeon on the wall.[67]

In spite of himself, the agnostic from Clifton and Oxford warmed to the Spurgeonite. Baxter was moved by the latter's account of an incident in his work for the Christian Instruction and Benevolent Society of which he was the leading member, and 'as he talked about the Society, the elderly and commonplace Deacon became to some extent transfigured and glowed with what I felt sure was a genuine enthusiasm for philanthropy.'[68]

George presented a distinctively Christian, and perhaps less than usually class-ridden, version of the values of this class.[69] But they could equally well take a form in which the religious element was incidental and George's humanitarian Nonconformity was either sentimental folly or a minor form of sedition. For instance many of the views of Archibald Brown, the minister of the East London Tabernacle, and a Baptist of strongly conservative theological views, might be taken as a polemic on behalf of the life-style of a particular class, with no hint that Evangelical religion was proposed as the solution to the sins of all classes:

> It is householders who are going, and room-holders who are coming. The difference does not only lie in financial position. There is a difference in manners, tastes and social life. Let the condition of our streets bear witness. We remember the Bow Road when it was a treat to walk along it, and when of a night quiet reigned, and all was respectable. Now night is made hideous, and sleep often an impossibility by the gangs of boys and girls that go shouting and roaring their music-hall songs. The right of respectable people to go to sleep is as nothing compared with the right of drunken blackguards to keep them awake. No weariness, no sickness, no dying scene, is any protection. All is sacrificed to noisy public-house scum. This is English liberty – the liberty of the debauched to make life intolerable to the sober and quiet. All this serves to drive the respectable families away, and with them goes the backbone of our churches.[70]

At Brown's packed services, there were 'no shabby waterproofs or battered bonnets; not a black eye visible on all these intelligent faces'. But it was 'encouraging to know that there is such a nucleus of good, honest, respectable English life in the midst of all this wilderness of seething poverty. . . .Traders, managers, foremen, overlookers, and skilled mechanics, the very bone and sinew of the land'.[71] Special services had to be held for the very poor, for, said Brown, 'if these people were to come to the ordinary Sunday services, the respectable congregation would be frightened away'.[72] He saw the '80s as a decade of retrogression after fifty years of progress: respect for parents was dying, there was less business honesty, religious indifference had deepened, and sensationalism had cheapened what religion there was.[73] He condemned 'politics in the pulpit' and had no sympathy with the involvement of many Nonconformist ministers in schemes of social amelioration – his church was for winning souls, which he did in a style uninhibited by modernist scruples[74] – but he allowed his support for

Liberal Unionism to be made public at the 1886 election.[75] He was merely contemptuous of new theological developments, and instead of refuting the arguments of their exponents, he was content to call in question their good faith.[76] If values of this sort were frequently identified (as Arnold identified them) with Nonconformity,[77] they could very easily be secularised and take the form either of purely conventional Anglicanism or of a practical man's contempt for the utopianism of all religions.[78]

Suburban Gentry

Only at the upper end of the middle class, among those who were unquestionably gentlemen, but preferred suburban spaciousness to West End fashion, did most men and women grow up with a consciousness of being born for power and responsibility. That the problems associated with the insufficiency of historical sources now largely disappear follows from this fact. This class provided a large proportion both of the reading and the writing public, and of those who were 'successful', and is accordingly richly documented in biography, memoirs, novels, and periodicals. The professional men, large employers, men and women of private means who occupied the mansions of Blackheath, Norwood and Putney, Hampstead, Highgate and Highbury, keeping three or four servants, had generally enjoyed a lengthy education, frequently culminating in university (which might be London, Glasgow or Edinburgh if they were Dissenters). One part of this education was the inculcation of an awareness of their status and responsibility as gentlemen, and another was an encouragement to adopt some sort of position on all issues of the day. If a knowledge of what was going on in

'the House' was one side of this, equally necessary was some knowledge of ecclesiastical affairs. In this section of society everyone had his religion – even if it were only that of 'moderate Churchman', just as everyone had his politics. In terms of church-going this was the most 'religious' class, and it was probably here that the effect of nineteenth-century 'seriousness' was most profound, though in the upper class 'religion' was less escapable, and in the lower middle class there were more people living in isolation from unbelievers. Superficially, this 'seriousness' was reflected in the multiplication of religious observances, designed to indicate a proper sense of reverence or at least of propriety; more deeply in a belief in Truth, and the necessity of discovering what it was, and in Duty, and the necessity of following it.

The content of upper middle-class religion varied widely, but the external forms were uniform: family prayers, regular attendance at church, the adoption of a distinctive pattern of behaviour on Sunday. All of this was a matter of 'decency' and betokened a regard for propriety rather than exceptionally strong religious convictions. The devout did two or three times what the conventional did once, and found offence in what seemed to others uncontroversial.

Walter Besant, fifty years afterwards, described this phase of upper middle-class religion as it appeared to those who were glad that it was over. He gave this account of Denmark Hill in the '50s:

> The road up the hill was somewhat gloomy on account of the trees; the houses with their gardens and lawns, and carriage drives, and smoothness and smugness betokened in those days the institution of evening prayers. I fear I may be misunderstood. At that time great was the power and authority of seriousness. To be serious was to be fashionable, if one may say so, in City circles. Respectability was nearly always serious: it was divided into two classes: that which had morning prayers only and that which had evening prayers as well. With the young, the latter institution was unpopular — no one of the present younger generation can understand how unpopular it was: a house that had evening prayers made a deliberate profession of a seriousness that was something out of the common, which the young people disliked as a rule; and it insisted on the sons getting home in time for prayers. This profession of seriousness generally belonged to a large house, beautiful gardens, rich conservatories, a large income and carriage and pair.[79]

It was a measure of the Evangelical achievement that for much of the century so many members of the upper and middle classes felt bound to attend church regularly, to observe Sunday, and to censor their conversation. It was a sign of the limits of this achievement that so much of this was hypocrisy. Men of these classes often lived in two worlds and compensated for the exemplary decorum that they displayed on the rare occasions that they were with their wife and children by their uninhibited conversation among men of their own class, and by helping to maintain the Great Social Evil. But even among those who were quite sincere in their religious observances, the beliefs behind the uniform facade were not generally those of the *Record*.

Representative of this middle ground of those who accepted many of the conventions in spirit and letter, but were far from being zealots, might be the family described in her autobiographical series by Mary Vivian Hughes. Here, the family religion, as exemplified by her father, was largely a matter of kindness and good temper, with the one absolute taboo being on rudeness to servants. His Cornish wife, whose family held prayers 'morning *and* evening', had somewhat inconsistently applied objections to any form of Sabbath activity, but he would take advantage of a bright Sunday morning to drop the usual journey from their Canonbury home to St. Paul's, and take the children to Hampstead Heath.[80]

The general impression is of a religion in which respectable standards and common kindness were sacred, but neither religious experience nor doctrinal questions raised any interest; there was an aunt who veered between extremes of Anglo-Catholicism and of Nonconformity, the only constant factor being a belief in hell, but even Mrs. Hughes' mother regarded her as bigoted, not to say curate-ridden.[81]

Within the family some of the range of religious positions within the class as a whole was reflected, so that a person growing up in such an environment was not only expected to adopt a position: a variety of alternatives was presented to him. If those like Mrs. Hughes' father represented a juste milieu, the spectrum extended from the utter repudiation of anything suggesting 'orthodoxy' or 'convention' in such circles as that of the Garnetts or in the environment described in the London chapters of Gissing's *Born in Exile* to the 'Christian feudalism'[82] of some families, where patriarchal authority was still a reality, order was the ruling principle of everyday life and a hint of 'unorthodoxy' provoked as much dismay as a suspicion of 'orthodoxy' in the circles described by Gissing.

Born in Exile might be taken as representative of one extreme as it was in the '80s and '90s. In the young, educated and fairly comfortably-off circle, many of them journalists, described by Gissing, 'emancipation' or 'enlightenment', meaning some form of religious heterodoxy, and implying an independence of middle-class conventions, was taken for granted in the case of men, hoped for in the case of women. But they still had some sense of being in a minority. Marcella Moxey, who was very self-consciously an 'emancipated' woman complained that 'most kinds of immorality are far more readily forgiven by people of the world than sincere heterodoxy on moral subjects', and the hero, Godwin Peak, felt that the 'isolation he was condemned to suffer' was epitomised in the fact that 'all his life he had desired to play games on a Sunday'.[83] Yet, in some aspects their attitudes were a mirror-image of those of the 'respectable' majority.

Buckland Warricombe, for instance, who was secretary to a Radical MP, and who came from an Anglican family 'could not without offence declare that no young man of brains now occupied a clerical career with pure intentions, yet such was his sincere belief. Made tolerant in many directions by the cultivation of his shrewdness, he was hopelessly biassed in judgement as soon as his anti-religious prejudice came into play – a point of strong resemblance between him and Peak'.[84] In this circle science was held totally to have discredited religion, and Warricombe's father, as a Christian scientist was of all beings the most absurd. No new creed had taken the place of Christianity: the tone of the Peak-Warricombe-Moxey group was sceptical and somewhat pessimist. Intellectual freedom and individual friendship (chiefly between men) were the main positive values.

The other extreme might be represented by the environment in which H. W. Nevinson grew up in the 1860s. At his grandfather's mansion at the top of Haverstock Hill, the butler rang a great brass bell at 8.30 each morning. All of the family would then file through one door, and when they were seated, all the servants entered through another, the housekeeper first and the butler last. Each in order of seniority would then read a verse of the chosen chapter of the Bible, and the head of the household provided a commentary at the end. In this way they made their way from Genesis to Revelation, omitting only Psalms, Levitical laws, genealogies and indecent passages.[85] This, like the Evangelical Sunday, could be a moving experience for the members of a family united in common beliefs. But, like the Sunday, it tended to become a meaningless and oppressive ritual because of the attempt to impose a fictitious unity on the household and on the nation. In his own family, Nevinson felt, the Evangelical preoccupation with the things of the soul had degenerated into morbid introspection, and he was relieved, on going to Oxford, to encounter the more 'joyous' religion of Scott Holland and the Broad High Churchmen.[86]

This was in the 1860s. By the '80s and '90s, not only had the facade of uniform orthodoxy cracked: even those who were at the heart of the Evangelical tradition were finding new symbols. Those like Albert Spicer who seemed to provide a link with the past, 'Victorian' certitude and calm faith personified,[87] had dropped some of the old taboos, and adopted a more extroverted and life-loving Christianity, in which 'character' – good citizenship, hard work, and a balanced personality – was the thing most highly valued.[88] This was one of the chief themes in the upper middle-class religion of this period; the others were the sense of service, which (together with an equally strong sense of proprietorship) was also said to be one of Spicer's characteristics,[89] and the desire for beauty, reverence and mystery in worship which was one of the sources of the growing strength of Anglo-Catholicism. In a strongly Nonconformist household George MacDonald might contribute as much as St Paul to the prevailing religious conceptions,[90] while a book specifically devoted to the 'human and cosmic education' of an upper middle-class child born in 1884, noted a strong sense of class identity, an interest in politics (encouraged by his father and grandfather), a mixture of social service and muscular Christianity (embodied in his headmaster) and 'an emphasis on the cultivation of habits of hard work — all of these having some logical connection — but nothing of conversion or 'the faith once delivered to the saints'.[91]

'Unconscious Broad Churchmen'

Most middle-class people might be termed 'unconscious Broad Churchmen'. Brought up to attend church and to assent to the doctrines they heard preached, their conception of religion remained largely practical. Taine in about 1860, quoted a friend who had polled the religious beliefs of a hundred Oxford and Cambridge undergraduates: only two claimed to be freethinkers, while the low and high churches found about fifteen adherents each, but as many as seventy claimed to be 'broad churchmen'.[92] This description probably covered a variety of views ranging from the ardent disciples of F. D. Maurice to the covertly sceptical, via many who were orthodox in a completely unreflecting way.[93] But all would probably have agreed as to what the essentials of religion were. Thirty or forty years later the number of avowed sceptics would certainly have increased, but most of them would have had many points in common with those inside the churches.

A guide to the state of middle-class opinion in Britain in 1904 is provided by the correspondence in the *Daily Telegraph* in the autumn of that year, selections of which were later published with an introductory note by the editor of the paper.[94] It began with a letter signed 'Oxoniensis' in which it was observed that the members of the Church Congress then meeting assumed a national faith that no longer existed. This provoked some 9,000 letters attempting to define the faith either of the nation or of the person writing.

The impression given is of large numbers of individuals, each working out a position for himself, and influenced in doing so both by particular ideas and by a general current of opinion in the circles in which they moved, but ignorant alike of contemporary theology and of the more radically anti-Christian thinking of the time. There was certainly none of the 'cosmic nervousness' that Neville Talbot, in 1912, was to define as characteristic of 'The Modern Situation'.[95] Believers and unbelievers alike held that Christianity was 'sublime'; the believers, however, held that it was so sublime that it was best to cast any doubts aside in confidence that full faith would come, while the unbelievers held that modern man was now so mature that he was largely able to do without religion. The words that occur in letter after letter are science, evolution, reason, progress. One letter claimed that Christianity had better be abandoned because the meek could not survive in a Darwinian universe.[96] But this aspect of evolution was generally overlooked. It was more commonly seen as a slow and painless process, whose course had been pre-arranged by a kindly deity, Christian or not, who aimed at the perfection of the race.[97]

Another point on which believers and unbelievers seemed to be in agreement was the incompatability between hell and a loving God.

Something else was common to both sides in the 'Do We Believe'? controversy: a belief in great men. 'When I call to mind', wrote one contributor, 'that the Bible, as it stands, was accepted by the late Dean Farrar and the late Mr. Gladstone, men of stupendous intellect and profound learning, I cannot believe otherwise than that it is the Word "which was, and is, and is to come".'[98] And for every Newman there was a Spencer, for every Paul a Marcus Aurelius.[99] A few might write that the course of history was predetermined, but most saw it as the creation of great men. The corollary of this was a belief in the importance of individual action. Randall Davidson, looking for a dominant theme in the correspondence, found it in the assertion that beliefs do not matter, only acts; as a Broad Churchman, he agreed, with the proviso that 'it is from the creed that I derive alike the motive to do it and the strength for the endeavour'.[100] This was where believers and unbelievers tended to diverge. If both saw ethics as the vital point, the terms in which they envisaged the problem differed. The unbelievers trusted in the innate goodness of man, the power of reason, the fruits of science, the law of progress. 'All impartial observers must admit,' wrote one correspondent, 'that sympathy and goodness have evolved beyond the need that rewards and punishments in a future state should be held up as an incentive.'[101] On the other hand, most Christian preachers saw life not as inevitable progress but as ceaseless battle against sin. Thus, R. F. Horton, after preaching on the various forms of fear that Christianity modified, concluded:

> Some men had a fear of dishonour, and that was a fear that ought to be cultivated. He could not trust a man who had no sense of shame. Every man ought to fear sin as he would fear a dreadful and terrible enemy.[102]

The themes of self-discipline and conquest of temptation were especially favoured by Winnington-Ingram, and in 1905 he chose these terms to condemn the growing practice of contraception:

> It is all part of the miserable gospel of comfort that is the curse of the present day, and we must learn ourselves and teach others to live the simpler and harder lives our forefathers lived when they made Britain what it is today and handed down the glorious heritage which, unless we amend our ways, must surely slip from our nerveless fingers today.[103]

It was the central importance attached to the idea of Character that was the nearest thing to a basic tenet, linking conversion-centred, sacrament-centred, and undogmatic liberal churches in late Victorian London. The ends to which the idea was put differed, but the central assumption remained the same, and set its exponents at odds alike with determinists and with those who adhered to some sort of ethic of neighbourly solidarity or the rule of custom. Thus, W. H. Lax defined himself as 'a worker in character',[104] and from theologically opposite wings of Nonconformity, Campbell Morgan argued that the Socialism implied in the gospel could only be achieved by 'a change in individual character',[105] while Bruce Wallace attributed the absence of interest in his Brotherhood Church to 'the lack of any moral ideals among the mass of the people'.[106]

The tendency of this sort of thinking was to produce a strong sense of individual responsibility, at some possible cost in terms both of sympathy and of spontaneity and self-expression. 'Character' always implied fairly strict views on the subjects of drink, gambling and sex. Beyond that, its implications were more varied. It might simply mean the sanctification of work.[107] On the other hand it could equally well be harnessed in favour of the growing militarism and interest in uniformed organisations of the early twentieth century or of the equally strong pacifism or near-pacifism widely current in chapel circles at this time.[108] In political terms, it could equally well be a weapon in the crusade against working-class drunkards or against 'the brewers, the capitalists, and the landlords'.[109] It tended to produce an unsectarian

Protestantism largely shorn of the insistence both on personal religious experience and on doctrinal orthodoxy characteristic of the Evangelicalism of the 'Revival' period. It retained a strong sense of sin (though often as much social as individual), but the salvation it offered was by works rather than by faith — and the criteria by which the worth of these works was to be determined were emphatically this-worldly.

If much of this stress on Character was a part of the general morality of the middle class, the criteria generally used tended to be more worldly. Horton's fear of dishonour tended to become a fear of failure, and Ingram's gospel of discomfort tended to be employed in the quest of social and financial success rather than of the Good pursued regardless of the cost. Both kinds of Character would be putting on airs in the terms of the typical working-class scheme of values. On the other hand there were parallels between the beliefs of those who wrote to the *Daily Telegraph* and those that were portrayed in such books as *The Ragged Trousered Philanthropists*: there was the strictly ethical conception of religion, and the insistence that if there be a God he must be kindly and forgiving by nature. In the middle class, these were often combined with an assent to various Christian doctrines, that had been taught them at school, church and home, and were regarded as at least possibilities. Moreover, religion was associated with institutions, religious personnel, and the various daily or weekly rituals which were bound up with them in people's minds.

Notes

1. For instance, Stanley Rd., Tottenham, in the 1920s, 'was considered to be a fairly respectable working-class street, especially at the top end where we lived'. T. Willis, op.cit., pp.8-9
2. G. Gissing, *New Grub Street*, Modern Library, New York, 1926, pp.243, 88, 185, (first published 1891).
3. G. Gissing, *In the Year of the Jubilee*, Watergate Classics, London, 1947, pp.1, 2, 328-9 (first published 1892).
4. G. Gissing, *Born in Exile*, Gollancz, London, 1970, pp.258-9 (first published 1892). Some clergymen claimed that middle-class people living in flats had less sense than other members of their class of duty to church and state. Booth Collection, B257, p.5; B263, pp.57-9. 'The new flats are insufferable. How can one live sandwiched between a music-hall singer and a female politician'? *Born in Exile*, pp.404-5.
5. *New Grub Street*, p.337.
6. *In the Year of the Jubilee*, pp.47-56.

7. R. Church, *Over the Bridge*, Heinemann, London, 1955, p.51.

8. This was as characteristically middle-class as day trips were typical of the working class or holidays in France or Switzerland of the gentry. The procedure is described in a memoir of an upper middle-class childhood in Thornton Heath in the '80s and '90s: Whitstable, Folkestone, Hastings, Eastbourne, Sandown, Ventnor were the favoured resorts; a furnished house would be rented for a month or so; a couple of servants would be sent down to make it ready; and a railway compartment for themselves, together with a family of cousins, would be reserved for the journey down. H. C. Barnard, *Were Those the Days?* Pergamon, Oxford, 1970 p.29.

9. 'The hearth', wrote Mayhew, 'which is so sacred a symbol to all civilised races, as being the spot where the virtues of each succeeding generation are taught and encouraged has no charms to them. The tap-room is the father's chief abiding place; whilst to the mother the house is only a better kind of *tent*. She is away at her stall or hawking her goods from morning to night . . .' (op.cit., I, p.43.) While the costermongers exhibited a particular form of family life in an extreme form, the same emphasis on the streets occurs in Acorn, op.cit., pp.14-23.

10. O. Sitwell, *Left Hand, Right Hand*! Macmillan, London, 5 vols., 1945-50, I, p.92.

11. Church, op.cit., pp.22, 73-5, 92-4.

12. M. V. Hughes, *A London Child of the Seventies*, OUP, London, 1934, pp.14-19.

13. Intensive study of eighteen Birmingham streets in 1871 shows twenty-two pubs and thirty-four small shops (rental less than £10 a year). See M. Hutsby, 'Focus on Winson Green: The Development of a Working Class Suburb, 1851-71', University of Birmingham, B.A. thesis, 1973 pp.46-7

14. Hughes, op.cit., p.92.

15. J. Kenward, *The Suburban Child*, CUP, Cambridge, 1955, pp.36-9, 72.

16. B. Willey, *Spots of Time*, Chatto, London, 1964, p.13.

17. The frontage was the best indication of the intended market for a house. With each stage from hovel to mansion the distance from the road was increased by steps, projecting windows or gardens, until in Highbury or Blackheath the house was almost hidden by trees. In the West End, trees were left to common gardens, but vast areas lay between house and street.

18. A memorandum by R. C. K. Ensor in 1907 noted the weakness of the ILP in many of the poorer districts and its strength in 'better class districts' of 'black-coated proletarians'. Among these, Paul Thompson notes Clapham and East Ham. In some working-class districts of London, the ILP was the main Socialist organisation but a large part of its London membership came from areas where the more purely working-class SDF was unable to take root. P. Thompson, op.cit, p.231.

19. C. F. G, Masterman, *The Condition of England*, Methuen, London, 1909, pp.71-73.

20. For an example of 'respectability' used in the positive sense: Ernest Aves' description of a Congregationalist deacon in Hampstead 'slight in build, bearded, quiet, inclined to precision in speech, liberal in his point of view, an excellent specimen of the highly respectable, religiously-minded citizen, who is thoughtful of the poor'. Booth Collection, B218, p.161.

21. Frederick Willis' family, who lived in a street of better-off City clerks in New Cross around 1900, were regarded as 'not altogether respectable' by the neighbours, and some of them might belong to this category — like his shabby, boozy, journalist uncle, and another uncle who was an actor. They were nonetheless conscious of being middle-class and 'aghast' at having to send Frederick to a board school. F. Willis, *Peace and Dripping Toast*, pp.13-28, 48.

22. Louis Staunton, a clerk, married a woman of very low intelligence who had inherited £2000 from a relative. They lived in various rooms in South London, where they had occasional visits from the woman's mother, who had strongly opposed the marriage, and now further antagonised both Staunton and his wife by complaints about inadequate furnishings, and the fact that they did not keep a servant. Then Staunton went to live with another woman and sent his wife to live with his brother, an artist, who lived in an atmosphere of picturesque squalor in a Kent farm-house with his wife and a cousin. Here she was confined to a bedroom, kept from the view of visitors to the house and fed on next to nothing. After a time they took her to Penge and placed her in lodgings, where she died almost at once. She was found to be in a state of extreme under-nourishment and the two brothers, together with Patrick's wife and Louis' mistress were charged with murder. They were tried in 1877 and all four sentenced to death, but there was a widespread feeling that they had been sentenced for wickedness rather than for murder, and that the judge in particular had allowed his conduct of the trial to be affected by his sense of revulsion; Louis' mistress was granted a free pardon, and the other three were reprieved. See J. B. Atlay, (ed.), *Trial of the Stauntons*, Hodge, Edinburgh, 1911.

23. Finding that just over half the working-class respondents claimed to be 'uninterested in politics', the authors of a study of the 1950 election in Greenwich argued that 'in the middle class all groups are induced by the patterns of culture to pay some attention to politics, whereas in the working class some groups (women and the uninterested) can remain comparatively cut off from political thought and discussion'. M. Benney, A. P. Gray, and R. H. Pear, *How People Vote*, Routledge, London, 1956, pp.161-2.

24. Gissing, *In the Year of the Jubilee* pp.214-5. Rather similar was his description of Amy Reardon in *New Grub Street*, p.384: 'though she could not undertake the volumes of Herbert Spencer she was intelligently acquainted with the tenor of their contents: and

though she had never opened one of Darwin's books, her knowledge of his main theories and illustrations was respectable. She was becoming a typical woman of the new time, the woman who had developed concurrently with journalistic enterprise.'

25. A more sympathetic account of a Literary Society is provided by William Kent, describing the society attached to the Congregational mission in Lambeth to which he belonged in his teens. W. Kent, *Testament of a Victorian Youth*, Heath Cranton 1938, pp.224-5.

26. This was Charles Masterman's slightly satirical description of the typical suburban Congregational minister (who 'faintly trusts the larger hope') in *The Condition of England*, p.75. Some twenty years earlier, the *Lewisham Gazette*, 21 November 1891, in one of a series of articles on local churches, reported that the congregation at Lewisham High Street Congregational Church 'appreciate a sermon on anything from the faith of Socrates to that of the recent 'vert from Nonconformity, the Rev. G. S. Reaney'.

27. E. Gill, *Autobiography*, Cape, London, 1940, pp.45, 57.

28. Ibid., pp.110-11.

29. Gissing, *In the Year of the Jubilee* pp.214-5.

30. D. G. Rowell, *Hell and the Victorians: A Study of the Nineteenth Century Theological Controversies concerning Eternal Punishment and the Future Life*, Clarendon Press, Oxford, 1974, pp.147-9.

31. *Clarion*, 20 February 1903, 13 March 1903, 1 May 1903, 15 March 1903, 17 July 1903, 31 July 1903, 4 September 1903. Ironically, a list of Clarion pamphlets and their sales published during the controversy showed that the most popular was 'Christian Socialism' by P. Dearmer. Ibid., 5 June 1903.

32. Compare Braintree, in the 1880s, a small town in a strongly Nonconformist area, where 'social ostracism' was said to await any large shopkeeper who did not appear at the Congregational chapel at the required times. F. H. Crittall, *Fifty Years of Work and Play*, Constable, London, 1934, p.55.

33. Another possible exception is J. R. Ackerley, *My Father and Myself*, Penguin, Harmondsworth, 1971.

34. D. Garnett, *The Golden Echo*, Chatto, London, 1953, pp.17-18, 44. Garnett was born in 1892.

35. I rather disapprove of (Lupin's wearing a check-suit on a Sunday, and I think he ought to have gone to church this morning: but he said he was tired after yesterday's journey, so I refrained from any remark on the subject.' G. and W. Grossmith, *The Diary of a Nobody*, Penguin, Harmondsworth, 1945, p.73 (first published 1892).

36. Soutter, op.cit., p.27.

37. I am told that the Scots are even more religious than the English ...Compared with Edinburgh, a Sunday in London is positively agreeable.' H. Taine, *Notes on England* (English

Translation), Thames and Hudson, London, 1957, p.283. Written 1862.

38. Maclaren, op.cit., pp.42-3. Scottish ministers were also very critical of 'half-day hearers' — those who only attended morning service.

39. Thus, Reardon 'made it a day of rest, and almost perforce for the depressing influence of Sunday in London made work too difficult. Then, it was the day on which he either went to see his own particular friends or was visited by them.' Gissing, *New Grub Street*, p.147.

40. Even J. M. Keynes once attended church in order to hear Hensley Henson preaching. C. Smyth, *Church and Parish*, SPCK, London, 1955, p.218.

41. Herbert Morrison in his teens spent Sunday morning at Brixton Discussion Forum, which was considered advanced because of its time of meeting, and in the evening he escaped the tedium of home by touring famous churches. H. Morrison, *Herbert Morrison*, Odhams, London, 1960, p.22.

42. Mudie-Smith, op.cit., p.7.

43. Booth Collection, B206, pp.67-9, describing a service attended 5 December 1897. By the '90s Morgan stood out among leading Congregationalist preachers for his doctrinal conservatism. According to a liberal interviewed by Booth's team, it was always easier for an old-fashioned Evangelical to draw great numbers, and Morgan was conservative enough to be really popular. Ibid., B218, p.153.

44. Ibid., B206, p.68.

45. The *British Weekly* published (18 March 1887) a poll in which readers were asked to decide who were 'the most popular preachers' of the five leading Protestant denominations. Some of those selected, such as Liddon, might have objected strongly to any suggestion that they were 'performers'. On the other hand another 'most popular preacher', Joseph Parker, impressed both of Charles Booth's reporters in this way, although their estimates of the performance differed. Thus Booth himself wrote that the minister of the City Temple 'is in truth a great actor and the whole service is an exquisite performance. . . He held his audience spell-bound and at times near us there were faint murmurings of conviction and assent. . . . Of course it was not what he said, but the way he said it that was remarkable — and I can only repeat that he brings to the pulpit all the arts of the stage.' George Duckworth, on the other hand, who thought Parker had taken Irving as his model (he was, in fact, an enthusiast for the theatre, and was criticised for this by Spurgeon), described him as 'an "entertainer", not a bad one, but not a very good one. Now and then he shouted out monosyllables with a bark and then dropped his voice and spoke quite low, though always perfectly audibly. At other times he lifted up his hands, spread out his fingers and then brought them together with a clap. At other times he sunk his chin into his coat,

shrugged his shoulders and started away from the pulpit, that was when he spoke of man being hunted by the hungry wolf of Heathenism.' Booth Collection, A423, p.3; A42.4, pp.16-17.

46. The following quotations illustrate the potential impact of two of the most powerful preachers on the theologically liberal wings of the London churches around the turn of the century. The first comes from the reminiscences of Miss G. M. Campbell, born in the 1870s, and subsequently a suffragette, Guardian, and manager of an Adult School, as quoted in Peel and Marriott, op.cit., pp.177-9: 'I was in the early twenties when I first went to Lyndhurst Road Church having lived, up to that point, the ordinary "sheltered" life of a "Young Lady", having little or no contact with reality. I associated "religion", for the most part, with old, rather weary clergymen; it was an arid, unreal business, divorced from one's every day life, and something quite out of touch with modern thought. My home upbringing had been on so-called "scientific" lines, and theology, as I understood it, was incompatible with an intelligent outlook. Lyndhurst Road was a revelation. Here was a minister, young, intellectually brilliant who had yet devoted himself to a life of religion and service. His sermons interested me intensely. He made me think: he appealed to my reason, which surprised and pleased me. He frequently used the expression , "I am persuaded": he did "persuade". And yet he appealed to something else besides one's reason. I began to discover the existence of a world of Truth, hitherto unsuspected. My eyes were opened by degrees to unseen Reality.' The second comes from the autobiography of Violet Markham, *Return Passage*, 1953, as quoted in Smyth, op.cit., p.216: 'An active agnostic with a haughty contempt for creeds and parsons I never went to church in those days. But it happened one Sunday morning that I was dragged under protest to St Margaret's when Hensley Henson was preaching. I returned the following Sunday, then again and again. His teaching worked by degrees a revolution in my own ideas . . . .'

47. *Lewisham Borough News*, 18 September 1914.

48. For two Nonconformist ministers who lost their pulpits as a result of their opposition to the war, see N. Micklem, *The Box and the Puppets*, Bles, London, 1957, pp.58-9; E. R. Richards, *Private View of a Public Man*, Allen and Unwin, London, 1950, pp.57-67. Those clergymen who initially supported the War, but opposed reprisal raids, or were considered over-sympathetic towards conscientious objectors, were also subject to violent criticism. See, e.g., Peel and Marriott, op.cit., pp.260-2; G. Bell, *Randall Davidson*, OUP, London, 1935, pp.777-8; and for reactions of church leaders generally to the outbreak of war see Mews, op.cit., pp.104-50.

49. At Hither Green, a district of medium-sized houses, built in the '90s, tenants were offered free season tickets. H. J. Dyos, 'The Suburban Development of Greater London South of the Thames, 1836-1914', University of London, Ph.D. thesis, 1952, p.279.

Large-scale building according to a uniform plan gave many lower middle-class districts of the later nineteenth century a more depressing appearance than working-class districts of intrinsically inferior houses.

50. S. Bullock, *Robert Thorne, The Story of a London Clerk*, Werner Laurie, London, 1907, pp.136-7.

51. He is shocked by the coarseness of his fellow clerks, and critical of the laziness of one who is his special friend. Ibid., pp.26-7, 44.

52. W. Kent, op.cit., Kent later became well-known as an author of London encyclopaedias, and a critical biographer of John Burns.

53. Of course, only some churches — mainly those with a large lower middle-class membership — fulfilled this function. For one example see K. Amis, *What Became of Jane Austen* Cape, London, 1970, p.193. Amis' parents attended Denmark Hill Baptist around the turn of the century, and it was 'literally at chapel that my father first met my mother'. The restrictions on middle-class courtship, and also some of the means of circumventing them, are illustrated in some of Gissing's novels of the '90s, such as *In the Year of the Jubilee* and *New Grub Street,*

54. Bullock, op.cit., pp.60-1.

55. Gill, op.cit., p.108.

56. Bullock, op.cit., pp.14-15, describes Thorne's friend, whose interests are football, hockey, cricket, tennis, theatres, music-halls, dances, parties, horses, boating, cards and slang. In January 1888, the Evangelical *Record* published a special supplement on 'South London: Its Religious Condition, Its Needs and Its Hopes'. In Brixton and Camberwell it noted 'a large number of unmarried young men, living at home or in boarding-houses, who have greater personal freedom than the attendants at places of business. It is largely, we presume, for their benefit that the newsagents find Sunday to be their heaviest day; and it is they too, who, skates in hand, flock to the railway stations on Sunday morning during a frost'.

57. Comments in Visitation Returns: 'In the new homes of rentals of £40 to £50 a considerable number seem to come to church occasionally, once perhaps in three or four weeks' (St Paul, Herne Hill, Rochester, 1894); 'The inhabitants of the newer and smaller houses on whom we rely to take the place of those who have left the larger houses many of which remain empty are the most difficult to get to church *regularly* (St Mark, Lewisham, Rochester, 1903).

58. Church, op.cit., pp.51, 73-6, 82, 135-40.

59. M. Arnold, *God and the Bible*, Smith, Elder, London, 1875, p.xxv.

60. M. Arnold, *Culture and Anarchy*, CUP, Cambridge, 1932, pp.157, 199; *God and the Bible*, loc.cit.

61. Ibid., loc.cit.

62. Gissing, *In the Year of the Jubilee*, pp.23, 61, 211.

63. It was thus that James Branch, a Bethnal Green boot manufacturer, and a leading Congregationalist and Radical

explained the rise of his firm from next to nothing at a party for three hundred employees to celebrate his son's coming of age. *East London Observer*, 7 January 1888.

64. Ibid., 29 July 1905.

65. Ibid., 2 July 1898. The only surprising point is that the chapel was Primitive Methodist. Booth's reports suggested the general character of Primitive Methodism in London was more proletarian. Booth Collection, B187, pp.51-2; Booth, op.cit., III, i, p.131.

66. *East London Observer*, 16 July 1887, reporting a meeting at Approach Road Congregational chapel.

67. Booth Collection, B183, p.95.

68. Ibid., pp.127-9.

69. In a speech of welcome to a new minister, George said: 'It was often said of their neighbourhood that the best people had gone (Laughter). Well let them go. (Hear hear, and laughter.) For his part, he thought the best people were those who had the best hearts, and certainly that qualification was not limited to the rich. (Applause.) . . . If the people did not turn to this church as a place of refuge and sanctuary, and as an ark, they might as well write up "Ichabod", and close the doors. (Hear, hear.)' *East London Observer*, 28 September 1901.

70. The Annual Report of the East London Tabernacle for 1889, as quoted in G. H. Pike, *Life and Work of Archibald G. Brown*, Passmore and Alabaster, London, 1892, pp.96-7.

71. A newspaper report of a service at the Tabernacle, as quoted in ibid., p.115.

72. Ibid., p.29.

73. Ibid., pp.97-8.

74. Long and eloquent hell-fire sermons by Brown (focussed on the sinner's death-bed, rather than on hell itself) were quoted in *East London Observer*, 20 February 1886, 18 February 1888.

75. Ibid., 10 July 1886, printed a letter from a member of the church condemning Brown's political stance.

76. Brown told the meeting to celebrate his 27th anniversary: 'When he did change in (the theological) sense – if ever he did – he would have the honesty to tell his congregation so; he would to God that some modern ministers who promulgated theories abhorrent to those who built the chapels in which they ministered, would have the decency to clear out. (Applause.) To him the Bible was the inspired word of God in the most literal sense; he did not care twopence what the higher critics said to the contrary, for he had the authority of the highest critic of all – Jesus Christ.' Ibid., 6 January 1894. In similar style, a speaker at Brown's Sunday School Anniversary condemned such 'wishy-washy trash as Theosophy and Buddhism'. Ibid., 30 May 1898.

77. The classic portrait of this type of Nonconformity is Mark Rutherford, [W. Hale White,] *The Revolution in Tanner's Lane*, 1887. It is represented by figures such as Mrs. Coleman and the Rev. John Broad, whose Nonconformist Christianity is a mere

conventionalism without humanity or imagination, and is contrasted with the real Nonconformity of those like the Allens and Zachariah Coleman, who are true to their radical heritage and conscious that it entails persecution by those in power and requires stoic courage.

78. An example of such an evolution by a single individual is possibly the miser, Tellwright, in Arnold Bennett's *Anna of the Five Towns*, 1902. Once a Wesleyan of the type described by Weber, whose religion was a guarantee of his financial integrity, he gradually loses all interest in anything but money. (For Weber's account of the advantages for American businessmen in the late nineteenth century of Baptist or Methodist church membership, see H. H. Gerth and C. W. Mills, (ed.), *From Max Weber*, Routledge, London, 1948, pp.302-6.)

79. W. Besant, *South London*, Chatto, London, 1899, pp.310-11.

80. M. V. Hughes, op.cit., pp.80-91, 121.

81. M. V. Hughes, *A London Girl of the Eighties*, OUP, London, 1936, pp.88-9, 156; *A London Child of the Seventies*, pp.97-8.

82. This phrase is used both by H. W. Nevinson to describe the regime at the Hampstead home of his Tory Evangelical grandfather, and by the biographer of Sir Albert Spicer, the Liberal M.P. and leading Congregationalist of a slightly later generation. H. W. Nevinson, *Changes and Chances*, Nisbet, London, 1923, p.19; *Albert Spicer, 1847-1934, A Man of His Time*, by One of His Family, Simpkin Marshall, London, 1938, pp.16-17.

83. Gissing, *Born in Exile*, pp.280-1, 288-9.

84. Ibid., p.227.

85. Nevinson, op.cit., pp.11-19. 'It is a scene from a vanished past. . . . In a few years the Christian feudalism which gave it character will seem as remote as the Crusades.' (Written in 1923.)

86. Ibid., pp.37, 43-5. He blamed his parents both for the wide range of prohibitions (including Shakespeare and à Kempis) that impoverished their own life and for their indifference to the world outside, and limitation of social contacts to the families of doctors, military officers and low church clergymen.

87. *Albert Spicer*, pp.811-2. This was how he appeared to his children, who saw themselves as part of the 'post-war' generation.

88. Ibid., pp.9, 16-17, 26-7, 66-7, 71. He was brought up to condemn dancing and the theatre, but as an adult he both gave dances and took parties to the theatre — this being not only a reaction against some of the ideas of his ancestors about legitimate pleasures, but also against their willing avoidance of Anglican 'good society'.

89. Ibid., pp.16-17.

90. E. Bligh, *Tooting Corner*, Secker and Warburg, London, 1946, pp.160-3.

91. Barnard, op.cit., pp.80-1, 116-23, 138, 158-61.

92. Taine, op.cit., p.116.

93. For the possible uses of the term 'Moderate Churchman' see this comment by Frederic Harrison on a speech by Fawcett: 'Then his

hypocrisy in calling himself a "moderate churchman"! Why, he is a notorious freethinker and religious indifferent. Some years ago he electrified Fitzjames Stephen as they were walking together, and the latter was airing his logic on the question of the existence of God — by saying in his noisy way — "Well you know, Stephen, the question of the existence of God is a thing *I never could take the smallest interest in*!" Very laudably positive, but hardly the view of a moderate churchman.' F. Harrison — J. Morley, 25 July 1873 (Harrison Collection.)

94. W. L. Courtney (ed.), *Do We Believe?*, Hodder and Stoughton, London, 1905.

95. 'This generation is modern in the sense that it never knew the world "before the flood". While it has been growing up the assumptions of mid-Victorian liberalism have been going bankrupt. Their capital has been running out. Even their last survivor, Progress, has been at grips with a doubt deeper than itself as to man's place in the universe. For the infection of a kind of cosmic nervousness has become widespread. Somehow the world is now felt to be less domestic than it was. The skies have darkened and men's minds have become more sombre'. B. H. Streeter and others, *Foundations, A Statement of Christian Belief in Terms of Modern Thought*, Macmillan, London, 1912, p.7. Talbot admitted, however, that 'the many', including 'certainly the majority of churchgoers' had yet to realise that it had passed into the post-Darwinian universe. Ibid., pp.10-11.

96. Courtney, op.cit., p.181.

97. Ibid., pp.67-8, 88-9, 96-7, 136-7, 246.

98. Ibid., pp.149-50.

99. This craving for great names with whom the ordinary confused individual could identify himself received this comment from Gissing's Godwin Peak: 'Two kinds of book dealing with religion are now greatly popular and will be for a long time. On the one hand, is that growing body of people who, for whatever reason, tend to agnosticism, but desire to be convinced that agnosticism is respectable; they are eager for anti-dogmatic books written by men of mark. They couldn't endure to be classed with Bradlaugh, but they rank themselves confidently with Darwin and Huxley. Arguments matter little or nothing to them. They take their rationalism as they do a fashion in dress, anxious only that it shall be "good form". Then there's the other lot of people — a much larger class — who won't give up dogma, but have learnt that bishops, priests and deacons no longer hold it with the old rigour, and that one must be "broad", these are clamorous for treatises which pretend to reconcile revelation and science. It is pathetic to watch the enthusiasm with which they hail any man who distinguishes himself by this kind of apologetic skill, this pious jugglery.' *Born in Exile*, p.119. This was written in 1892, but this particular scene was supposed to have taken place in 1884.

100. Courtney, op.cit., pp.293-9, from a sermon at Canterbury Cathedral.
101. Ibid., pp.192-3.
102. New Year Message to City Men in Bishopsgate Chapel, as reported in *Hampstead and Highgate Express*, 9 January 1909.
103. Winnington-Ingram, op.cit., p.33.
104. Lax, op.cit., pp.20-1.
105. Booth Collection, B206, p.51.
106. Ibid., B195, p.25.
107. Thus, Pedr Williams, a Congregational minister in Lower Clapton, was said not to 'bother with theology at all — preaching simply Christ our leader — and a life of honest work.' Ibid., B190, p.124.
108. For the former, *Scouting for Boys* would provide a good text with its stress on discipline and those who are, and are not, worth their salt; for Nonconformist semi-pacifism, see Mews, op.cit., pp.107-10, 119-22, and for anti-militarist rhetoric, see the section on the Boer War in the next chapter.
109. This list of parasites comes from a PSA address by a Spitalfields curate, Rev. T. Collings, quoted in *East London Observer*, 7 November 1896. For claims that drink is 'the chief cause of poverty', see a considerable proportion of Booth's interviews with clergymen; also Lax, op.cit., p.108: 'At the back of most of the troubles of the East End is drink. If you could abolish drink, you would largely cure the ills of Poplar.'

CHAPTER VI THE CHURCH IN THE SUBURBS: LEWISHAM

The metropolitan borough of Lewisham, which came into existence in 1900, was formed of the ancient parishes of Lee and Lewisham, which had been gradually suburbanised in the course of the nineteenth century. In 1777, Lewisham High Street was already the home of 'opulent merchants and traders of London',[1] and in the early nineteenth century the village of Sydenham in the south-west of Lewisham parish won a certain reputation as a spa, while Blackheath, with its fine hill-top position on the borders of Lee and of Greenwich, established itself as a southern Hampstead, much favoured by retired generals, successful businessmen, Evangelical ladies of independent means. The first of the railway lines that were eventually to turn Lewisham into the characteristic home of the lower middle-class commuter came in 1839. The population of the two parishes was 30,000 in 1861. Between 1861 and 1881 the larger villas had multiplied and a new working-class district had arisen around the gas works at Bell Green. The population was now 68,000. In the next fifty years, first the speculative builder, then the LCC, filled in gaps. The population had reached 127,000 in 1901 after the pulling down of the old houses in Lewisham High Street and the development of the railway-based suburbs of Catford and Hither Green. In 1931 it was 215,000 after the electric-tram based LCC estates had driven the farmers from Southend and the successful businessmen from Grove Park.

The borough is trisected by the Ravensbourne and its tributary, the Quaggy, two apparently insignificant streams that become quite formidable in time of flood. In 1900, its wealthier inhabitants were concentrated on the heights of Blackheath and of Sydenham and Forest Hill in the north-eastern and western thirds; the central section belonged to the six- to eight-room villa of the City clerk or the 'respectable' working man, though working-class terraces squeezed between the main roads and the rivers, and there were concentrations of poverty at Bell Green and in the brickmakers' colony round Loampit Vale.[2] By the turn of the century, seven railway lines connected the borough with central London: at the time of the Work-places Census in 1921 persons living in Lewisham and working outside outnumbered those doing the reverse by more than five to one, a far higher ratio than that in any other metropolitan borough. It was essentially a middle-class district: medium-sized houses, occupied by people with medium-sized incomes, healthy, respectable and unremarkable.[3] 'Lewisham', wrote William Margrie, the Sage of Camberwell, 'is chiefly noted for its virtue. On an average not more than three murders a week take place in Lewisham.'[4]

In a sample of three hundred and ninety-six men married at Anglican churches in Lewisham in 1898-1901, 52.0 per cent were manual workers. In 1913, in a sample of the same size, the proportion was 48.7 per cent. The chief change between the two dates is in the increased proportion of clerical workers, and the reduced proportion of retailers and of unskilled workers. Otherwise, the changes are very small. In the 1898-1901 sample, the group highest in the social scale — gentlemen and officers in the armed forces — made up 2.3 per cent, while professional men and employers and managers were 11.1 per cent; 10.9 per cent were retailers and 23.7 per cent were in other lower middle-class occupations; 26.0 per cent were skilled manual workers and 26.0 per cent in other types of manual work.

In view of its social composition, it is scarcely surprising that the level of church attendance in Lewisham was among the highest in London. In 1886-7 it was 45.5 per cent as against an average of 28.5 per cent; in 1902-3, after a good deal of levelling out, it was 30.5 per cent, as against an average of 22.0 per cent. Both the Church of England and the main branches of Nonconformity had a large local following; only the Roman Catholics had fewer worshippers than the London average. It was a good illustration of Nonconformist strength in the suburbs and Catholic strength in the centre, as Lewisham was better provided with Nonconformist chapels than any other district of London.[5] (See Table 18.)

These borough averages concealed considerable differences between the many partly separate communities within Lewisham. For instance, attendances were very low in the working-class district of Lower Sydenham. But there is a clear enough contrast between the groves of Blackheath and Lee, with their largely upper middle-class population, and the vast uniform estates of Catford, representative of the new lower middle-class districts. In 1902-3 the adult[6] attendance rate for the whole of London was 21.3 per cent, but in Blackheath, Lee and Eltham it was 43.4 per cent — almost higher than in any other district. In Catford it was only 18.2 per cent — though it might have been a little higher but for the attractions of churches in Lewisham village. The difference was very largely accounted for by the Church of England: in

Catford, Nonconformists slightly outnumbered Anglican worshippers; in the wealthier district the number of chapel-goers was about the same, but the proportion of Anglican church-goers in the population was three times as high. There is also a difference between the branches — and perhaps the kinds — of Nonconformity represented. In Lee and Blackheath, Baptists and Congregationalists predominated, and both denominations had churches with well-known preachers, and attended by the local dissenting aristocracy; in Catford, the best attended chapels were Wesleyan and no preacher had a similar reputation. (See Table 19.)

Churches and the social order

At the top of the social scale was a small class whose relationship with the Established Church was hereditary. The Earls of Dartmouth were Lords of the Manor of Lewisham, the Earls of Northbrook Lords of the Manor of Lee. Although by 1900 the one lived in Staffordshire and the other in Hampshire, they continued to choose the incumbents both of the old parish churches and of several of the daughter churches, and to support them with their money and occasionally their presence. For much of the nineteenth century, indeed, the Vicar of Lewisham was a member of the Dartmouth family, the last of these being the Hon. Augustus Legge, who became Bishop of Lichfield in 1891.[7] At St John's, Southend, a proprietary chapel within the parish of St Mary, until it became a parish of its own in 1916, the relationship between landowner and clergyman was even closer, for the Forster family actually paid the incumbent.[8] And in the late nineteenth century there was still at least one member of this class of hereditary patrons who was very active in the affairs of the Lewisham Church: Mayow Adams of the Old House, Sydenham. 'Good Mayow Adams!' wrote a local historian. 'He was so greatly beloved by Guardians, officers and the poor, and was in every respect a typical English gentleman.'[9] When he died aged ninety, in 1898, he was described as churchwarden of St Bartholomew's, Sydenham, and prime mover in the building of Christ Church, Forest Hill, Treasurer of the National Schools, Chairman of the Lewisham Guardians, and leader of local Conservatism.

> Mr. Mayow Adams has held a unique position in Sydenham. When the place was a simple village, Mr. Adams was its squire, and since it has grown to be a populous and fashionable suburb,

something like the same position has been occupied by Mr. Adams by the common consent of all classes of the community. Mr. Adams has been the recognised leader of all social and philanthropic movements in the locality, and has ever been ready to assist by his influence and presence every good and useful undertaking on many occasions when, perhaps, a due regard for his own comfort and health would have kept him at home.[10]

For Mayow Adams and his like, support for the Church was a part of their inherited duty to the community, and of a kind with public service on the Board of Guardians or the committees of charities, or defence of the Constitution through the Conservative Party. For those who accepted the sort of society that he represented, he was an 'influential' name on a committee or a subscription list, and a guarantee that the cause was deserving.

The newer commercial and professional aristocracy of the borough were mainly church-goers and Anglicans, and some of them occupied an analogous position, bearing both the responsibility and the power of patrons. But they occupied the position by the choice of both parties rather than by hereditary right. There were two reasons for this system: the fact that the expense of building and running a church usually outran the combined means of their average members, and that this led to heavy pressures on a few individuals who were known to be both zealous and wealthy; and the fact that Church and Chapel were the chief basis of two rival elites competing for political control of the community. In consequence of the former fact, Nonconformist chapels, especially, could come to depend very heavily on one or two of their members – with the double effect that their death might be followed by a financial crisis and possible closure, and that the minister might feel himself constrained to preach in ways acceptable to these powerful individuals;[11] at the same time each denominational and church party had its leading laymen, who were continually meeting requests for help from struggling churches.[12] In Lewisham, the Congregational chapel in the High Street was said to have been built largely with the money of Henry Wood, a gentleman of independent means living nearby; while George Parker, a solicitor and a J.P., living in Lewisham House, was said to have financed single-handed the building of St George's, Catford.[13]

Patrons of Church and Chapel were also leaders of two mutually hostile sections of the community at a time when this particular cleavage was of greater political significance than any other. The contrast in religious affiliation between leaders of Liberal and Conservative parties was far more striking than the difference in social class.[14] Thus in the 1903 election to the borough council a local paper stated the affiliations of twenty successful Progressive candidates: three were Anglican, one Roman Catholic, five Congregationalist, two Baptist, four Wesleyan, two Primitive, one Bible Christian and two simply 'Nonconformists'.[15] In 1909, when the affiliations of twenty Moderate candidates were stated, seventeen were Anglicans, one a Roman Catholic, one a Wesleyan and one a Presbyterian.[16] There were many councillors whose religious affiliation was never mentioned in the press, and there must have been others who were only marginally involved in the work of their church and chapel. But religion and politics were so closely linked that the one could follow as a matter of course from the other. Thus there were figures like W. H. Le May, a hop factor, with a business in the Borough and a home at Grove Park, who was Mayor of Lewisham, a churchwarden, and a member of the British Empire League, the Primrose League and the Kent Yeomanry, or H. P. Stebbing, J.P., a City importer living at Inglemere House, Forest Hill, Mayor of Lewisham in 1908-9, a member of several charitable committees and of the Rochester Diocesan Society and a churchwarden.[17] Conservative MPs and County Councillors presided at Anglican church meetings as an integral part of their duties[18] — though as MPs they represented all their constituents, and they might lay the first stone of a new Nonconformist chapel.[19] On the Nonconformist side were figures like George Lidgett of Grove Lodge, Blackheath, a ship-owner, who divided his time between Liberal politics and religious and charitable work,[20] or the Congregationalist Warmington brothers, one of whom was the first Liberal Mayor of Lewisham the other a London County Councillor and founder of a Home of Rest for lady Sunday School teachers.[21] Two figures were pre-eminent in the aristocracy of Lewisham Dissent, and they might stand as counter-types to Mayow Adams: Sir Nathaniel Barnaby and Judge Willis. They added 'influence' to a Nonconformist platform as surely as the Earl of Dartmouth gave it to a Conservative or a Church cause. Both were attached to Lee Baptist, the unusual position of which within its own denomination can be deduced from the fact that its Literary Society invited an Anglican parson to address it on the Oxford Movement and a rabbi to speak on Judaism.[22] Barnaby, the son of a Chatham dock-yard official was an apprentice shipwright at fifteen and eventually became director of naval construction. A life-long abstainer, he was a Sunday School teacher for seventy-two of his eighty-six years — a 'piece of devotion that few of the aristocrats of the Church can have felt called upon to imitate. When he died in 1915, the words chosen by a local paper to describe him were 'kindliness', 'thoroughness' and 'inflexible integrity'.[23] Judge Willis, the son of a Dunstable hat manufacturer, was a former Liberal MP. Unlike Barnaby, who opposed the pro-Boer section of local Nonconformity during the South African War, his favourite cause was Peace, and he was particularly severe on General Gordon, who, he thought, would have been far better advised to have stayed at home and found himself a useful occupation; an authority on Burke and Milton, he was contemptuous of those who read the *Times* instead of *Hansard* – their minds were fed on snippets. When he died he was said never to have borrowed money, never to have looked at the price of consols, never to have ridden in a motor car, and never to have read anything of the Crippen Trial.[24]

If money and 'influence' gave a small class of the very wealthy an important role both in the Church-Conservative and the Chapel-Liberal worlds, another rather small group was also important because of the exceptional strength of its local ties: those with business in the borough. For instance, out of forty-six councillors and aldermen elected in 1903 about whom such information is available, twelve would seem to come into this category – most of the others being professional men or else connected with businesses in the City.

Less well represented, certainly among the leadership of the political parties, and probably in the leadership of the churches, about which there is much less evidence, was the new 'villadom' of lower middle-class commuters, together with those, such as board school teachers, of similar social status. Several of the most active individuals, especially in Chapel and Liberal Party belong to this category, but their number was relatively small. It was also noted by some Anglican incumbents that members of this class often came occasionally to their churches, but without the degree of regularity characteristic of the upper middle class. This probably reflects a distinctive attitude both to churches and to political parties. Where tradesmen might participate as a matter of course because of strong local ties (and sometimes self-interest), the gentry and many of the upper class because of what they saw as the responsibilities inherent in their social position, 'villadom' saw them as being among several organisations of a comparable type which they might or might not choose to belong to. It would be an exaggeration to say that churches were on a par with cycling clubs and debating societies. But those who were active in churches were so by personal choice rather than as a matter of course. There were in fact a number of teachers among the leading Nonconformists in the borough — such, for instance, as Arthur Hiscox, a Baptist and a Liberal Mayor of Lewisham, and Clifford Smith, a Liberal councillor and Bible Christian Circuit Steward.

The working class, which formed about half the Lewisham population, was even less involved in the rival elites. A few working men became Liberal councillors and a carpenter, Mark Cottell, was among the trustees of a Wesleyan church. I have found no examples of working men who were Conservative councillors or who were Anglican churchwardens. Among the few Labour councillors in Lewisham before 1914 one was an active Roman Catholic and another an Anglican.[25] But a degree of anti-clericalism, or even anti-religion, was quite common among those who claimed to speak for the working class. In 1908, for instance, the Sydenham and Forest Hill SDF and the South London Right-to-Work Committee held a meeting at a Baptist mission in Lower Sydenham, during which the Rev. G. W. Thompson made what the minister in charge of the mission termed 'a revolutionary and bloodthirsty speech'. Before the revolutionary spoke, however, he had to listen to the chairman declaring that, Comrade Thompson excepted, he had little time for parsons, and that they 'worried more about teaching children the story of the whale swallowing Jonah than about what the children themselves swallowed'.[26] And when in 1891 and 1892 the *Lewisham Gazette* published large numbers of letters on 'Why Working Men Don't Go To Church', among them was the following which, while not overtly political was still self-consciously proletarian in attitude:

It is generally kept out of sight that unbelief in Church teaching, and aversion to the humbug and insincerity of the humbugs who play at believing they believe what they do not believe has any share in keeping people from the house of God. It is easy to see why those who are obliged to keep up social pretensions should attend church; but the working man can afford, during his few hours of leisure to assert his manhood, and why should he attend church to feed on the few dry husks of withered dogma from which all nutriment has long departed, when he can gather the living science of to-day, which will be of practical use to him in his own life? Why should he support antiquated superstition which has been the most powerful instrument of the oppression of his class? The voice of the church is evermore heard crying 'Give! Give!' and the working men properly think those should subscribe who derive advantage. What a

revelation is that made by the Bishop of Dover as to the results of
Bible Sunday School training. Of one hundred of his own scholars he
could trace but seventy-seven, and of those two only were attending
church regularly, and thirty-nine were confirmed drunkards. At
Pentonville Prison, seven hundred and fifty seven out of a thousand
prisoners had been Sunday Scholars, their average time of attendance was three years. What facts should better show that religion
debases and corrupts the people.[27]

Church v. Chapel

For another twenty-five years or so this cry of 'a plague on both your
houses' would be politically irrelevant: Lewisham still divided on lines
that were basically Church v. Chapel, and the many who were neither
had to choose between them. The clergy split in much the same way as
the laity: between 1885 and 1914, at least thirteen Anglican incumbents in Lewisham appeared on Conservative platforms, stood as
Conservative candidates, or declared their support for the Conservative
Party, as against two who were Liberals and two who were Socialists.[28]
In the same period at least eleven Nonconformist ministers were
Liberals, and another minister, the Rev. F. W. Aveling, stood as Liberal
candidate for the borough in 1906, while E. T. Carter (Wesleyan) was a
Conservative, and one of the Liberals, W. C. Pope (Unitarian), was also
a Fabian. The size and importance of the Church-Chapel division is
obvious, but it was far less complete than, for instance, the analogous
division between Catholic and anti-clerical in France at the same time,
and the slow growth of the Labour Party emphasised differences within
the middle class that were often more apparent than real. For instance,
although political parsons (except for a few Anglican ultra-radicals)
were generally those who ran true to denominational type, there were
also many who were genuinely non-party. In Lewisham they found a
platform in the Municipal Association, whose leading members included
the Vicar of Lewisham, the minister of Lewisham High Street
Congregational Church, and the Roman Catholic priest, and which tried
to encourage voting on non-party lines for 'men of high character,
without any private interests to serve'.[29] There were also many of the
general public who were sufficiently indifferent to Church-Chapel
conflicts to be willing to attend services at either: one Evangelical
incumbent complained in 1889 that 'too many Churchmen' were
'Honorary members of Nonconformist places of worship',[30] and

another had noticed in 1881 that 'a strong leaning towards work carried on on undenominational lines is painfully prevalent among professing members of the Church of England whose personal piety is conspicuous'.[31] Except on the part of a few Anglo-Catholics, Church-Chapel antagonism was a social and political rather than a theological matter, and there were fair numbers of those whose sense of religious affinity seemed more relevant to them than these differences. The controversies provoked by the 1902 Education Act and the 1909 Budget also showed that Nonconformists were divided between intransigents, bitterly hostile to Church and Conservative Party and tending to identify the two as part of a common aristocratic conspiracy, and moderates who were prepared to compromise, or who even proposed common action against the Socialist threat.

In the first instance, the Church-Chapel divide was a matter of ignorance, of two cultures that barely touched. When, in 1899, the Bishop of Rochester asked what the relations of the clergy were with 'ministers and members of other Christian bodies', two Lewisham imcumbents simply said that relations were friendly, three had co-operated in non-religious matters and two said that their relations were friendly, but based on frank opposition to the rival doctrines; on the other hand, two blamed the Nonconformists for bad relations, one kept clear of 'all outside bodies', one answered 'Don't know much about them', and seven answered 'None' or made no reply at all.[32] On the other side were men like the Baptist, the Rev. J. T. Dawson, who believed that ministers of the State Church lived in a world of hunting, gambling and Sabbath desecration: 'In God's name let them leave the care of souls to be managed by the ambassadors not of King Edward but of the King of Heaven.'[33]

In spite of more tangible cultural differences, such as the Nonconformist shibboleth of temperance, the chief basis of antagonism was that Nonconformists felt themselves to be outsiders, despised and discriminated against by the Establishment and its supporters, while Anglicans saw themselves as loyalists, defending the fundamental institutions of the country against vulgar and unprincipled agitators. Because of this view of their own position Nonconformists were thus predisposed to be more sympathetic towards smaller nations in conflict with Britain, towards the cause of peace generally, towards trade unions and towards the Labour movement generally, and towards attacks on vested interests.[34] The conflicts of the late nineteenth and early twentieth centuries over Ireland, South Africa, education, the 1909 Budget and labour militancy, were to show that for some Nonconformists their religious Dissent provided the unifying principle of a more general radicalism, while for others it was an isolated act within a general conformism.

In part, the dividing line was social. During the Boer War the one religious body in Lewisham unmistakably opposed to British policy was the Bible Christian, whose members were at the lower end of the Nonconformist status hierarchy.[35] The Lee Stop the War Committee met at Lee Bible Christian chapel, whose minister was its chairman, and the Bible Christian minister at Forest Hill also preached against the war.[36]. On the other hand Burnt Ash Congregational church, whose minister, the Rev. G. Critchley, was an outspoken pro-Boer, and one of whose members was secretary of the anti-war committee, was bitterly divided. The minister was forced to resign, although a large minority of members supported his stand. Some of the latter resigned with him.[37] The only other ministers publicly to oppose the war seem to have been the Primitive Methodist, Rev. H. Kendall, and the Congregationalist, Rev. F. W. Aveling, the headmaster of a Blackheath school, who, like Critchley, had his windows smashed on Mafeking Night.[38]

Bible Christians and Primitive Methodists were again active in the campaign of passive resistance to part of Balfour's Education Act, that was among Nonconformity's central concerns for several years after 1903. All four ministers of those denominations in Lewisham in 1904 were summoned for failure to pay a part of their rates, as against four out of eight Congregationalist ministers and a smaller proportion of Baptists and Wesleyans.[39] In the Methodist sects social status and religious allegiance combined to produce a monolithic radicalism;[40] the more socially established sections of Lewisham Dissent were in a more complex situation. The two leading Congregational ministers in the borough, both moderate men, were summoned for non-payment, but the Rev. F. G. French of Lee Baptist accepted the principle of passive resistance without, apparently, practising it, and Nonconformist magistrates expressed sympathy with the resisters called before them, but did not join them.[41]

If Methodist sectarians, as well as some of the Baptists, tended to be radicals of an aggressively working-class or lower middle-class type, the Congregationalists and Unitarians were chief recruiting grounds for middle-class progressivism. If the first type of political Nonconformity was socially based, the basis of theirs was theological. Rebels against hell tended to apply the same humanitarian principles to politics, and to reject the view that worldly failures were such because of their own moral inadequacy;[42] those who repudiated a preoccupation with

personal salvation found an alternative centre for their religion in the
fight against injustice and suffering. If such sects as the Unitarians and
Quakers were more solidly identified with such a form of Christianity,
its largest body of adherents was to be found on the liberal wing of
Congregationalists. From this denomination came several of the leading
pro-Boers in the borough and some of the more vehement critics of the
House of Lords in 1910.[43] Their views were represented in 1913, when
the Sydenham, Forest Hill and Catford Free Church Council took a
monthly page in the *Lewisham Borough News* and used it to attack the
'respectability' and 'canting humbug' of too many of their fellow
Nonconformists, and to advocate the view that the social order was
unjust, that the cause lay partly in individual sin, but partly in a false
individualism, as disastrous in economics as in religion, and that the
cure to many of these ills was to be found in the policies favoured by
the ILP.[44]

If such ideas were commonplace among Nonconformists ultra-
liberals (most of them members of such Congregational churches as
Anerley Road, Penge) in the early twentieth century, and attractive to
many of the more orthodox, there were also many middle-class
Nonconformists who were finding their position on the political Left
increasingly anachronistic. In 1886 large numbers of Nonconformists
had become Liberal Unionists, and in the period of extreme social
tension after 1909 many more became Conservatives. So closely were
party and denomination linked that many of these left their chapels, or
even joined the Anglican Church.[45]

On the Anglican side most of the clergy were Conservatives by
instinct and by education, but there were differences in the meaning
they gave to Conservatism. There were romantic Conservatives, like
A. E. Green, the extreme High Church Vicar of All Saints' Sydenham,
and Conservative social reformers, like Councillor the Rev. J. C. Morris,
as well as reactionary Conservatives, like Kenneth Clarke, Morris'
successor at St Mark's.[46] The more outspokenly reactionary speeches
at church conferences tended to be made by laymen.[47] Patriotism
came as naturally to the Anglican clergy as anti-militarism came to a
large section of Nonconformity: it was appropriate that on Mafeking
night, while the homes of two Congregationalist ministers were being
attacked, Lewisham Vicarage should be festooned with Union Jacks.[48]
Terms such as 'loafer' would be used fairly freely at ruri-decanal
conferences: the principle of free education was repeatedly rejected in
the late '80s,[49] and when, in 1887 the Deptford unemployed marched
to St John's to attend morning service, they were treated to a sermon

on 'Let every soul be subject to the higher powers.'[50] The schools issue appeared to make support for the Conservative Party a simple matter of loyalty: there were Anglican clergy who opposed sectarian education, just as there were Nonconformist ministers who were 'moderate drinkers', but the other side made itself heard much more easily, and could resort with impunity to purely emotive arguments.[51] The way in which a strong emotional reaction to a single issue might colour a whole political outlook was suggested in the anti-Birrell tirade of a South London vicar who implicitly associated the attitude of the Non-conformists with that of the improvident classes: 'Churchmen are to be punished for their keenness and self-sacrifice, and the Nonconformists, who have always refused to build schools of their own, are to be rewarded with the gift of other people's. It is monstrously unjust.'[52]

Up to about 1890 the few clerical opponents of the dominant attitudes in the Lewisham area seem to have been Broad Churchmen, like Brooke Lambert, Rector of Greenwich, and Russell Wakefield, Vicar of St Michael's, Sydenham, both of whom argued for free education against general opposition. From the 1890s, the local press made known the existence of a number of High Church clergy of the moderate social reforming type associated with the Christian Social Union or of the more iconoclastic and self-consciously anti-puritan type associated with the Guild of St Matthew and, later, the Church Socialist League. Although they were generally outvoted at Church conferences they were less isolated than their predecessors on the radical wing had been. Thus a conference of clergy on the Poor Law in 1909 showed a majority favouring moderate reforms, but a minority, including the Vicar of Lewisham, supporting the Minority Report,[53] and the wave of strikes in 1912 found at least two Lewisham incumbents severely critical, but a third strongly in favour of the strikers.[54] In 1914-5 most Lewisham clergymen reported in the local press were ultra-patriotic, but others were emphasising the general principle of national self-determination as the only legitimate end to the fighting, or were even adopting apparently pacifist positions.[55] The sermon at St John's, Deptford, in 1887 must have been amongst the last of its kind,[56] though there were, no doubt, many of the clergy who continued to think in similar ways. In 1908, two hundred Lewisham unemployed marched to the parish church and cheered at morning service while the vicar called for a programme of public works and condemned 'a Christianity that has told the suffering and the oppressed that they must bear their burdens patiently because it is the will of God; such teaching is contrary absolutely to that of our Lord and Master, the

Founder of our religion'.[57]

The Church v. Chapel basis of Lewisham politics had thus survived into the second decade of the twentieth century. But it depended on the continuing position of such issues as education at the centre of party politics, and on the relative unimportance of economic issues. As these came to the fore from 1909, and more especially after the War, the Church/Chapel distinction rapidly became politically irrelevant, and the Chapel lost one of its chief functions as a centre for middle-class dissidents, and a means towards political power.

Church as Sub-Community: Liberty and Discipline

The churches in Lewisham were generally parts of larger organisations with their leaders, their officials, their conferences, their attempts to influence national policy. The concerns of these national leaders were often quite different from those of the average member or minister. A well-known and especially dramatic example was the conflict within the Wesleyan Connexion in the early nineteenth century between officials at the centre, chiefly concerned with preserving the Connexion from anti-itinerant legislation, and thus Tory in politics, and Local Preachers, who saw their political radicalism and their religious dissent as part of a consistent opposition to the established order.[58] In a less clear-cut way at the end of the nineteenth century there was a contrast between Anglican bishops who were disturbed at the alienation of a large section of the population from the institution of which they were among the leaders, and were consequently prepared to sacrifice much of their Conservatism, and large numbers of Anglican laymen and parish clergy, who saw their Anglicanism and their Conservatism as parts of a general belief in hierarchy, deference, and loyalty to established institutions, and would not have thought of sacrificing one in the interests of the other.[59] As a different example of a similar situation: at the Pan-Anglican Conference in 1908 the bishops advanced from the cautious ecumenism of the two previous conferences to suggest ways in which Anglican and Nonconformist ministers and congregations could establish friendly relations; but when in 1915 the Bishop of Southwark asked incumbents in his diocese what they had done to put the resolution into effect only one out of twenty-four in Lewisham had done anything.[60] It was in the local religious community that the individual found or failed to find a form of Christianity that gave his life more meaning, and the actions of denominational hierarchies did not necessarily have much bearing on the matter.

What kind of community the individual was looking for varied as much as the forms of Christianity which he could find within them. The differing functions of the church can be illustrated from the experience of William Kent: brought up as a Wesleyan, he became attached in his early teens to a Congregational mission, which for several years provided him with a complete range of friends and leisure activities, until at nineteen his 'advanced' theological ideas led him to join Bernard Snell's Brixton Independent, where he attended services for eight years, admiring Snell's preaching, but scarcely speaking to another member and continuing to belong to the Bible Class and Literary Society at the Wheatsheaf mission.[61] The importance for many people of the bonds formed at their church is instanced by a note in the minute-book of the Church Council of St Cyprian's, Brockley; it is written by a member of the congregation and thanks them for support during the illness and after the death of his wife. It ends:

> It was a St Cyprian's man who has stood by me the last seven weeks and when the blow fell, he took me home to his house and he and his wife were more than brother and sister could have been. Christianity is a real thing when it can see a man through such a time and I am more than ever assured that it is the only hope for such a tribulation.[62]

On the other hand there were many people whose conception of their church's place in their lives and of their relationship with fellow-members was much more limited. Most churches probably acted in such a way for at least a few of their members, but all except the smallest, also entered in a smaller way into the lives of a much larger number of people – for some merely enabling them to fulfil their Sunday duty. Mary Vivian Hughes and her mother, for instance, lived in Lee for a time and attended George Critchley's Congregational church on the grounds that: 'We get something to think about anyhow. Of course the hymns are too emotional and the praying a bit *outré;* but that man Critchley has some fine ideas.'[63] Like many middle-class people they attended church as a matter of course, and chose that which provided the best sermon or the most beautiful music, but they regarded what they were given with detachment, and not in a spirit of intimate involvement. For others, the church provided facilities for particular types of leisure, and they belonged to it only in that aspect: many churches, for instance, had excellent debating societies,[64] which probably attracted some who were not otherwise attached, and many deliberately provided Girls' Clubs or Saturday Nights for the People, which provided for one of the needs of a given class of non-member.[65] To say what kind of community the churches provided for those most fully involved is not, therefore, adequately to represent their role in Lewisham.

For those marginally involved in Lewisham churches one was probably fairly much like another. But the range of forms of Christianity embraced by the committed was wide. At opposite extremes there were Anerley Road church, a centre of ultra-liberal Congregationalism and St. Stephen's, Lewisham, the leading Anglo-Catholic church in the borough. Burnt Ash Congregational in Critchley's time and Lewisham Unitarian would have been close to Anerley Road at one extreme, and there were several less well known Anglo-Catholic churches resembling St Stephen's. The extremes they represented were those of liberty and of discipline as religious principles. Both were in revolt against the religion born of the Evangelical Revival – but where one rejected the individualism, the puritanism and the austere worship of Protestantism, the other rejected all creeds, and wished to push individualism in theology – though not in economics – still further.

The pastors at Anerley Road were Joseph Halsey from 1867 to 1904, and, from then until the church closed in 1940, H. C. Wallace, assisted for a time by Joseph Warschauer. According to its constitution, the fellowship was 'open to all sincere disciples of Christ', and all members recognised 'the right to private judgement, free from all external authority in matters of religion'. The declaration continued: 'The members of this congregation admit that there exists among them considerable diversity of opinion on several important doctrines of Theology; but they do not regard that difference as a bar to Christian Union, either among themselves or with other communities.'[66] It was on this very issue of the terms of fellowship that Spurgeon and Archibald Brown seceded from the Baptist Union, and it was for similar reasons that Gore opposed the entry of Modernists to the Anglican ministry. For a conservative Evangelical as for a conservative Anglo-Catholic, a Christian was only a Christian by virtue of his acceptance of certain 'doctrines of theology'. Liberal Protestant anti-dogmatism was in the first instance a form of self-protection, but it also introduced a positive change of emphasis – its chief concern was with action, and liberal Protestants often found more congenial company in those outside the churches who shared their attitude to social progress than in those inside the churches who did not.[67] Halsey himself saw his church as a place where 'Christian worker' and 'Christian capitalist' could meet on equal terms and he condemned that indifference of the churches to the secular well-being of the people that had led to Secularism; he claimed to teach a 'rational theology' with no 'Romanizing doctrines and ritualistic practices'.[68] When in 1907 R. J. Campbell and the City Temple became a focus for the previously somewhat isolated forces of Nonconformist ultra-liberalism, Anerley Road was one of the centres of the New Theology. Campbell's movement collapsed within a few years, many of his followers leaving, or being pushed out of, the Congregational ministry and Campbell himself becoming an Anglican; Wallace was for several years excluded from the London Congregational Union.[69] But the movement was only an extreme development of a much more general trend in English Nonconformity at the beginning of this century: the attraction of a Christianity based on the spirit of fellowship, devotion to Christ and a common passion for the improvement of the human condition, and unencumbered by dogmatic tests, pedantic attachment to forms or any sacramentalist or sacerdotalist survivals.[70]

Attractive as this kind of religion was to those emotionally bound to the chapel, its power was short-lived. Many of those whose intellectual position was fairly similar longed to be free of the restraints that any religion, however free, imposes;[71] on the other side were many who found liberal Protestantism too insubstantial, and longed for the security offered by tradition and dogma, for the beauty and mystery of Catholic worship. The latter might have been drawn to St Stephen's, Lewisham. This church was built at the top of the High Street in 1865, and drew its distinctive character from R. Rhodes Bristow, vicar from 1867 to 1897. It was based on the Catholic idea: that of an ordered religious society, with common rules, a common discipline, a systematic body of shared doctrine, and officers who were obeyed. In the late nineteenth century, Anglo-Catholicism had a strong appeal to men of radical temperament, reacting against the respectability, the individualism and the puritanism of English Protestantism.[72] Bristow and his associates also reacted, but for different reasons: their co-operative society was hierarchical; in Church and State they emphasised order, authority and tradition to a degree that left little scope for novel or independent thought; all the answers, they said, were already there. When leading members died, the qualities that the Parish Magazine chose to stress were 'devout example on such points as the Fast before Communion' or willingness to take as the 'unfailing test of right and wrong' the question 'What does the Church order?'[73] These leading members were also apt to be described as 'an ardent Church Defence advocate and a thorough Conservative'.[74] For one of Bristow's followers Liberalism and Socialism meant infidelity and loose morals as surely as Toryism, for one of Halsey's followers, would have meant brewers and landlords. Thus, an early issue of the Magazine published an address on religious education by one of the churchwardens, in which he argued as follows:

> Against this common enemy [Satan], it is that you are asked to erect a barrier. And how shall you do it but by taking means to impart to the rising generation of the masses of this country, who come under the influence of our Church Schools, a religious education such as will bring them up to be loyal to the Church of England at the same time that they are loyal to the Crown; loyal to their rights and liberties as Englishmen, and loyal to the Constitution.

In listing Satan's many forms, he mentioned 'the subtle mask of speculative and rationalistic enquiry', 'pure scepticism disguised under the specious forms of ethnological and archaeological research', 'the alluring mask of ease and indolence', 'unsound political economy', 'the engrossing race for wealth', 'the coarse features of spiritualism and imposture', and 'the plainer garb of communism'.[75]

At the St Stephen's Guild, fifteen years later, the speaker asserted that 'the Church is not, as some would have us believe, an institution useful enough in its own way, but one we could get on fairly well without. Rather it is the condition without which we are unable to do anything except mischief.'[76] This Anglican sectarianism – though not the extreme form of Conservative politics that went with it – was common enough in Lewisham, where the chief Church patrons, the Lords Dartmouth and Northbrook, seemed to prefer High Churchmen.

Parson and People: Common Ground and Points at Issue

But, whatever church party they belonged to, an emphasis on 'the Church' seems to have been common to most of the Lewisham clergy, and one of the most important elements in their view of the world. Nonconformist ministers, though for varying reasons, seldom attached great significance to sectarian boundaries: they usually distinguished between the 'great truths' common to all true Christians, and the minor differences separating them.[77] On the other hand, a large section of the

Anglican clergy were strongly conscious of the special identity of their own church, of the need for parish organisations 'on definite Church lines',[78] with the assistance of 'staunch churchmen'[79] brought up in schools where the teaching has been 'calculated to make the scholars churchmen or churchwomen when they grew up'[80] — whether they thought in terms of 'Christ's Catholic Church',[81] 'the law',[82] or less exclusively, of 'the inconsistent English Church', than which there is no more glorious Church in Christendom ... nor one that has shown such wonderful proofs of the Christian life'.[83]

Among Nonconformist ministers in Lewisham the point most nearly common to those at different points on a wide theological spectrum was a tendency to present the issues of the day in high-charged rhetoric and to see their solution as a matter of ethical imperatives. The press exaggerated this tendency. A Congregational minister such as J. Eames of Lewisham High Street church, a disciple of F. W. Robertson, noted for his 'subdued earnestness',[84] made less colourful reading than, say, John Clifford, and his pronouncements accordingly received less publicity. During the period of passive resistance, Eames, who was among those summoned for non-payment was less often quoted than a neighbouring Baptist fire-eater, the Rev. R. Walker, whose ranting tones thus became those in which the resisters' case was characteristically heard. From Parnell to the Education Bills, from the Boer War to the People's Budget, politics were seen to present moral choices. The essential was not popularity or worldly success — indeed a fair measure of the reverse could be expected by those who chose aright, and those who appeared to have chosen wrong were accused not of faulty judgement but of moral failure. 'Let them not run away', Halsey told his congregation, 'with the idea that their's was a popular church or that he was a popular preacher, because they were nothing of the kind. Let them rather feel that their church had a mission and that their preacher had a message, and that, come what may, that mission would be discharged and that message delivered.'[85] It was an attitude that came easily to Nonconformists, brought up on the story of the long struggle against Anglican privilege, though it mixed rather oddly with an alternative version according to which the Nonconformists were the voice of 'half the nation'.[86]

It was in these terms of clear-cut moral choice that the Rev. R. Walker declared (to loud applause from fellow Baptists) 'If I were not a passive resister under present conditions I would be ashamed of myself',[87] that the Congregationalist Rev. J. Morley Wright insisted that Britain's continuing greatness depended on the departure of the 'admitted and convicted adulterer, liar and sneak', Parnell,[88] and that George Critchley pronounced the Boer War 'a great question of moral righteousness' presenting the Free Churches with a choice between condemning British policy, or being reduced to the utterance of 'a set of flimsy pious platitudes, meaning nothing, good for nothing, serviceable for nothing except to cover the guilt and selfishness of a people with a thin veneer of Christian sentiment upon them'.[89]

Whatever the origin of particular crusades,[90] the general Non-conformist propensity for moral crusading followed naturally from liberalised Protestant theology, from their historical experience and from their social situation. For those who had rejected predestination and justification by faith alone but kept the Protestant emphasis on personal commitment, moral choice was of crucial importance.[91] For those who had known something, and probably heard a great deal more, of social exclusion, the role of persecuted warriors for principle came easily, and those who refused to join the struggle could easily be branded as self-interested turn-coats.[92] And as men of intermediate social status, they were particularly inclined to oppose upper-class traditionalism and lower-class communitarianism with a politics based on morality and a morality based on choice.[93] Anglican ecclesiasticism probably affected the clergy far more deeply than the laity, while Nonconformist moralism affected all parts of the Free Churches. Both could find themselves under attack from laymen with their own definite ideas of what the church was for.

Baptist, Congregational and Unitarian churches, because of their democratic character, were necessarily subject to secessions, expulsions, ministers forced out of their pulpits. But these were not entirely unknown in the Church of England: for instance, St Mark's, Lewisham, was built by Protestant parishioners who could not stand the Popish goings-on at St Stephen's.[94] The immediate cause of such disputes was often ritual, the protesters being laymen who objected even to the slightest 'Romanisation'. But behind these conflicts there often lay different ideas as to what the Church of England was. Thus, when C. E. Escreet, the Socialist and 'Romanising' Rector of Woolwich (later Archdeacon of Lewisham) proposed to introduce a new altar the Vestry tried to stop him doing so on the grounds that 'it was for the parishioners and not the two or three who attended the church to decide these things (cheers).'[95] For those Anglicans who had not become 'Catholics', the parish church was seen not as a unit in a divinely created society, but as a local amenity providing useful services including good preaching, acceptable versions of the Anglican liturgy and a competent parson. 'Catholics' saw the exercise of discipline over the laity as part of the functions of the priest;[96] many laymen had a less clearly articulated, but nonetheless potent, sense of their own right to discipline the clergy. Thus, at the ruri-decanal conference in 1889 a layman from Lee made these comments on the prosecution of the Bishop of Lincoln:

> The Church of England was as much the church of the laity – (cheers) – as of the clergy, and this question would never have arisen if the clergy had known what the people thought. The poor and the middle classes did not go to church because they cared nothing for all these things – (oh, oh,) – they could not understand the services and were opposed to anything that approached to Popery (laughter). The point that he wished to impress was that the crime of the Bishop of Lincoln was that he had disobeyed the law (hear, hear).[97]

If the sense of 'the Church' meant very little to many Anglican laymen, Nonconformist ministers, who were far more vulnerable, often found the members of their churches hostile to their moral crusades. For instance, campaigns against the Armenian atrocities would at least meet with little opposition, but when Nonconformist ministers applied similar principles to British policy in South Africa, many of their congregations put their loyalty to their country before their alleged duty to their conscience. The Johnson-Wells fight, as Stuart Mews points out, was an excellent means of promoting Nonconformist unity, but the more urgent contemporary issue of industrial conflict, which some Nonconformists saw in equally moralistic terms, could only divide.[98] The conclusion was sometimes wrongly drawn from this that Nonconformists only applied their moral principles to relatively minor issues: the point, however, was that their principles took them to differing conclusions, and that it was within the more limited areas that united action was possible.[99] Those ministers whose conclusions put them sharply at odds with the majority of the middle class, or even with public opinion in general, could find themselves bitterly opposed. One example was Critchley, who lost his pulpit, although a substantial minority of the church supported him. Another Lewisham minister lost nearly half the members of his church in circumstances that are more mysterious, but which he regarded as plainly political: when A. L. Baxter interviewed him in 1901 he was described as 'a political minister on strongly advanced, if not socialistic lines', who 'cannot think of administration of the Poor Law without his blood boiling', and he in turn described his opponents as 'people who are very glad to have the working man at their church if they may condescend and patronise him, give him half a crown and pat him on the back and patronise him, but who don't at all like being made equal with Tom, Dick and Harry.'[100]

If by 1899 such secessions were becoming rather unusual, it was a sign that most people were taking their church membership more casually. As a vicar in the neighbouring borough of Greenwich told Booth's representative: 'they all take their religion much more lightly: there is much more tendency to believe it will all come right in the end. . . . [Twenty years ago] a week would not pass without letters of praise, inquiry or abuse with regard to sermons: they have completely ceased.'[101]

Notes

1. S. Byrne, *The Changing Face of Lewisham*, Lewisham Public Libraries, London, 1965, pp.8-9.
2. Description based on Booth's maps and section on 'Housing and Rents', in Booth op.cit., III, vi, pp.157-8.
3. Booth in 1891 found Lewisham, Sydenham and Eltham to be the least crowded district of London (the percentage of the population living in such conditions being 7 per cent, as against 57 per cent in South Shoreditch). In 1911 the proportion of the population living in tenements of six and seven rooms (a typically lower middle-class size of house) was higher than in any other metropolitan borough. Pevsner's comment on the borough is: 'There is so little of note that it is hardly worth working out an elaborate itinerary.' Booth, op.cit., Final Volume, p.17; *London Statistics, 1912-3*, p.66; N. Pevsner, *London, except the Cities of London and Westminster*, Penguin, Harmondsworth, 1952, p.290.
4. W. Margrie, *Roses and Kippers*, Watts, London, 1930, p.259.
5. Lewisham had one Wesleyan, Baptist or Congregational church or mission for every 2779 adults in 1903, Woolwich and Camberwell ranking second and third, and Paddington, with one for every 10,993 adults standing at the opposite extreme.
6. Adults are those who appeared to the enumerators to be fifteen or over.
7. For examples of the offering of sites for churches by the lords of the manor, see Ecclesiastical Commissioners' Files, 64,910 and 67,208. *Lewisham Borough News*, 20 December 1912, reported that the Earl and Countess of Northbrook had come up from Hampshire to open a sale of work at the church of the Good Shepherd, Lee. When attacks were being made, said the Earl, on the Church of Wales (and it would be England's turn next) everyone had a duty to pull together.

8. Ecclesiastical Commissioners File 50,975. Report dated 29 February 1912.

9. H. C. Mott in *Lewisham Journal*, 10 March 1911.

10. *Lewisham and Lee Gazette*, 25 February 1898.

11. A well-documented case of the former is Greville Place Congregational Church in Kilburn, the records of which are in the Greater London Record Office. Formed in 1858, it depended heavily on the support of the Callard confectionery family. From the early '80s it was in financial difficulties, and by 1908, when the last of the Callards left Kilburn, these were acute. The church was dissolved in 1923, after expenses had been cut to two inescapable items — a minimal salary for the minister and the upkeep of the chapel buildings. The latter was much discussed by critics of Nonconformity, but I have not come across clear examples of individuals using their power in this way. In 1909, the minister of Newington Green Unitarian church was forced to move because an influential minority objected to his Socialist sermons. (M. Thorncroft, *Trust in Freedom*, (n.d.), p.28). Cases where a majority told the minister what he could preach are common enough.

12. The best known example was the Congregationalist Samuel Morley, for whom see Inglis, op.cit., p.101. The more active Anglican and Roman Catholic clergy in poor areas were usually expert 'beggars'. E.g. the parish magazine of St. Peter's, London Docks, January 1886, reported that the Countess of Cheltenham was holding a Drawing Room Meeting in support of their schools, and that others present would include the Bishop of Bedford, the Duke of Newcastle and Earl Nelson. For claims on rich Roman Catholics, see S. Gilley, 'English Catholic Charity and the Irish Poor in London', in *Recusant History*, Vol. XI, no. 4, January 1972, pp.187-8.

13. *Lewisham Journal*, 3 January 1911.

14. N. Blewett, *The Peers, The Parties and the People: The General Elections of 1910*, Macmillan, London, 1972, pp.229-33, states that Liberal and Unionist candidates 'were not sharply distinguished by age, occupation or education', most of them being drawn in each case from 'the solid and upper-middle classes', but that 35 per cent of Liberal candidates were Nonconformists, as against 3 per cent of Unionists.

15. *Borough of Lewisham Gazette*, 6 November 1903, 13 November 1903. Some biographies did not mention religion, although in at least one such case the councillor concerned was an active Nonconformist.

16. *Borough of Lewisham Gazette*, 9 – 23 October 1909, 6 November 1909, 4 December 1909.

17. See biographies in T. Bavington Jones, *Kent at the Opening of the Twentieth Century*, Pike, Brighton, 1904.

18. *Lewisham Borough News*, 22 May 1908, reported that Major Coates, the Tory MP for Lewisham, had presided at a rally in

support of the Pan Anglican Conference and that he, together with the local County Councillor, had spoken at the opening of the Ladywell Mission Hall.

19. *Hampstead and Highgate Express*, 28 October 1905, reported that the daughter of the local Conservative MP had laid the foundation stone of a new Salvation Army citadel. However, Salvationists were seldom interested in politics, and this might be ranked as an uncontroversial good cause.

20. See biography in Bavington Jones, op.cit., and the *Reminiscences*, Epworth, London, 1928, of his nephew, J. Scott Lidgett.

21. Bavington Jones, op.cit.

22. *Lewisham Borough News*, 13 December 1907; *Lewisham Journal*, 20 January 1911. The Anglican parson was a moderate High Churchman.

23. *Lewisham Borough News*, 18 June 1915.

24. *Lewisham Gazette*, 16 March 1900; 25 August 1911.

25. In 1903 William Dawtry, a steam engine maker, who described himself as an Anglican, and Robert Farrell, a GPO sorter, and one of the leading Roman Catholic laymen in the borough, were elected as Progressives, but they later formed part of a distinct Labour group, before losing their seats in the Moderate clean sweep of 1906 (*Borough of Lewisham Gazette*, 13 November 1903; *Lewisham Borough News*, 7 June 1907). Charles Lewis, a printer, described by the *Lewisham Borough News* (10 May 1907) as the leading Socialist in Brockley, and an unsuccessful Council candidate in 1909 was a Free Methodist (*Borough of Lewisham Gazette*, 23 October 1909).

26. *Lewisham Borough News*, 18 December 1908.

27. *Lewisham Gazette*, 21 January 1892.

28. The Liberals were Russell Wakefield (St. Michael's, Sydenham), later Bishop of Birmingham, and J. C. Gill (St. Augustine's, Grove Park), both in the '80s and early '90s. The Socialists were both High Churchmen: C. E. Escreet (Archdeacon of Lewisham in 1906, and Vicar of the Ascension, Blackheath, in 1909) and J. Drew Roberts (Vicar of St Swithun's, Hither Green, 1902-8).

29. *Borough of Lewisham Gazette*, 30 October 1903.

30. Rochester Visitation, 1889. Reply of Vicar of St John's, Blackheath.

31. Rochester Visitation, 1881. Reply of Vicar of St Michael and All Angels, Blackheath.

32. Rochester Visitation returns, 1899.

33. *Lewisham Borough News*, 23 November 1906.

34. The connection was made from the opposite side by a Conservative councillor, speaking at the Lewisham Ruridecanal Conference, who condemned the Liberal Licensing Bill in these terms: 'The Government were attacking vested interests. What would they attack next? Our dear, dear Church!' *Lewisham Borough News*, 13 March 1908.

35. The minister of Lee Bible Christian church, interviewed by Booth

claimed that the members were working-class, together with a few tradesmen. Booth Collection, B315, pp.73-7. The only members to be mentioned in the local press were Clifford Smith, a teacher, and Herbert Baker, a grocer, both of whom were active Liberals.

36. *Lewisham Independent*, 22 February 1900; *Lewisham Gazette*, 23 February 1900. The Rev. H. W. Horwill (Forest Hill Bible Christian), preaching at Lewisham High Street Congregational chapel on 'the root of all evil', claimed that 'the real Commander in Chief in this unjustifiable and iniquitous war' was the Stock Exchange. There were some cries of 'No!' and the organist included bars of 'Rule Britannia' in his voluntary.

37. At a church meeting in April 1900, a motion 'entreating' Critchley to withdraw his resignation was lost by thirty-four votes to thirty-two. In February 1900, a sermon at Critchley's church by the pro-Boer, Rev. F. W. Aveling, had provoked a shout of 'traitor', which some of the congregation followed with 'rotten tomfoolery' and 'let him go and preach that to old Kruger'. *Lewisham Independent*, 22 February 1900; *Lewisham Borough News*, 10 May 1900; Church Minute Book, 28 March 1900, 10 April 1900; 30 May 1900.

38. *Lewisham Borough News*, 10 May 1900.

39. These are minimum proportions, and depend on reports of appearance by resisters in court in the local press. These were occasions for speeches by one or more of those summoned, and tended to be prominently reported both by sympathetic and by hostile papers. I have only found one Wesleyan and one Baptist minister among those summoned in the borough, though one Baptist minister, R. Walker, was a particularly uncompromising resister, and several Baptist laymen were locally prominent in the movement.

40. The Methodist sects were probably also the section of Nonconformity most completely identified with tee-totalism. The Bible Christian minister at Lee told Booth's representative that seven-eights of the members of his church and all ministers of the denomination were total abstainers: 'There is no rule about it, but sentiment is so strong it comes to the same thing'. Booth Collection, B315, p.73.

41. *Lewisham Borough News*, 21 January 1904, reported a debate on passive resistance at St Mary's Debating Society, in which a wide spectrum of opinion was represented. French argued that obedience to the law could not be absolute, but reserved his own position on the matter immediately at issue. At a local Free Church Council meeting (ibid., 22 June 1905), a Nonconformist J.P. admitted that passive resisters 'stood on a higher moral platform than he did'. But passive resistance was certainly not limited to 'noisy extremists' as Marjorie Cruickshank claims in *Church and State in English Education*, Macmillan, London, 1963, p.87.

42. In the pamphlet warfare of the 1820s a Unitarian had compared

Evangelical champions of eternal punishment to those who
'oppose the amelioration and happiness of whole nations lest
they should lose any of their exclusive privileges by a change in
the situation of the multitude'. Rowell, op.cit. p.44.

43. The members of the Lee Stop the War Committee seem all to
have been Congregationalists or Bible Christians, and the fund
raised on Critchley's behalf was organised by W. Betts, a Fabian
deacon at High Street Congregational Church (*Lewisham Borough
News*, 2 August 1900). Ibid., 7 January 1901 reported strongly
worded attacks on the Lords from Liberal platforms by the Revs.F.
Aveling and G. Darlaston, the latter demanding that they be
'wiped out'.

44. *Lewisham Borough News*, 28 March 1913, etc. Contributions to
these pages included declarations of general social principles,
advocacy of specific policies such as the minimum wage, the
highlighting of conditions of work in such industries as tailoring,
and items of gossip publicising the work of reformers.

45. The Lewisham press does not provide much evidence on this
movement. But in the wealthy suburb of Hampstead the
involvement of many Nonconformists in Liberal Unionism was
well reported and in 1909-10 several letters were published written
by Nonconformists complaining of their ministers' radicalism.
Hampstead and Highgate Express, 18 June 1887, reported the
formation of a Liberal Unionist group under mainly Unitarian
leadership, with a Congregationalist chairman. In 1910 'thousands
of Nonconformists' were said to have been 'driven out' by the
Budget League oratory of R. F. Horton and others. Ibid., 8-22
January 1910.

46. For a remarkable sermon by Green on the coronation of George
V, see *Lewisham Journal*, 30 June 1911; it is surprising that he
was also (*Borough of Lewisham Gazette*, 12 March 1909) an
advocate of women's suffrage. Morris (ibid., loc.cit.) successfully
demanded a ruri-decanal Social Service committee which, in his
view, should organise enquiries into such subjects as sweating.
Clarke (*Lewisham Borough News*, 5 March 1915) opposed the
idea that the peace settlement should be on the basis of national
self-determination on the grounds that what was granted to the
Czechs could not be denied to Irish, Welsh and Indians.

47. At the Lewisham ruridecanal conference in 1894, a motion
suggesting that the Church should take a greater interest in social
questions was passed nem. con., but not before one layman had
suggested that the Church's chief concern should be to teach the
working class 'their duty to their betters'. *Lewisham Gazette*, 9
March 1894.

48. *Lewisham Borough News*, 14 May 1900.

49. In 1890 the Lewisham conference rejected the principle by 51-7.
In 1887 it had only one supporter, the chief objections being that
the rates would rise, that board schools would chiefly benefit,
and the working classes would become less independent.

Lewisham Gazette, 14 March 1890; *Lewisham Courier*, 18 March 1887.

50. *Lewisham Courier*, 4 February 1887. There were no interruptions beyond the hissing of the Queen and Prince of Wales during the prayers. After the service, the leader of the unemployed told a reporter that he never remembered attending church before, but he liked it so much he was thinking of going again.

51. *Lewisham Courier*, 22 May 1885, reported a Greenwich ruri-decanal conference at which only Rev. Brooke Lambert had defended board schools and opposed a motion of support for the Moderate candidates in the coming school board elections.

52. St Stephen's, Lewisham, Parish Magazine, June 1906, quoting the Vicar of St Peter's, Streatham.

53. *Borough of Lewisham Gazette*, 11 December 1909.

54. Rev. J. H. W. Kane preached on 'The Dangers of Socialism' and Rev. A. E. King, also a High Churchman, condemned the foreign agitators who had organised the current wave of strikes, while Rev. C. E. Escreet, at the Representative Church Council, attacked employers; Rev. W. P. Holmes, in his parish magazine, thought that each side was right in some ways and wrong in others, while Rev. A. E. Green called for co-partnership as the solution to industrial conflict. *Lewisham Journal*, 1-8 September 1911; *Borough of Lewisham Gazette*, 12 July 1912.

55. *Lewisham Borough News*, 6 November 1914, 5 March 1915. At the ruri-decanal conference in November 1914, a motion was passed calling for compulsory military training and drill at schools. Two clergymen opposed the idea in terms tantamount to general pacifism.

56. Chartist church paraders were frequently subjected to such sermons in the 1830s and '40s. See H. U. Faulkner, *Chartism and the Churches*, Columbia University, New York, 1916, pp.35-9.

57. *Lewisham Borough News*, 30 August 1908.

58. W. R. Ward, *Religion and Society in England, 1790-1850*, Batsford, London, 1972, pp.56-62, 85-104.

59. From 1880 onwards papers on 'social' subjects and references to 'social' themes from a reforming point of view became increasingly frequent at the annual Church Congress. By 1911 these had become so much of a cliche that Bishop Winnington-Ingram, in his opening sermon, praised the Labour Party and preached the 'great gospel of Brotherhood, Love and Equality of Opportunity'. On the other side was the Evangelical *Church Family Newspaper*, which in 1908 asserted that 'the working classes need much plain and courageous speaking from the Church today', and that 'the "Socialism" meeting' at the Church Congress was 'no fair expression of the views of the majority of Churchmen'. *Official Report of the Church Congress*, 1911, pp.7-14; Mayor, op.cit., pp.235, 239.

60. Southwark Visitation, 1915. Most emphasised that relations were nonetheless friendly (mostly as a result of sitting on the same war

relief committees), and none was as unashamedly sectarian as the Vicar of St Peter's, Eltham, who wrote: 'We have, happily, no Dissenting Conventicles in this Parish.'

61. W. Kent, op.cit., pp.217-24.
62. Minute-book of the Church Council, St Cyprian's, Brockley, 26 May 1910.
63. Hughes, *A London Girl of the Eighties*, p.156.
64. Debates on capital punishment, passive resistance and 'Christianity and Socialism' at the St Mary's Debating Society or Men's Society were notable for the comprehensive range of views expressed — ranging in the last case from those of a Conservative councillor to an atheist-Socialist speaker on Hilly Fields. *Lewisham Gazette*, 19 December 1890; *Lewisham Borough News*, 21 January 1904; ibid., 1 March 1912.
65. For instance, St Mary's had in 1886 a clothing club (192 members), a coal club, a provident bank (197 deposits), a medical insurance scheme, etc. St Mary's, Lewisham, Year Book, 1886.
66. Annual Report for 1900, included in Booth Collection, B315.
67. An example of this was an article in the *Christian Commonwealth*, the organ of R. J. Campbell's New Theology, 27 January 1909. Reporting a Women's Labour League meeting at the Memorial Hall the paper found it ironical that 'not a single Free Church leader was there to champion the cause of the down-trodden women'. It concluded that 'churchianity' faced 'complete extinction', and replacement by 'the great new movement that is sweeping the country' which 'does not speak in terms of hell and heaven, but of starving children and crushed women'.
68. Sermon reported in *Lewisham Gazette*, 10 April 1891. This was in reply to letters he had invited from working men stating their religious views and criticism of the church. He partially accepted the criticisms, but complained of 'a lack of spiritual aspiration' in the letters. The church was said to have been packed and the congregation to have applauded at the end of the seventy-minute sermon.
69. London Congregational Union Minutes, 18 May 1914, 15 June 1914. His name reappeared in the *Congregational Year Book*, in 1921. The reason for the expulsion (by fifty-seven votes to five) was not stated.
70. The best account of this trend is in J. W. Grant, *Free Churchmanship in England, 1870-1940*, Independent Press, London, n.d., Chs.3-4. Although Grant's chief purpose is to show how far the liberals deviated from the authentic 'Reformed tradition', he allows Clifford, Fairbairn and Horne, as well as less formidable exponents — whom he tends to dismiss as 'naive' or 'genial' — to speak for themselves through frequent quotation.
71. The Ethical Movement in particular, and even the Humanist movement in general, seem to have suffered similar problems. Arising out of the utopian ferment in the '80s and '90s, the

Ethical Movement sought to become a church for the agnostic; by 1905, if not earlier, it was losing members to the ILP which seemed to be 'doing' something; when in the 1950s it revived it was as a pressure-group, with much more limited aims. Budd, op.cit., pp.380, 456-63.

72. See, for example, Reckitt, op.cit., a collection of studies of Anglo-Catholic Socialists.

73. St Stephen's Lewisham Parish Magazine, May 1918, October 1910.

74. Ibid., February 1905.

75. Ibid., January 1873, printing an address to the English Church Union.

76. Ibid., August 1888. Address by Rev. W. H. Lucas, Rural Dean of West Fordingbridge.

77. It was in such terms that Spurgeon, after seceding from the Baptist Union, insisted that he had 'never sought to intrude upon it any Calvinistic or personal creed', but merely such a statement of belief as that of the Evangelical Alliance 'which includes members of well-nigh all Christian communities'. *Sword and Trowel*, February 1888.

78. *Borough of Lewisham Gazette*, 24 September 1910, reported that the new Rector of Lee specialised in Men's Meetings run on such lines.

79. The Vicar of St Laurence's, Catford, saw his chief need as 'working men evangelists who could work as staunch churchmen among their own class'. Rochester Visitation, 1889.

80. The Vicar of St Swithun's, Hither Green, defined the religious teaching in board schools as not being so calculated. Rochester Visitation, 1889.

81. Articles in St. Mary's, Lewisham, Parish Magazine, September 1880 and July 1882, condemned 'innovations', such as Popery and trans-substantiation and 'schisms' — Wesleyans, Plymouth Brethren, etc.

82. When the vicar of Christ Church, Forest Hill, complained to the bishop (Rochester Visitation, 1881) of a breakaway congregation formed by some of his parishioners, he was particularly upset by the fact that 'numbers of the inhabitants seem to be indifferent to whether a clergyman is licensed or unlicensed'.

83. Dean Church, as quoted by D. Voll, *Catholic Evangelicalism* (English Translation) Faith Press, London, 1963, p.95.

84. *Lewisham Gazette*, 18 October 1901.

85. *Lewisham Gazette*, 31 January 1890.

86. The heroic version of English Nonconformist history — a ceaseless struggle against tyranny, privilege and inequality led by the Church — is presented in C. S. Horne, *Nonconformity in the XIXth Century*, Free Church Council, 1905. The 'success-story' version of Nonconformist history was especially favoured by H. P. Hughes. See D. Hughes, *Life of Hugh Price Hughes*, Hodder and Stoughton, London, 1904, pp.442-4. For the coalescence of

majority and minority-consciousness in the thinking of F. B. Meyer, the Baptist leader who successfully campaigned for a cancellation of the Johnson-Wells fight in 1911, see S. P. Mews, 'Puritanicalism, Sport and Race', in G. J. Cuming and D. Baker (eds.), *Studies in Church History*, **8**, CUP, Cambridge, 1972.

87. *Lewisham Borough News*, 12 November 1903.
88. *Lewisham Gazette*, 28 November 1890.
89. *Lewisham Borough News*, 2 August 1900.
90. Mews, 'Puritanicalism, Sport and Race', explains the Johnson-Wells agitation in terms of the Free Church Council movement's need for 'some national issue on which it could unite and fight'. J. Kent, 'Hugh Price Hughes and the Nonconformist Conscience', G. V. Bennett and J. D. Walsh, (eds.) *Essays in Modern English Church History*, A. and C. Black, London, 1966, p.204, sees the 'Nonconformist Conscience' as an instrument of the rise to power through the Liberal Party of the Nonconformist lay elite.
91. Glock and Stark, in their study of North California in the 1960s, found a great emphasis on ethics among the more theologically liberal religious groups. They suggested that 'ethicalism and orthodoxy can be mutually exclusive roots of religious identity' C. Y. Glock and R. Stark, *American Piety*, University of California Press, Berkeley and L.A., 1968, p.75.
92. Like Eric Gill's father, who left the Nonconformist for the Anglican ministry — with financially disastrous effects. E. Gill, *Autobiography*, 1940, pp.65-6.
93. F. Parkin, *Middle Class Radicalism*, Manchester UP, Manchester, 1968, pp.40-5, notes the continuing tendency for a section of the middle class to see politics in terms of moral issues — though environmental determinism has changed the style in which these are presented.
94. St Stephen's, Lewisham, Parish Magazine, May 1900.
95. *Lewisham and Lee Gazette*, 18 November 1898.
96. The Anglo-Catholic Rev. A. E. Green, who had been subjected to Kensitite demonstrations, told his Sydenham congregation: 'First he must put before them their plain duty, that those who were Catholics should obey their parish priest'. *Lewisham Borough News*, 16 February 1912.
97. *Borough of Lewisham Gazette*, 17 May 1889.
98. Mews, 'Puritanicalism, Sport and Race', pp.315-6. Charles Brown, the President of the Free Church Council believed that 'the Church should openly ally itself' with the strikers, but many Free Church leaders disagreed.
99. Thus when, in the early twentieth century, Anglicans took to organising demonstrations in Hyde Park, the two issues they chose were defence of the church schools and of the Church of Wales. The choice of two such apparently selfish issues gave an unfortunate, but largely misleading, impression of bigotry. In fact the Anglican clergy were involved on both sides of a much wider range of social conflicts, but it was only on such relatively

peripheral issues that a united stand was possible.
100. Booth Collection, B315, p.107. The minister was the Rev.
     Newton Vanstone of Catford Bridge Baptist church, and, in 1899,
     154 out of some 350 members resigned and formed a church at
     Perry Rise. The report in the *Lewisham and Lee Gazette*, 16
     September 1899, and the *History of Catford Hill Baptist Church*
     do not throw much light on the causes of the dispute.
101. Vicar of St Paul's, Greenwich, interviewed 29 May 1900. Booth
     Collection, B287, pp.5-7.

It was gloomy and inconvenient, with large drawing-rooms, bad bedrooms, and very little accommodation for servants. But it was the old family town-house, having been inhabited by three or four generations of Longestaffes, and did not savour of that radical newness which prevails, and which was peculiarly distasteful to Mr. Longestaffe. Queen's Gate, and the quarters around were, according to Mr. Longestaffe, devoted to opulent tradesmen. Even Belgrave Square, though its aristocratic properties must be admitted, still smelt of the mortar. Many of those living there and thereabouts had never possessed in their families real family town-houses. The old streets lying between Piccadilly and Oxford Street, with one or two well-known localities to the south and north of these boundaries, were the proper sites for these habitations. When Lady Pomona instigated by some friends of high rank, but questionable taste, had once suggested a change to Eaton Square, Mr. Longestaffe had at once snubbed his wife.[1]

The Longestaffes were a Suffolk gentry family, with a town-house in Bruton Street, off Berkeley Square, to which they came for the 'Season', and financial problems that made it hard for them to live in the style that they regarded as their right. They were an unpleasant family, exhibiting the prejudices of their class in quite exceptional measures. Yet much in the caricatured views of the family's head was general to West London: a sense of minute distinctions of social status and of their reflection in local geography; a sense of family and of family traditions; an awareness of the appropriate and the 'proper' and a willingness to impose social sanctions on those violating these standards.

In 1885, Sweet Escott, the editor of the *Fortnightly Review*, defined Society as 'the social area of which the Prince of Wales is personally cognisant, within the limits of which he visits, and every member of which is to some extent in touch with the ideas and wishes of His Royal Highness.'[2] During the London season, the members of this select group were all to be found within a short distance of the eastern extreme of Hyde Park. In the autumn and winter they were to be found at their country seats. Most of this inner circle occupied their position by virtue of heredity, and drew their incomes from land, though the agricultural depression was obliging them to shore up declining finances by buying shares and acquiring directorships.[3] A few had forced their way in by outstanding success in politics, law, business, or social climbing. At one side, Society merged into St John's Wood — often brilliant but more than a little *risqué*.[4] At the other, it merged into South Kensington — estimable, but not quite fashionable.[5] St John's Wood, besides being the proverbial home of the 'kept women' of those living in Mayfair and Belgravia, was also favoured by 'advanced thinkers', such as George Eliot, T. H. Huxley and Herbert Spencer. Kensington was the characteristic place of residence of professional men, politicians, businessmen, rentiers, who were wealthy but did not aspire to a place in Society. Bayswater belonged to the same category, while Bloomsbury, isolated among several of the poorest districts in London had a literary flavour, even before its post-War heyday.

Common to all these areas were high levels of church attendance and Anglican predominance.

The Upper-Class Pattern of Life

In nineteenth-century England it was usually held that the middle class was the religious class *par excellence*. If the criterion were the number of individuals whose life centred round their religion or who were isolated from intimate acquaintance with the worldly or the sceptical, this was perhaps true. But it was among the gentry that religious observances were an integral part of the life of a whole class. Those of a religious turn of mind distinguished themselves by devoting their lives to philanthropy, by joining the Church of Rome, or by an ostentatious abstention from the prescribed rites. But sceptics, and even avowed unbelievers, had their children baptised, sent them to schools staffed substantially by clergymen, and themselves attended church regularly. Working- or lower middle-class children of non-church-going parents were sometimes attracted by a choir or a club: Lady Tweedsmuir, who came from the Grosvenor family, records that although her parents were both agnostics her mother actually encouraged her to attend church, and arranged for Scott Holland to prepare her for confirmation.[6] She grew up to be a Christian and a practising Anglican. Lytton Strachey, who soon made his mother's scepticism appear reverent and respectable by comparison, was sent by his agnostic parents to schools where 'a special emphasis was laid on Christian teaching', and he claimed to have been a 'devout Christian' up to the age of sixteen.[7]

In the village, the landowner, whatever his convictions, was likely to be on intimate terms with the parish incumbent.[8] In town, bishops, as much as painters and rising MPs were likely to be met at dinner parties.[9] The Anglican clergy were, for the most part, 'gentlemen', drawn from the same classes that populated the West End and the wealthiest suburbs; close acquaintanceship with clergymen was as much the common inheritance of all in the upper class as christening, confirmation, church marriage and education in a chapel-centred public school. Agnostics often had their favourite bishop or canon. Beatrice Webb got on particularly well with prelates — though she probably saw them, in the first instance, as commanding heights to be conquered. Mandell Creighton was her favourite.[10] Cosmo Lang was especially popular in Society:[11] Lady Cynthia Asquith was confirmed by him and married by him; he promised to bury her, but died too soon.[12] Contempt for clergymen in general was quite common, but there were few people who were not linked to clergymen, and thus to the church that they represented, by ties of blood and friendship.

If Anglicanism was an integral part of the life of the upper class this was primarily because most members of the class still saw the Established Church as an essential part of the social order within which they held privileged positions, and which they felt a duty to uphold. In a study of 'An Englishman's Religion' published in 1911, it was said of the Old Squire that 'he does not ask whether he needs the comforts of religion, he is sure that society needs religion, and if society needs religion he, as one of the first in the social organisation, must be there at his post'.[13] Those who had no such sense of what 'society' needed were still conscious of what was required of people in their own social position, and of the sanctions that could be imposed on those who failed to conform. In the country, even a republican and unbeliever, such as Frederic Harrison, might attend church, to keep up, as he said, the family credit.[14] And thoroughly conventional families, such as the Longestaffes, had a highly developed consciousness of what was and was not 'done', and a readiness to inflict any amount of pain on themselves or on others, if only the standards of correct behaviour were observed:

Of course they were all going to church. They always did go to church when they were at Caversham ... The three ladies knelt on their hassocks in the most becoming fashion, and sat during the sermon without the slightest sign either of weariness or of attention. They did not collect the meaning of any one combination of sentences. It was nothing to them whether the bishop had or had not a meaning. Endurance of that kind was their strength.[15]

This sort of pressure bore more heavily in the country than in London, and on women and married men than on bachelors. The latter were, in any case, subject to counter-pressures to prove their manliness. But all members of the upper class were subject to particularly strong pressures to behave in approved ways, with the threat of losing the social acceptability on which their ability to move in fashionable or near-fashionable circles depended. Furthermore, routine and formality were essential to the upper-class way of life, and into this routine little bits of formal religion got mixed in, as matters of 'good taste' and 'correct behaviour'. Of the latter the supreme arbiter was the Prince of Wales who, according to Escott, ruled over Society as 'a benevolent despot':

> He wishes it to enjoy itself, to disport itself, to dance, sing, and play to its heart's content. But he desires that it should do so in the right manner, at the right time and in the right places; and of these conditions he holds that he is the best, and, indeed, an infallible judge.[16]

Routine characterised the life of the Prince of Wales — a routine often pleasant, often enlivened by brilliant company, but nonetheless orderly and predictable. Everything had to be done correctly and with propriety. 'He attaches great importance to the ordinances of religion, attends church regularly, digests and criticises the sermon, has a quick eye for the *mise en scène* of the ecclesiastical interior.'[17] This preoccupation with formality assisted the turning of formal observances into shibboleths. It also fostered a variety of hypocrisy. While standards of 'correctness' were applied to public behaviour, quite different standards might be applied to private behaviour. 'Everyone, society argues, has a clear interest in suppressing anything which might lead to social disturbance. Externally therefore, the proprieties must be respected.'[18] But within society, 'they love to parade their own vices', and the sexual irregularities of a Hartington are not held against him.[19]

In this respect there was a tension between the expectations of Society, in which propriety and discretion were ranked highly, and those of Male Society, in which a degree of daring was looked for, and a prowess in matters of drink, sex and sport that involved the risk of impropriety. It was not a difference so much between the expectations of men and of women, as between what both thought admissible in the world of aristocratic males and in the great world where women of their own class were present and where a censorious public looked on. Those like the Prince of Wales who themselves sailed very close to the wind were strongly conscious of such distinctions. There was also a tension between the beneficence expected of the upper class, the reality of which provided the chief of the arguments advanced in favour of social hierarchy, and the very expensive business of maintaining the style of life demanded by their social equals. The latter weighed sufficiently heavily on the upper middle class.[20] In the more claustrophobic world of fashion, 'Society', its view of any given subject, its standards and requirements, the character of its members, tended to become an obsession. On the one hand, therefore, landlords were expected to take a personal interest in their tenants and to provide help in difficult circumstances, and women of the upper class were expected to devote a certain amount of time and money to charity. On the other hand, the one really absorbing subject was 'Society' and it was there that success or failure was to be had. The public service and the acts of charity might become in fact the individual's chief business in life;[21] they could do so only at the cost of a reputation for eccentricity among social equals, and consequent loss of caste. For those whose chief business was 'entertaining and being entertained'[22] such good works tended to become a rather perfunctory appendage to life.

Varieties of Upper-Class Religion

Four types of religious attitude were typical of those in Society and on its fringes around the end of the nineteenth century: the purely conventional, the devout, the intellectual and the sporting. The latter three corresponded to particular upper-class sub-cultures, but they were not so much exclusive categories as tendencies more than one of which might be present in any given individual.

The purely conventional attitude was that which took what 'everyone' did as the sole standard of behaviour, and was oblivious of all considerations of abstract principle. Again, Trollope provides a good example. The scene is Belgravia in the mid-'70s, and Georgiana Longestaffe is discussing with Lady Monogram, her chief authority on the ways of Society, the proposal of marriage she has received from a wealthy Jewish banker named Breghert:

> 'But, really, Julia, when you tell me that Sir Damask cannot
> receive Mr. Breghert, it does sound odd. As for City people, you
> know as well as I do that that kind of thing is all over now. City
> people are just as good as West End people.'
> 'A great deal better, I dare say. I'm not arguing about that. I
> don't make the lines, but there they are; and one gets to know in a
> sort of way where they are. I don't pretend to be a bit better than
> my neighbours. I like to see people come here whom other people
> who come here will like to meet. I'm big enough to hold my own
> and so is Sir Damask. But we ain't big enough to introduce
> new-comers. . . . I go pretty well everywhere, as you are aware, and I
> shouldn't know Mr. Breghert if I were to see him.'

Later, Georgiana puzzles out her own attitude to her intended (for
totally unromantic reasons) marriage, and the rooted objection of her
parents, and, apparently, of Society:

> For herself she regarded the matter not at all, except as far as it
> might be regarded by the world in which she wished to live. She was
> herself above all prejudices of that kind. Jew, Turk, or infidel was
> nothing to her. She had seen enough of the world to know that her
> happiness did not lie in that direction, and could not depend on the
> religion of her husband. Of course, she would go to church herself.
> She always went to church. It was the proper thing to do. As for her
> husband, though she did not suppose that she could ever get him to
> church, – nor perhaps would it be desirable, – she thought that she
> might induce him to go nowhere, so that she might be able to pass
> him off as a Christian.[23]

It was in similar spirit that in the mid-'80s, 'most of the smart people'
went to church, 'to the Chapel Royal, or to St Margaret's, Westminster,
if they belonged to the political set; and many other shrines are
specially set apart for Society's elect.'[24] In this scheme of things, the
duties, pleasures and prescribed ordinances of life were determined by
the impersonal forces of tradition and convention. Religion entered
these in the form of various rites and observances and a certain amount
of charitable activity. For some, as with Trollope's characters, it had no
interest at all in itself. For others who were very conventional, their
religion still had some independent force. An example of this might be
Lady Monkswell, whose diaries extend from her marriage in 1873 until
her husband's death in 1909.

Lady Monkswell was a woman of average intelligence living on the edge of Society, a keen Churchwoman but no zealot. Both she and her husband were children of Liberal MPs. Her father-in-law had become Attorney-General, a Judge, and then a peer, and had built Monkswell House on Chelsea Embankment. As far as her religion is reflected in her published diaries, it is in a horror of scandal and a love of Anglican worship. Wilde, Dilke and Parnell all receive a good kick — though she thought that adultery was pretty small beer compared with Parnell's other sins. She cut off relations with a brother-in-law who went to Norway in order to marry his deceased wife's sister. She was not afraid to lead a church party in company that was often fairly apathetic. For instance, in a large party at Sir George Trevelyan's in 1905, where 'the conversation was extremely brilliant; I chiefly sat and listened and was well amused', 'among these Privy Councillors and Cabinet Ministers, the only church-goers were Lord Goschen and myself'.[25] (Unfortunately, the sermon was in defence of the Athanasian Creed, and Lord Goschen 'snorted a good deal' during it, so they decided not to say anything about the service to the other guests.) In Lady Monkswell's case, we seem to see a religion that is more than a mere convention, though tending at many points to overlap with the social custom of her class, but less than the central unifying principle described in the memoirs of the conspicuously devout, such as George Russell.

There is much in the diaries about awe-inspiring cathedrals, fine musical services, powerful sermons. But there is no idea of the church as a community. For the poor, churches were sources of money, for the middle class they were social centres; but for the upper class they were places of worship first and last. Their community already existed in the form of the branch of Society to which they belonged; moreover life in Society permitted local ties only in the form of patronage. Religion, in spite of the pressure to attend public worship, was a private matter. The emphasis was on beautiful services and private prayer. People in other classes, of uncertain theological orientation, went to church for the sense of community, the Sankey hymns, the pulpit rhetoric. Here they were more likely to see a church as a place of calm for meditation on holy things. The former idea was extroverted and communal, the latter introverted and individualistic. This was the sort of distinction that one of Charles Booth's more aristocratic assistants, George Duckworth, was making when he complained that there was no sense of the 'Presence' in the City Temple.[26] And it was in the same spirit that the agnostic Frederic Harrison could hold that there was no experience equal to evening service at a cathedral,[27] or that an aristocratic memoirist found it easy 'to feel religious in an atmosphere of lovely music and good singing at the Temple Church or at St Paul's Cathedral, or Westminster Abbey, or when I stayed with my uncle, the Hon. James Leigh, at the Deanery at Hereford', although she did not consider herself 'a religious person', and her real love was for fox-hunting.[28] Lord Courtney gave his reasons for attending church regularly in spite of his unorthodox beliefs:

> We go to church and we enter into an atmosphere of calm. The distilled wisdom of the ages is about us. The oldest narrations of human history are read in our hearing . . . The sense that we are at one with the singers of countless generations is an uplifting. Paul's exhortations stimulate our courage. In the teaching and the passion of the gospels we follow the way of perfect life which leads to victory over death. . . . So I remain a church-goer, though it may be my proper place in the outermost court of the Gentiles.[29]

Courtney very seldom felt able to take Communion, and it may be that many members of the upper class attached a special significance to this act, while regarding attendance at services as a social matter or as a means of 'entering into an atmosphere of calm'.[30]

How the religion of many of those moving in similar circles appeared to the Evangelical incumbent of an upper middle-class parish can be seen from his answer to the question, 'Is there any profession of Infidelity among your people?' at the London Visitation in 1883:

> Abundance of that vague but scarcely avowed scepticism which prevails amongst men in the upper and middle classes. The outward morality of the neighbourhood is above the average. Yet there is much latent licentiousness and an increasing tendency to laxity in regard to Sunday observance. I believe that our teaching (I include my own) has been in times past so *indefinite* in regard to what the claim of Christ on our hearts and lives is that it has been possible even for those who have been our constant hearers to remain at ease in a quite unsaved state. . . .Ours is a church-going neighbourhood, though there is not a large amount of religious vitality.[31]

Those who lived in a 'quite saved state' were almost invariably Anglicans or Roman Catholics — though the Congregationalist magnate, Sir Albert Spicer, had much of the outlook of the Anglican squire, and deliberately adopted an upper-class style of life as a challenge to the exclusion of Nonconformists from the higher ranks of the social hierarchy.[32] They included some of those who were socially qualified for membership of Society, but who were excluded by Society's taboo on enthusiasm,[33] and by their own taboo on many of the things that Society took for granted. An extreme case might be Sir Osbert Sitwell's grandmother, a baronet's widow, living with her equally Evangelical daughter and large numbers of servants in Surrey, Scarborough or the family seat in Nottinghamshire. She ran a home for fallen women, a small hospital, a club-room, and a Christmas morning breakfast for postmen; her daughter spent Saturday evenings trying to evangelise a neighbouring gypsy encampment. Even if they had had time for the fashionable round, their strict sabbatarianism[34] and their taboos on such things as theatre and opera would have made life difficult.[35] They therefore kept largely to a circle whose members, mostly clergymen, had views similar to their own, and within which they acted as patrons of the needy and deserving. They remained true members of their own class in the ritualisation of life and their extensive notions of propriety, but the ritual was now charged with religious emotion, and the notions of correct behaviour were supported by religious sanctions.[36] And nothing could be further from the religion even of the more devout members of Society than their insistence on the need for a 'crisis' and the knowledge of having passed from darkness into light.[37]

If the whole way of life of those like Lady Sitwell tended to set them apart from the majority of their class, Anglo- and Roman Catholicism fitted more comfortably into the general upper-class environment. The appeal of Roman worship, Roman Catholicity, and Roman succession from the Apostles was greatest in this class – whereas, most members of the working and middle classes were content, as Arnold complained, to live a hole-in-the-corner provincial existence if they happened to be right, and their own masters. Rome also had a special attraction for reformed rakes, retired courtesans, and so on: while the Christian sailor or the converted coster was almost inevitably an ultra-Protestant, his upper-class equivalent was as certainly a Roman Catholic.[38] The West End boroughs were in fact those with the highest proportions of Catholic worshippers – next to the small borough of Holborn, with its large Irish and Italian population – and such notable Catholic centres as Westminster cathedral, the Brompton Oratory, and the Jesuit church in Mayfair – 'a church for the rich, and especially for propaganda amongst the rich'[39] – were all in the heart of West London.

One aristocratic convert to Catholicism was the Liberal politician, George Russell – though he was converted to the Anglican variety, and his Evangelical parents had been as devout as himself. Like Lady Sitwell he was at home only in 'an atmosphere where the salvation of the individual soul was the supreme and constant concern of life',[40] and he regarded with some hostility 'Smart Society', which 'keeps the sphere of private life absolutely free from the invading forces of religion'.[41] There were however, others 'in Society' with an interest in religion, and personal positions ranging from the undemonstrative High Anglicanism of Lord Salisbury to the Positivism of Frederic Harrison. But constant intercourse with those for whom the individual soul was *not* the chief concern of life, forced on them a degree of detachment and openness to alternative possibilities and points of view of which Lady Sitwell was scarcely capable.

This detachment was, however, combined with a serious interest in religion, and some sort of personal commitment. Detachment became total indifference only in the sporting sub-culture of the upper class. Of this, rather similar pictures are provided in the Beargarden Club of Trollope's *The Way We Live Now*, and in Douglas Sutherland's account of the circle of the fifth Earl of Lonsdale in the '70s and '80s. In the latter, 'bottom' was the chief requirement, and this could be demonstrated by extraordinary feats of drinking, gambling and seduction, by winning improbable bets, and by an attitude of insouciance while taking risks and acting in ways that upset normal ideas of propriety.[42] Lonsdale, like Trollope's Sir Felix Carbury, overstepped the mark, as far as Society in general saw things, and it was only gradually that he rehabilitated himself. On the other hand, the young Lonsdale only represented in extreme form attitudes very similar to those of men at the centre of Society such as the Marquis of Hartington. Lonsdale 'worshipped physical fitness and virility in men. For him life was a matter of the survival of the fittest.'[43] In this scheme of things, ideals were derided, ideas dismissed as tedious speculation; strength was the chief virtue in a man; sexual and social hierarchies were regarded as equally inevitable, and the double standard was vigorously maintained. As Lonsdale's behaviour became more overtly conventional, the double standard found concrete expression in the distinction between his home at Carlton House Terrace where his wife ruled supreme, and only those guests who were acceptable to her found admittance, and the Pelican Club, where he could meet racing and boxing enthusiasts and fellow men of the world.[44] As a 'conventionalist' who 'flouted convention' he was happy to let his wife maintain a more orderly and unexceptionable regime, and as he grew older routine and formality became as much his concern as hers.[45] For the upper-class rake was usually a firm believer in roles – morality was not a matter for humans, to be determined on

general principles, but a matter for old men and young men, men and
women, patron and client, each with standards of correct behaviour
determined by custom. And the contemptuous view of religion as a
matter fit for women and children merged into the 'high esteem' for
'the Church as an institution' that Escott believed to characterise
Society.[46]

On all sides of the upper class — except perhaps the circles of the
conspicuously devout — this respect for the Anglican Church as an
institution, and acceptance of some sort of inherited duty to support it,
combined with a fair degree of anti-clericalism. In the working class this
tended to take the form of rabid hostility, here of superior contempt. A
clerical career, it was held, was most suitable for that member of the
family who was least equipped in body and mind.[47] One stereotype
presented the clergy as industrious, unselfish, and possessing a complete
understanding of the problems of the poor.[48] But an equally common
conception was that of well-meaning but narrow men, whose orthodox
interpretation of Christianity was evidence of their mental rigidity,[49]
and whose strict notions of morality painfully inhibited whatever
company they were in.[50] The views of the Prince of Wales were
probably representative of a large section of his class, though few others
would have dared to express them in his peculiarly brazen way: the
Prince found long church services so intolerable that he and his male
house-guests at Sandringham would arrive half-way through the service,
to the sound of a fresh peal of bells, in time for a sermon that, it was
understood, would not last more than ten minutes.[51] And if the Prince
of Wales represented the Fast Set, the notebooks of Charles Booth and
his associates show that similar views were to be found among the
earnest young. The most active of Booth's collaborators in the
'Religious Influences' series was Arthur Baxter, a barrister educated at
Clifton and Oxford. In his case familiarity with the Church of England
had bred contempt. A curious result of his work for Booth seems to
have been that he left it with his prejudices against the clergy largely
confirmed, but with a degree of respect for Nonconformist ministers.
They were *men*, even if they were not *gentlemen*.[52] After interviewing
ministers of all denominations in Hackney and Islington he reported:
'whatever may be the case elsewhere the Nonconformists here are on
the whole stronger men than the Clergy; am I right in suggesting that as
a body they are more intelligent, better educated and better trained?'[53]
Support for the Church of England was general in West London, and
any other form of explicit religion or irreligion — possibly excepting
Roman Catholicism — highly eccentric. But the attitude to the church

of the church-going class was often highly ambivalent.

Notes

1. A. Trollope, *The Way We Live Now*, OUP, London, 1941, I, p.119, (first published, 1874-5).
2. A Foreign Resident (T. H. S. Escott), *Society in London*, 1885, p.31. In quoting this book twenty-five years later, George Russell referred to the 'Foreign Resident' as 'an anonymous writer, who at the time when his book was published, was generally admitted to know the subjects of which he discoursed'. G. W. E. Russell, *One Look Back*, Wells Gardner, London, 1912, p.125.
3. F. M. L. Thompson has shown how the Earls of Verulam maintained a very high standard of living, in spite of sharply falling rents, between the 1870s and the First World War by buying mining shares and acquiring directorships of a wide range of companies. The 'rush to get peers on the boards' started in the '80s, and he thinks it 'highly likely' that the general movement of landowners to invest in stock exchange securities began at this time. F. M. L. Thompson, *English Landed Society in the Nineteenth Century*, Routledge, London, 1963, pp.303-7.
4. When Jolyon Forsyte visited his son in St John's Wood, 'he looked about him with interest; for this was a district no Forsyte entered without open disapproval and secret curiosity', and he left, walking 'between little rows of houses, all suggesting to him (erroneously no doubt, but the prejudices of a Forsyte are sacred) shady histories of some sort or kind'. J. Galsworthy, *The Man of Property*, Penguin, Harmondsworth, 1951, pp.84, 89. (first published 1906).
5. 'Yet the society in which you will see no one whom after a time you have not seen before is less tedious on the whole than the society in which new faces abound. It is not merely the best, but perhaps the only, the sole society that it is worth taking the trouble to enter. . . . What Bloomsbury was, South Kensington is; and though there are many persons who have recognised position in London society and who live in Queen's Gate and its neighbourhood, you will do well to hesitate before you accept the ordinary invitations that emanate to you from that quarter.' Escott, op.cit., p.116.
6. S. Tweedsmuir, *The Lilac and the Rose*, Duckworth, London, 1952, pp.86-7.
7. The two schools he attended between the ages of thirteen and sixteen were distinguished by, in the one case, 'brazen religiosity' and, in the other, 'pompous mummery and faked emotions', according to M. Holroyd, *Lytton Strachey*, Heinemann, London, 1967-8, I, pp.65, 70, 84.
8. 'As he will periodically come into personal proximity with myself

and my wife, it is, of course, essential that he should be a
gentleman' — Curzon on the qualifications for being vicar of
Kedleston. K. Rose, *Superior Person*, Weidenfeld, London, 1969,
p.95.

9. Though Escott thought that no bishop in the '80s was of Society
in the way that Wilberforce had been. Escott, op.cit., pp.161-2.

10. Webb, op.cit., p.350.

11. J. G. Lockhart, *Cosmo Gordon Lang*, Hodder and Stoughton,
London, 1949, pp.145-6.

12. C. Asquith, *Haply I May Remember*, Barrie, London, 1950,
p.222.

13. W. K. Lowther-Clarke (ed.), *Facing the Facts*, Nisbet, London,
1911, pp.43-5.

14. An added attraction was that Matthew Arnold lived nearby. ('It is
beautiful', wrote Harrison, 'to see him pray'. Harrison—John
Morley, undated letter in Harrison Collection with pencilled on
top 'c. August 20, 1876'). Lytton Strachey's mother had become
a freethinker at nineteen, after reading *On Liberty*, and was also
an advocate of women's rights, a smoker and an expert on
billiards, but she attended church regularly when in the country.
Holroyd, op.cit., pp.20-4.

15. Trollope, op.cit., I.p.194.

16. Escott, op.cit., p.33.

17. Ibid., p.29.

18. Ibid., p.108.

19. Ibid., pp.58-9, 208-9.

20. In 1858, a series of letters to *The Times* discussed the question of
what sort of income a young man should be able to marry on.
Most agreed that 'social position is the touchstone of the matter'.
One correspondent, for instance, granted that £300 a year could
'maintain a young couple in respectability and comfort', but he
denied that 'a young man belonging to a rank in society which
renders him eligible for admission to a West-End club can
maintain a wife of similar rank (to say nothing of a family) on an
income of £300 a year without practically abdicating that
position.' J. A. Banks, *Prosperity and Parenthood*, Routledge,
London, 1954, pp.41-3.

21. S. Gilley notes the asceticism and absorption in charity of such
converts to Rome as the 16th Earl of Shrewsbury and Lady
Georgina Fullerton. Elsewhere he describes the charitable activity
of those Catholic gentry who were less totally committed but
nonetheless had 'a sense of social responsibility'. 'Heretic
London, Holy Poverty and the Irish Poor, 1830-1870', *Downside
Review*, Vol.LXXXIX, no.294, January 1971, p.78; 'English
Catholic Charity and the Irish Poor in London, 1700-1840',
Recusant History, Vol.XI, no.4, January 1972.

22. For a woman in Society in the '70 and '80s, this was, according
to Beatrice Webb, 'The very substance of her life before marriage,
and a large and important part of it after marriage'. Webb, op.cit.,

p.70.
23.   Trollope, op.cit., II, pp.89, 92-3.
24.   Escott, op.cit., pp.162-3. Another of Trollope's characters,
       Lady Carbury 'always went to church when she was in the
       country, never when she was at home in London. It was one of
       those moral habits, like early dinners and long walks, which
       suited country life, and she fancied that were she not to do so,
       the bishop would be sure to know of it and would be displeased.
       She liked the bishop. She liked bishops generally; and was aware
       that it was a woman's duty to sacrifice herself to society. As to
       the purpose for which people go to church, it had probably never
       in her life occurred to Lady Carbury to think of it'. Trollope,
       op.cit., I, p.158.
25.   Collier, *A Victorian Diarist, 1895-1909*, p.101.
26.   Booth Collection, A42.4, p.21.
27.   F. Harrison, *The Creed of a Layman*, Macmillan, London, 1907,
       p.9.
28.   V. Hardy, *As It Was*, Johnson, London, 1958, pp.117, 185-6.
29.   [L. H. Courtney], *The Diary of a Church-Goer*, Macmillan,
       London, 1904 [published anonymously], pp.224-5.
30.   L. Courtney, op.cit., p.70. Cf R. Jenkins, *Sir Charles Dilke*,
       Collins, London, 1958, p.24: 'In the course of 1863 I ceased my
       attendance on Holy Communion, and fell into a sceptical frame
       of mind which lasted several years, was modified in 1874, and
       came to an end in 1875. ... From 1885 to 1888 the Holy
       Sacrament was a profound blessing to me, but in 1905 I ceased
       again to find any help in forms.'
31.   Reply of the Vicar of St. Thomas', Paddington, London
       Visitation, 1883.
32.   Spicer, born into a wealthy family of wholesale stationers in 1847,
       moved in 1893 from Woodford Green to Bayswater, where he
       had a butler, coachmen and footmen. *Albert Spicer 1847-1934. A
       Man of his Time*, pp.16-17, 23-4.
33.   According to Escott, op.cit., p.181, 'to talk politics, to proclaim
       one's own political faith and argue against one's opponents when
       politicians are off duty, is looked upon as a mark of the
       enthusiast, and in London society the enthusiast is considered to
       be only one degree less intolerable, if even that, than the bore.'
34.   Escott reported (op.cit., pp.162-3) that by 1885 London still
       appeared to be 'the only capital of Europe entirely given over to
       the rule of Sabbatarianism', but that Sunday dinner parties were
       now universal in Society, and that the behaviour of the upper
       class was much less restrained in private than in public.
35.   Sitwell, I, pp.154-5. Sitwell's grandmother, who was born about
       1830, attended her last opera in 1857. The music was 'delicious',
       but 'there were many things that shocked and offended me'. It
       seems to have been the licentious associations of the stage, rather
       than worldly amusements as such, to which she objected. She
       remained a devotee of the Romantic composers, and a keen

reader of poetry, and of political and philosophical books (except on Sundays).

36. Lady Sitwell 'would tolerate no least evasion of propriety or respect, either due to herself or to others'. Ibid., I, p.156; II, pp.89-91.
37. Ibid., I, p.153.
38. Skittles Walters was the outstanding example. She claimed in fact to have been brought up as a Catholic, though this aspect of her personality remained concealed until fairly late in her career.
39. Booth, op.cit., III, iii, p.100.
40. Russell, op.cit., pp.11-12.
41. G. W. E. Russell, *An Onlooker's Notebook*, Smith Elder, London, 1902, pp.174-5.
42. D. Sutherland, *The Yellow Earl*, Cassell, London, 1965, pp.21-2.
43. Ibid., p.29.
44. Ibid., p.91.
45. Ibid., pp.54, 152-4.
46. Escott, op.cit., pp.162-3.
47. These attitudes were shared even by some members of the clergy. Of the two Deptford clergymen who made the best impression on A. L. Baxter, one refused to attend clerical conferences because of the nonsense that was spoken, and the other described the clergy as 'so bigoted', 'amazingly unwise', Booth Collection, B284, pp.21, 43.
48. As in P. Lyttelton Gell's pamphlet, *Work for University Men In East London*, 1884, (Toynbee Hall Collection, 9): 'I have seen something of the noble life lived by the East End Clergy – I am not going to say lived only by the clergy – but it is they who in their official position bear the burden and heat of the day . . . '.
49. *Daily Telegraph* editorial (29 August 1905) on diocesan conferences: 'A number of blameless clergymen, very earnest and devout, but also very narrow, make statements no doubt valuable to those who admit their premisses and sympathise with their mode of interpreting life, but almost meaningless to others whom they would stigmatise as worldly, but who are, at all events, more experienced and more tolerant . . . .'
50. Thus Escott (op.cit., pp.137-8) compared two leading lawyers, Sir Henry Hawkins and Lord Justice Coleridge, in these terms: Hawkins who dined at the Turf Club, had 'no wish to pose as a latter-day edition of a father of the early Christian Church, a Greek sophist, or a medieval anchorite', while Coleridge tended to dine 'with prelates' or with 'titled laymen more severe in their notions than the prelates themselves.'
51. P. Magnus, *Edward the Seventh*, John Murray, London, 1964, p.78.
52. The exotic nature of Nonconformity for someone with Baxter's background is illustrated by the interview quoted in Chapter V, beginning: 'I had never before consciously met a Deacon in the flesh . . . ' (Booth Collection, B183, p.95).
53. Booth Collection, A37, Report on districts 14 and 16, pp.73-4.

The theme of 'lost certainties' was recurrent in the late nineteenth century. Matthew Arnold was only one of many who looked back to some assumed, though unspecified, time, when the 'Sea of Faith' was full, and contrasted their own bleak disenchantment with the blissful ignorance of their ancestors. The years of complacent confidence were usually assumed to be fairly recent. Charles Masterman, in 1909, quoted Bishop Gore to the effect that 'some thirty years ago' there had been 'a sort of Protestant religion, with a doctrine of the Trinity, of Heaven and Hell, of Atonement and Judgement, of Resurrection and Eternal Life, which for good or evil could be more or less assumed', but that now 'religious opinions are in complete chaos'.[1] Masterman, like everyone else, looked around for reasons. He argued that: 'Fear, which is the beginning of wisdom no longer terrifies a society which, seeing orderly arrangements everywhere, accepts the secure as the normal.'[2] Some, in rather similar vein, saw 'chaos' as self-indulgent evasion of duty, while others welcomed it as an inevitable result of advancing knowledge.[3] But whether they looked back nostalgically to an 'Age of Faith' when there was a moral and dogmatic consensus, or whether they celebrated humanity's escape from error, nearly everyone believed that such a consensus had once existed, and most believed it to be desirable – granted only that it were founded on truth. Yet it could equally be argued that if the great majority of people are agreed on any matter of importance, this is a sign not that the present state of knowledge demands such agreement, but that legal or social pressures are limiting what is thinkable.

Religion and the State: Coercion

From the seventh to the nineteenth century, such authoritarian and hierarchical versions of Christianity as fitted the requirements of the state were in England used as instruments of political discipline, and any deviation from the current orthodoxy was subject to official harassment. Until the seventeenth century, hanging or burning was the fate of large numbers of heretics. In the eighteenth century they were no longer hanged, or even, in more than a few cases, imprisoned, but they were still denied the rights of citizens. And when, in the 1790s and the decades following infidelity became deeply rooted in the radical working class, the persecution of blasphemers as presumed organisers of sedition revived.[4] Neither uniform orthodoxy nor any kind of personal faith could be imposed by such means. But such means could ensure that heresies remained localised, largely inarticulate and generally private. The effect of a religious terror that is being pursued from similar motives in our own day has been described by an Englishman who spent a year at Moscow University. He found students who took a cynical view of all they were told; students who clung defiantly to beliefs condemned by those in authority; even students who instinctively adopted anything they were told to reject. But such rebellions remained incoherent and even non-rational, as the rebels had little or no access to alternative systems of ideas, and little opportunity of discussing their doubts with other people.[5] The English Ecclesiastical Courts, whatever may have been the case in, for instance, Louis XIV's France,[6] were scarcely in the same league as their Soviet equivalents. In the remoter parts of England, in the sixteenth, seventeenth and eighteenth centuries, pre-Christian customs survived in isolation from the state and its priests, and it is unlikely that many people attended any sort of church until the arrival of the Methodists. Among the rural poor of South and East many of the same customs may have survived, together with a good deal of anti-clericalism, in combination with external conformity to the official religion.[7] The point, however, is not that the officially imposed doctrines were generally known or believed, but that the suppression of all alternative systems of belief made it difficult for heterodoxy to develop beyond a vague scepticism. The official formulae received the status of that which none but a few outcasts had openly challenged. Nagging doubts might persist, but it was difficult to conceive of any very developed alternative. Such systematic heterodoxy as existed usually took a Christian, or at least deistic form, an overt denial of God in a Christian state being no more possible than overt denial of socialism in a Marxist-Leninist state. The 1640s and '50s showed that radical critiques of the state-imposed orthodoxy could develop fast enough in conditions of freedom, and given the stimulus of social upheaval. Just as in the Reformation period, artisan sects proliferated, with common tendencies to political and religious democracy, the abolition of property, pacifism and universalism.[8] After 1660, they were pushed underground once more. Their ideas only survived through the medium of a modified Quakerism, and these ideas still had the power to shock when revived by Unitarians and Secularists in the nineteenth century. Even so, their rationalism and humanitarianism, though less frequently their democratic principles, were gaining increasing favour among the educated in the late seventeenth century.

Religion and Society: Informal Pressure

Nowhere could this be better seen than in the changing status of the doctrine of hell. Denied by Anabaptists, Socinians, Ranters, Quakers, it had been reaffirmed as vigorously by Luther and Calvin as by the Catholic Church.[9] By the late seventeenth century many of the older arguments for hell had been discredited: the idea that the happiness of the blessed was enhanced by their contemplation of the just sufferings of the damned was 'almost obsolete', and the torment of unbaptised infants was a possibility vehemently repudiated even by many of those who accepted the torment of adults.[10] Not only artisan sectaries but Anglican bishops and Dutch Calvinists were now beginning to doubt that *anyone* could be subjected to everlasting punishment. But 'secrecy and dishonesty'[11] still surrounded the debate. Some, like Locke, who were known by their friends to deny the doctrine, did not publish their opinions on this subject; and Thomas Burnet who published his opinions in Latin, argued that 'the populace', 'which is inclined to vice and can be deterred from evil only by the fear of punishment', should still be threatened with hell.[12] Although religious liberalisers were restrained by a fear of the political concomitants of their theology, their ideas obtained wide currency throughout the Protestant world in the course of the eighteenth century. While the educated were frequently converted to deist or sceptical views, a pelagian theology was increasingly adopted by the clergy.[13] In the seventeenth century, heterodoxy of many kinds had flourished in the relatively free atmosphere of Holland; by the late eighteenth century, even the Spanish government was finding it hard to stop the flow of heretical books from abroad.[14]

The tide turned in the last years of the eighteenth century. In France 'philosophical' views of religion, whether Liberal Christian, deist or atheist, became entrenched at every social level, except perhaps that of the aristocracy, during the civil war of the 1790s.[15] In Britain, the United States and Scandinavia, on the other hand, the 'Awakenings' converted whole communities to Evangelical Protestantism, and won a dominant influence over the culture of the middle and upper classes.

About 1800, numbers of these brought up in eighteenth-century rationalism were undergoing spiritual crises and adopting Evangelical principles.[16] Revivalist preaching was converting groups previously little touched by organised religion, Cornish miners, Lapps, Scottish Highlanders.[17] In the same year, 1796, that McGready began preaching in Kentucky, Hauge started in Norway, and four years later Laestidius, whose followers were to form the largest body of Free Churchmen in Scandinavia, began his work in Northern Sweden.[18] Equally international was the conversion of the educated and the upper classes: the success of the Clapham Sect in England was paralleled by the conversion of a third of the student body at Yale in 1802, and by the circles of Pietist nobility in Pomerania, such as that to which Bismarck belonged in the 1840s.[19]

No satisfactory account has yet been offered of the origins of this movement. The explanations commonly offered in terms of the reaction against the French Revolution or the particular economic circumstances of individual countries scarcely allow for the movement's scope, however much these factors may have affected its local forms. It is easier to explain the peculiar force that the movement developed. All successful movements have a coercive aspect: as they increase in numbers pressure begins to be directed at those who are not yet members, but might be; suddenly they find that all their neighbours are saying the same things, that the papers they trust are continually arguing a particular case — their ability to argue the contrary gradually dissolves until willy-nilly they are drawn in too. It is in such an atmosphere that political parties move within a very short period from the periphery to the centre, and in similar, though more subtle ways, new shibboleths, be they temperance in the 1830s or population control in the 1970s, establish their sway over classes and communities. But if all successful movements are coercive, Evangelicalism was more so than most. It limited the intellectual alternatives open to the potential convert by filling his mind with the question of his own Salvation, with the absolute need for personal religious experience, and with the hell that lay in the background. And what internal compulsion could not achieve might be brought about by the appeals of parents and fiancées, the finger-pointing of neighbours or the mass emotion of revivalist meetings in communities where the unconverted could become marked men.[20] Legal pressure against religious deviants was by now relatively limited, and where it was attempted it was no longer very effective. Social pressure could, however, become intolerable.[21]

In spite of the attempts in England from the 1790s onwards to use the law to hinder the distribution of anti-religious literature to working-class radicals, legal repression was powerless to stop such literature reaching radical working men, superfluous if intended to protect other sections of society. From the 1790s there was a large section of the population deeply hostile to all the established institutions of society. Governments could harass its members, plant police spies to report on their conversations, imprison the more prominent among them — but they could not destroy them; and as long as this large radical sub-culture survived, it provided a medium for the diffusion of every kind of dissenting idea, including deism and atheism. If the majority of the working class were protected against such ideas by a lack of interest in systems or abstractions of whatever kind, the majority of the middle and upper classes were protected by the gulf that divided respectability from unrespectability, and ensured that whatever was said in one world was not heard in the other. For the first seventy years of the nineteenth century overt heterodoxy within the respectable world was largely limited to fairly isolated intellectual and radical circles; elsewhere it was private and seldom publicised. There was a stigma attaching even to Unitarianism.[22]

The effects of the religious revival were most far-reaching in small and relatively isolated communities, where Evangelical Protestantism might come to pervade the whole atmosphere, and almost the entire population could be in some degree influenced.[23] Elsewhere, converts were likely to be in a minority, but 'respectability' was the instrument through which a facade of uniformity could be maintained. As the concept of respectability became more democratic, admitting of a measure of earned status, so it became more morally exclusive, and those who failed to conform with certain standards were threatened with a loss of caste. For a large part of the working class, born with very little status in a society that remained, in spite of the ideologists of opportunity, highly stratified, such a threat meant very little; there were also, perhaps, a few of the aristrocracy whose inherited status rendered them indifferent to such sanctions. But for most of the upper and middle classes, as well as the more prosperous section of the working class, the fear of loss of status enforced at least outward conformity to the dictates of respectability. For most of the nineteenth century, these included decorous behaviour on the Sabbath, including, preferably, attendance at church. Its concomitants were listed by J. W. Croker in 1843, in an article welcoming 'the visible, and we trust, substantial increase of religious feeling which has recently developed itself so extensively and vigorously among the members of the Established Church':

> The more willing adhesion to reverential forms — the more exact observance, both public and domestic of the Sabbath — the growing disfavour and discouragement of profane or even idle amusements — the spread, we had almost said the fashionable vogue, of religious literature, and the diffusion of, if we may venture to employ a metaphor on such an occasion, a kind of Christian tint over the general aspect of society.[24]

The movement was 'vigorous' and 'substantial', but at the same time the 'tint' was often no more than a tint. Those who became 'serious' were numerous,[25] but there were far more who partially adapted their habits and thoughts to the new seriousness without becoming fully converted to Evangelical religion. For many people, whether Evangelicals themselves or merely worshippers of propriety, conformity in externals was better than none at all. Both therefore conspired to encourage forms of religion that were often very superficial, and might be positively hypocritical.

This phase of English Christianity, in which the majority of the middle and upper classes attended church regularly, observed Sunday, and adhered at least nominally to the basic Evangelical doctrines (even though most had not experienced conversion), lasted for about three generations. While it lasted there were many forces combining to keep the potential deviant in line. Of these the most basic was the gossip of social equals. There were many of those like Reardon's mother-in-law in *New Grub Street* who was terrified when her daughter, Amy, separated from Reardon (although she never liked him) because:

> Like her multitudinous kind, Mrs. Yule lived only in the opinions of other people. What others would say was her ceaseless preoccupation. She had never conceived of life as something proper to the individual; independence in the directing of one's course seemed to her only possible in the case of very eccentric persons, or of such as were altogether out of society. Amy had advanced, intellectually, far beyond this standpoint, but lack of courage disabled her from acting on her convictions.[26]

More subtle, because strictly self-imposed were the pressures arising from the individual's sense of his social position and of what this required in terms of setting an example. Thus the Evangelical vicar of a South London parish, incidentally exemplifying the tendency of many believers to look for the forms of religion even where the substance was lacking, looked back in these terms from 1912 with its shrunken congregations to the crowded churches of earlier days:

> Amongst my earliest recollections is the delightful sight of heads of families accompanying their children to church and worshipping together in the family pew. Even in those cases where religious convictions were not very deep they thought it their duty to attend church, if only to set an example to their children and servants. Husbands and wives, realising the uncertainty of life and the shortness of the time they might be permitted to spend together, would make a practice of kneeeling side by side in the house of God, and mingling their prayers at the mercy seat.[27]

But the crucial role in the system of control was that of women. In those societies where the status of a family depends on the chastity of its individual members, it is female chastity that is required, while attitudes to male chastity are much more ambivalent.[28] Similarly in nineteenth-century England it was the women of the middle and upper classes whose religious orthodoxy was most carefully watched,[29] the women who determined the tone of the home – to which the head of the household (who might behave quite differently when with other men) conformed[30] – and the women who passed on the approved religion to the next generation. In some families husband and wife adhered whole-heartedly to the same standards. But in many others some sort of compromise was reached between the newer conceptions of morals and mores and older values based on the double standard. Men drank, swore and womanised in the company of other men, but would still have been shocked by any public avowal of habits they willingly admitted in private. Women accepted the role of upholders of purity, but still expected their sons to adhere to the stereotype of the virile aggressive male. The public standards of behaviour, however, were those of which women were the guardians. The chief embodiment of this compromise between an ideal of uniform piety and the only half-admitted reality was the English Sunday. The Sabbath lay at the heart of the Christianity born of the Evangelical Revival and its due observance, at least in externals,[31] provided the clearest test of respectability. For Evangelicals the Sabbath was not only a divine institution. It was also a symbol: it was the day on which the members of the family reaffirmed their common commitment to God and to one another; it was the day on which they worshipped in the same 'family pew', the day of the Sunday Dinner, a meal that had a ritual character even for those who had not worshipped together first,[32] of hymns round the piano after tea. Thus E. H. Bickersteth linked 'the Holy Day of Rest binding men to God' with 'Holy Marriage, the bond of human love' as one of the 'two sacred ordinances that have come down to us from Eden';[33] and when R. F. Horton, sent by his Nonconformist parents to Shrewsbury, reported on the numerous repellent aspects of life at the school – games, Latin and Greek verse, drink and swearing, Toryism – his mother wrote back: 'and in Christian England to spend such Sundays must lead to misery and danger'.[34] Similarly, the general observance of Sunday, imposed if necessary by force, became the means by which 'reformers of manners' could assure themselves that 'Christian England' still was 'Christian'. And this was where a celebration meaningless except to the convinced Evangelical became an empty symbol of compulsory conformism. Unsabbatarian working men simply ignored the demands of 'Christian England', and, except in the matter of public house opening hours, there was little that the law could do, hard as it might try, to limit their freedom.[35] But the middle-class rebel was much more effectively coerced by public opinion than the working-class rebel by the law. Thus the scene in *Born in Exile* where Sunday becomes a symbol of the oppression both of deviants by the respectable majority and of everyone by convention. Alone, in his Exeter lodgings, the hero reflects on his status as a life-long 'lodger':

> Was he never to win a right of citizenship, never to have a recognised place among men associated in the duties and pleasures of life?
> Sunday was always a day of weariness and despondency. . . . Until mid-day he lay in bed. After dinner, finding the solitude of his little room intolerable, he went out to walk in the streets.
> Not far from his door some children had gathered in a quiet corner, and were playing at a game on the pavement with pieces of chalk. As he drew near, a policeman, observing the little group, called out to them in a stern voice:
> 'Now then! What are you doing there? Don't you know *what day* it is?'
> The youngsters fled, conscious of a shameful duty. There it was! There spoke the civic voice, the social rule, the public sentiment! Godwin felt that the policeman had rebuked him, and in so doing had severely indicated the cause of that isolation which he was condemned to suffer. Yes, all his life he had desired to play games on a Sunday; he had never been able to understand why games on a

Sunday should be forbidden. And the angry laugh that escaped him as he went by the guardian of public morals, declared the impossibility of his ever being at one with communities which made this point the prime test of worthiness.[36]

There were many other members of the middle and upper classes who shared this desire to 'play games on Sundays', but being less socially isolated than Godwin Peak, or than Gissing, they accepted without complaint the dictates of convention, and perhaps did not even consider the possibility that convention could be changed.[37]

If the observance of Sunday was the prime symbol of the ostensible religious consensus within the respectable world, and a convention that anyone with claims to respectability defied at his peril, there were other formal observances which became important parts of middle- and upper-class life. In small quantities they betokened a proper regard for the proprieties; in larger quantities a piety beyond that demanded by mere convention, and on a scale that the merely conventional might find embarrassing. Besides attending church more or less frequently,[38] these included saying Grace at meals and the holding of family prayers. Thus in 1901, when customs had changed, George Russell looked back to his childhood, when 'religious people regarded church-going as a spiritual privilege, but everyone recognised it as a civil duty', and when Sunday observance in 'Society' was 'universal'.[39]

But these were no more than outward signs. Ostensibly they betokened a reality of uniform 'orthodoxy' and of Christian living beneath the surface of formal observances. In fact, large numbers of those who behaved with propriety in public had no intention of adopting any form of Christian morality, and their theology, though less well-defined than their morality, could not be reduced to the same sort of uniformity as their public observance of Sunday. The essentials of 'orthodoxy', distinguishing it from 'unorthodox' forms of Christianity were the fall of man, the divinity of Christ, man's redemption through Christ's atoning death, the inspiration as a whole and in every detail of the Bible, and the everlasting torment of sinners. Thus Tractarians, though quite possibly objectionable on other grounds, were not 'unorthodox', but many varieties of liberal Protestant, and most notably Unitarians, who could be cruelly ostracised, were. On the other hand, there were many 'respectable' people who had private doubts about aspects of 'orthodoxy' and many more who accepted it only in a fairly passive spirit.

Thus the 70 per cent of Oxford undergraduates whom Taine claimed to be 'Broad Churchmen' would probably have sympathised with F. D. Maurice rather than with the authorities of King's College, with the authors of *Essays and Reviews* rather than with those who prosecuted them; like Taine, they would probably have attached more importance to 'ethics' than to 'ritual and dogma'.[40] They would have enjoyed satire at the expense of Stiggins and Chadband, but they would not on this account have voiced public disagreement with any of the 'orthodox' doctrines, or have shown much sympathy for atheists or even for Unitarians. Between the small minority of rebels in the respectable classes and the larger minority of those deeply attached to some form of 'orthodox' religion, were large numbers of those who were not very 'serious' or very intellectual, but who were good citizens and good Christians in their own way. Their latent dissatisfaction with the prevailing religion only began to find overt expression in the last quarter of the century.

Latent Dissatisfaction

The latent dissatisfactions are easy enough to find, and acknowledged by those writing from every point of view in the middle decades of the century. Trollope, for instance, tended even to exaggerate the purely formal character of the religion (and the total lack of Christian feeling or principle) in most of the gentry families that he described.[41] In such circles the one point of reference was 'everyone', meaning the arbiters of correct behaviour within their own little clique of Society. Even where religious convictions rested on slightly less ephemeral found-ations, overt piety, or almost any public observance beyond the obligatory church attendance might cause a certain degree of embarrass-ment. Thus Mary Vivian Hughes remembered the discomfort which family prayers caused the barrister father of a school-friend when she stayed in their Camden Road house in the early '80s. This family gathering was 'conducted in the same off-hand style in which he used to look into his hat for a few moments before the Service in the Temple', and took the form of 'a few short prayers mumbled so hastily that I had the impression of his being ashamed to bother the Almighty and that he was hoping not to secure attention'. Like Mrs. Hughes' own father, an equally undemonstrative Anglican, he disliked Non-conformists because of 'an objection to anything openly perfervid in the religious line'.[42] The point was that many people whose religion played a fairly small part in their lives and who found certain parts of it oppressive, nonetheless considered it to be a social necessity, and were certainly far from any kind of heterodoxy.

It was the 'objection to anything openly perfervid' and the sense of 'discomfort'[43] involved in the various observances required and prohibitions imposed by the dominant religion of the mid-nineteenth century that represented the greatest area of latent dissatisfaction. But the weakest link of the religious consensus was the doctrine of hell. For here those who were 'serious', 'unserious', or neither could join hands. The idea that *anyone* should consciously suffer a punishment that was to last for all eternity was disturbing, often agonising, even for those who felt obliged to believe it.[44] The fact that those destined for such a fate included not only 'murderers and a person who had destroyed a girl's character',[45] but 'saints of rationalism' such as J. S. Mill, and the adherents of Judaism, Hinduism and Buddhism en masse, made it an issue of justice, as well as of humanitarian scruple. Yet the prestige of hell was also a matter of priorities. Its renewed power in all Protestant countries between about 1790 and 1850 was not accompanied by a general slackening of humanitarian feeling. On the contrary, those who were involved in the revival of Evangelical religion were also, in many cases, involved in campaigns against slavery, and for legal reform and factory control. But they were even more involved in preaching the authority of the Bible, and above all, the awfulness of sin, and the necessity for conversion to God. They were thus inclined to accuse those who doubted the possibility of eternal torment of minimising the seriousness of sin, and of a generally frivolous outlook. If the Unitarians, in the pamphlet warfare of the early nineteenth century, accused their opponents of inhumanity, and of creating a God in their own repulsive image, the Evangelicals claimed that the critics of hell were 'altogether men of the world', who 'spent most of their evenings in cards' and 'seldom conversed in religious topics',[46] or they accused them of having a very low idea of heaven — 'for they march up to its doors proclaiming "We are worthy." '[47] So, if many of the arguments that had been used to justify hell had been discredited before 1700, the doctrine was likely to be revived at times when the otherness of God, the hopelessness of the human condition, and the necessity for the experience of conversion were the main burden of Christian preachers.[48] Thus the decline of hell in the second half of the nineteenth century reflected a more optimistic view of human capacity, a broader conception of the sacred, and a more sceptical view of the personal experience of God that was the central concern of Evangelicalism.[49]

The fear of hell had been one of the chief means by which revivalists had secured mass conversions and doubters were induced to 'put themselves right with God'. Only a coercive form of religion, maintaining its influence by the imposition of social penalties in this world, and threats of very much worse in the world to come could maintain the external religious uniformity that prevailed in most Protestant countries in the middle decades of the nineteenth century. Those who had doubts on the subject of hell did not usually care to voice them publicly. It involved the emotions in a way that made rational discussion difficult. Anyone who denied the ultimate deterrent was open to charges both of amorality and political subversion.[50] Thus 'secrecy and dishonesty' continued to surround the debate in the nineteenth century. Certainly, in religious circles, unless they were conspicuously liberal, the eternal punishment at least of some tended to be assumed at least until the '70s, even if it were regretted. The part played by the belief in people's lives varied considerably. Some parents considered frequent reference to the fires of hell to be an essential part both of religious education and of household discipline.[51] On the other hand, many of those who had an Evangelical upbringing in the second half of the nineteenth century stress the benevolent character of the religion of their childhood, and the tendency for hell, though accepted in principle, to be pushed into the background, whether because as E. E. Kellett, the son of a Wesleyan minister, suggests, they privately hoped that no one would actually go there,[52] or, as in Basil Martin's Congregationalist family, 'All the emphasis was laid on the love of God in providing a means of escape'.[53] Of course, in a household like that in which Mary Vivian Hughes grew up in the '70s, where they 'did not take religion *too* seriously', it is unlikely that hell was mentioned at all.[54]

There was an old woman in Basil Martin's congregation at Hereford who remembered the day in the 1840s when Edward White, then minister at the church, had first expounded his doctrine of conditional immortality:

> She recalled the discussions afterwards at dinner, and how, while her parents were expressing their amazement and horror, her heart leaped for joy that she need no longer think that people were going to suffer an eternity of misery in hell.[55]

At that time, most Congregationalists took the same view as the woman's parents, and White's *Life in Christ*, published in 1845, was coldly received.[56] Meanwhile, revulsion from the doctrine was playing an important part in the 'conversions' of many working-class Secular-ists,[57] and in the growing doubts of J. A. Froude and F. W. Newman.[58] Yet, in spite of the stir caused in some circles by *Essays and Reviews*,[59] and the prosecution of one of the contributors, the Rev. H. B. Wilson for, among other things, his denial of everlasting torment,[60] it was only in the 1870s that 'secrecy and dishonesty' became things of the past, and hell was attacked by those to whom 'respectable' people would listen. Of these, the most widely popular was F. W. Farrar, whose sermons in 1877, published the year after as *Eternal Hope*, revealed the existence of large numbers of people who, like the woman in Hereford, had previously kept their hopes to themselves. The sermons provoked both a hostile reply from Pusey and a large, and mostly favourable correspondence.[61] One London corres-pondent wrote that: 'there is no one thing which oppresses the mind of thoughtful men at the present day more than the popular idea that Christianity is committed to the affirmation of the everlasting damnation of the overwhelming majority of mankind. . . . It is one of the most fruitful sources of modern unbelief.'[62] And even among the Baptists, soon to be known as the chief remaining champions of hell, there were now some who doubted or denied eternal torment.[63]

Within a few years, a sermon in favour of hell would provoke as much surprise (unless it were preached in a church with a special reputation for old-fashioned views) as a sermon against hell (in any but a notably advanced church) might have done twenty years before. When in 1884 the Nottingham congregation of the Baptist universalist, Samuel Cox, made their minister a presentation, they noted 'a marked change of religious thought' in the seven years since the publication of his *Salvator Mundi*.[64] From the late '70s the taboo on discussion of the subject was broken, and the change of opinion was indeed rapid. Thus the surprise of the Hampstead man just returned from holiday in Scotland in September 1886:

> There was something very refreshing in the English service after the dry formality of some of the Scotch services at which I had recently been present; but I was certainly not prepared to hear the doctrine of everlasting punishment so glibly laid down in the heart of liberal London. Had this view been expressed in the northern land from which I had just returned, I should have regarded it as the legitimate result of the parson's upbringing, but surely one may look for something different to this from our modern English clergy?[65]

The Consensus Breaks Down

If, as Marx suggested, the criticism of religion was the beginning of the criticism of society, hell occupied an analogous position within Evangelical Christianity. It was a bold man who said that the pit from which every converted sinner had been saved had never been there at all; but once the first step had been taken the rest was comparatively easy. Depose personal salvation from its position as the central concern of every Christian and the way was prepared for a reconsideration of every orthodox doctrine. 'The orthodox hell', as D. P. Walker shows, 'has its strong and its weak points.'[66] The fact that within any given milieu at any particular point in time the doctrine has tended to be generally accepted or generally repudiated arises from the exclusive consideration of one side of the case. As the doctrine revived in the early nineteenth century and gained at least the passive acceptance of most of the 'respectable' classes, certain scriptural texts (notably Matthew XXV) were held to clinch the matter, critics of hell were accused of a frivolous view of the divine justice, and in social terms they could be branded as morally dubious. As with equal rapidity it declined in the last quarter of the century it became generally accepted that hell was an immoral means of cajoling people into a self-interested virtue, and that it was incompatible with the divine love, while an equally coercive public opinion branded those who still upheld the doctrine as misanthropic bigots.

For some the questioning of hell was the beginning of the process that led to more liberal forms of Christianity. For others, like Susan Budd's working-class Secularists, it was the beginning of the dissolution of all religious beliefs. Thus, in the Do We Believe? correspondence published in the *Daily Telegraph* in 1904, one writer claimed that his reaction against hell-fire preaching had led him to discover 'the impossibilities and contradictions in the Bible';[67] and in W. L. Courtney's selection of letters, hell was the most widely quoted objection to Christianity. It was actually mentioned in eleven out of ninety letters in which specific criticisms were made, and an objection to hell was also implicit in those letters which defended the moral and spiritual qualities of agnostics, Hindus, Buddhists, etc.[68]

But the most significant conclusion to be drawn from this correspondence was that the majority whose beliefs were not altogether clearly defined could not be coerced by a threat that was no longer credible. 'If', wrote one contributor, 'there be a God of Justice and of Love, He will not condemn me to everlasting torment or any unendurable retribution because I am unable to convince myself of His reality, and so lack the comfort and moral strength which that conviction would inspire'.[69] Arguments both for and against Christianity usually assumed not the inexorable divine justice of the Evangelical scheme or the Tractarians' impassable barrier between the sinner and a Holy God, but a God who was easy-going and made allowances. It was Pascal's wager in reverse: enjoy yourself; if there is no God, you have had a good run for your money, and if there is, he would do the same in your place.

The foundations of this humanitarian optimism lay more in new unargued assumptions than in new knowledge. H. R. Murphy and Susan Budd have shown relatively isolated individuals questioning 'orthodox' tenets that conflicted with their ethical assumptions, and only subsequently discovering the scientific basis for an alternative system. In the '80s and '90s, when rebels against 'orthodoxy' were seldom so isolated the abolition of hell no longer required an anguished search for scriptural support: it was being announced on all sides, and accordingly was accepted gladly and with scarcely a thought for the arguments that had seemed so weighty to the previous generation. And as the taboo on the public expression of heterodox opinions lost its power and the 'orthodox' consensus broke down, mere lack of conviction tended to become Doubt. 'Doubt' was not necessarily related to intellectual advance: it was an inevitable product of the new freedom of religious debate. Where debate is severely restricted simple faith tends to coexist with an incoherent scepticism. Where a variety of opinions are freely canvassed simple faith cannot flourish, and incoherent scepticism may give way to a conscious relativism. Any doctrine claiming exclusive validity is then open to both the charge of inhumanity, and to the counter-assertion that knowledge is in continual progress and that creeds must progress with it. In the late nineteenth century both human and natural sciences were, indeed, making spectacular progress. But the criticism of Christianity depended less on new discoveries than on arguments of an *a priori* nature, often current for a century or more.

This tendency can be also illustrated from the Do We Believe? controversy. Out of ninety letters in Courtney's selection that made specific criticisms of Christianity, there were forty-six in which these criticisms could be termed 'scientific' — eleven of these being sociological or anthropological, two being textual (arising from inconsistencies in the Bible) and the rest of a philosophical nature, or drawn from some knowledge of the natural sciences. But in many cases these rested on assumptions about, rather than conclusions from, the sciences. Thus, six letters considered that religious beliefs were sufficiently condemned by being termed 'anthropomorphic'; seven condemned those who believed what they could not prove; six asserted a general objection to miracle; one singled out for criticism the concept of free will; and six asserted that creeds improve as knowledge advances, and none, therefore, can claim absolute validity. This tendency to produce arguments which claimed to be drawn from science, but were in fact *a priori* assertions, can be seen in a letter from an undergraduate at Hertford College, Oxford, which could have been a composite production, combining in slightly incongruous fashion the most representative arguments from each of the contributors to the correspondence.

The argument ran as fellows: no one knows anything about 'the Deity' beyond the fact that he is 'an absolute being', 'absolutely free' from human limitations; it would in any case, be 'impertinent' to offer him 'our puny advice on the government of the Cosmos'; all conceptions of God are merely reflections of current modes of thought, and will change as these change; if God is good, he cannot, having made his creatures as they are, condemn any of them; free will is an absurd delusion in a world where everything is governed by 'the inevitable working of natural laws'; the idea of a Fall is inconsistent with the evolutionary story of 'a long and painful struggle upwards'; the ideas of Incarnation and Resurrection are found in 'mythologies far older than Christianity'; the good should be done for its own sake and not for hope of ultimate reward; faith is mere self-indulgence – 'it is the choking of the reason by the blind acceptance of what we are told to take for granted without any possible proof.'[70]

Two of these arguments draw on information acquired through scientific advance, and one assumes scientific modes of thinking; the others are of a 'moral' kind, and whether or not they convince depends entirely on what the reader is prepared to accept as self-evidently true.

It remains true, however, that two scientific developments were frequently mentioned in these letters, and might be assumed to have influenced the ways of thinking of those contributing to the correspondence: Darwin's theory of evolution, and the study of non-Christian religions.

Darwin's theory challenged existing beliefs most obviously by undermining biblical literalism (as the geologists had already done), and this was the aspect of his work that received the most general publicity.[71] On the other hand, few of the contributors to *Do We*

Believe? seem to have regarded this as one of the matters at issue. Biblical literalists there still were in large numbers but such views had by now been dropped even by many of those whose view of inspiration was otherwise conservative.[72] When contributors to the correspondence referred to evolution they were usually thinking of 'the rise of man',[73] 'the indisputable law of evolution and general progression'[74] or 'that Nature is uniform in action and that the law of causation is universal'.[75] The meanings attached to evolution fell into three chief categories: progress, the uniformity of nature, and the impossibility of absolutes. Those in the first category, certainly, and often those in the other categories too, were among those classified by Morse Peckham as 'metaphysical evolutionists', who claimed Darwin's warrant for their views, but who actually held to a form of evolutionism current before Darwin, and contrary to his own theory.[76] For Darwin himself, the most shattering implication of his researches seems to have been the apparently random way in which natural selection worked, and the lack of evidence for design.[77] Yet the popular meaning of evolution, for the religious and for the anti-religious, seems to have been the very reverse. It meant the process onward and upward, ordered, progressive, and, in most people's opinion, planned.[78] It is hard to believe that such facile progressism could have been derived from Darwin – more probable that a garbled version of Darwinism was used to re-inforce pre-existing ideas.

More significant as a derivation from recent scientific advance was the conception of a creation in perpetual flux and the relativism which intermingled with the interest in comparative religion that formed the other main 'scientific' theme of the correspondence. Correspondents were chiefly interested in parallels between religions, and these were used to show either that all were equally true, or that they were equally false. On the one side was the contributor who combined 'metaphysical evolutionism' with the new comprehensive world religion, referring to the 'basic and fundamental truths whether taught by Buddha, Plato or Christ', and insisting that 'although the progress may be slow, the time required for the evolution of a perfect humanity compared with the time we have already existed must be very great indeed'.[79] On the other side was the writer who claimed that 'comparative theology and mythology' had shown all religions to be 'purely human products, strivings of the mind to explain its relation to the universe, all charged with the legendary and with assumptions about supernatural agencies the advance of disbelief in which is the measure of the advance in knowledge of "the eternal order which never dies", belief in which is man's one sure foundation.'[80] Of course, no one had proved, or could, that all religions were 'purely human products'. The point, however, was that by offering explanations in such terms anthropologists shifted the burden of proof on to the believer.

It is unlikely that many of those who quoted such arguments had made much study of the Hindu scriptures or of studies of comparative mythology, any more than they had made much study of Darwin. But arguments drawn from these sources formed part of the complex of ideas and attitudes that was undermining the religious consensus. A usually distorted Darwinism was used to support belief in relativism and in the 'law of progress'; knowledge of the fact that Christian moral teaching was paralleled in other religions reflected ill on Christian exclusiveness, while parallels between Christian and pre-Christian mythology favoured a sociological interpretation of all religious phenomena; horror at the idea of hell — which in the light of these developments seemed to be a survival from a more primitive phase of human development — gave impetus to the revolt against the existing 'orthodoxy'. 'Orthodoxy', I have argued, rested on a basis of informal social coercion. As this ostensible uniformity disintegrated in the later '70s and '80s, and more obviously in the '90s and thereafter, and a variety of religious positions acquired social acceptability, many people had the sensation of discovering that the emperor had no clothes, that beliefs they had accepted without any great thought had no foundation; others were forced painfully to reconstruct their beliefs, with little of the massive social support that had enabled members of various religious traditions to take vast areas of their belief for granted, and to argue only over details.[81]

The Transitional Period

Some of the external signs of these changes were: the less strict observance of Sunday, declining church attendance, the greater freedom with which religiously heterodox opinions were expressed in the press. In London, the first signs of widespread change appear between about 1875 and 1885: for instance, the London diocesan Visitation in 1883 suggested that the externals of religion, though still observed by most of the upper class, were being more widely ignored than in 1862;[82] a *Punch* article in 1877 satirising the Sunday non-observance of the fashionable seemed to hint at changing fashions;[83] when in 1881 religious censuses were organised in a number of provincial towns, London editors chose the occasion to declare that there was 'much more religious feeling that is growing up outside the religious organisations, and that does not look to the pulpit for sustinence' – although there was little statistical evidence of a decline in the number of worshippers since 1851.[84] Meanwhile, agnosticism had become staple fare in the 'monthlies'.[85] What had been a significant trend in the early '80s became a flood in the '90s. After 1883, the next surviving London Visitation is that of 1900,[86] and the replies of the incumbents on this occasion made it clear that the changes indicated seventeen years before had now gone much further. But they had been anticipated by the incumbents in the diocese of Rochester (including all of South London) who had for the first time been asked in 1894 about Sunday observance and about 'any changes in religious faith or feeling':[87] now even the most sanguine suburban vicar qualified his report that all was well, and many reported rapid and recent change. At St Giles', Camberwell, for instance: 'Less come to church than did ten or even four years ago. The tendency seems to be in this direction increasingly.' And this was confirmed by the *Daily News* religious census of London in 1902-3, which showed a spectacular fall in church attendances in middle- and upper-class districts since the last such census in 1886. Meanwhile, in the early '90s, sexual morality replaced agnosticism as the question of the day in the intellectual reviews.[88] The critics of 'orthodoxy' had now sufficient confidence to attack the most deeply entrenched of conventional ideas – ideas far less vulnerable than hell or vicarious atonement, which many Christians were only too glad too drop. But the general press seems as yet to have been little touched by such themes. When, for instance, the local press in London editorialised on the 'church' in the '90s, it was generally to commend the Anglican clergy for their expanding 'social' concern, or else to engage in the sort of sectarian disputes that had continued for decades.[89] The weakening of the conventional sanction for religious observances and the spread of 'doubt' were apparent to the clergy, and taken for granted in the novels of such writers of the time as Gissing and Mrs. Humphry Ward, but they still seemed to belong to the sphere of that which was known but not freely admitted.[90] It was just past the turn of the century that 'the decline of the churches' became in London at least, a cliché, and part of the regular matter of sermons, letters to the press and editorials. For instance, the *Borough of Lewisham Gazette* published an editorial on the subject in 1905,[91] and the *East London Observer* in 1907.[92] Hampstead had been a home of agnostics and 'advanced thinkers' long before 1900, but it was only about then that the *Hampstead and Highgate Express* began publishing letters from an avowedly anti-Christian point of view in any significant numbers[93] (and at the same time restricting the space allowed for sectarian controversy).[94] In 1904 it reported R F. Horton's opinion that 'there was a great deal to be said for the view that the great majority of the English people were drifting towards a state of "non-religion" '[95] and in 1906 it published a sermon which may be taken as the epitaph for a phase of Hampstead's history that was now unmistakably ended. It was delivered by the minister of Haverstock Congregational Chapel on the death of a particularly stalwart member:

It has become a common thing for Christian people – even members of churches – to make their presence at public worship entirely a matter of inclination. If they think well to be there they will; if, from any cause whatever, they choose to be absent, they will be absent. A fine morning will decide them to take a walk, a wet morning to stay at home. The visit of a friend for tea will fix them for the evening. The playing of a band on Parliament Hill will draw them there.

The extent to which Sunday is used, not only by people who make no religious profession, but by professing Christians as a day of convenience is one of the most depressing features of our times. The plea that they are so hard pressed on the six days that rest and recreation on the Sunday are a physical necessity is often the merest excuse. People are no busier than their grandfathers and they have vastly more leisure. It is simply a lax sense of religious obligation. It does not seem to be recognised that public worship is the first of duties to God, and that no light thing should stand in the way of its discharge. One does not like to think that the race of those who have a passion for the house of God, who would as soon think of neglecting their meals as their worship, is dying out. To Mr. Gard, the Sunday was shorn of much of its brightness and inspiration – was almost a dies non – if he could not be here; and I would that the younger generation could preserve his ideal and perpetutate his habit.[96]

I will first consider the changes in mores, in social custom that were proceeding rapidly after about 1875, and then the profounder changes in ideas, values, conceptions of the world, of which these were the external signs. If some of the former seem trivial, the part they played in the life of the 'respectable' classes in nineteenth-century England was nonetheless great, and for some people they had immense emotional significance. There were, on the other hand, many people for whom these customs were no more than conventions, accepted while they were socially required, and dropped when they went out of fashion. There were also those who, consciously or not, found such customs burdensome, and who, when customs began to change, soon became aware of their latent discontent. Not only the response to these changes, therefore, but also their importance within the individual's life varied widely.

The change in mores took the form of the widespread abandonment of those externals of religion, the multiplication of which J. W. Croker had noted in 1843. Most generally dropped was the custom of family prayers, while that of weekly church attendance remained fairly common, and the observance of Sunday was in an intermediate position. It was because so many of the upper and middle classes had been bored or embarrassed by customs which they had none the less accepted, perhaps taken for granted, that these were so widely dropped once the movement had begun. The memoirs of Lady Diana Cooper, for instance, convey some of this sense of painful duties performed unquestioningly, which would be gladly forgotten if someone in authority were to say that it was permissible:

> Confirmation I had dreaded because to talk of God to anyone but oneself was taboo. Even the word God stuck in my throat, as I feel it might have done in Mr. Knox's outside his pulpit. To be instructed about the unmentionable appalled me.[97]

Similarly, there must have been many upper-class people who were relieved when, in 1888, a book intended for those who 'do not wish to appear singular, eccentric, old-fashioned, unconventional',[98] advised its readers that saying Grace was now 'a matter of feeling rather than etiquette':

> It used to be very much the custom to say 'grace', but of late years it is oftener omitted than not, especially at large dinner-parties in town.
> In the country, when a clergyman is present, he should be asked to say grace. When grace is said by the host, it is said in a low voice, and in a very few words; the guests inclining their heads the while.[99]

It was probably at about this time that new middle- and upper-class households were dropping family prayers.[100] George Russell, in 1901, thought the custom now very rare in Society although in the '50s and '60s a devout family, like his own, would have held prayers *twice* daily.[101] By about 1920 many members of the upper and middle classes seem to have regarded the custom as almost spectacularly anachronistic.[102] But the timing of the change remains obscure, hidden away, perhaps, in diaries, and not sufficiently public to attract the volume of comment through which the parallel decline in Sunday observance can be plotted.[103]

Sunday was at the centre of 'Victorian' religion, both in its essential and its merely conventional forms. By the same token, it was a prime target of Anglo-Catholics, who believed that Evangelicalism had given England the wrong sacred days and the wrong taboos; of liberal religionists, who wanted a Christianity freed from *all* such superstitions; of hedonists and of aesthetes; of rebels against cant, formality and hypocrisy; of the apostles of common sense, who wanted all things, Christianity included, in strict moderation. Nonetheless, its passing was in several stages. Family prayers you either held or did not hold; on the other hand you might abandon strict sabbatarianism without feeling free to do exactly as you liked on the day. Around 1860 strict sabbatarianism still seems to have been the rule.[104] By 1883, some London incumbents were reporting that Sunday was being observed 'with less and less earnestness, especially by the upper class'.[105] In the mid-'90s, Sunday had become 'simply a day of physical rest' for many of the middle class of Herne Hill, a day for 'private parties down the river or lawn tennis parties at home' for the wealthy of Wimbledon.[106] Yet there was a tendency for Sunday to become a day of compromises. When, in 1905, the *Daily Telegraph* investigated the British Sunday, there was a gap between law and custom, and between healthy recreation and amusements so worldly as to trouble the conscience even of the most moderate sabbatarian. Thus at Stoke Newington it was reported that: 'Billiards is entirely tabooed on Sundays, but the happy owners of motors take advantage of the day of rest to have a run in the country.' And at Putney, boating on the river was popular and golf was permitted by the private Ranelagh Club, but the LCC banned football and cricket on the Heath.[107]

Something of the flavour of this period of transition can be got from two lapsed Nonconformist family histories. In one example, sent to me by Fr. Ralph Gardner, Nonconformist traditions remained deeply engrained even in those who had ostensibly rejected them. He was born in 1893, and brought up in Harlesden, where his father who left orthodox Nonconformity for Theosophy, was in business as a builder and decorator:

My branch of the Gardner family was nurtured in the firmest

tradition of mid-Essex Independency. A considerable part of Sunday was spent in the Congregational Chapel, and games, amusements and 'profane' reading were taboo on that day . . . .

My parents had grown up in the same tradition of Sunday as a day of special duties and prohibitions which still prevailed at Brentwood; but during the first few years of my life my father was moving away from the form of religion that gave sanction to such practices. However, Sunday was still treated as a special day, though with rules less rigid than of yore. Gardening, sewing, walking, and even bicycling were permissible, and a wider range of books for Sunday reading was allowed. (I remember *The Fairyland of Science* which made the best of both worlds in that it was written by a clergyman.) Sunday evenings were especially distinguished by my father's reading aloud to my brother and myself, and I remember particularly his rendering of The Tales of Uncle Remus, the Ingoldsby Legends, and the poems of Bret Harte. I do not recollect finding this imposition of a pattern on the week, with Sunday being a day of special seriousness, as being at all oppressive. In my late teens, when I became a Churchman, I came to think of Sunday as the weekly Easter festival, rather than as the Jewish sabbath transferred from the seventh day to the first; and in the early years of my priesthood a desire to emphasise the joyousness of Sunday and the goodness of earthly things made me severely critical of the Puritan Sunday of my forefathers. I certainly don't think that this was wrong; but I do wonder whether the present age, with what may be called its loose end, unserious Sunday, is not missing something of genuine value.

The other example is taken from an autobiographer whose family were in comfortable circumstances, and had for several generations lived in south-east London. Around 1880, when his mother was young, his grandfather would stump on to his lawn on Sunday afternoon, and, if he heard the click of croquet mallets further up the street, would mutter 'Disgraceful!' By the mid-'90s, or thereabouts, when the author's father had appeared on the scene, croquet was the accepted Sunday afternoon game, though the Congregational chapel still took up a good deal of the time of his mother and her friends. By 1908, when the author was born, home-made model soldiers had taken over the house for the whole of Sunday – these being the chief passion of his father and uncle – and the chapel had been dropped. His parents 'outgrew it simply and naturally as a child outgrows its nurse, and felt as warmly towards it afterwards'. They were 'not anti-religious': 'they respected and openly acknowledged their debt to the Christian ideal'. But 'they valued intellectual freedom above all things, and they hated dogma'.[108] 'Simple and natural' was the accent here, and if his parents revealed any symptoms of Nonconformist survival or if they had any qualms, the author does not mention it.

Church attendance remained fairly high in middle- and upper-class areas, though it too fell in the '80s and '90s and the decades following. The number of regular Anglican communicants was probably increasing with the advance of the Catholic wing of the church in the later nineteenth century; the declining force of the other kinds of compulsion to attend church can be traced through the national religious census of 1851 and the *British Weekly* census of London in 1886-7 to the *Daily News* census of Greater London in 1902-3. Twicers were a fairly small minority even among church-goers by 1902-3 — about 15.5 per cent of those attending church on census Sunday, or 3 per cent of the total population in Inner London — though we have no figures from an earlier date with which to compare these.[109] This small section of church-goers might be regarded as the hard-core of convinced sabbatarians. The percentage of church attendances to population in Inner London on a single Sunday was slightly under 30 per cent in 1851, 28.5 per cent in 1886-7 and still 22.0 per cent in 1902-3.[110] But this is to understate the significance of the '80s and '90s in the West End and suburbs of London. Between 1851 and 1886 church attendance rates changed little in most districts, though the Church of England appeared to have lost ground, and attendances had dropped in Hampstead, the wealthiest of the suburbs.[111] (For figures in detail, see Tables 20 and 21.) Between 1886-7 and 1902-3, attendance rates rose in two working-class districts, Finsbury and Bermondsey, and fell only slightly in Bethnal Green. On the other hand, they fell from 43 per cent to 25 per cent in Kensington, a very wealthy district on the fringes of Society, from 41 per cent to 25 per cent in upper middle-class Hampstead, from 53 per cent to 33 per cent in middle and lower middle-class Stoke Newington, from 36 per cent to 28 per cent in the City of Westminster, which housed many of the capital's poorest inhabitants, but also most of the Upper Ten Thousand. There were also substantial drops in attendance in the suburbs of declining social status, crossed by one of London's 'moving frontiers': from 33 per cent to 25 per cent in Hackney, from 28 per cent to 21 in Lambeth. Partial exceptions to the rule were the wealthy districts of Chelsea and St Marylebone, where the fall in attendance was relatively moderate; but these were areas of declining population, declining because of the gradual elimination of their working-class population pushed out to make way for railway termini, offices and shops, and new blocks of flats.[112] Working-class Londoners had never been great church-goers, but the energetic activity of the clergy, especially Anglicans and Wesleyans, in working-class areas was sometimes being rewarded with greatly increased congregations. The decline in church-going in this period was limited to 'the upper and middle classes (those whom we term church-goers)'[113] but within these classes the movement was so powerful that the most vigorous clergymen could do little to stop the shrinking of his congregation.[114] All the major denominations lost worshippers, but the Church of England, which had always been preferred by those who, like Mary Vivian Hughes' family, 'did not take religion *too* seriously', suffered most heavily.[115]

Middle- and upper-class people were becoming increasingly ready to take pleasure as their first consideration, even when it conflicted with what they had been taught to regard as duty. Sometimes this was expressed in a fully articulated gospel of self-development. More often this took the form of an 'unconscious hedonism', which broke free from some of the more irritating restraints imposed by convention, without attempting to apply any general principles. In such cases, mores rather than underlying values were changing. Thus in 1910, when several Hampstead Nonconformists had delivered stirring attacks on their ministers, whose radical partisanship was driving them from the chapels where they loved to worship, another defaulting Nonconformist brought the debate down to a more mundane level:

> It may be there are some whose whole or partial estrangement from their places of worship is due to their objection in this matter, but I fear that, as in my own case, so in most, the reason will be found in the allurements of the country, river, or sport, either for the sake of health, pleasure or both.[116]

'England without Sunday', wrote a High Churchman in 1902, 'will mean sooner or later England without God.'[117] That is a matter of opinion. What, however, is certain, is that England with Sunday was not on that account England with God. The calm tones of the Hampstead Nonconformist are scarcely those of a man who has been subjected to a 'crisis of faith'. They are those of that large section of the middle and upper classes whose religious ideas were never very fully formulated, and whose habits adjusted easily to new fashions. Thirty years earlier *Punch* conveyed some of this unideological insouciance in its enquiry into 'How to spend a Pleasant Sunday':

'Pleasant can't be wrong' is the motto of the Upper Ten — as for instance: —

LADY MILLEFLEURS HAUTON (Grosvenor Square). — Church, of course, you know, in the morning, and then a gentle ride to Twickenham on my Lord's drag, a dinner at the Orleans Club, and a pleasant journey home in the cool of the evening.

MRS. SMITH FITZ-SMITH SMYTHE   (Bayswater). — Westminster Abbey or the Chapel Royal (when we get a ticket) in the morning and then a stroll to the Zoo. Nice little dinner for the girls and their friends afterwards, you know, because we must think about the future.

THE HON. BERTIE DANGLE (Noodle's Club, St. James's). — Oh get up at twelve, don't you know? Breakfast at one, and then if its a really jolly day, take the train to Maidenhead, go up the river to Henley in a steam-launch, and dine at SKINDLE'S afterwards.

MRS. GOLIGHTLY FASTWAYS (Mayfair). — Can't do better than take a coach from Slough, and pic-nic at Burnham Beeches. Drive back in the moonlight with a pleasant party — particularly jolly — at least I always find it so myself, dear.[118]

To talk of changing mores in this context is to talk of nothing that is deeply rooted or capable of arousing strong emotion. But custom and fashion, however ephemeral, still gave life a lot of its special colour, and the consequences of their changing could sometimes be important.

'The Divine Right of Self-Development'

At the same time, the principle of self-development was the chief point in the attack on all religions of the prophets of pleasure, and in the attack on Evangelicalism of many religious reformers. It is the less obvious, but the more effectively handled, of the two leitmotifs in Mrs. Humphry Ward's novel, *Robert Elsmere*, published in 1888, and immensely popular both in Britain and in the United States. Religious families, especially those whose traditions were Evangelical, had tabooed a wide range of amusements because they savoured of 'the world': the theatre and all games or sports associated with drink or gambling were generally banned; fiction was often barred, though some authors might be exempted; the ban on operas often extended to oratorios; and some rigorists saw even licit pleasures as an irresponsible waste of invaluable time.[119] By about 1880, however, even strongly

Evangelical families were extending their ideas both of what pleasures were licit, and of the time that might be spent in enjoying them.[120] Sharply conflicting attitudes to pleasure in this time of transition were personified in the characters of Mrs. Ward's novel.

The older values are represented by the heroine, Catherine Leyburn, 'brought up in the austerest school of Christian self-government', who devoted her life to the well-being of the poor in the remote mountain district where she lived. She was carrying on the work of her schoolmaster father, who had given Catherine's musical sister a violin, but who 'thought it wicked to care about anything but religion', and had retired to Westmorland because 'he thought the world was getting very wicked and dangerous and irreligious' and 'it comforted him to know that we should be out of it'.[121] Yet both Catherine and her father had a warmth, and a humility, that forced even those who rebelled against their principles to love them. In Newcome, a Ritualist priest, who makes occasional brief appearances in the story in order to declaim against modern religious ideas, conviction becomes bigotry, and hatred of sin becomes hatred of life. The rebellion against these values, whether in their Protestant or in their new Catholic form, is represented by Catherine's sister, Rose the violinist, who longs for her 'artistic' circle in London, Berlin, or even Manchester, and for whom her sister's name meant 'everything at this moment against which her soul rebelled — the most scrupulous order, the most rigid self-repression, the most determined sacrificing of "this warm kind world", with all its indefensible delights, to a cold other-world, with its torturing inadmissible claims.'[122] She and Catherine were tied to one another by strong feelings of love, but they were perpetually at loggerheads, and each had the power to hurt. When Rose spoke: 'Catherine felt a shock sweep through her. It was as though all the pieties of life, all the sacred assumptions and self-surrenders at the root of it, were shaken, outraged by the girl's tone. ... This language of a proud and tameless individuality, this modern gospel of the divine right of self-development — her soul loathed it.'[123] And, if Catherine was caricatured by Newcome, Rose's cry for freedom was caricatured in the 'hard self-confidence' of the politicians and littrateurs who filled Mme de Netteville's salon, 'where everything is an open question and all confessions of faith are more or less in bad taste'. Catherine's husband is partly attracted by 'the free play of equal mind' that he finds in the salon. But their brilliance is ultimately 'glittering and arid' to his enthusiastic unworldliness.[124] It is Catherine's husband, Robert Elsmere, who unites Catherine's moral commitment with Rose's impulse to freedom. He indignantly repudiates the remorseless asceticism of Newcome, a fellow-parson in Surrey: 'Where you see temptation, I see opportunity. I cannot see God as Arch-plotter against His own creation'.[125] As a country parson his enthusiasms were 'dirt, drains and Darwin': campaigns for sanitary improvements, lectures on natural history, readings from the classics at his Institute, organising the villagers' Sunday cricket. The 'Puritan distrust of personal joy as something dangerous and ensnaring', that was deeply engrained in Catherine had no hold on him.[126] His religion was one of delight in the Creation, fight against the cruelty, intolerance and ignorance that prevented its full enjoyment by all, and confidence in the possibilities of education. When he left the Church of England and formed his New Brotherhood, his religion changed very little though he became yet more earnest.

But, it was the earnestness, quite as much as the puritanism, of Evangelical Christianity that many conventional people of the middle and upper classes found oppressive, and the neo-Christianity of an Elsmere, however inspiring to perplexed idealists, was no answer to their discontents. For many of those growing up at the end of the nineteenth century even the most Liberal form of Christianity belonged with the cant and the rant, the hypocrisy and the ugliness that had for too long darkened English life and violated the sacred laws of self-development. Thus, Eric Bligh, who later described his early years in a book called *Tooting Corner*, was born about 1890 in the well-known South London suburb, beloved of *Punch* humourists, in which his father was a medical practitioner. He was descended on both sides from a line of Nonconformists stretching back for several generations. He was very attached to his father who was a convinced Evangelical Christian, broad in his sympathies and tolerant in his attitudes, but showing no signs of ever having suffered doubts or been tempted to heresies. Yet, when the son was sixteen he happened to open a book by Pater, and as he read it he realised that he had heard a new gospel, after which the old would never seem the same again, and that he was seeing expressed in words his latent dissatisfaction with the religion of his fathers. This dissatisfaction he expressed in terms of atmosphere rather than of dogma:

> I knew that the Christian religion needed the supplementing manna of the philosophy of sensation, and in this at the age of seventeen I was perfectly right. My recent preoccupation with the religious youth of my ancestors has filled me with distaste and

depression. How I bore the actual world of it I do not know. I was never in the least danger of following in their footsteps, but I find it difficult to surmise in what dreary and uncertain wastes I should have found myself if I had not by chance discovered the larger world of *Marius* and the *Renaissance*. 'On a sudden the imagination feels itself free. How facile and direct, it seems to say, is this life of the senses when we have apprehended it! Here, surely, is the more liberal life we have been seeking so long, so near to us all the while.' Difficult and ironical doctrine, surely, for a stammering and isolated boy in Tooting? Well, such clarion sentences made possible my seemingly endless cul-de-sac. It was Pater and not the ancestral strait path of religion, which enabled me to greet the problematical and threatening day.[127]

Some, therefore, were sliding into an easy-going disregard for 'Victorian' conventions, while others were formulating the principles of revolt. But unconsidered as this revolt sometimes was, its consequences could be momentous. The most notable example of this fact is the continuous drop, from the 1870s to the 1930s, in the middle-class birth rate. Even specialists in the field are cautious in advancing explanations of how or why the change took place. But it is clear that in England and Wales, as well as in several other West European countries, the birth rate was falling by the 1880s, and that in England, at least, the change was due to the deliberate restriction of births, either more effectively than hitherto, or by a greater number of couples, and that it was most marked among the relatively well-to-do.[128] In the 1930s the managers of birth control clinics were able to interrogate new patients on their 'contraceptive histories'. But in the 1870s these were still a private matter, and only the occasional reference in a diary or a volume of letters written long after the event exists to indicate whether the contraceptive revolution of the '70s and '80s was the product of new methods or of the increasing popularity of old.[129] Whatever the answer to this question, it clearly was a rebellion against the standards of propriety as they had been understood for several decades, and a rebellion regarded with abhorrence by most of the Anglican clergy.[130] So vehement was their opposition, and so close the parallel in timing between the contraceptive revolution and the other developments that were undermining the Evangelicalism of the Protestant world in the last quarter of the nineteenth century, that there seems good reason to regard this revolution as part of the same movement.

The Bradlaugh-Besant trial in 1877 provoked many national and provincial papers to violent attacks on the accused. The few papers that defended the sale of *The Fruits of Philosophy* generally did so on the grounds of the freedom of the press or of the importance of the matters of issue, rather than of the desirability of 'mechanical' contraception.[131] Nonetheless, the taboo on public discussion of the subject had been broken.[132] The attack by a section of the clergy on the new habits seems to have begun in the late '80s, when it was clear that the birth rate was dropping. The first such attack that I have seen is in the opening sermon to the Church Congress of the liberal Bishop of Ripon, Boyd Carpenter, in 1890. 'It is ill,' he warned, 'when men make passion safe and vice easy, shirking the responsibilities that make nations strong, and give to peoples the benediction of the Almighty.'[133] This particular form of grandiose and empty rhetoric was a speciality of Winnington-Ingram, Bishop of London from 1901 to 1939, and in his 1905 Visitation Charge, he chose very similar terms to condemn a practice that was clearly spreading rapidly.[134] Winnington-Ingram may have been cruder than most in the way that he expressed his views, but his hostility to contraception seems to have been shared by the majority of the bishops, who affirmed their opposition to 'artificial' methods in 1908 and again in 1916.[135] Even in 1930, according to the admittedly hostile Hensley Henson, who tended to exaggerate the stupidity of his brother bishops, the Bishop of Exeter was 'loudly cheered' at the Lambeth Conference for 'a passionate diatribe against contraceptives, which he clearly placed in the same category as abortions and infanticides'.[136]

The anti-Malthusians had three main lines of attack: that the availability of contraceptives encouraged fornication; that a high birth rate was a sign of national vigour, and a falling rate both a sympton and a cause of national decline; and that unnatural intrusions cheapened what was beautiful and desecrated what was holy. The first two arguments were peripheral: Malthusians were by no means all advocates either of fornication or of national decadence, while those who argued against them on those grounds were generally anti-Malthusian on other grounds as well. The third argument was basic: while respectable people regarded any method of cheating nature as an affront to female delicacy and the degradation of a wife to the level of a mistress or a prostitute, there would be no need for other arguments.

Contraception was very far from being a nineteenth-century invention. That methods of population control – presumably *coitus interruptus*, abortion and infanticide – were used to some effect by sections of the English and French rural populations in the seventeenth and eighteenth centuries has been demonstrated by studies of variations in fertility in small communities.[137] It seems probable that these were among the rural customs called in question by the 'reformation of manners' in the later eighteenth and early nineteenth century, which established standards of decency in the middle and upper, and a part of the working class. Those who publicly questioned the taboo on contraception during the first eight decades of the nineteenth century were largely drawn from those who rejected the forms of religion that provided a sanction for these standards.[138] When, from the '70s onwards, the birth rate was falling in the 'respectable' classes, and far more rapidly than in the rest of the population, this probably indicated both a weakening of the influence of this religion, and the adoption of more effective methods of birth control than those favoured by the rest of the population.[139]

J. A. Banks has shown that the middle-class style of life responded to rising incomes in the 1850s and '60s, and that the threat to this style of life and its associated 'paraphernalia of gentility' posed by the Great Depression, the rising cost of education and (from the 1890s) the diminishing supply of domestic servants, provided strong motives for family limitation – once the idea had become 'thinkable'.[140] The problem is: why had such a remedy become 'thinkable' to many middle-class couples marrying in the '70s and '80s, whose parents and grandparents, although they enjoyed child-bearing and the raising of large families no more, had responded either (in the fashion of Irish farmers) by raising the age of marriage yet further, or by simply making the best of what could not be helped.[141] Since, as J. A. and Olive Banks put it, 'child-rearing usually weighs more heavily on wives than on their husbands',[142] the most plausible reason would seem to be greater independence, willingness to assert their interests, and desire for satisfactions beyond those of motherhood on the part of wives; but their study of the feminist movement suggests that, at least until about 1890, its tendency was to *discourage* the use of contraceptives,[143] while the fall in the birth rate preceded the appearance of wider economic opportunities for middle-class women.[144] In an earlier study, Banks had tentatively suggested that the decisive factor in facilitating the acceptance of economic logic may have been 'the spread of ideas of evolution culminating in the Darwinism of the 1860s', and the consequent conviction that 'humanify itself was really only part of nature'.[145]

Evolution, according to this argument, assisted the adoption of 'mechanical' contraceptives by demystifying Man and allowing human behaviour to be studied more 'rationally'. This may exaggerate the direct influence of scientific ideas, and the extent to which individuals made connections between them and their own behaviour. It may also be that this argument allows insufficiently for the distortion of such ideas in the popular mind. If the Do We Believe? correspondence is any guide, the chief effect of evolutionary ideas, as they were popularly understood, was to encourage grandiose statements about 'the Race' and the perfectibility of Man. The objection to Christianity was not that it exalted Man too far by placing him 'a little lower than the angels', but that it degraded him by admitting the idea of Original Sin — or even of any sin at all.[146] After noting that some middle-class couples practised contraception long before the 1870s,[147] and that many others continued long afterwards not to do so, an alternative theory can be suggested as to why the most effective method of reducing middle-class economic problems became more thinkable at this time: that the religious revival of the early nineteenth century led to the adoption (by men, as well as by women) of very strict standards of sexual behaviour within a certain section of the population; that this section was sufficiently large and influential to be able to impose certain standards of behaviour, at least in externals, on the majority of the middle and upper classes; that the women of these classes, as guardians of the family's respectability, were the chief instruments for ensuring the observance of these standards; that these standards involved restraints that many people, consciously or unconsciously, found irksome; that the system of control began to break down in the late '70s as the doctrine of hell, which had been essential to its ability to command widespread acceptance, lost plausibility; that the breakdown of this system of social control and of the religious fear that had supported it led to the formulation and systematic application by a few of doctrines of self-development, replacing those of self-restraint in obedience to a God and a public opinion both highly coercive, to the rejection by many of those proprieties that they found burdensome — among which they soon found the prohibition on birth control to be one; (by this time, relatively effective methods of birth control were available, so that as the newer attitudes asserted themselves, the middle-class birth rate steadily dropped).

This theory has the advantage of being apparently applicable to the United States and Scandinavia, where the chronology of falling births and of religious change appears to be similar to that in England. But the nature of the evidence makes it difficult to draw confident conclusions. J. A. Banks has devoted two substantial books to the causes of the contraceptive revolution, but remains exceedingly hesitant in offering explanations. There does, however, seem to be sufficient evidence to suggest that the religious changes of the '70s and '80s contributed significantly to this revolution, and that without them it would not have been possible.

This-Worldly Religion

The chief effect, therefore, on the mass of unideologically-minded people in the upper- and middle-class of the breakdown of the religious consensus would seem to have been the dropping of unwelcome restraints, and the more conscious acceptance of pleasure as a chief motive — together with the fading from the consciousness of some of a God who, when he ceased to be feared, lost the only form of reality he had held for them. But new systems of values were also developing, and offering coherent alternatives to 'orthodox' religious doctrines and moral standards.

These took divergent forms: new formulations of Christianity; religions of humanity, whether defined as such or not; individualist mysticism and individualist hedonism. At the same time, the more conservative forms of Evangelicalism continued to have a large although shrinking, following: from the late '70s 'progress' was clearly moving away from them, but their opponents for long remained in a minority within the churches, and often in society at large.

Common to most new formulations of Christianity, whether Catholic, Evangelical or ultra-liberal was the influence of F. D. Maurice. The saving of souls from damnation had given churches a clearly defined purpose, and the fear of hell had provided a motive for belief. The slowing down of church expansion and the decreasing frequency of mass conversion after 1859[148] suggested that the effectiveness of this approach was diminishing. Most of the abler church leaders, Anglican or Nonconformist, born in the '40s and '50s, were following Maurice in rejecting the doctrine of hell as incompatible with the divine love and with the divine plan of self-revelation. Those clergymen who were not defiantly old-fashioned were now attempting, with a Maurician identification of the secular with the sacred, to provide for the whole human personality, body and soul, citizen and seeker after truth. F. H. Stead, who combined the maximum of political and social work with the minimum of orthodox doctrine, expressed the new order of priorities by asserting that he had more sympathy with Roman Catholics than with the kind of Nonconformist whose 'one thought is to save his dirty little soul and get to heaven at last'.[149] A very similar thought was attributed to Hugh Price Hughes, the most influential Nonconformist of his generation, as well as a critic of the doctrine of hell which, he considered, had led to a disastrously unbalanced presentation of the Gospel:

> His heart was stirred within him at the thought of the degradation and misery in the slums, which Christians intent on singing hymns and the saving of their own miserable souls had so long and shamefully neglected.[150]

The same trend can be seen in the Institutional Churches, introduced from American models, which attempted to provide for all the legitimate social needs of the neighbourhood,[151] in the Wesleyan Central Missions of the '80s and the apparatus attached to them, and even in the extensive network of guilds associated with the ritualistic churches.[152] All of these developments reflected a partial turning away from the preoccupation with individual salvation that is associated with the doctrine of hell.

At the same time, this-worldly religion reflected a shrinking from the personal experience of God that had been religiously obligatory and the familiarity with him that had been socially obligatory for several decades. One aspect of this was the 'Secularisation of the Pulpit' described by George Barrett in his address from the Chair to the Assembly of the Congregational Union in 1894. In the last fifty years, he said, much dead wood had been cut away: the theology of the '90s was in many ways 'truer and nobler' than that of the mid-century; the pulpit language was less formalised. But he missed 'the sounding of the deep things of God'.[153] The area of human freedom was being enlarged; the trivial decisions of everyday life were no longer said to be the work of the Holy Spirit. The Minutes of a Congregational church in Kilburn show this process at work even where the Holy Spirit was most taken for granted. The letters by which pastorates were accepted or resigned were always recorded, and from the church's inception in the late 1850s until the end of the century these letters changed very little: they were long, they were full of hackneyed phrases, they were written in a peculiarly stilted style, and they gave a fairly detailed account of the soul-searchings that had preceded the decision. Such decisions were, of course, taken very seriously, and many of the associated emotions were entirely genuine, but the letters often give the impression that their authors, knowing how such a letter ought to be written, were more concerned with satisfying the convention than with writing what was true.[154] A change was first noticeable in 1906, when the letter of acceptance written by the new minister was brief and to the point: it stated his conviction that he had received a call from God, but did not enlarge upon the point. His successor, who came in 1909, was chosen chiefly because of his enthusiasm for the New Theology. His letter, though rather longer, was very largely free from the conventional vocabulary; if he was sure that he had received the divine call, he left it to be assumed. The letter was mainly concerned with his theological sympathies and his interest in social work. 'I come to you as a Progressive, trusting to receive the freedom I am willing and anxious to extend to others. I have to make either "Authority" or "Liberty" my principle, and I unhesitatingly choose the latter, for it seems to me that "Authority" ecclesiastically construed is not only foreign to the spirit of Congregationalism but injurious to the Truth.'[155]

If large numbers of Nonconformists were finding in 'Liberty' a solution to their perplexities, there was also a large group of religious rebels who demanded more 'Authority'. As Anglo-Catholics realised, God the Great Clock-maker was a remote being who had lost all immediacy, while the God of T. H. Green, however pure and morally beautiful his religion might be, was unlikely to capture the mass imagination. Thus their insistence on a God 'who does things in particular',[156] and their attempts to exclude from the Anglican ministry those who took a symbolic, or simply a sceptical view of the New Testament miracles.[157] The miracles (to Liberals materialistic accretions, and by Evangelicals accepted more because they were there than because they were necessary) were, for Anglo-Catholics, God's way of working in the world. Yet their demand for visible means of communication with God – the Church whose ministry and traditions provided a direct link with the apostolic age, the sacraments, the splendour of Catholic worship – was a sign that God had become more remote, that the personal experience of him required of every Evangelical convert was less easily attained. Thus the following statement of faith by a Congregationalist convert to Anglo-Catholicism:

The Mass and the Confessional were bugbears to Protestant England; their reappearance in the National Church was viewed with horror and gave Dissenters further reason for separation from it. They were in fact the two things that I needed. The rather cultured Nonconformity in which I was brought up gave me a picture of Christ as of someone long ago who told us the truth about God, bringing home his love, and strengthening us by His example, but it was a tale of long ago. I wanted Someone here and now. Catholicism taught the real Presence of Christ among us through the Apostolic Sacraments.[158]

This searching for authority at a time when old authorities were collapsing was certainly one reason for the attractiveness of Anglo-Catholicism in the late nineteenth century, and familar to those who have tried to explain conversions of intellectuals to the Roman Catholic Church in the twentieth century. But this is not enough to explain the range of the Catholic appeal: an appeal to ultra-democrats as much as to ultra-conservatives, to the theologically liberal as much as to the authoritarian. Catholicism answered to a need of beauty and a need for community, felt to be lacking in Protestantism. It also appealed to those who longed for a sense of 'the Church' and its true grandeur, and those who wanted a religion freed from the respectability and the puritanism of the churches in which they had grown up.

The Anglo-Catholics were thus, rather paradoxically, among the beneficiaries of the revolt against authoritarian religion. But the natural beneficiaries would seem to be the Unitarians. Unitarians, like Catholics, tended to see every disturbance within the other churches as a sign that the conversion of England was at hand. Thus, in 1882, the minister of Rosslyn Hill chapel in Hampstead saw that belief in the biblical Creation story and account of the fall of man was weakening, and 'multitudes are silently giving up Christianity and religion altogether, and are passing into agnosticism and materialism'. He therefore pleaded on behalf of the 'rational' alternative of liberal religion, based on 'the fatherhood of God and the brotherhood of Man'.[159] For a time his alternative seemed to be finding support. In 1883, he noted some 'favourable "signs of the times" ' and argued in favour of enlarging the church:

> At no previous time have there been so many strangers at the services or so many applications for sittings from those who previously belonged to orthodox churches. I am, moreover, deeply impressed with the change in the tone of feeling in our neighbourhood in religious matters. From some from whom I should least have expected it, I have heard opinions and liberal sentiments very much in accord with my own.[160]

On the one hand, 'orthodox' pulpits were being filled by men like R. F. Horton, who was far from being a Unitarian, but also far from being a Spurgeonite, and who, in his more ecumenical moods, would extend the hand of fellowship to almost anyone. On the other hand, even Horton was losing members who thought his Liberalism too Evangelical.[161] Unitarianism, however, seemed in perfect accord with the spirit of the age. It preached duty without sin; self-development without hedonism; progress through public service.[162] Its adherents had a highly developed urge to put the world to rights,[163] and minimal attachment to those religious doctrines that offended modern tastes.[164] Yet the revival at Rosslyn Hill, marked by large recruitment in the '80s and '90s proved to be no more than a transitional phrase. The number of subscribers reached a peak of about 350 in the late '90s and thereafter fell steadily to 247 in 1929, and more sharply to 71 in 1953, by which time deaths each year took away several members.[165]

In the long run, the Unitarians probably lost more members to 'orthodoxy' than they gained. Like the Labour and Brotherhood Churches, which working men with similar beliefs were forming at about this time, they were especially vulnerable to the reaction against public worship as such, for the very reason that their members were not isolated by beliefs radically different from those of non-church-goers.[166] As Henry Gow, minister from 1902 to 1921, reported in 1904:

> The old unreasoning habit of Public Worship which took our forefathers to church or chapel has been broken down. There is a tendency for good men to care for Practice without Prayer, to believe in morals without religion.[167]

He often returned to this theme. In 1913, he was welcoming the social work undertaken by members of his chapel, but deploring the tepidity with which they worshipped – it was 'an age when Public Worship is regarded as of slight account in comparison with social usefulness'.[168] And in 1911, he had identified a new field of conflict, in which Unitarians were as much under attack as members of the most authoritarian or superstitious of churches: 'Christian morality as well as Christian doctrine has been challenged by many modern writers. We are told that a new morality, that to some of us looks like old immorality, is needed'.[169]

Outside the Church

To judge why the heyday of Liberal religion proved so short we should look at some of those who were advocating similar ideals outside the organised church. Three important currents of opinion may be represented by Grant Allen, by Robert Blatchford, and by the team who produced Charles Booth's 'Religious Influences' — the first of these being overtly and essentially opposed to institutional Christianity, the second not being so at first but becoming so, and the third being so only partially and by implication.

Charles Booth himself came from one of the leading Liverpool Unitarian families, but seems in later life to have adopted a 'reverent unbelief'.[170] Instinctively sceptical, he none the less accepted worship as an end in itself, and wherever it was 'genuine' (a word that occurs frequently in the 'Religious Influences' series) he was attracted towards it; he was catholic both in his likes and his dislikes, and set no store by numbers.[171] On the other hand, his chief assistants, Arthur Baxter and Ernest Aves, would seem to have been agnostics of Anglican family. Their opinions of the work of the churches are stated in the note books on which the published volumes were based, and probably represent a large section of the Settlements generation of upper middle-class reformers, to which both belonged.

Aves (born 1857) was Vice-Warden of Toynbee Hall and subsequently responsible for organising the Trades Boards; Baxter (born 1862) was a barrister who had organised boys' clubs at Notting Hill. When Aves was himself interviewed by the Booth team as a representative of Toynbee Hall, he described it 'corporatively' as 'non-religious but not irreligious' and added that 'the bulk of the residents do not go to any place of worship, but most of them are religiously minded men, and some devout Christians'.[172] This might fairly suggest Aves' own attitude to the churches: independent, critical, but fairly benevolent.[173] Baxter was less dispassionate: he was strongly attracted by a few of the clergy and active laymen whom he interviewed, bitterly critical of many others. Their criticisms were those of practical men. They wanted 'social influences' that would make better citizens in a better society, and they were impatient of work directed primarily towards the salvation of souls. They were not over-optimistic about human capacity, but neither did they believe in a sense of sin or a radical change of heart. They wanted facts, social surveys, a level-headed, dispassionate approach, skilful social engineering. The chief instruments of social progress were schools and enlightened local authorities; but clergymen could help by inspiring those around them with high ideals. In general, according to the judgement of Aves and Baxter, they failed to do this, and Baxter accordingly ranked 'religion' as the least important of his 'social influences'.[174] There were, however, some clergymen who won their enthusiastic approval, most of these being Nonconformists of the more liberal type. They tended especially to be Congregationalists such as the Evangelical pulpit-star, Campbell Morgan, the ultra-liberal Fleming Williams, or the more main-line William Pierce.[175] Even so, some of these were open to the charge of 'making some particular connexion or membership an object, as though it were something good in itself', instead of limiting themselves to assisting 'men and women to live their own lives independently as good citizens, in the best way possible'.[176] In other words, the ends of Aves and Baxter, if not always their means, were similar to those of many Broad Churchmen and liberal Nonconformists (Aves, of course, as a leading member of Toynbee Hall, was an admirer of Canon Barnett), but they had no sympathy with those whose main purpose was to win souls. Such preachers might be excellent men, but the benefits of their work would be incidental. Aves and Baxter did not completely lack Booth's appreciation of worship as an end in itself, but they were readier to condemn what was hollow than to admire what was real.[177]

Their criticism of the churches fell in two main areas: questions of tone, and differing views of how social change could be achieved. As far as tone was concerned, Baxter especially was equipped with a number of hostile clerical stereotypes, which certainly in many cases failed to fit, but which in others led him to make critical generalisations about particular types of clergymen. The Anglican clergy in general he was apt to dismiss as 'poor creatures', members of 'the large class who are fit for no career but the Church'.[178] Catholics, Anglican or Roman, were often admired as individuals, but were suspect as a class because they threatened freedom.[179] On the whole they were kinder to Nonconformist ministers, in spite of one or two references to 'actors' and 'Chadbands', but the whole milieu was one to which they only adjusted with difficulty.

As for their differing views on social change: Aves was prepared to brand politicians and religious workers alike as busy-bodies who turned to sorting out other people's problems because they could not face their own – though there was probably an element of self-mockery in this, for if anyone was a busy-body it was surely a Vice-Warden of Toynbee Hall. He was inclined to a gentle deflation of the churches' efforts by the suggestion that everyone would be best if left to muddle along in their own unheroic way[180] – though the objections he made to the work of churchmen would presumably be as applicable in practice to the school-teachers and local administrators by which he set such store. Baxter felt that 'morality is simply a question of temperament modified by environment'.[181] The churches, on the other hand, whether they were concerned primarily with individual character or with attacking vested interests, usually saw the chief means towards change as the mounting of moral crusades.[182]

Finally, there was Baxter's recurrent pessimism. In Hackney he chose to emphasise 'how much devotion and self-sacrifice is being shown in religious and philanthropic work among the poor', but he was inclined to conclude:

> that all these good people are spending their lives in almost vain endeavours to mitigate the brutality of God, in futile strivings to mend the pots that he has marred in the making, or has placed in surroundings where they could not fail to break.[183]

Of course, large numbers both of religious and of secular reformers, saw such 'broken pots' as victims of human rather than divine brutality, and looked to human action for a remedy. But Baxter's own view of social progress was cautious:

> We only advance in certain directions as a condition of going backwards in others; the important point is that for each step back we should take a larger step forward; so shall we reach, not indeed the Utopia of which some have dreamed, but the furthest point which the Higher Powers, who have formed us of such conflicting elements, intend that we should touch.[184]

Those who dreamed of Utopia included many of his middle-class contemporaries, for whom, from the early '80s onwards, socialism or hedonism offered more enchanting visions than this rather bleak level-headedness. The most eloquent example of this mood was Robert Blatchford, whose half-earnest, half-facetious, quipping, slightly beery *Clarion*, added a fourth, and perhaps the most powerful current, to the more heavily chronicled forces of Marxism, Nonconformity and Fabianism, that came together in British socialism. And if Blatchford's main constituency was artisan and Manchester-based, his ideas, and something of his style, were echoed at many other points in the social scale. In the early days of the *Clarion*, Blatchford was a Christian of an anti-clerical and anti-dogmatic kind. Around the turn of the century he became a militant unbeliever, convinced that socialism required atheism, and he published a series of articles on 'Science and Religion', subsequently published as *God and my Neighbour*. The emotional basis of his antipathy to Christianity was a dislike of 'formality', 'cant',[185] 'sterile and manless . . . yeaforsooth prudes',[186] and 'lily-livered, tee-total Methodists'.[187] Its rational basis was a determinism, which asserted that if God made Man, God was responsible for all human actions, and thus the author of all evil – this argument Blatchford termed his Christian-eating wolf.[188] Socialism was an alliance of humans against an environment whose author was probably hostile: his opinions should, in any case, be ignored.[189] 'Not Guilty!' he was to declare in the book that he himself regarded as his masterpiece, 'A Defence of the Bottom Dog.' The Bottom Dog's actions were a product of this cruel environment, and the need was not 'to divide men into good and evil'[190] but to change the environment.

Blatchford's criticism of society was echoed at many points by liberal Nonconformists and by High Anglicans of the Guild of St Matthew type. An ironical feature of the 'Science and Religion' controversy was the number of letters of protest from ministers who claimed to be avid *Clarion* readers.[191] His criticism of religion overlapped with that of the hedonists, some of whom were Socialists, but many of whom were primarily individualists. Shaw, in 1891, attributed the popular hostility to Ibsen to his 'acceptance of the impulse to greater freedom as sufficient ground for the repudiation of any customary duty, however sacred, that conflicts with it', and he took Strindberg, Nietzsche, Wagner, and Schopenhauer as part of the same world-wide movement.[192] A notable English prophet of self-development was Grant Allen, whose article, 'The New Hedonism', was published in 1894, and his novel, *The Woman Who Did*, in 1895. In 'The New Hedonism', Allen foresaw a humanity 'sound in mind and limb', 'educated', 'emancipated', 'free', 'beautiful', and dubbed his opponents 'ascetics'. Duty was not entirely banished by Allen: it survived in the form of a duty to self to maximise one's achievement in each of these dimensions. But the most notable feature of the article was his insistence that sex was the crucial area of debate.[193]

Earlier in the century Evangelical religion, Liberal politics and Utilitarian social philosophy intermingled to form some of the characteristic complexes of attitudes. At the end of the century, Liberalism and Evangelicalism were considerable survivals, but were not winning many new converts, though the views of those like Booth and his colleagues could be taken as revived Utilitarianism. It intermingled with the newer forces of liberal religion, catholicism, hedonism and socialism to form the attitudes characteristic of the period 1880-1914. Among those reacting against a Protestant upbringing, but still ardently

Christian, the Catholic-Socialist-anti-puritan syndrome, of which Stewart Headlam was the outstanding exemplar, was typical of this period. Equally characteristic, among those reacting against *all* kinds of religion, was the scientism, socialism and sexual rationalism of H. G. Wells.[194]

There is a splendid account of how these currents intermingled to make up one person's understanding of the world in London at the beginning of the twentieth century in the *Autobiography* of Eric Gill.[195] In the office of the Ecclesiastical Commissioners the ideas on which he had been brought up disintegrated under the attack of his office-companions, and it was only some years later that the stock of principles and prejudices he learnt from them gave way to his own more idiosyncratic view of the world. The components of the view of life he learnt in the office included a Rationalist Press Association attitude to nature — a sense of its uniformity and impersonality, and of the infinite smallness of Man; a form of socialism inspired by revulsion against the 'damned ugliness' both of the social system and of the environment to which it gave birth — and influenced by Ruskin and Morris; and a view of sex, stripped of the romanticism and the conventional restraints he had previously assumed. Above all was the sense that the existing social order, the conventional politics and the conventional religion, the conventional architecture, in the production of which he was assisting, were all a sham, and that, almost regardless of what was to replace them, there could be no progress until all had been cleared away.[196]

It is of course a feeling that some in every generation have experienced, and for many others growing up at this time it was the conventional religion — sometimes all religion — that was the supreme expression of the hypocrisy on which society was founded. An extreme example of such total disenchantment was Richard Aldington's *Death of a Hero*, published in bowdlerised form in 1929, which was an assault on 'the "Victorians" of all nations', and on the 'regime of Cant before the War which made the Cant *during* the War so damnably possible and easy'.[197] Religion was only one among many targets, but he was comprehensive in the range of religion that he attacked . it was *all* Cant. Charles Gore's religious 'chaos', with which this chapter began, was at least in part a misnomer, since many other such rebels against conventional religion solved the problem in the same fashion as Aldington. Aldington's own alternative, however, seems to have been an individualist hedonism which may have answered his needs, but was not intended to answer anyone else's.[198] The sort of socially reinforced communal certainty that supported many 'orthodox' Christians earlier

in the century was from the 1880s increasingly becoming the special
preserve of Socialists, although forms of scientism (merging at some
points into forms of socialism) offered their more isolated adherents
the same happy sense of being on the side of history.

The religion of science as it appealed to her in the late '70s is well
described in Beatrice Webb's *My Apprenticeship* – the belief in a
universe governed by law and in the inevitability of continuous progress
if humanity should but discover and recognise these laws: 'what seems
to me clear is that we are at a very early period in man's existence, and
that we have only just arrived at the true basis of knowledge: and that
bright and glorious days are in store for our successors on earth'.[199]
Though Beatrice Webb soon claimed to have lost faith in the inevitability of progress, on the grounds that science 'lends herself indifferently
to the destroyer and to the preserver of life, to the hater and to the
lover of mankind',[200] the Do We Believe? controversy in 1904
demonstrated the continuing attractiveness of the progressist creed. It
was, however, by its nature an individualist creed, since it was not a
matter of general agreement what lessons science did teach or what
direction progress ought to take, and it was a particularly vulnerable
creed, because of the tendency both of science and of progress to take
wrong turns.[201] Scientism was more effective as a support for a more
explicit creed, usually some form of socialism.

Just in the last quarter of the nineteenth century as many members
of the middle and upper classes were experiencing that loss of belief not
only in 'specific systems of ultimate meaning' but also in 'the
possibility of *any* definitive system of answers to such questions' which,
in the inimitable phraseology of Glock and Stark, 'seems to be one of
the marks of emerging modern man',[202] many members of the working
class were discovering the ultimate meaning that had been previously
denied them. The autobiography of Tom Jackson describes – perhaps
in unusually clear-cut form – the experience of many. Jackson was to
be severely critical of the 'sentimental pacifist'[203] element in the
British Socialist movement. It was therefore appropriate that his
conversion began at an anti-Boer War meeting where he was impressed
by the fashion in which SDF strong arm men disposed of attempted
Tory disruption. He went home to re-read *Merrie England*, and within
an hour he had become a Socialist. 'When I say that I "became a
Socialist" I mean simply that I was struck as by a thunderbolt with the
realisation that a society built upon the private ownership of land as an
alienable "property" – with all the developed consequences of that
private ownership – must be a radically immoral society and one

increasingly oppressive'.[204] He at once joined the SDF, and shared with his fellow members 'intense conviction', 'deep passionate earnestness' and 'fervid exaltation' in winning 'converts'. He then (though without any encouragement from the branch Literature Secretary, who had never heard of Marx), turned to *Socialism, Utopian and Scientific* and the *Communist Manifesto*, and found there the systematic world-view that his earlier reading of Darwin and Hegel had led him to desire:

> It gave me as in a flash of blazing realisation a completely inter-related Universe, in which mankind and human society and their history were details in an endlessly developing whole — the triumphant Revolution and realised socialism emerging as sub-details in the magnificent sweep of its irresistibly compelling whole.[205]

All he needed now to protect his 'completely inter-related Universe' from alternative theories was a formula for explaining the motives of opponents and the reason for the setbacks that the movement from time to time suffered — and this he found in 'the astuteness with which the ruling class manage things',[206] The fact that a large and increasing section of the working class, together with some from the middle and upper classes, shared this Socialist faith, although differing over matters of details, meant that Jackson would not need to fall back on this formula too often. Far from his being an 'emerging modern man', his system of ultimate meaning was as completely protected as that of any pre-Vatican II Portuguese priest.

Jackson, and thousands like him, enjoyed the total certainty of having found the meaning of life that was becoming rare among Christians — except in some protected enclaves chiefly of working-class Roman Catholics. What had gone was the appearance of consensus that Evangelical Christians had succeeded in imposing on the middle and upper classes generally (and in Wales and Cornwall on the population as a whole) during the first three-quarters of the century. Class solidarity was the secret weapon of the Socialists, as respectability had been of the Evangelicals, by means of which doubters were kept in line. But it could only be invoked in critical situations, such as those of a strike, and not every day, and working-class sceptics remained aloof from the dominant ideology, even when the Socialist tide reached its high-water mark in 1919 and the years following, far more easily than the 'practical men' and exponents of the double standard in the middle and upper classes had escaped the attentions of the dominant Evangelicalism in its early Victorian heyday.

Notes

1. Masterman, op.cit., pp.88-9.
2. Ibid., p.267.
3. The *British Congregationalist* 13-27 February 1913, published a symposium on the decline of church membership and attendance. It is an interesting example of contrasting reactions within the same church. There were three main attitudes: to blame the people, like the Rev. B. Nightingale, who mentioned 'the prevalence of the materialistic spirit', 'inordinate passion for pleasure', 'undue eagerness to become speedily rich', and 'lowered conception of Christian responsibility'; to blame the church, like the Rev. F. J. Powicke, who thought his brother ministers too strict about 'doctrinal standards', and too loose about 'loving the Lord Jesus'; or to welcome the change, like the Rev. R. Briggs, who noted a 'wider and deeper spiritual freedom', a 'purer' 'spiritual atmosphere', and was glad that people no longer joined a church 'for custom's sake, or as the hall-mark of respectability'.
4. Prosecutions of those selling *The Age of Reason* began in 1797, after it appeared in a cheap edition. E. Royle, *Radical Politics, 1790-1900: Religion and Unbelief*, Longmans, London, 1971, pp.20-5, 29.
5. M. Bourdeaux, *Opium of the People*, Faber, London, 1965, pp.137-150.
6. In the diocese of La Rochelle, now substantially 'dechristianised', 99 per cent of the Catholic rural population are calculated to have done their Easter Duties in the 1660s. In the 1680s the dragonnades turned the majority of the Protestants into nominal, though not in many cases very good, Catholics. L. Pérouas, *Le Diocèse de La Rochelle de 1648 a 1724*, Paris, 1964, pp.162, 419.
7. Thomas, op.cit., pp.159-66, has collected numerous examples of ignorance of religion, non-attendance at church, reluctant attendance, and irreverent conduct during services in rural England in this period. Like others he makes special mention of the North and of heath and forest. Cf. C. J. Hunt, *The Lead Miners of the Northern Pennines*, Manchester UP, Manchester, 1970.
8. C. Hill, *The World Turned Upside Down*, Temple Smith, London 1972, Chs.8-10.
9. D. P. Walker, *The Decline of Hell*, Routledge, London, 1964, pp.3-23. Walker stresses the obscurity (Origen excepted) of those who challenged the doctrine of eternal punishment before the end of the seventeenth century, the rarity of such challenges and the cautious manner in which they were made. Hill, on the other hand, (op.cit., pp.140-2), lists large numbers of attacks on the doctrine in England in the 1640s and '50s, and notes two sixteenth-century examples of what was to become a cliché in the nineteenth century – that hell was 'a torment of conscience' or 'poverty in this world'.

10. Walker, op.cit., pp.29, 37-8.
11. Ibid., p.5.
12. Ibid., pp.93-5, 159.
13. See, e.g., for England, R. N. Stromberg, *Religious Liberalism in Eighteenth-Century England*, OUP, London, 1954; for Scotland, T. C. Smout, *History of the Scottish People, 1560-1830*, Collins, London, 1969, pp.213-22; for Denmark, J. O. Andersen *Survey of the Danish Church*, Copenhagen, 1930, pp.35-42.
14. K. H. D. Haley, *The Dutch in the Seventeenth Century*, Thames and Hudson, London, 1972, pp.94-9; H. Kamen, *The Spanish Inquisition*, Weidenfeld, London, 1965, pp.249-70.
15. To take two examples from local studies: in the Loiret in the mid-nineteenth century, 'throne and altar' were part of the common consciousness of the aristocracy, even though the men did not necessarily go to Mass themselves; but in all other classes, especially the grande and petite bourgeoisie, anti-clerical feeling was strong even among many of those who did go to Mass. In the Var, the peasants remained devout until the 1840s, but the bourgeoisie in town and country were often avowed freethinkers. C. Marcilhacy, *Le Diocèse d'Orléans au Milieu du XIXe Siècle*, Sirey, Paris, 1964, pp.6-8, 192, 202-17; M. Agulhon, *La République au Village*, Paris, 1970, pp.168-72, 182.
16. Thus in Denmark, Mynster and Grundtvig, two of the outstanding figures of the century evolved in such a way and underwent crises in 1803 and 1810 respectively. Andersen, op.cit., pp.44-6, 48-53.
17. Rule, op.cit., pp.287-301; L. J. Saunders, *Scottish Democracy*, Oliver and Boyd, Edinburgh, 1950, pp.264-7; O. Vornen and E. Manker, *Lapp Life and Customs* (English Translation), OUP, London, 1962, p.130.
18. K. S. Latourette, *Christianity in a Revolutionary Age*, Eyre and Spottiswoode, London, 1962, IV, pp.154-5, 172.
19. W. S. Hudson, *Religion in America*, Scribner, New York, 1965, p.135; Latourette, op.cit., IV, pp.70-5.
20. The process by which Evangelical Protestantism moved into a dominant position, during the first half of the nineteenth century, in the culture of the mining villages of Cornwall and of the farms and small towns of Western New York has been described by Rule, op.cit., and by W. Cross, *The Burned-Over District*, New York, 1950. Rule notes the important position of the local preachers (rather like that of the Irish priest), resting on friendship and loyalty, but enforced by the occasional use of 'moral terrorism'; Cross describes the ultra-Evangelical of the 1830s as very intolerant not only of outright evil, but of 'the indifferent, cautious, or merely less than supremely zealous person' (Rule, pp.279-83, 310-9; Cross, p.205).
21. The uncomfortable position of the doubter in a revival-bound Pietist community has been mentioned by Ibsen (who came from South-East Norway) and Engels (who came from the Wuppertal). M. Meyer, *Henrik Ibsen, The Making of a Dramatist*, Hart-Davis,

London, 1967, p.70; H. Desroche, 'Athéisme et Socialisme dans le Marxisme, Classique', *Archives de Sociologie des Religions,* no.10, juillet-décembre 1960, p.80.

22. As one example: Mary Vivian Hughes in the 1890s was friendly with two old women, governors of Bedford College, one of whom had been 'embittered about all kinds of religion. You see, we are Unitarians and are looked upon as atheists, and by many people as inferior socially.' M. V. Hughes, *A London Home of the Nineties,* OUP, London, 1937, p.142.

23. In West Cornwall in the early nineteenth century there were said to be villages where 90 per cent of the adult population attended Methodist meetings. In South Cardiganshire, the 1859 revival completed the process by which the great majority of the non-gentry population was brought into connection with a Nonconformist church; by 1900 it is calculated that over 90 per cent of the adult population of the parish studied by David Jenkins were either church members or Church of Wales communicants. M. S. Edwards, 'Cornish Methodism: A Study in Division, 1814—57', University of Birmingham M. A. thesis, 1962, p.19; Jenkins, op.cit., pp.207-14.

24. *Quarterly Review,* CXLIII, May 1843, p.232.

25. It was about 1810, according to a historian of the subject, that children began to reproach their parents with frivolity. M. Jaeger, *Before Victoria,* Chatto, London, 1956, p.71.

26. Gissing, *New Grub Street,* p.256.

27. Rev. W. H. Langhorne in the parish magazine of Holy Trinity, Sydenham, as quoted in *Lewisham Borough News,* 9 August 1912.

28. See, for instance, two recent studies of rural communities in Spain, in which the insistence on female chastity is contrasted with the demand for 'Don Juanism' on the part of young men, and for 'manliness', including most notably an aggressive sense of honour, on the part of all men – J. A. Pitt-Rivers, *The People of the Sierra,* Weidenfeld, London, 1954, and C. Lison-Tolosona, *Belmonte de los Caballeros,* OUP, London, 1966.

29. To give one example, Thomas Okey, who at one stage in his life lived in the same Kent village as H. M. Hyndman and his wife, reported that Mrs. Hyndman could not get domestic help until she had made a few appearances at the parish church. Of course, no one insisted on Hyndman going. Okey, op.cit., p.110.

30. Taine quoted the case of a wealthy businessman who dropped all pretence of Sabbatarianism when he visited Paris alone, but behaved just as he would have done in England when going there with his wife and daughters. When his host came to see him in London, the Frenchman started practising at the billiard table on Sunday morning and was stopped at once. Taine, op.cit., p.194.

31. Anglican incumbents, when replying to Visitation Queries concerning Sunday observance, were well aware of the distinction. Typical replies were: '*Externally* it is observed with great

propriety' (Minister of Regent Square Chapel, London Visitation, 1842); 'Very well outwardly' (Vicar of St Peter's, Notting Hill, London Visitation, 1862).

32. See Thomas Wright's account of the prosperous artisan's Sunday in *Some Habits and Customs of the Working Classes*, London, 1867, p.214.

33. F. K. Aglionby, *Life of Edward Henry Bickersteth*, Longmans, London, 1885, pp.191-4. Bickersteth was Vicar of Christ Church, Hampstead, 1855-85, and Bishop of Exeter, 1885-1900. He was a leading representative of the more theologically conservative Evangelicals.

34. Peel and Marriott, op.cit., p.53.

35. Sunday morning was, of course, the time when the poor bought their meat at reduced prices, as well as much else. (See, for instance, H Mayhew, op.cit., I, pp.10-11). The failure of all attempts to stop such trading by persuasion can be seen from any volume of City Missions Reports or Visitation Returns. The failure of an attempt to limit such trading by law is described in B. Harrison, 'The Sunday Trading Riots of 1855', in *Historical Journal*, vol. VIII, no.2, 1965. The limited effect of legislation intended to restrict Sunday drinking is noted in Wright, op.cit., p.226, where a Sunday morning session in a back-street pub is interrupted by a policeman, who turns out to be one of the 'tolerably numerous sort' who accept shillings and drinks on the house. Bye-laws often restricted Sunday recreation in parks, but this did not stop fishing and boating in or on rivers, football or pigeon-flying on waste-ground, or, in many cases, anything short of fully organised sport in the park. Visitation Returns provide much evidence of the local forms of Sunday non-observance. For instance, the Vicar of Trinity, Twickenham (London Visitation, 1842) complained of a general 'desecration of the Sabbath' and the Vicar of St Mary's mentioned fishing, work in market gardens, pleasure boats (and 'indecent behaviour' on them), barges, steamers, seventy vans going through the parish on a summer Sunday often with twenty or thirty people in each. Trippers were complained of by incumbents of riverside parishes and of those on main roads out of London generally. Roger Homan, in a study of 'Sunday Observance and Social Class', correctly points out that Sabbatarian legislation and the abstract 'Victorian Sunday' could bear heavily on working men with very little leisure, but does not raise the question of how far it affected them in practice (D. Martin and M. Hill (eds.), *Sociological Yearbook of Religion in Britain, 3*, SCM Press, London, 1970, p.89).

36. Gissing, *Born in Exile*, pp.288-9.

37. One example of the middle-class sabbatarian who is unconvinced, but nonetheless respects convention, has been quoted from Taine. Another is Professor Blackie's account of an afternoon with Lord Amberley in 1860: 'I owe two things to him not at all to be de-

spised. He taught me a new game called croquet and he gave me the new sensation of playing at a game on Sunday, doing what to our Scottish conscience should appear as a sin.' B. and P. Russell, *The Amberley Papers*, Allen and Unwin, London, 1937, I, p.218.

38. Melbourne asserted that 'once is orthodox, twice is puritanical', whereas Gladstone coined the terms 'oncer' and 'twicer' He was emphatically a 'twicer' (W. B. Trevelyan, *Sunday*, Longmans, London, 1902, pp.277-8).

39. G. Russell, *For Better? For Worse?* Fisher Unwin, London, 1902, pp.59-60; *An On-lookers Notebook*, p.175.

40. Taine, op.cit., p.290.

41. See above, Chapter VII.

42. Hughes, *A London Family of the Eighties*, pp.88-9.

43. As with the 'Old Squire' (Lowther-Clarke, op.cit., p.45), who appeared in his pew on Sunday morning, 'clothed in a frock coat, and an immaculate silk hat in his hand which bespeak both the respect that he deems right to show and also the sense of discomfort inseparable from social obligations'.

44. Edward White and Henry Dobney, two Congregational ministers who in the 1840s advocated conditional immortality in books largely ignored or condemned at the time, had both endured periods of mental torture because of their belief in hell. (Dobney later became a universalist). Liddon who, of course, believed in hell, regarded the desire to deny its eternity as a temptation to be fought against. Rowell, op.cit., pp.110, 182-8.

45. An Irish definition of the damned. See C. Arensberg and S. K. Kimball, *Family and Community in Ireland*, Harvard UP, Cambridge, Mass., 1940, p.217.

46. Rowell, op.cit., p.50.

47. Ibid, p.46.

48. Thus Luther at a time when the doctrine of hell was under various forms of attack from radical reformers, insisted that no unbeliever could be saved, and, if this seemed harsh in some human eyes, 'musz man unszer duncken und Gottis warheyt gar weyt sundern'. He concluded that we should 'far rather allow that all men, angels and devils will be damned than that God should not be truthful in his words'. Walker, op.cit., p.6.

49. D. W. Howe, 'The Decline of Calvinism', *Comparative Studies in Society and History*, vol.XIV, no.3, June 1972, suggests a rather extreme version of the theory that religious doctrinal systems are a reflection of the social situation of those who adhere to them. Thus, he argues that Calvinism arises from a 'social mood of fear', and declines as capitalism, and, with it, man's control over his environment advances. In support of this he instances the fact that in the early nineteenth century the merchant elite of Boston were 'Liberals', often Unitarians, while Calvinism flourished in the 'lonely isolation' of rural Scotland or the American back-woods (ibid., p.323). In nineteenth-century Britain, however, although most Unitarians were rich, most rich men certainly were

not Unitarians. They were far more likely to be Evangelical Anglicans, a particularly conservative group. For most of the century, in fact, Calvinism was most characteristic of the higher social strata, and though Howe grants that the 'threat of militant secularism coming with the French Revolution provoked a Calvinist reaction in a few quarters', (ibid., p.322), this reaction does seem to have been unduly prolonged.

50. In 1853 a worker at the locomotive shop at Swindon was sacked after he declared his disbelief in hell in a letter to the press and, as late as 1878, a pamphlet condemning the views on hell of F. W. Farrar argued that it was only this fear that restrained the poor from orgies of class violence. Royle, *Victorian Infidels. The Origins of the British Secularist Movement, 1791-1866*, Manchester UP, 1974, p.288; Rowell, op.cit., pp.150-1.

51. Authors who mention hell as an important part of their childhood include William Kent (op.cit., p.28), who was born in 1884 in a lower middle-class Wesleyan family; Thomas Okey (op.cit., pp.6-7), 'the religious atmosphere' of whose 'school and home was of the narrowest Victorian Evangelicalism, although I remember none of our elders who attended service at church', and who was born in 1852; and Robert Graves *Goodbye to All That*, Penguin, Harmondsworth, 1960, p.20, (first published 1929), who was born in 1895, whose parents were Anglican, upper middle-class and literary, and who claimed to have been 'perpetually tortured by the fear of hell'.

52. E. E. Kellett, *As I Remember*, Gollancz, London, 1936, pp.126-31.

53. B. Martin, *An Impossible Parson*, Allen and Unwin, London, 1935, p.16. This is interesting, as Martin rejected most of his parents' Calvinist theology. However, it was sufficiently notable to be worth remembering when at eleven (about 1870) he met his first universalist (a Bible Class teacher).

54. *A London Child of the Seventies*, p.80.

55. Martin, op.cit., p.99.

56. Rowell, op.cit., p.188.

57. Budd, 'The Loss of Faith', pp.118-9.

58. H. R. Murphy, 'The Ethical Revolt Against Christian Orthodoxy in Early Victorian England', *American Historical Review*, vol.LX, no.4, July 1955, p.801. Like Budd, who has also traced the process by which individuals lost their faith, he notes the fact that moral objections – chiefly to hell, to some aspects of the Old Testament and to substitutionary atonement – preceded 'scientific' objections. This is a valuable point, but he gives Froude, Newman and George Eliot more of representative character than they deserve. His castigation of the millions of Evangelicals, High Churchmen and Nonconformists who failed to accept the 'spirit of the age' suggests criteria for defining that spirit comparable to those of the 'grass-roots Democrat' who claimed that McGovern could not lose if he chose a black woman

as his running-mate.

59. Thus in Sidgwick's circle the adoption of 'more sceptical and less Christian' views dated from 'the discussions started in 1860 by *Essays and Reviews'*. B. Willey, *More Nineteenth Century Studies*, Chatto, London, 1956, p.101.

60. O. Chadwick, *The Victorian Church*, A. and C. Black, London, 1966-70, II, pp.75-90. In 1864, 10,906 out of 24,805 Anglican clergymen signed a declaration reaffirming belief in among other things everlasting torment. But very few clergymen were prepared unequivocally to defend the Essayists.

61. Rowell, op.cit., pp.147-9. The correspondence is now preserved at Canterbury Cathedral.

62. Ibid., p.354. Edward White's conditionalist doctrine had become well known through a controversy in the liberal Nonconformist *Christian World* in 1870, (ibid., p.196).

63. This was to be one of the major issues in the Down-Grade controversy in 1887, which led to Spurgeon's secession from the Baptist Union, on the grounds of its being insufficiently exclusive. See E. Payne, *History of the Baptist Union*, Carey Kingsgate Press, London, 1959.

64. Rowell, op.cit., p.133. During the '70s and early '80s a number of Congregational chapels in the Eastern Counties were split by the preaching of young ministers with a 'kindlier and more imprecise theology'. Some of these conflicts have been analysed by Clyde Binfield, who concludes that: 'Many in the 1870s and 1880s must have found the experience of their first pastorate strangely like the hell in whose disbelief lay their undoing'. C. Binfield, 'Chapels in Crisis', *Transactions of the Congregational Historical Society*, vol.XX, no.8, October 1968, pp.238, 246.

65. Letter published in *Hampstead and Highgate Express*, 18 September 1886.

66. Walker, op.cit., p.4. These strengths and weaknesses are discussed in chapters two and three of his book.

67. W. L. Courtney, op.cit., pp.285-7.

68. Out of the ninety letters, there were thirty-two in which the main point was the excessive harshness or exclusiveness of Christianity, of which, besides the eleven directed against hell, there were four directed against doctrines of atonement, three arguing for the excellence of non-Christian religions, three for the moral excellence of non-Christians generally, and thirteen advocating a non-dogmatic humanism (two of which also fell into one of the other categories).

69. W. L. Courtney, op.cit., pp.182-3.

70. Ibid., pp.263-4.

71. It was presumably this that E. E. Kellett, brought up in an atmosphere of 'fatal bibliolatory', had in mind when he claimed that 'there is far more difference between the mind of 1900 and that of 1880 than between 1880 and 1640'. Kellett, op.cit., pp.101, 105-6.

72. See e.g., J. Kent, *From Darwin to Blatchford*, and Chadwick, op.cit., II, pp.23-25. There is one letter from a believer condemning Darwin (Courtney, op.cit., pp.153-4) and one from a doubter whose faith had been shaken by attacks on the historicity of Genesis and Jonah. (Ibid., pp.242-3).

73. Ibid., pp.199-201.

74. Ibid., pp.271-3.

75. Ibid., p.250.

76. M. Peckham, 'Darwinism and Darwinisticism', *Victorian Studies*, vol.III, no.1, September 1959. Among the leading 'metaphysical evolutionists' he includes Spencer, Browning, Tennyson, Carlyle, and the authors of *Essays and Reviews*.

77. Chadwick, op.cit., II, pp.19-20; W. Irvine, *Apes, Angels and Victorians*, Weidenfeld, London, 1955, pp.108-11.

78. Thus, one contributor, whose views were indeed paralleled in a number of other letters, claimed that 'though Englishmen have lost faith either in the absolute truth of the Gospel, or in the orthodox creed of the Churches, a very large and increasing number of them' believed that 'a great inscrutable, living force and intelligence is slowly evolving order out of chaos, and bringing about that state of human perfection which we call "Heaven" ' (Courtney, op.cit., p.245).

79. Ibid., pp.96-7.

80. Ibid., pp.232-3.

81. Thus the great heat generated by such issues as infant baptism in an overwhelmingly Protestant society, such as South Wales in the mid-nineteenth century, and exemplified in the Rhymney Baptismal Fair of 1844, where huge crowds gathered for a debate between Baptist and Independent champions that turned into a riot. See E. T. Davies, op.cit., pp.51-2. The studies by Glock and Stark of the varieties of religious commitment in the United States have illustrated the difference between belief as integration into a community whose tenets are uniform and exclusive, and belief as personal affirmation in an environment of wide-ranging scepticism. 99 per cent of Southern Baptists, but only 41 per cent of Congregationalists claim to be 'certain' of God's existence. Glock and Stark, op.cit., pp.22-56.

82. Unfortunately no records of London Visitations in the intervening period appear to have survived.

83. *Punch*, 23 June 1877.

84. The declaration was that of the editor of the *Nonconformist* (2 February 1882), who also noted that church-going had become 'more than was formerly the case perfunctory'. The *Daily Telegraph* (quoted in the *Nonconformist*, 23 February 1882) expressed similar views in more apocalyptic terms. The editor of the *Hastings and St Leonard's Times*, (26 November 1881), emphatically agreed, but most of the papers organising the censuses offered no opinion on the subject. Partial exceptions were the *Bolton Journal*, (10 December 1881) which noted a

'sifting of old beliefs', and the *Northampton Guardian* (12 November 1881), which referred to a decline in 'twicing'. In fact, a difference in method between the 1851 census and those held in 1881 made direct comparison fallacious. My own comparisons suggest that there was little change in the level of church-going.

85. In 1880 the *Nineteenth Century* was debating 'Agnosticism and Women'. The first article (April 1880, pp.626-7) claimed that the desire 'to be in the front ranks of progress' was drawing women towards 'the atheism of the day'.

86. These are both in the Fulham Papers at Lambeth Palace, the catalogue of which also includes the Returns for 1905 and 1911, though they are said to be 'lost'. Two sets of returns from Visitations held in the 1890s are at the Guildhall Library, but they appear to include only the replies of churchwardens to questions about church fabric.

87. Returns from 1881, 1885 and 1889 are also available. They include the question 'Does the Church of England appear to be fairly holding her own among you?' It was generally answered in terms of the relative strength of Nonconformity.

88. P. T. Cominos, 'The Late Victorian Revolt', University of Oxford, D.Phil. Thesis, 1958, pp.586, 590-3; H. Jackson, *The Eighteen Nineties*, 3rd edition, 1931, pp.22-3.

89. As an example of the former, the *Lewisham Gazette*, 19 April 1895: 'While the Church is certainly not losing her hold on the "classes", she is making headway with the "masses" with a rapidity unknown for generations.'

90. There is an obvious parallel in the new freedom with which Fleet Street — as opposed to papers with a specialised readership — has discussed pre- and extra-marital sex in the last five years or so.

91. 10 March 1905: 'All branches of Christians are conscious that the Church in these days is losing its hold . . . '

92. 12 October 1907: On 17 June 1905, it had published an article headed 'Why not abandon Christianity?' which had advocated the conversion of the Church into a non-sectarian social service body.

93. In the period 1885-1900 I have only come across two such letters, (*Hampstead and Highgate Express*, 12 May 1888 and 16 June 1888), both from the same correspondent, both in criticism of a local High Church vicar, and largely phrased in terms of a fairly conventional anti-clericalism. (Certain passages concerning the distinctive views on religion of the correspondent were cut by the editor.)

94. In reporting a series of anti-Catholic lectures (10 March 1900), the editor announced that no further correspondence on the subject would be allowed, and this announcement was thereafter repeated in the years following whenever speeches of a sectarian nature were reported. Previously the matters at issue between Protestants and Catholics, Ritualists and Kensitites, etc., had been debated *ad nauseam* in the paper's columns.

95. Ibid., 10 December 1904. R. F. Horton, whose church was in

Hampstead, was a pundit of national significance, whose views on every subject were convassed by the press, and eagerly followed by many readers.

96. Ibid., 29 September 1906. It may be worth mentioning that Haverstock Chapel, fashionable some three decades earlier, had long been overshadowed by Horton's Lyndhurst Road. Its members and ministers were probably more politically and theologically conservative, and this may have predisposed them to jeremiads of this sort. Horton, like the liberal Baptist Newton Marshall, at Heath Street chapel, no doubt deplored the decline in the observance of Sunday, but he was committed to emphasising the positive aspects of new developments.

97. D. Cooper, *The Rainbow Comes and Goes*, Hart-Davis, London, 1958, pp.75-6. She was born in the 1890s and her father was Duke of Rutland. Mr. Knox was his chaplain.

98. A Member of the Aristocracy, *Manners and Rules of Good Society*, (1888 ed.,) p.112.

99. Ibid., p.111. This passage does not appear in the 1879 edition of the book, in which there is no mention of Grace.

100. The only example I have come across is in the autobiography of Lady Violet Hardy (op.cit., p.14), whose father was a successful barrister and son of a peer, and whose husband was a Warwickshire landowner. She thought that family prayers interfered with the servants' breakfast preparations, and 'I fear I had to abandon the practice after marriage [in 1900]. Our small but definite household could not stand up to it, a lapse for which we were reproved by my husband's two spinster aunts, the Misses Gladstone, who were nieces of the G.O.M.'.

101. G. Russell, *For Better? For Worse?*, pp.155-8.

102. Thus, Sonia Keppel, who was born in 1900 into West End Society, describes the first account she received in a letter from a friend of the bizarre goings-on at the Surrey home of her future parents-in-law, Lord and Lady Ashcombe: family prayers every morning was ranked with girls having to wear gloves in the house, smoking being banned in the drawing-room, and cards on Sunday anywhere (S. Keppel, *Edwardian Daughter*, 1958, p.184).

103. In 1889 the Provost of King's College, Cambridge, still took it for granted that most freshmen came from homes where family prayers were the custom. S. Andrews, *Methodism and Society*, Longmans, London, 1971, p.71, quoting an unidentified circular.

104. Taine, op.cit., pp.156-7; replies by incumbents, London Visitations, 1858 and 1862.

105. London Visitation 1883, reply of minister of Brunswick Chapel, Marylebone.

106. Rochester Visitation, 1894, replies of Vicars of St Paul's, Herne Hill, and Emmanuel, Wimbledon.

107. *Daily Telegraph*, 6 October 1905. A ban on Sunday games in LCC parks had been imposed, with very little opposition, in 1901. Pressure for at least a partial lifting of the ban was initiated in

1913 and succeeded in 1922. London County Council, *Minutes of Proceedings*, 12 March 1901, 8 July 1913, 22 July 1922, 10 July 1923. Conservative councillors had supported the ban in 1913, but opposed it in 1923, when a motion to stop Sunday games was lost by 83-33; Labour was strongly anti-sabbatarian on both occasions; while the Liberals were evenly divided, a small majority opposing the ban on each occasion.

108. Kenward, op.cit., pp.23-4, 32-3, 72.

109. The percentage of 'twicers' was high among Baptists (about 20 per cent), slightly lower among Wesleyans and Congregationalists, and much lower among Anglicans (about 12 per cent).

110. None of these figures is exact: in 1886-7 and 1902-3 we have an exact number of church-goers, but population has to be estimated; in 1851 we have exact population, but some of the congregational totals are estimates, and all of them include Sunday School children in proportions that can only be discovered by working through the original schedules – my sample suggests that on average they made up 20 per cent of the total, but that the proportion varied widely (it was 28 per cent in Bethnal Green, but 6 per cent in St. George's, Hanover Square).

111. To compare 1851 with 1886-7 I have taken five registration districts, for 1886-7 and 1902-3 the 28 metropolitan boroughs. The former comparison shows little change in Bethnal Green, Lambeth or St. George's, Hanover Square, but drops from 19 per cent to 17 per cent in St George's in the East and 55 per cent to 41 per cent in Hampstead. In all five districts Anglican attendances had dropped.

112. Westminster, Chelsea, and St. Marylebone were the only metropolitan boroughs in which the number of female domestic indoor servants per 100 families increased between 1901 and 1911. For the changing character of the inner West End, see Booth, op.cit., III, iii, p.130.

113. A pamphlet of 1858, quoted by Inglis, op.cit., p.322.

114. In Bethnal Green, where the population only increased slightly between the *British Weekly* and *Daily News* censuses, eight Anglican congregations increased and eight decreased; in Lewisham, where population increased substantially, there were four new Anglican churches, six in which the congregation increased and nineteen where it decreased.

115. Anglican attendances as a percentage of total population fell from 13.5 to 9.4, or by 30.3 per cent, the loss being greatest in the wealthiest districts, and slightly greater at evening than at morning services. Corresponding losses for the major Nonconformist bodies were: Baptists 20.4 per cent, Congregationalists 19.8 per cent, Wesleyans 13.1 per cent. Two smaller denominations, Presbyterians and Salvation Army, suffered as heavily as the Anglicans. The Roman Catholic share of the total population probably fell by about 25 per cent, but the incompleteness of the 1886-7 figures makes it impossible to be

certain.

116. Letter to *Hampstead and Highgate Express*, 15 January 1910. The Hampstead Nonconformists, whose chief targets were Horton and Newton Marshall, were not alone. Lloyd George's budget brought to a head long-standing antagonism between leading ministers, who tended to be ardent Radicals, and wealthy laymen, whose Liberalism was often very luke-warm. See Blewett, op.cit., pp.346-9.

117. Trevelyan, op.cit., p.5.

118. *Punch*, 23 June 1877. The article was presumably intended as an indictment of those who supported sabbatarian legislation while not observing Sunday themselves, as it ended with Bill Jones (Seven Dials) reporting that he spent the day in the public house, "Cos you nobs ain't left me nothing else for to do'.

119. For a general discussion of changing Evangelical attitudes to pleasure, see M. Hennell, 'Evangelicalism and Worldliness, 1770-1870', in G. J. Cuming and D. Baker (eds.), *Studies in Church History*, 8, CUP, Cambridge, 1972. He notes a greater strictness in the generation of Evangelicals born about 1800 than in their fathers. John Venn, for instance, ordered all of Scott's novels as they came out, and though he did not have his children taught to dance, he claimed to have 'religious friends' whose children did learn dancing; his son, however, took for granted a ban on all 'worldly amusements'.

120. For one example, see P. Scott, 'Cricket and the Religious World', *Church Quarterly* vol.III, no.1, July 1970. Scott notes that several leading Evangelicals of the early and mid-nineteenth century had been outstanding cricketers at university, but 'silently renounced' the game on being ordained, as part of putting away childish things. But from the 1880s onwards, the cricketing prowess of C. T. Studd, and of his successors, up to David Sheppard, was exploited for evangelistic ends.

121. Mrs. H. Ward, *Robert Elsmere*, Nelson, London, 1952, pp.103, 185-6, (first published, 1888).

122. Ibid., p.91.

123. Ibid., p.209.

124. Ibid., pp.492-5, 500-8.

125. Ibid., p.165.

126. Ibid., pp.169-70, 176-80, 158.

127. E. Bligh, *Tooting Corner*, pp.333-4. A contemporary of his, brought up in a Welsh mining village, tied to the chapel by strong family loyalties, has described his revulsion from the 'thick Ulster coat' type of religion prevailing in Glamorganshire Nonconformity which preceded his subsequent Darwinian and Marxist objections. W. J. Edwards, *From the Valley I Came*, Angus and Robertson, London, 1956.

128. The sources of information are (i) the Fertility Census of 1911, included in the decennial census of that year, in which married women were asked in what year they had married and how many

children they had had, and (ii) the totals of births registered annually. The latter are not completely reliable, both because of incomplete registration and because of the difficulty of estimating the size and composition of inter-censal population, but J. W. Innes, *Class Fertility Trends in England and Wales, 1876-1934*, Princeton UP, 1938, p.14, dates the decline in the legitimate birth-rate per 1000 married women aged 15-45 from 1877. The former source shows the size of completed family (5.71) as slightly greater for women born 1841-5 than for those born 1846-50 (5.63), and the rate of decline increasing between each subsequent five-year period. Among women marrying 1851-61, the least fertile group, middle- and upper-class wives had a completed family 86 per cent of the average, while the most fertile group, wives of miners, stood at 110 per cent. Among those marrying 1881-6 the differential was much greater. For figures for other countries, see D. V. Glass and E. Grebenik, 'World Population, 1800-1950', H. J. Habakkuk and M. Postan (eds.), *Cambridge Economic History of Europe, VI*, CUP, Cambridge, 1965, pp.68-9, 90-119; A. J. Coale, 'The Decline of Fertility in Europe from the French Revolution to the Second World War', S. J. Behrman and others (eds.), *Fertility and Family Planning: A World View*, Michigan UP, Ann Arbor, 1969, pp.3-24.

129. The 1870s saw improvements in synthetic rubber moulding in Germany, which facilitated the manufacture of cheap sheaths, and in 1885 Rendell's quinine sulphate spermicide was invented. J. Peel, 'Manufacture and Retailing of Contraceptives in England', *Population Studies*, vol.XVII, no.1, July 1963, pp.116-7. But the Royal Commission on Population claimed that *coitus interruptus* remained the most important method for long after the late '70s. *P.P.*, 1949, XIX, paras. 92-3. For examples of the use of old-fashioned methods by H. H. Asquith, W. T. Stead and the 'respectable' working class in Tottenham, see O. Mosley, *My Life*, Nelson, London, 1968, p.114; J. A. and O. Banks, *Feminism and Family Planning*, Liverpool UP, Liverpool, 1964, p.92, fn 1; T. Willis, op.cit., pp.8-9; for a combination of new and old by a somewhat unrespectable middle class, Ackerley, op.cit., p.43. I am indebted for the first of these references, and for other suggestions on this subject, to Professor J. R. de S. Honey.

130. I have found less evidence of Nonconformist attitudes. As early as 1893 (Banks, op.cit., pp.99-100), the liberal *Christian World*, Spurgeon's *bête noire*, was denouncing those who failed to take advantage of the 'safe period'. But it was not necessarily representative of Nonconformists in general.

131. J. A. and O. Banks, 'The Bradlaugh-Besant Trial and the English Newspapers', in *Population Studies*, vol.VIII, no.1, July 1954. Conservative papers were most likely to be hostile to the defendants.

132. When in 1854-5 the decline in the French population was much

discussed the reasons suggested were sometimes so bizarre as to suggest that the extensive practice of birth control in the country was either not known or else not a fit subject to mention in print. Banks, *Prosperity and Parenthood*, pp.139-42.

133. *Official Report of the Church Congress, 1890*, p.28.

134. See above, Chapter V.

135. B. R. Wilson, *Religion in Secular Society*, Watts, London, 1966, pp.65-6. The Lambeth Conference in 1958 reversed these positions.

136. H. H. Henson, *Retrospect of an Unimportant Life*, OUP, London, 1942-6, II, p.274.

137. E. A. Wrigley, 'Family Limitation in Pre-Industrial England'. *Economic History Review*, vol.XIX, no.1, April 1966, showed that the fertility of married women in Colyton, Devon, followed a cyclical pattern between 1538 and 1837, and the fall in the number of baptisms between about 1650 and 1730 was apparently due both to a rise in the mean age of marriage and to the lower fertility of the married. The French literature on this subject is extensive. See, for instance, J. Dupaquier and M. Lethivier, 'Sur les Débuts de la Contraception en France, ou les deux Malthusianismes', *Annales*, vol.XXIV, no.6, nov-dec 1969. Their study of a small town in the East of France shows that the proportion of families in which the mean interval between the birth of children exceeded four years increased from 10 per cent in the period 1660-1739, to 21 per cent between 1740 and 1789, and 52 per cent between 1790 and 1839. According to V. Bourgeois-Pichat, the gross reproduction rate in France fell almost continuously from 1770 to 1935, except 1850-70. It fell from 2.45 in 1770 to 1.65 in 1851-5. See D. V. Glass and D. E. C. Eversley, (eds.) *Population in History*, Arnold, London, 1965, pp.475-89. Unfortunately, it may be that Wrigley is analysing fluctuations in the proportion of babies baptised, rather than in the number of births. T. H. Hollingsworth (*Historical Demography*, Hodder and Stoughton, London, 1969, pp.193-5) has constructed an alternative explanation of Wrigley's figures, based on this assumption. But it seems to me less convincing than Wrigley's original explanation.

138. This would be true, for instance, of Place, J. S. Mill, Bradlaugh, Besant and Amberley. R. S. Neale, in a criticism of 'ideologically homogeneous' conceptions of the mid-Victorian middle class, associates advocacy of contraception, and other heterodox attitudes to sex, with 'the politically Radical beliefs characteristic of the middling class' (i.e. the 'uneasy class' of those who were not members of the working class, but lacked the security and status of the middle class) (*Class and Ideology in the Nineteenth Century*, Routledge, London, 1972, p.141). There is an interesting contrast of attitudes in a book of family history, the milieu of which is the upper working and lower middle classes of Manchester and Rossendale, into which the author was born in

1895. Her family by marriage, who were Secularists, campaigned for Bradlaugh and shared his views on birth control, but '*my* father and mother', who were Wesleyans, 'regarded birth control as an impious indecency'. C. S. Davies, op.cit., p.101.

139. For the newer methods, see above, footnote 129. As for the older, there is scattered evidence from various points in the nineteenth century suggesting that alleged abortifacients were fairly widely available. Banks quotes a middle-class example of their use from 1807, and notes that they were extensively advertised, appropriate euphemisms being used, in the 1890s. (*Prosperity and Parenthood*, pp.143, 157-8). When J. R. Ackerley's parents wished to induce the premature arrival of his elder brother in 1895, 'doctors were confidentially consulted, various homely remedies prescribed, and all manner of purges, nostrums and bodily exercises employed to bring about a miscarriage' (op.cit., p.43). And when, in 1885, a Bethnal Green girl accused the curate of being the father of her illegitimate child, she claimed that 'when she found she was pregnant, she told the curate, and he gave her 1s. and a note to take to Mr. Jeremy (chemist) for a draught to procure an abortion.' Although the story was probably untrue, it suggested that Bethnal Green girls had their well-tried remedies in such circumstances. *Prosperity and Parenthood*, pp.143, 157-8; Ackerley, op.cit., p.43; bundle of papers in Spitalfields Box, Temple Collection.

140. *Prosperity and Parenthood*, pp.198-201. *Pace* many of those who have quoted Banks' conclusions, he does *not* assert that 'the rising standard of living was the *major* factor in the spread of family limitation'. In fact (ibid., pp.202-4), he exposes the 'implausibility' of this view and terms it 'something of a non sequitur'.

141. Banks (ibid., pp.144-5) quotes Jane Austen and Queen Victoria on the pains and inconveniences of frequent childbearing. The latter is particularly illuminating in this context, as she wanted a small family, but would accept a large one if it were God's will.

142. *Feminism and Family Planning*, p.5.

143. Ibid., pp.120-1, 92-6, 100-4.

144. Ibid., pp.50-1.

145. *Prosperity and Parenthood*, p.204.

146. Two of the letters in Courtney's selection do mention the relationship between Man and 'lower animals' as the chief lesson of evolution (Courtney, op.cit., pp.184-5, 232-3). They are, however, considerably outnumbered by those drawing grand progressist conclusions. E.g., 'History disproves the alleged fall of man. Evolution substitutes for it the rise of man'. 'I base my firm belief in a future state on the indisputable law of evolution and general progression, the upward aspiring principle of the universe'. 'All impartial observers must admit that sympathy and goodness have evolved beyond the need that rewards and punishments in a future state should be held up as an alternative'.

And – most remystified of all – the correspondent whose God 'prepares each, by the experience of one or more earthly lives, for the next school of training in the great evolutionary march of embryonic souls from chaos towards that perfected state which can gaze upon the face of God himself'. Ibid., pp.199-201, 271-3, 192-3, 136-7.

147. Neale, op.cit., p.126, noting the evidence on this score, raises the question of how far this was due to the influence of Knowlton, Drysdale, and others who published information on the subject when it was still taboo. The evidence is, of course, scanty, but there may not always have been any connection. Overtly to challenge established standards of decency in the mid-nineteenth century was to be branded as subversive; but many of those who execrated such rebels silently defied those standards. This form of hypocrisy, as it existed in Society, is discussed in Escott, op.cit., pp.108-9.

148. For which, see Currie, op.cit., pp.93-100.

149. As quoted unfavourably in *British Weekly*, 3 February 1898.

150. D. Hughes, op.cit., p.194.

151. Percy Alden of Canning Town Settlement (the future Liberal and Labour MP) saw this as the church form of the future: place of worship, centre for healthy amusement and social reforming force. See his contribution to Mudie-Smith, op.cit., pp.43-4.

152. Their purpose was not to increase the sum of wisdom, love or happiness in the community, but to create a feeling of solidarity between the communicants and to bind them more closely to the church. But, by the standards of Conservative Evangelicalism, much of their activity was thoroughly 'secular'.

153. *Congregational Yearbook*, 1895, p.27.

154. The following letter is an example. It was written in 1880 by Rev. Bevill Allen, then about thirty, and later a well-known member of the LCC. 'Dear Christian friends, Your earnest and cordial invitation to become pastor of the Church you severally compose was received by me on the first inst. with very mixed feelings. I was glad and thankful to discover that the decision was arrived at with such unanimity and heartiness, sorry that choice had fallen on one who himself is so conscious of insufficiency and incompetence, and it may be right to say that had I allowed my first impulse to dictate my reply, I should have answered in the negative rather than the affirmative; but calmer reflection and more prayerful consideration of the many attendant circumstances, all of which seem so clearly to point to the dealings of an All-Wise and Ever Watchful Providence, have brought me to the conclusion that it is the "Voice of God, and not the voice of man", and consequently with the deepest humility and profoundest reverence, I in response to His command would say, "Here I am, for *Thou* didst call me" – Thus, dear friends, in the same spirit of love and earnestness in which I feel confident that the invitation was proffered, would I accept it, trusting that your

prayers on our behalf may be fervent and unceasing. It shall be my aim and ambition as Divine help shall be granted, to "commend myself to every man's conscience in the sight of God", to preach frankly and earnestly the "glorious Gospel of the blessed God" in all its simplicity and native purity; with honest plainness of speech rebuking, reproving and exhorting all men without respect to state or condition, and I trust that by a faithful loving and conscientious discharge of my pastoral duties I may ensure to you as a people the fulfilment of God's gracious promise, in which the windows of heaven are to be opened, and such a blessing outpoured that there shall not be room enough to receive it. – (D. V.) I shall commence my ministry among you on the first day of February, and may God bless the union by causing His face to shine upon us and by establishing the work of our hands.' Greville Place Congregational Church Minute Book, 28 January 1880.

155. Ibid., 31 January 1906, 11 November 1909.
156. J. Carpenter, *Gore, A Study in Liberal Catholicism*, Faith Press, London, 1960, p.110. Gore wrote: 'All my life has been a struggle to believe that God – the only God – is love. That is to me, as to many others, not only the governing dogma of the Christian religion, but the only difficult dogma. . . . in the Bible, I contend, it is wholly bound up with the conception of God as transcendent and sovereign and over and above nature.'
157. See Chadwick, op.cit., II, pp.132-50. For the views of the principal advocate of exclusion, see G. L. Prestige, *Life of Charles Gore*, Heinemann, London, 1935, and for those of his chief opponent, Henson, op.cit., I, pp.154-69, 214-70. For the fate of the historian, J. M Thompson, the best known of those whom Gore and his party did succeed in excluding from the ministry, see S. P. Mews, *Liberalism and Liberality in the Church of England*, unpublished Hulsean Prize Essay, 1968.
158. S. Miles, *Portrait of a Parson*, Allen and Unwin, London, 1955, p.104. The subject of this book, W. C. Roberts (1873-1953) was Vicar of St George's, Bloomsbury, 1917-38, and had much of Stewart Headlam about him, being unsectarian, both 'liberal' and 'orthodox', anti-puritan, and to the Left in politics.
159. A sermon printed in T. Sadler, E. Squire and H. Sharpe, *History of the Rosslyn Hill Congregation*, Hampstead (n.d.), pp.25-6.
160. Thomas Sadler–Edmund Squire, 12 April 1883: a letter of which a printed copy is in the Church Minute Book, Rosslyn Hill Collection.
161. In the late '90s Horton had tried unsuccessfully to persuade his 'orthodox' colleagues to give the Unitarians a place on the Hampstead Free Church Council, and about this time, his aunt, with whom he lived, left his church on the grounds that he preached 'unitarianism'. But when a member left his church to join Rosslyn Hill, he remarked that 'he would rather see the church depleted than have as members any who had lost vital

faith in the divinity of our Lord Jesus' *Hampstead and Highgate Express*, 2 October 1897; Peel and Marriott, op.cit., pp.159-62; Lyndhurst Road Congregational Church Minute Book, 2 June 1898.

162. See, for instance, a sermon preached by the Rev. Brooke Herford, then minister at Rosslyn Hill, on the opening of a new chapel in West Hampstead: 'As he washed the feet of his disciples, so they might build baths and wash-houses; as he healed the sick, so they might best follow him by supporting the hospitals . . . [etc.]'. *Hampstead and Highgate Express*, 18 January 1896.

163. For the remarkable contribution of Unitarians, and members of the effectively Unitarian Church of the Saviour, to local government in Birmingham, see. E. P. Hennock, *Fit and Proper Persons*, Arnold, London, 1973, pp.91-7.

164. Thus, when Robert Elsmere decides that the impossibility of miracle is the great religious question of the day, he finds his closest ally in a Unitarian minister, and Catherine's great fear is that he will join that outcast body himself. Mrs. H. Ward. op.cit., pp.402-3.

165. Figures taken from Annual Reports in Rosslyn Hill Collection.

166. Membership of the Brotherhood Church in Hackney declined from 140 in 1906, to 25 in 1929. (See annual statistics in *Congregational Year Book*.) The decline of the Labour Churches seems to have begun rather earlier. The lack of a distinctive religious standpoint on the part of most members was underlined by the President of the Union, D. B. Foster, who toured branches in 1902, and reported 'loud and persistent demands' for economic change, but little interest in 'the development of the human soul'. K. S. Inglis, 'The Labour Churches', *International Review of Social History*, vol.III, 1958, p.459.

167. Rosslyn Hill Calendar, May 1904.

168. Annual Report for 1913.

169. Rosslyn Hill Calendar, October 1911.

170. T. S. Simey and M. B. Simey, *Charles Booth, Social Scientist* OUP, London, 1960, p.60. He remained, however, sufficient of a Unitarian to chair the annual meeting of the London Domestic Mission. *Hampstead and Highgate Express*, 21 May 1904.

171. In 1893, he had written enthusiastically about a Catholic service he had attended in Italy. During the work for the Religious Influences series, he was highly eulogistic both of the Christian Socialist, Bruce Wallace, whose politics he can scarcely have agreed with, and of an evangelist called Richardson, who ran a Free Church in Bermondsey, and whose theology presumably differed considerably from Booth's own. Richardson he typically described as 'this seemingly vulgar little man earning his living as an employee of the Western Telegraph Company' who 'is able so to use his Sundays and week-nights as to have become a really great spiritual force'. M. Booth, *Charles Booth*, Macmillan, London, 1918, p.71; Booth Collection, B195, p.28; A46, 3, p.83.

172. Booth Collection, B225, p.217. It all depended on what was meant by religion: Barnett's successor as vicar of St Jude's, Whitechapel, was interviewed by Baxter in the late '90s, and described Toynbee Hall as 'an irreligious influence' on the grounds that 'none of the residents' went to church, and his parishioners accordingly got the idea that 'infidelity is the swagger thing'. He thought that the distinctively Christian character of most other Settlements led to a concentration of agnostics on Toynbee Hall. It also happened that the particular values characteristic of the first and most famous of the Settlements tended in the '90s to be associated with agnosticism. Ibid., B221, p.193.

173. This, according to most accounts, seems to have been his attitude to everything. An obituary in the *Economic Journal*, June 1917, referred to his 'judicial mind', 'delicately balanced, and quivering under perhaps too heavy a load of facts and possibilities'.

174. Booth Collection, A37, Report on districts 14 and 16, pp.62-4.

175. Baxter described Williams as a 'genius', and Pierce as 'one of the best ministers of any denomination that I have met for a long time: intelligent, level-headed and practical'. Ibid., B195, p.18; B218, p.157.

176. Ibid., A33, Report on district 12, p.56 (c).

177. Baxter made these comments on a prayer meeting at H.P. Hughes' West London Mission: 'Altogether I never felt so strongly as I did last night that the truest prayer must be private and practically wordless, and that if public prayer there must be, far the best and wisest course is to make it liturgical when dignity and reverence can be assured and the banal and flippant banished. Only a genius can make extempore prayer tolerable: the prayers of these good people are in essence and almost in every word every bit as well worn and hackneyed as those of the English liturgy and I cannot conceive that their emotional appeal is greater to any single soul'. Ibid., A42. 4, pp.16-21.

178. The Vicar of St Jude's, Whitechapel, quoted above, fell into the latter category.

179. Baxter reported as follows on the Church of England in Shoreditch: 'With very few exceptions the finest characters and the hardest workers among the clergy that we have met are men whose beliefs – apart from the non-recognition of the "Bishop of Rome" – differ little if at all from those of Roman Catholics . . . But hateful as are the methods of Mr. Kensit and his followers, I am not persuaded that the protests that have been raised against the danger of the growth of "superstition and sacerdotalism" are not justified.' Ibid., A40.7, p.24.

180. Ibid., A37, Report on districts 15 and 17, pp.89-90.

181. Ibid., A37, Reports on districts 14 and 16, p.65.

182. The difference in approach is illustrated in two sympathetic accounts of interviews. Fleming Williams, interviewed by Baxter delivered rhetorical attacks on various current evils, notably

alcohol and Anglo-Catholicism ('the school of authority'), and Baxter, though generally eulogistic, admitted that he might be 'emotional, sentimental, unpractical, possibly a bit of an actor'. Aves found John Clifford 'a zealous, optimistic Christian Socialist', 'a powerful and commanding figure, interesting, attractive and genuine', but 'a few touches in the course of a long interview made me think that if he were confronted with a practical industrial problem he would be found wanting in real mastery of it'. Ibid., B195, p.18; B249, pp.31-57.

183. Ibid., A37, Report on districts 14 and 16, pp.113-5.
184. Ibid., A37, Report on districts 14 and 16, p.62.
185. From a letter in which Blatchford defined his earlier religious position, cited in L. Thompson, *Robert Blatchford*, Gollancz, London, 1951, pp.44-5.
186. Ibid., p.170.
187. H. Pelling, *Origins of the Labour Party*, Macmillan, London, 2nd edition, 1966, p.174. Different drinking habits seem to have been one reason for the mutual antipathy between Hardie and Blatchford. It may also explain the difference between Hardie's rather grandiloquent style 'and Blatchford's short, pithy sentences: the 'labour leader' did not need to stop for gulps of whisky.
188. The *Clarion* series began on 2 January 1903 and ended on 28 October 1904. From 29 January 1904 to 5 August 1904, George Haw was allowed to edit two columns a week of Christian replies. So convinced was Blatchford that his 'wolf' could gobble up the adherents of 'any religion of which I have heard', that he made no serious attempt to answer the objections raised by G. K. Chesterton and others against this rigid form of determinism – including, of course, the claim that it made nonsense of Blatchford's own moral indignation against Liberals, Conservatives, clergymen, Keir Hardie, etc.
189. R. Blatchford, *God and my Neighbour*, Clarion Press, London, 1903, pp.188-97.
190. L. Thompson, op.cit., p.182. The tendency of Socialists.so to divide men he saw as arising from the fact that 'so many of the women and men in the movement have been saturated with the false and unjust philosophy of the Bible'.
191. The first batch of critical letters included one from the High Church anti-puritan, Rev. J. Cartmel Robinson, who had been among the originators of the Clarion Cyclists. In the same issue was an article by the Congregationalist, Rev. Ambrose Pope, who had been in trouble with his congregation for a sermon on 'The *Clarion* as a Christian newspaper'. *Clarion*, 20 February 1903.
192. *The Quintessence of Ibsenism*, p.25, in *The Works of Bernard Shaw*, Constable, London, 1930, XIX.
193. G. Allen, 'The New Hedonism', *Fortnightly Review*, New Series, no.327, 1 March 1894, pp.380, 383.
194. Wells (born 1866) regarded this group of attitudes as typical of a

large part of the intelligentsia of his generation. H. G. Wells, *Experiment in Autobiography*, Gollancz, London, 1934, I, p.186.

195. For his early life, see Gill, op.cit., Chapters 1-3.

196. Ibid., pp.94-130, 266.

197. R. Aldington, *Death of a Hero*, unexpurgated edition, Sphere, London, 1965, p.222.

198. According to Aldington's autobiography, *Life for Life's Sake*, Cassell, London, 1968, (first published 1941), p.78, 'In religion and even in politics I was more or less a Gallio, caring nothing. What I wanted was to enjoy life, to enjoy *my* life in *my* way . . . I wanted to know and to enjoy the best that had been thought and felt and known through the ages — architecture, painting, sculpture, poetry, literature, food and wine, France and Italy, women, old towns, beautiful country.'

199. Webb, op.cit., pp.89-105. The quotation comes from Beatrice Webb's diary, in the entry for 31 March 1878.

200. Ibid., p.105.

201. Susan Budd points out that popular scientific interest has run through four characteristic phases: biology in the later nineteenth century, anthropology around 1900, physics and chemistry in the 1920s and '30s, and social sciences since the Second World War. Whereas the first two phases were highly favourable to the Rationalist Press Association understanding of 'science', the popular scientists of the third phase tended to be theists, dedicated to demonstrating that the universe was a product of mind. See Budd, 'The British Humanist Movement', pp.241-69.

202. Glock and Stark, op.cit., p.58.

203. T. Jackson, op.cit., p.165.

204. Ibid., p.49.

205. Ibid., p.59.

206. Ibid., p.94; cf. p.165.

CHAPTER IX SOME IMPLICATIONS

Some books are based on the discovery of startling new evidence which, their authors claim, demands that the subject be seen in a new light. Most of the material used in the present book, however, will be familiar to anyone with much previous knowledge of Victorian social history. Any novelty that it has will lie less in the evidence presented than in the manner of its interpretation. Rather, then, than drawing conclusions, I shall suggest some of the implications of my approach.

First, in what way are events in London representative of anywhere else? A basis for comparing the religious characteristics of nineteenth-century towns exists in the church attendance censuses, and these show that while the class-based pattern of attendance was repeated in every part of England, its level and denominational distribution varied quite widely even between the larger cities.[1] Thus, in every town church attendance was considerably lower in working-class districts than in middle- and upper-class districts, and explanations of this fact that are valid for London will probably be valid for other towns too; but both working-class and middle-class church-goers were far more numerous in, for instance, Bristol than in Sheffield. Thus, part of the difference between towns can be attributed to differences in class composition, but other factors were clearly at work. Among these, only one is clearly established: an only partly explained regional factor. While church attendances were generally more numerous in country than in town, the range in both cases was considerable, and attendances both in town and in country tended to be above the urban and rural averages in the East, East Midlands and South-West, below the average in the North, West Midlands and South-East. London lay within a zone of low rural attendance, but with a zone of high attendance not much further to the north. Another factor is often mentioned – the size of town[2] – but its importance seems to be less clearly established. Other factors which might prove to be significant – such as the character of local industry, the proportions of migrants from the countryside in the local population, or the varying effectiveness of missionary and pastoral work by the churches[3] – can only be evaluated when the 1851 census returns have been subjected to much more intensive analysis. The censuses of 1851 and 1886-7 showed that attendance in London was below the average for large towns, and that Nonconformity was especially weak, but that London was in no way unique: for instance, Birmingham was very similar both in the level and in the distribution of attendances.[4]

If our view of late Victorian London tends to be distorted by the assumption that London is 'the unique city', the religious history of the period is also distorted by assumptions that emphasise the novelty of the changes then in progress. The cities appeared yet more godless if set against the background of a devout countryside, and the 'crisis of faith' of which contemporaries were so aware is made the more dramatic by the legend of a past in which 'All of our ancestors were literal Christian believers, all of the time.'[5] These assumptions, taken as established fact, provide 'problems' to be solved by such formulae as Luckmann's law that 'the degree of involvement in the work processes of modern industrial society correlates negatively with the degree of involvement in church-oriented religion.'[6] In fact, both the assumptions and the formula are open to serious question. Even where the external evidence suggests a population of 'literal Christian believers', the definition is not a very helpful one, so widely do conceptions of Christianity vary. But the external evidence does not all point in the same direction. If the migrant to Manchester or to Bradford in the eighteenth or early nineteenth centuries (like the Andalusian coming to Barcelona or the Highlander to Glasgow) might find there more churches and priests than ever he had known in his homeland,[7] even in those parts of England where the Established Church was well rooted 'literal Christian belief' was not necessarily the characteristic attitude of the population. While G. V. Bennett has shown that the number of Easter communicants in some parishes fell sharply after the Declaration of Indulgence in 1687, and Clive Field has shown that non-attendance at church by nominal Anglicans was already fairly widespread before that date, the work of Keith Thomas and James Obelkevich suggests that many of the rural poor in seventeenth- and nineteenth-century England knew more of the magical uses than of the Christian significance of the church's ceremonies.[8] If formal religion for many nineteenth-century city dwellers extended little beyond the rites of passage and attendance at Watch Night services, this may have been a continuation of habits well established in the countryside. On the other hand, those who see the 'city' as intrinsically 'secular' overlook the fact that *middle-class* areas of great cities in nineteenth-century England and twentieth-century America have been strongholds of institutional religion, and that if this has ceased or is ceasing to be so the time-lag has been rather considerable; those who associate religious 'survivals' in the modern city with backward forms of production or with the survival of groups 'peripheral to the structure of modern society' ignore the well-established links between Evangelical Protestantism and the pioneers of industrial capitalism in such countries as Scotland and the United States.[9]

The chief theme of this study has been not the uniform impact of an 'industrial society' or the adoption of an 'urban way of life', but the division of a city into separate worlds, marked by radically different styles of life, and between which there was little communication. The differences between those within the three basic status-groups was particularly clear-cut in the area of formal religious practice, and should be understood primarily in terms of the varying degrees to which the members of each felt a sense of obligation to 'society' and possessed status or 'respectability' that could be lost through deviant behaviour. In matters of religious belief and commitment, however, the effect of social status or class membership is less easily defined. In such countries as France, Spain and Ireland, bloody conflict divided the population into selfconscious religious communities, united by common loyalties and hatreds. In England, religious boundaries were much less rigid (except, perhaps, in Lancashire).[10] The nearest equivalent to the civil wars of the 1790s, 1848 and 1871 in France had been the acute social conflicts of the early nineteenth century. W. R. Ward has shown how Methodist revivalism capitalised on the hostility to the clergy in the Midlands 'enclosure country', and how the class warfare of the 1810s in the North divided the Wesleyan Connexion, placing the travelling preachers and wealthy laymen (on whose financial support they depended) on one side of the fence, and a large proportion of local preachers and working-class members on the other, the result being that the radicals left or were expelled in their thousands, some to join Methodist sects, and others to leave organised religion altogether.[11] It seems likely that the suspicion of churches in general and the Established Church in particular which, though weak by French or Spanish standards, was still quite widespread in the English working class at the end of the nineteenth century, was a legacy of this period.

There is abundant evidence of the association between social and religious cleavage in nineteenth- and twentieth-century Europe.[12] When the members of a community are divided into classes, always separate and often antagonistic, meeting only in relations of authority and subordination, it is futile to expect that they will meet in the same church. The great majority of the London working class were not, therefore, potential converts to the Church of England or to denominations, such as the Wesleyans or Congregationalists, dominated by the middle class, though outstanding ministers of these churches could still win some working-class following. The more interesting and difficult question is why working men did not respond to exclusion from the major denominations by forming their own sects, and why such bodies as the Primitive Methodists and the Salvation Army were even weaker in London than the Anglicans or Wesleyans. It may be that the democratic sect makes greater demands on its members than most people are prepared to meet, but the fact remains that religion of this kind did attract a significant following in some parts of the country.[13]

One possibly relevant factor was the working-class ethos of communal solidarity: the strongholds of working-class Nonconformity were in rural areas or in industrial villages, where some form of Methodism (most commonly) was able to identify itself with the community as a whole, and while many adult males did not attend services, most people sent their children to Sunday School, were acquainted with the leading members of the chapel hierarchy and took some part in activities associated with the chapel.[14] In London, however, the only parallel was within the Irish Roman Catholic community. Elsewhere, to join any sort of church was to mark yourself out as an individualist, someone who, even if liked and respected, was trying to stand out from his neighbours, and might be suspected of looking down on them. A second possible explanation for the religious indifference of so many members of the working and, to a lesser extent, lower middle class, who were committed to no anti-religious ideology, lies in proletarian parochialism, the source of which lay in hereditary subordination, and the consequent limitation of the area within which the individual was accustomed to knowledge, responsibility and power. Engels asserted that God was a personification of the mysterious forces controlling society, and the more men felt helpless, the readier they were to seek an explanation for their situation in the arbitrary will of God.[15] According to my interpretation, the reverse was true: those who felt powerless in a world dominated by mysterious alien forces tended to respond by withdrawing into a more local world, within which their words and actions *were* of some consequence, and questions concerning the general nature of society, let alone of the universe, they tended to dismiss as irrelevant speculation; the arbitrary ruler of their world was not God but Fate.

If this argument is correct it would scarcely support the common theory according to which the typical working-class believer is drawn from among the most disadvantaged, in search of 'other-worldly compensations'. This theory has been given even wider application in an interesting essay on German socialism, in which it argued that in the later nineteenth century the myth of a Marxist utopia replaced the myth of a Christian heaven as 'heart of a heartless world' in the minds of working men whose present misery could only be mitigated by dreams of paradise to come.[16] Yet all the evidence suggests that in nineteenth-century London, at least, most religious activists, like most political activists, were drawn from the more prosperous sections of the working class – those whose lack of status and power was more acute than their material need, and whose style of life was closer to the lower middle class than to the 'rough' working class.[17] Though there may be individual exceptions to the rule, the destitute were generally too absorbed in the struggle to remain alive to look for 'other-worldly compensations', and if they thought of the Creator at all they were likely to blame him for their sufferings.[18] Working-class religious converts were mainly drawn from those with ideas, in search of meanings, systems, explanations, or from those in revolt against the way of life of their neighbours. In either case, questions both of personal morality and of the nature of the social and cosmic order were likely to bulk larger in their conception of religion than the contemplation of bliss to come.

While it is possible to generalise about the *type* of religion prevalent in a given milieu, I have tried to show that the actual beliefs of individuals, let alone of large groups, tended to be fluid and ambivalent. To illustrate from the case of one particularly articulate individual: two of the largest collections of letters in the Frederic Harrison Collection at LSE present two quite different religious faces. In writing to Mrs. Hadwen, the Anglican wife of a northern industrialist, and the recipient of many letters from Harrison in the '60s, the Positivist became the earnest agnostic, conscious of the beauty of Christianity and its capacity to inspire, sorrowful that on the path onward and upward humanity had been obliged to leave this sublime religion behind. The face seen by John Morley in the '70s, however, was that of a radical iconoclast, with a taste for blasphemy and a fierce hatred of priests, reactionaries and Gladstone. Meanwhile, a third face appeared to Harrison's son and biographer, Austin – that of the austere 'Victorian' parent, both an intransigent moralist and an observer of tiresome conventions, a stern critic of tobacco, detective stories, Oscar Wilde, music-halls, and all forms of tomfoolery.[19] In part, these may reflect phases in Harrison's own development but they might also be seen as different attempts, because triggered off by differing personalities, to interpret an imperfectly understood reality and to define incompletely perceived responses to this reality. If Harrison could be carried away by his own eloquence to extravagant statements of contradictory positions, I have argued in Chapter III that many far less articulate people were capable of a considerable range of religious positions, and that different aspects of a rather incoherent complex of attitudes came to the front in varying situations. The historian's task is to determine thè range of attitudes of which an individual or a group was capable, the range of actions it was prepared to sanction.

If this fluidity of religious position was characteristic of the working class, where individuals were seldom tied to the official formulae of organised bodies, members of the 'church-going classes' often, consciously or not, held beliefs at variance with the doctrines of their churches. A common-sense Christianity or a purely conventional Christianity would be combined with a suspicion of dogmas, zealots and parsons, or sincere Christian convictions might coexist rather incongruously with the values of a businessman, a gentleman or a member of Society.[20] After about 1875 these contradictions were increasingly recognised, and resolved sometimes by the reassertion of Christian ideals or the adoption of new religious and ethical systems, but more often by the dropping of those religious conventions or ideas that conflicted with more deeply-held convictions or with hitherto suppressed desires. The 'church-going classes' were entering a period of reaction, in which the prevailing religion began to appear as hypocrisy and cant, its daily and weekly rituals merely embarrassing. This did not necessarily involve a change from one set of beliefs to another: it might mean placing new emphasis on one part of an existing set of conflicting values.

Although the hold of 'Victorianism' over the middle and upper classes had been maintained by the force of 'respectability' and the threat of its withdrawal, it seems unlikely that the decline of 'Victorianism' followed from a slackening of this force or from changes in the material basis of middle- and upper-class life. For very similar changes were taking place at exactly the same time in Scandinavia and the United States, as well as in Scotland. One of the most remarkable and baffling features of eighteenth- and nineteenth-century religious history is the fact that the chronology of change in the Protestant countries of Northern Europe and North America was so similar. The Great Awakenings of 1800 and the years following had reached all parts of the Protestant world, while temperance had swept across the same

countries in the 1830s and the decades following.[21] Equally international was the reaction of the 1870s and '80s, marked by
well-publicised attacks on Christianity, a decline in church attendance
and Sunday observance, and the development of liberal theology. It was
in the '70s, for instance, that Brandes emerged as the chief exponent of
intellectual atheism in Denmark, and Ingersoll as the champion of
Secularism in the United States.[22] And it was in the late '70s that
Norwegians suddenly became aware of the fact that their own religion
was under attack.[23] Where the leaders of the great awakenings had
often been brought up in the spirit of eighteenth-century rationalism, a
common evolution was now out of Pietism, into Liberalism or
scepticism: in Norway, the '80s and '90s were the decades of the
'transition theologians', bred in Pietism, who had partly adapted
themselves to the new ideas; Naumann, who in the '90s was chief
advocate of a *rapprochement* between Lutheranism and Social
Democracy in Germany, was a 'child of the awakenings'; and many
American Protestants, born around the mid-century, developed in a
similar way.[24]

The obvious implication of these facts is that however local patterns
were moulded by social and political circumstances, the primary source
of the religious changes of the period must be sought in the flow of
ideas rather than in situations peculiar to particular regions and
countries. The economic and social environment should be seen not as
inexorably moulding the individual's forms of thought, but in a more
negative role, controlling the flow of ideas current in a given society at
a given time, and making some more accessible to given sections of the
population than others. Such formulae as 'industrial society', or
'secularisation' may be useful as long as it is recognised that they are no
more than concepts. But they can be given a spurious reality, and thus
become vehicles for a mechanical theory of human motivation, in
which human thoughts and actions merely reflect their environment, or
those aspects of the environment that the historian chooses to select.

The question arises: how far can changes in religious beliefs be
attributed to new knowledge? The implied argument of this book has
been that the chief catalyst of religious change in the later nineteenth
century was a shifting of perspective in three areas that seems to have
been largely independent of any change in the scientific knowledge that
was generally available. These shifts were: an increased awareness of
extreme social inequality, and of its overwhelming importance; a more
widespread desire to be free of 'puritan' restraints; and a revulsion from
those aspects of 'orthodox' theology, especially hell, that made God

appear cruel and vindictive.[25] The roots of the first of these shifts of perspective lay in social change; but the only necessary precondition for the second and third shifts was the ending of the state-enforced religious monopoly, which in England dated from the Declaration of Indulgence in 1687 and the abolition of censorship in 1695. The rationalism and anti-puritanism of the later nineteenth century was a continuation of trends well-established in the eighteenth century, and its mass character, as much as the mass character of early nineteenth-century Evangelicalism was due less to a flood of new knowledge than to the coercive power of public opinion.

Commitment to a religion – or, indeed, to any movement whose aims are not very narrow and specific – involves an element of 'act of faith'. This is because the evidence potentially relevant to the individual's choice is so extensive that he is forced to choose on the basis of a limited selection of this evidence – or never choose at all. Those considering 'leaps of faith' in late Victorian England were moved less often by such abstractions as Darwin's theory of Evolution, which was known to most people only in very garbled form, and the implications of which were not a subject of general agreement, than by more practical questions of human relations and human priorities. Leaps of faith have to be consistent with the knowledge of the world that is available to the potential convert, but the decisive considerations in the making of such commitments tend to be: which of the multitude of human problems is most urgent, and who seems most likely to solve them; whom does such a choice place him with, and whom against; the existence or not of equally attractive alternatives.

Two examples can illustrate this process. At about the time that Nunquam was delivering his famous attack on Christianity in the columns of the leading Socialist weekly, one nationally known Socialist was rejoining the Church of England after several years as an agnostic and another Socialist, unknown outside of Huddersfield, was severing his connection with 'the Christian movement' for reasons that were basically similar, although his train of reasoning had led him in a different direction. The first was George Lansbury, who a decade earlier had been an Anglican Sunday School teacher, with unorthodox views on the Resurrection, and had left the Church after reading *Robert Elsmere*.[26] The process of reappraisal that ended with his return to the Church of England in 1901 was initiated not by a sudden conviction of the reasonableness of miracle, but by a period in which he lost much of his will to continue in political work that produced no apparent results and separated him from his wife and family: the end of his depression was not a retreat into private life, but a revived interest in Christianity which, he felt, provided a motive for continuing in spite of setbacks and a more solid basis for the movement than material interest.[27] The considerations that led Wilfred Whitely, the son of a Huddersfield mill engineer, and then in his early twenties, to leave organised Christianity in 1904 were equally pragmatic – he had in any case been simultaneously a teacher at a Socialist Sunday School and a Wesleyan Adult School, a member of a Baptist congregation, and an occasional occupant of Unitarian pulpits, and so can hardly have been a doctrinal pedant. He remained an 'ethical' Socialist, more interested in 'Human Brotherhood' than in Marxism or the class war, and his heroes in the ILP seem to have been mostly of the 'religious Socialist' type, such as the Rev. W. E. Moll. His reason for leaving was: 'I didn't feel that the churches and chapels were meeting the needs of the situations so far as the needs of the people were concerned. I wanted them to be interested in the economic welfare of the people and the social welfare of the people. I think that I could almost say that I made Socialism my religion.'[28]

Notes

1. This paragraph is based on my article, 'Class, Community and Region: The Religious Geography of Nineteenth Century England.'

2. See H. Perkin, *The Origins of Modern English Society, 1780-1880*, Routledge, London, 1969, p.200.

3. Birmingham has a history of below average church attendance continuing to the present day. A study which emphasises organisational defects as a factor in Anglican weakness for most of the nineteenth century is R. Peacock, 'The Church of England and the Working Classes in Birmingham, 1861-1905', University of Aston M.Phil. thesis, 1973.

4. Censuses in 1886 and 1892 showed that although the overall level of attendances was higher in London than in Birmingham, because of the larger middle- and upper-class populations in the capital, the rate was in both instances about 15 per cent in the poorest areas, with Anglican and Nonconformist worshippers roughly equal in number; about 20 per cent in working-class and 30 per cent in socially mixed suburbs, with Nonconformists in both cases the majority; and about 40 per cent in the wealthiest districts, where Anglicans easily outnumbered chapel-goers.

5. P. Laslett, *The World we have lost*, Methuen, London, 1965, p.71.

6. This comes from T. Luckmann, *The Invisible Religion*, English

translation, Macmillan, New York, 1967, p.30. Luckmann's views are quoted with approval and further developed by P. Berger, *The Social Reality of Religion*, Penguin, Harmondsworth, 1973, Chapters 5-7.

7. In Andalusia, where parishes are large, there are said to be many villages where no one has been catechised for 200 years. Similar conditions seem to have prevailed in many parts of the Scottish Highlands until the early nineteenth century. R. Duocastella, 'Géographie de la Pratique religieuse en Espagne', *Social Compass,* vol.XII, 1965, pp.261-3; T. C. Smout, *A History of the Scottish People*, Collins, London, 1969, p.312. For the prevalence of large parishes with inadequate endowments in northern England before the mid-nineteenth century see D. Sylvester, *The Rural Landscape of the Welsh Borderland*, Macmillan, London, 1969, Chapter 8, and an important thesis that I saw only after completing this book, A. Gilbert, 'The Growth and Decline of Nonconformity in England and Wales', University of Oxford D.Phil. thesis, 1973.

8. Thomas, op.cit., and Obelkevich, op.cit., passim. Obelkevich, while noting the superstitions associated with churching and with certain days in the Christian year, is chiefly impressed by the fact that most of the magic in rural Lincolnshire in the mid-nineteenth century had no connection with the church at all (op.cit., pp.439-71). For seventeenth-century church attendance: Bennett, 'The Conflict in the Church', pp.157-65; C. Field, 'Some Aspects of religious Practice in England, 1600-1750' (unpublished paper, 1973).

9. Luckmann's assertion (op.cit., pp.39-40) that the survival of 'church-oriented religion' in West Europe is to be explained by the survival of groups 'peripheral to the structure of modern society' ('the peasantry, the remnants of the traditional bourgeoisie and petite bourgeoisie') appears to be based on a study made of Reutlingen, a medium-sized town in South Germany in 1955-6, which showed that government employees and the self-employed were the groups most involved in the activities of the Protestant church. (F. Tennbruck, 'Diè Kirchengemeinde in der entkirchlichten Gesellschaft: Ergebnisse und Deutung der "Reutlingen-Studie" ', D. Goldschmidt, and others, *Soziologie der Kirchengemeinde*, Ferdinand Enke, Stuttgart, 1960, p.127). Luckmann's explanation for differential rates of church involvement accords with the view standard among East European sociologists that religion is associated with backward forms of production. Yet there is a far greater body of evidence to suggest that the reasons for differential rates of church participation lie in differences of class and social status, or in the political situation of particular groups, rather than involvement in different types of production. A similar point has been made by a Yugoslav sociologist, who compared Yugoslav studies finding a positive correlation between education and

atheism with an Italian study showing the reverse: the crucial difference, he argued, lay not in the effects of education as such, but between the social systems that education was a means to upward mobility within. (See S. Vrcan, 'Implications of the Religiosity as a Mass Phenomenon in a contemporary Socialist Society', *International Year Book for the Sociology of Religion*, vol.VII, 1971, p.161).

In most East European countries religion is inevitably concentrated on the 'periphery', because religious affiliations are a disqualification for most positions of power. In other industrial societies – for instance, the United States in the later nineteenth century – the position was almost the reverse, and the religiosity of such notably unperipheral figures as John D. Rockefeller and Cyrus McCormick has been plausibly attributed to the affinities between Evangelical Protestantism and a 'gospel of wealth'. See Hudson, op.cit., pp.294-5, 302-7; also L. Pope, *Millhands and Preachers*, Yale UP, New Haven, 1942, pp.16-23; and MacLaren, op.cit., passim, where it is argued that Free Presbyterianism was the ideology of the new urban-based bourgeoisie in nineteenth-century Aberdeen. Luckmann's stimulating and wide -ranging, but sometimes rather flimsily based essay should also be compared with one of the very meticulous and rather narrow specimens of French 'sociologie religieuse' that he so much despises – G. Cholvy, *Géographie Religieuse de l'Hérault Contemporain*, PUF, Paris, 1968. In what must be one of the most exhaustive studies ever made of Mass-attendance statistics, Cholvy showed conclusively that the dividing lines between the levels of Catholic practice in different occupational groups were those of class and social status, and that the sometimes considerable variations within the 'middle class' group had no connection with 'industrial work processes'. The most 'dechristianised' groups were miners and fishermen, while farm labourers (6 per cent of adult males practising) were far closer to 'ouvriers' (3 per cent) than to farmers (21 per cent). 'Patrons, industrie et commerce' (7 per cent), most, presumably, being small shopkeepers, and 'instituteurs' (9 per cent) were the least practising middle-class groups while engineers (20 per cent) ranked third after professional men and farmers. The fact that engineers – who by Luckmann's reasoning should be the least 'church-oriented' group – are in fact one of the *most* 'church-oriented' occupations in France is also noted by E. Pin, 'Hypothèses rélatives à la Désaffection religieuse dans les Classes inférieures', *Social Compass*, vol.IX, no.5-6, 1962, p.528.

10.   For which see the chapter on 'The Conservative Party at Prayer' in P. F. Clarke, *Lancashire and the New Liberalism*, CUP, 1971. Here, as in Ireland, 'religious' conflict was primarily conflict between natives, on the one hand and, on the other, migrants and their descendants.

11.   Ward, op.cit., pp.9-12, 85-94.

12. F.-A. Isambert, in *Christianisme et Classe Ouvrière*, Casterman,
     Tournai, 1961, pp.43-53, asked 'L'abstention religieuse des
     classes ouvrières est-elle générale?' and concluded that in Western
     Europe and the Americas it was, although in some areas such as
     the Catholic South of the Netherlands working-class religious
     practice was low only by comparison with the extremely high
     levels found in other sections of the same community. Ireland,
     Poland, and the Catholic Rhineland might be in the latter
     category. For studies of lower-class alienation from churches
     dominated by higher strata, see E. T. Davies, *Religion in the
     Industrial Revolution in South Wales*, which is especially
     interesting, as it describes an area where working-class particip-
     ation in the life of the Nonconformist chapels declined only after
     the onset of acute social conflict in 1898; J. Cutileiro, *A
     Portuguese Rural Society*, OUP, London, 1971, which is about
     agricultural labourers in the latifundist South-East; Maclaren,
     op.cit., pp.142, 165-202, where the author attributes the
     non-attendance by working men at Presbyterian churches
     (established or free) to their 'class-conscious nature', and
     contrasts this with the Episcopalians, Congregationalists and
     United Christians, all of whom had a large working-class
     membership; B. Gustafsson, *Social demokraten och Kyrkan
     1881-90*, Stockholm, 1953, as summarised in English in *Excerpta
     Historica Nordica*, III, Copenhagen, 1959, pp.168-71, in which he
     argues that the first 'dechristianised' groups in Sweden were
     workers on manorial estates and artisans threatened by
     mechanisation, who were thus made acutely conscious of their
     inferior social status and of the church's commitment to a
     hierarchical society. But evidence published since Isambert's book
     suggests possible exceptions to his general rule that working-class
     religious practice is lower than that of other social groups in the
     same community: in Sweden, where there is no social pressure on
     the higher strata to make formal religious observances, there is
     now no difference between the proportions of manual workers
     and of the upper middle class claiming to attend church (though
     the former are predominantly supporters of the free churches, the
     latter supporters of the state church); and in Eastern Europe,
     where education has a strongly atheistic slant and members of
     religious organisations may find it difficult to go to university or
     to obtain the kind of job that they want, a higher proportion of
     manual workers than of clerical workers or 'intelligentsia' claim
     to be 'believers' (though statistics of church attendance, the
     subject best documented in the West, do not appear to be
     available). R. F. Tomasson, *Sweden: Prototype of a Modern
     Society*, New York, 1970, p.77, (quoting a public opinion poll of
     1955-6); E. Kadlecova, 'Religiosity in the North-Moravian District
     of Czechoslovakia', *Social Compass*, vol.XIII, no.1, 1966;
     S. Vrcan, 'Implications of the Religiosity as a Mass Phenomenon
     in a Contemporary Socialist Society', *International Yearbook for*

the *Sociology of Religion*, vol.VII, 1971; D. A. Martin, *The Religious and the Secular*, Routledge, London, 1969, pp.139-52.

13. Those northern towns, such as Hull, where church attendance was relatively high, and those towns, such as Bristol and Leicester where working-class attendance was above average, included large numbers worshipping either at services held by the Salvation Army or at the chapels of the Methodist sects. See my article, 'Class, Community and Region'.

14. The outstanding example of such an area would be West Cornwall, where Methodism, led by the local preachers, moved from a minority position to a dominant position in the culture of the mining villages during the first half of the nineteenth century. See Rule, op.cit., pp.279-83, 310-19.

15. K. Marx and F. Engels, *On Religion*, Schocken Books, New York, 1964, pp.147-9.

16. V. L. Lidtke, 'August Bebel and German Social Democracy's Relation to the Christian Churches', *Journal of the History of Ideas*, vol.XXVII, April-June 1966.

17. For working-class church-goers and religious activists, see chapters II, III, and IV of this book; for political activists, see Stedman Jones, op.cit., Chapter 19, and Paul Thompson, op.cit., pp.115-16 (though Thompson notes evidence that the Deptford and Clerkenwell branches of the SDF included very poor members).

18. Robert Allerton, a Hoxton man brought up in great poverty, who blamed his law-abiding father for the family's privations and turned to crime as the easiest road to relative prosperity, put it as follows, when a Church Army captain tried to convert him: 'I said I didn't believe there was a God, and if there was, he must be a stupid bastard, who couldn't make things go right'. R. Allerton and T. Parker, *The Courage of his Convictions*, Hutchinson, London, 1962, pp.61-2.

19. A. Harrison, *Frederic Harrison, Thoughts and Memoirs*, Heinemann, London, 1926, pp.106-29.

20. Beatrice Webb (op.cit., pp.6-7) described her Unitarian father, 'honourable', 'loyal' and 'generous' in all personal relationships, and also very rich, as tending 'to prefer the welfare of his family and personal friends to the interests of the companies over which he presided, the profits of these companies to the prosperity of his country, the dominance of his own race to the peace of the world.' Obelkevich (op.cit., pp.57-66) notes the paradoxical nature of the concept of 'Christian gentleman', and argues that the ideal of the gentleman, from its association with traditionalism and worldly-wisdom to its emphasis on 'temperament, moderation, balance', was incompatible with the ideal of the Christian. As an example of the tension in practice, Trollope's Suffolk squire, Roger Carbury, (*The Way we Live Now*; I, p.75), who is a sincere Anglican, and about as near to being an honest man as anyone in an almost uniformly uninviting collection of

characters, 'did not quite believe in the forgiveness of injuries', it being 'weak, womanly and foolish'.

21. In England, temperance found many of its strongest exponents among Nonconformists and Secularists in the towns, whereas in Scandinavia and the United States it was predominantly a rural movement, and thus tends to be interpreted as an embodiment of 'anti-urban values'. Compare B. Harrison, *Drink and the Victorians*, pp.148-9, with S. Rokkan and H. Valen, 'Regional Contrasts in Norwegian Politics', E. Allardt and V. Littunen (eds.), *Cleavages, Ideologies and Party Systems*, Helsinki, 1964, p.189.

22. J. O. Andersen, *Survey of the History of the Church in Denmark*, Copenhagen, 1930, pp.63-4; Hudson, op.cit., p.265.

23. E. Molland, *Church Life in Norway*, English translation, Minneapolis, 1957, pp.66-76. He quotes a clerical observer, who made annual reports on the religious situation. In 1874, he was welcoming the fact that the 'streams of unbelief' had not reached Norway, but in 1877 he was more pessimistic, and by 1882 he was admitting that 'modern unbelief' was advancing at a pace 'no one would have thought possible a few years ago'.

24. Molland, op.cit., pp.81-6; Latourette, op.cit., IV, pp.124-7; C. H. Hopkins, *The Rise of the Social Gospel in American Protestantism, 1865-1915*, Yale UP, New Haven, 1940, pp.61-3, 216-32.

25. Cf S. E. Ahlstrom, 'The Radical Turn in Theology and Ethics: Why it occurred in the 1960s', *Annals of the American Academy of Political and Social Science*, vol.CCCLXXXVII, January 1970, pp.7-8. Much of what he wrote about America in the 1960s ('a growing attachment to a naturalism or "secularism" that makes people suspicious of doctrines that imply anything supernatural or which seem to involve magic, superstition or divine intervention in the natural order', etc,) might be equally applicable to England in the 1880s and the decades following. In so far as he is able to suggest reasons for the 'radical turn', it is largely in terms not of new knowledge, but of the catalytic effect of Vietnam and of racial violence.

26. Booth Collection, B 178, p.115.

27. G. Lansbury, 'Why I returned to Christianity', *Clarion*, 29 July 1904.

28. Interview with Wilfred Whitely, *Bulletin* of the Society for the Study of Labour History, no.18, Spring 1969, p.16.

Table 1   Manual workers as a percentage of men marrying with a given type of ceremony. (The size of the samples is given in brackets.)

Bethnal Green	1880–1901	Nonconformist	(443) 48.8%
	1888	C. of E.	(506) 82.2%
	1913	Civil	(141) 80.1%
Lewisham	1899–1914	Nonconformist	(629) 38.5%
	1898–1901	C. of E.	(792) 50.4%
	1913		
	1899, 1913	Civil	(244) 74.2%

Marriages in Lewisham 1898-1903

Table 2   Rates of intermarriage between the larger occupational groups. The number of marriages between those of each group are given, with the 'expected' number (on the assumption that choice is determined solely by chance) in brackets.
Some of the smallest occupational groups are included in the manual and non-manual totals, but are not given separately.

Non-manual		Own Group		Other non-manual		Skilled manual		All manual	
1. Professional									
On Husband's Side	(19)+	6	(0.8)	11	(6.7)	0*	(6.2)	2**	(11.4)
On Wife's side	(22)			13	(9.0)	3	(7.4)	3**	(12.2)
2. Clerical & 'junior' professional									
On Husband's side	(56)	12	(4.7)	20	(17.6)	18	(18.1)	24**	(33.7)
On Wife's side	(42)			19	(14.0)	8	(14.1)	11	(23.3)
3. Owners & managers of businesses									
On Husband's side	(92)	20	(14.0)	36**	(22.6)	24	(29.8)	36**	(55.4)
On Wife's side	(76)			33**	(19.9)	16*	(25.5)	23**	(42.1)
4. Retailers									
On Husband's side	(52)	6	(5.8)	22*	(14.9)	18	(16.9)	24*	(31.3)
On Wife's side	(56)			24	(19.2)	23	(18.8)	26	(31.0)

Manual	Own Group		Other manual		Retail		All non-manual	
1. Skilled								
On Husband's side (168)	60	(54.4)	58	(46.7)	23	(18.8)	50**	(66.9)
On Wife's side (162)			42	(35.3)	18	(16.9)	60	(72.3)
2. Semi-skilled								
On Husband's side (25)	4	(1.6)	17	(13.5)	0	(2.8)	4*	(10.0)
On Wife's side (32)			20	(16.1)	3	(3.3)	8*	(14.3)
3. Unskilled								
On Husband's side (46)	15**	(6.2)	30*	(21.5)	1	(5.2)	1**	(18.3)
On Wife's side (67)			46*	(31.0)	2*	(7.0)	6**	(29.9)
4. Personal Service workers (private & public)								
On Husband's side (26)	1	(1.5)	19	(14.1)	2	(2.9)	6	(10.4)
On Wife's side (29)			21*	(14.6)	0	(3.0)	7*	(12.9)

*   Difference from 'expected' figure significant at 5% level, using Chi Square with 1 degree of freedom.

** Significant at 1% level.

+   These numbers indicate the number of individuals in each category.

Source: Marriage registers in district register office, Lewisham High Street, S.E.13.

In Tables 2 and 3 379 weddings in Bethnal Green and 500 from Lewisham have been taken from the period 1896-1903. In each case, both bride and groom have been assigned to the manual or the non-manual category according to the occupations of their fathers, and these groups have then been sub-divided by type of occupation. All weddings where the occupation of one parent has not been given, or where he is described as 'gentleman', have been excluded. The Bethnal Green sample has been taken from 3 Anglican churches; that from Lewisham has been taken from 3 Anglican churches, 1 Wesleyan, 1 Congregationalist and the District Register Office, in the proportions 350 Anglican, 100 Civil,.50 Nonconformist.

The purpose of the test is to discover whether members of each occupational group show a preference for marriage partners from some groups rather than others. If no such preference exists, we could expect that the number of marriages between members of any one group and of any other to be roughly proportionate to the number of partners from each available. The extent to which the actual number of marriages deviates from the number predictable on these lines is an indication of how far class affects the choice of partner, and thus of the nature and location of the status divisions in society.

Although I owe the idea of this test to J. O. Foster's thesis, I have used a different method of presenting the results, as his Index of Association can be misleading when there are considerable differences between the numbers in each category. The Chi Square Test (M. J. Moroney, *Facts from Figures*, 3rd ed., Penguin, Harmondsworth, 1956, p.250) has been used to determine the probability of the observed number of marriages in each category arising by chance. If the level of significance is 5 per cent the probability of such a distribution arising by chance is not higher than 1 in 20; if it is 1 per cent, the probability is not higher than 1 in 100.

My classification of occupations is based on that used in *The Classification of Occupations*, published by the General Register Office in 1966. My 'Employers and Managers' is equivalent to S.E.G. 1-2, 'Professions' 3-4, ' "Junior" Professional' 5, 'Clerical' 6, 'Skilled' 8-9, 'Semi-skilled' 10 'Unskilled' 11. 'Service' is equivalent to S.E.G. 7, but consists largely of coachmen, chauffeurs and gardeners. 'Retail' includes owners and managers of shops, restaurants and public houses, but not salesmen, who go in the 'Clerical' category. The agricultural and extractive categories have not been used: farmers go with employers, farm labourers with unskilled and miners, quarrymen and fishermen with semi-skilled. Of those occupations that no longer existed in 1966, the most important was that of carman: they have been placed with the unskilled on the basis of their social status rather than of any estimate of the degree of skill that the job required. (In 1891, according to Booth, the majority of carmen lived in crowded conditions, and the proportion was only exceeded by that of costers, street-sellers, coal-porters, dockers, and labourers doing so [Booth, op.cit., II, v, p.8].) The only group of occupations that I have reclassified have been security workers who have been detached from S.E.G. 6, police being placed with skilled manual workers, park-keepers, etc., with semi-skilled. The problems of classifying occupations that changed in character between 1861 and 1891 or varied between one area and another have been discussed by Stedman Jones (op.cit., pp.352, 357): he decided that one occupation (brush-making) that had been skilled in 1861 had unmistakably ceased to be so by 1891, that painters, though generally classified as 'skilled' could not be regarded as such in London, while tailors, bootmakers and coopers could be termed artisans in some parts of London but not in the East End. I have not felt that the gain in accuracy from a similar investigation of the changes in the character of each occupation between 1900 and 1966 justified the labour involved. Two unavoidable sources of inaccuracy remain: the fact that the 'employer' and 'retail' categories are too comprehensive to be very informative, and that occupational definitions are ambiguous: such groups as bakers have been divided between retailers and manual workers in the proportions given by the 1901 census for the borough concerned; engineers have been assumed to be manual workers, unless it has been stated otherwise.

Table 3 Marriages in Bethnal Green 1896–1902.
Rates of intermarriage between largest occupational groups. (Some of the smaller groups, such as clerical workers, are not given separately).

Fathers of husbands   **Fathers of wives**

Fathers of husbands		1.(25)†	2.(199)	3.(38)	4.(92)
1. Retailers	(30)†	5 (20)	14 (15.8)	5 (3.0)	5 (7.3)
2. Skilled manual	(164)	10 (10.8)	90 (87.3)	10 (16.7)	40 (40.3)
3. Semi-skilled	(43)	1 (2.8)	27 (22.6)	8 (4.3)	7 (10.4)
4. Unskilled	(96)	4 (6.3)	42 (50.4)	11 (9.6)	33*(23.3)

Fathers of husbands   **Fathers of wives**

Fathers of husbands		Manual (339)	Non-manual (40)
Manual	(328)	297 (293.38)	42 (45.62)
Non-manual	(51)	31 (34.62)	9 (5.38)

† These numbers indicate the number of individuals in each category.
* Difference from 'expected' figure significant at the 5% level, using the Chi Square test with one degree of freedom.

Source: Marriage registers in district register office, Bow Road, E.3.

Table 4 Addresses of couples marrying in certain London parishes, 1896–1905

St Clement, Notting Hill, 1901–3
Total sample 187
Giving same address 107 (57.2% of total sample)**
Others 80

Living in the same neighbourhood	66	(82.5%)*
Others less than ½ mile apart	2	(2.5%)**
Elsewhere in London	7	(8.75%)
Outside London Postal District	5	(6.25%)

St Andrew, Bethnal Green, 1899–1902

Total sample 129
Giving same address 51 (39.5% of total sample)**
Others 78

Living in the same neighbourhood	51	(65.4%)
Others less than ½ mile apart	13	(16.7%)
Elsewhere in London	12	(15.4%)**
Outside London Postal District	2	(2.6%)**

St Mary, Lewisham, 1898–1902

Total sample 149
Giving same address 39 (26.2%) of total sample)
Others 110

Living in the same neighbourhood	28	(25.5%)
Less than ½ mile apart	18	(16.4%)
Elsewhere in London	47	(42.7%)
Outside London Postal District	17	(15.5%)**

St John, Paddington, 1896–1905

Total sample 180
Giving same address 39 (21.7% of total sample)
Others 141

Living in same neighbourhood	28	(19.9%)
Less than ½ mile apart	10	(7.1%)
Elsewhere in London	54	(38.3%)
Outside London Postal District	49	(34.8%)

* Difference from equivalent percentage in district immediately below significant at 5% level, using Standard Error (M. J. Moroney, *Facts from Figures*, 3rd ed., 1956, pp. 222–3).
** Significant at 1% level.
Source: Parish registers in Greater London Record Office, County Hall, S.E.1.

Each of the categories relates to the distance between the addresses of bride and groom. In each case, one of them lives in the parish. Thus, 'Outside London Postal District' means that either bride or groom lives in the parish in question, while the other lives outside London. The reasons for excluding those couples giving the same address are given in Chapter 1.

Table 5   Addresses of couples marrying in certain London parishes, 1896–1905, divided by occupational groups.

Notting Hill	Neighbourhood	Less than ½ mile	Elsewhere in London	Outside L.P.D.
Non-manual	(6) 4	–	1	1
Servants	(3) 2	–	1	–
Skilled manual	(26) 16 (61.5%)	2 (7.7%)	6 (23.1%)	2 (7.7%)
Other manual	(45) 43 (95.6%)	–	–	2 (4.4%)
Bethnal Green				
Non-manual	(9) 9	–	–	–
Skilled manual	(39) 24 (61.5%)	6 (15.4%)	8 (20.5%)	1 (2.6%)
Other manual	(30) 18 (60.0%)	7 (23.3%)	5 (16.7%)	–
Lewisham				
Clerical/Retail	(48) 14 (29.2%)	7 (14.6%)	21 (43.8%)	6 (12.5%)
Other non-manual	(23) 6 (26.1%)	2 (8.7%)	9 (39.1%)	6 (26.1%)
Manual	(39) 11 (28.2%)	7 (17.9%)	18 (47.2%)	3 (7.7%)
Paddington				
Clerical/Retail	(39) 11 (28.2%)	4 (10.3%)	12 (30.7%)	12 (30.7%)
Other non-manual	(50) 7 (14.0%)	3 (6.0%)	20 (40.0%)	20 (40.0%)
Servants	(21) 6 (28.6%)	–	7 (33.3%)	8 (38.1%)
Other manual	(31) 4 (12.9%)	3 (9.7%)	15 (48.4%)	9 (29.0%)

Table 6 Attendances by adults at all churches in 1902–3 as percentage of adult population: Greater London.

A Social Index has been drawn up by averaging the rank numbers in the tables of domestic servants per 100 households and of percentage of population enumerated in tenements of 8 or more rooms. Position on the Social Index is significantly related to the relative level of church attendance. Using Spearman's Rank Correlation co-efficient (Moroney, op.cit., p. 335): R = 0.70; t = 6.86 with 49 degrees of freedom; p < 0.001.

	Female domestic indoor servants per 100 households 1901	Percentage of population enumerated in tenements of a given size, 1911		Adult church attendance
		8+ rooms	6–7 rooms	
1. Ealing	68.6	25.4%	28.6%	47.4%
2. Hornsey	43.8	33.4	27.6	40.6
3. Bromley	47.8	25.4	22.0	38.0
4. Croydon	31.6	17.0	26.7	37.5
5. St Marylebone	51.4	23.8	8.5	37.1
6. Ilford	23.2	6.2	43.1	37.0
7. Finchley	42.9	22.9	33.4	36.1
8. Wood Green	16.3	9.1	31.9	32.9
9. Wimbledon	38.8	21.2	27.6	32.8
10. Enfield	19.7	8.7	24.4	32.7
11. Stoke Newington	27.8	21.8	19.8	32.1
12. Richmond	49.8	28.5	23.5	30.6
13. Lewisham	36.2	20.0	29.4	30.5
14. Hendon	28.8	15.5	25.5	30.3
15. Westminster	65.8	27.1	8.9	27.0
16. Hampstead	81.4	46.8	12.6	26.04
17. Chiswick	33.5	23.2	23.9	25.96
18. Kensington	80.0	34.7	10.9	25.46
19. Barnes	36.9	18.3	30.8	25.45
20. Twickenham	37.4	19.0	27.2	25.3
21. Walthamstow	9.6	3.3	23.7	24.4
22. Woolwich	14.4	6.2	23.9	24.2
23. Isleworth	22.3	9.4	26.3	23.9
24. Hackney	17.9	11.8	18.1	23.8
25. Holborn	22.3	11.3	7.0	23.5
26. Camberwell	15.3	10.5	19.8	23.2
27. Greenwich	24.5	11.9	19.7	22.8
28. Wandsworth	35.2	20.0	21.3	22.32
29. Paddington	50.2	21.7	9.8	22.29
30. Leyton	18.6	5.0	37.1	22.0

	Female domestic indoor servants per 100 households	Percentage of population enumerated in tenements of a given size, 1911		Adult church attendance
		8 + rooms	6-7 rooms	
31. Chelsea	55.2	25.1	11.5	21.60
32. Islington	15.5	10.1	11.2	21.57
33. Lambeth	18.1	13.5	16.1	20.6
34. Acton	24.5	9.3	24.2	20.2
35. East Ham	8.4	1.4	26.1	19.9
36. West Ham	9.1	3.0	17.4	19.6
37. Edmonton	10.3	3.5	14.9	18.6
38. Stepney	8.8	2.7	10.4	18.5
39. Finsbury	8.2	3.5	5.8	18.3
40. St Pancras	16.9	9.8	8.5	17.7
41. Deptford	15.4	10.0	19.4	16.9
42. Bermondsey	6.6	2.1	13.1	16.8
43. Willesden	22.0	12.8	15.1	16.4
44. Tottenham	10.7	4.1	22.6	16.1
45. Southwark	7.8	3.0	8.9	15.7
46. Battersea	13.1	6.8	16.6	15.2
47. Hammersmith	19.3	12.3	16.2	14.8
48. Poplar	8.1	2.4	11.9	14.4
49. Bethnal Green	5.8	1.3	6.7	13.3
50. Shoreditch	5.7	1.8	6.7	12.2
51. Fulham	18.6	7.8	15.1	11.8

Source: Figures for housing taken from *London Statistics*, 1912–13, pp. 62–7, and for domestic servants from the 1901 census.
Adult church attendances taken from Mudie-Smith, op.cit.
Population for Inner London: the estimates given in *London Statistics*, 1911–12, p. 49, for 1 July 1903. Population for Outer London: estimates kindly made for me by Mr. J. G. Heal on the basis of the figures at each census between 1881 and 1921.
The proportion of adults in the population of each district has been assumed to be the same as at the 1901 census.

Table 7   Attendances by adults at services of the Church of England, 1902–3, as a percentage of adult population: Greater London.
The numbers in brackets represent the position of the district in the Social Index.
R = 0.85; t = 12.46, with 49 degrees of freedom; p<0.001

1.	Ealing	28.5	(5)	27.	Walthamstow	9.6	(42)
2.	Bromley	20.7	(6)	28.	Lambeth	9.4	(25)
3.	Richmond	18.8	(4)	29.	Woolwich	9.0	(39)
4.	Croydon	18.2	(19)	30.	Leyton	8.8	(37)
5.	Hornsey	17.7	(7)	31.	Holborn	8.1	(24)
6.	St. Marylebone	17.4	(9)	32.	Edmonton	8.0	(41)
7.	Twickenham	16.6	(14)	33.	Islington	8.0	(34)
8.	Barnes	16.5	(16)	34.	Hackney	7.9	(28)
9.	Enfield	16.4	(30)	35.	Camberwell	7.7	(33)
10.	Lewisham	15.6	(15)	36.	Deptford	7.4	(31)
11.	Westminster	15.5	(3)	37.	St. Pancras	6.8	(32)
12.	Finchley	15.4	(11)	38.	Battersea	6.7	(38)
13.	Kensington	14.9	(2)	39.	East Ham	6.6	(48)
14.	Chiswick	14.5	(12)	40.	Willesden	6.3	(22)
15.	Wimbledon	14.4	(13)	41.	Hammersmith	6.0	(23)
16.	Isleworth	13.6	(27)	42.	Fulham	5.7	(36)
17.	Hampstead	12.9	(1)	43.	Tottenham	5.5	(40)
18.	Hendon	12.6	(20)	44.	West Ham	5.4	(43)
19.	Stoke Newington	12.1	(18)	45.	Poplar	5.4	(46)
20.	Paddington	11.7	(10)	46.	Bermondsey	5.3	(49)
21.	Chelsea	11.5	(8)	47.	Bethnal Green	5.3	(51)
22.	Ilford	11.0	(29)	48.	Shoreditch	4.9	(50)
23.	Greenwich	11.0	(21)	49.	Southwark	4.8	(47)
24.	Wandsworth	10.9	(17)	50.	Finsbury	4.8	(44)
25.	Acton	10.5	(26)	51.	Stepney	4.2	(45)
26.	Wood Green	9.8	(35)				

Table 8 (a)   Metropolitan Boroughs, ranked according to the number of adult attendances at Anglican services per cent of adult population in 1902—3. Numbers in brackets represent the position of the borough in the Social Index for Inner London.

R = 0.90; t = 10.52 with 26 degrees of freedom; p<0.001

1. St. Marylebone	(5)	11. Lambeth	(13)	21. Fulham	(19)
2. Lewisham	(7)	12. Woolwich	(21)	22. Poplar	(24)
3. Westminster	(3)	13. Holborn	(12)	23. Bermondsey	(26)
4. Kensington	(2)	14. Islington	(18)	24. Bethnal Green	(28)
5. Hampstead	(1)	15. Hackney	(14)	25. Shoreditch	(27)
6. S.N.	(9)	16. Camberwell	(17)	26. Finsbury	(22)
7. Paddington	(6)	17. Deptford	(15)	27. Southwark	(25)
8. Chelsea	(4)	18. St. Pancras	(16)	28. Stepney	(23)
9. Greenwich	(10)	19. Battersea	(20)		
10. Wandsworth	(8)	20. Hammersmith	(11)		

Table 8(b)   Boroughs and Urban Districts of Outer London, ranked according to the number of adult attendances at Anglican services per cent of adult population in 1902—3. Numbers in brackets represent the position of the district in the Social Index for Outer London.

R = 0.85; t = 7.11 with 21 degrees of freedom; p<0.001

1. Ealing	(2)	9. Finchley	(5)	17. Walthamstow	(21)
2. Bromley	(3)	10. Chiswick	(6)	18. Leyton	(18)
3. Richmond	(1)	11. Wimbledon	(7)	19. Edmonton	(20)
4. Croydon	(10)	12. Isleworth	(14)	20. East Ham	(23)
5. Hornsey	(4)	13. Hendon	(11)	21. Willesden	(12)
6. Twickenham	(8)	14. Ilford	(15)	22. Tottenham	(19)
7. Barnes	(9)	15. Acton	(13)	23. West Ham	(22)
8. Enfield	(16)	16. Wood Green	(17)		

Table 9   Attendances by adults at Nonconformist chapels in
1902–3 as a percentage of adult population: Greater
London.
The numbers in brackets represent the rank number of
the district in the table of percentage of population
enumerated in tenements of 6 or 7 rooms at the 1911
census.
$R = 0.56$; $t = 4.72$ with 49 degrees of freedom; $p < 0.001$

1.	Ilford	22.6	(1)	27.	Greenwich	9.26	(26)
2.	Hornsey	21.9	(9)	28.	Richmond	8.7	(20)
3.	Wood Green	20.5	(4)	29.	St. Pancras	8.52	(47)
4.	Finchley	18.4	(3)	30.	Wandsworth	8.51	(23)
5.	S.N.	17.7	(25)	31.	Acton	8.3	(16)
6.	Croydon	17.1	(11)	32.	Isleworth	8.1	(12)
7.	Ealing	16.4	(7)	33.	Southwark	8.0	(45)
8.	Bromley	15.6	(22)	34.	Deptford	7.73	(27)
9.	Wimbledon	13.8	(8)	35.	Tottenham	7.72	(21)
10.	Walthamstow	13.7	(19)	36.	Bermondsey	7.5	(36)
11.	Enfield	13.6	(15)	37.	Twickenham	7.0	(10)
12.	Camberwell	13.3	(24)	38.	Battersea	6.84	(30)
13.	Hackney	13.2	(28)	39.	Poplar	6.82	(38)
14.	Lewisham	13.0	(6)	40.	Bethnal Green	6.792	(50)
15.	East Ham	12.1	(13)	41.	Westminster	6.785	(44)
16.	Leyton	12.0	(2)	42.	Paddington	6.6	(43)
17.	Islington	11.5	(41)	43.	Stepney	6.3	(42)
18.	Finsbury	11.1	(51)	44.	Chiswick	6.2	(18)
19.	Woolwich	10.9	(17)	45.	Hammersmith	6.15	(31)
20.	Hendon	10.8	(14)	46.	Holborn	5.9	(48)
21.	Lambeth	10.5	(32)	47.	Chelsea	5.74	(39)
22.	West Ham	10.4	(29)	48.	Shoreditch	5.7	(49)
23.	St. Marylebone	10.38	(46)	49.	Kensington	5.1	(40)
24.	Hampstead	9.9	(37)	50.	Barnes	5.0	(5)
25.	Edmonton	9.4	(35)	51.	Fulham	4.2	(33)
26.	Willesden	9.33	(34)				

Table 10   Total church attendances by adults in 1902–3 as percentage of estimated adult population in 81 areas classified according to their colouring on Booth's Social Map of London, 1900.

Poor

1. Waterloo	22.6	8. Borough	14.1	15. City Road	7.5
2. Peckham N.T.	21.8	9. St. Georges in E.	13.3	16. Somers Tn.	7.3
3. Clerkenwell	18.5	10. Walworth	11.7	17. Bromley	6.9
4. Bethnal G.West	18.2	11. Battersea Park	11.6	18. B.G., S.E.	6.4
5. Rotherhithe	15.7	12. Kensal N.T.	10.2	19. Hackney Wk.	6.2
6. Lisson Grove	14.2	13. King's Cross	9.4	20. B.G., South	6.0
7. Deptford Creek	14.1	14. Vauxhall	7.7		

Working Class

1. Kentish Twn	23.7	5. Plumstead	15.4	9. Camden Twn.	9.7
2. Soho	19.3	6. Peckham N.	13.2	10. Camberwell N.	9.6
3. Bermondsey	17.0	7. Isle of Dogs	12.6	11. Barnsbury	7.6
4. Nine Elms	16.3	8. Clapham Jnctn.	10.2	12. Stepney	5.8

Upper Working Class

1. S.N., South	23.1	5. Holloway	17.7	10. Stockwell	13.8
2. Peckham Rye	21.4	6. Plumstead Cmn	16.3	11. S. Bermondsey	13.0
3. Kentish Tn, N.E.	20.0	7. Queens Park	16.1	12. Dalston	12.5
4. DeBeauvoir Tn	18.0	8. Lavender Hill	15.4	13. Fulham	11.7
		9. Deptford	14.6		

Lower Middle Class

1. Lewisham	42.8	5. Catford	18.2	8. Camden Tn W.	12.6
2. Bow	24.7	6. W. Hampstead	18.1	9. Camden N.T.	11.7
3. S. Battersea	22.3	7. W. Kensington	17.5	10. Shepherds B.	11.3
4. E. Dulwich	18.6				

Middle Class

1. Clapham	36.7	4. Wandsworth	24.5	7. S. Hackney	18.8
2. Kilburn	35.3	5. Balham	22.7	8. Brockley	18.7
3. W. Hackney	26.0	6. U. Holloway	20.4	9. Brixton	18.4

Wealthy–Suburban

1. Blackheath & Lee	43.4	4. Sydenham	36.8	6. Hampstead	28.8
2. Eltham	40.4	5. Dulwich and	33.4	7. St. John's Wood	25.1
3. Highbury	38.7	Herne Hill			

Wealthy – West End

1. Kensington	43.2	5. Belgravia	33.8	8. W. Brompton	27.3
2. Marylebone	40.1	6. Knightsbridge	31.5	9. Bayswater	26.1
3. Upper Chelsea	38.7	7. Earls Court	29.3	10. Mayfair	23.4
4. S. Kensington	37.7				

Notes to Tables 10 to 12

Each of the 81 districts has been formed of a group of three or four parishes. Parish populations for 1901 and 1911 are stated in the censuses for those years: but it has been necessary to estimate both total populations for 1903, and the proportion of this population aged 15 and over. The first has been done by simply adding or subtracting a fifth of the amount by which the population of each parish changed between the two censuses. The second has been slightly more complicated and the method used was as follows: comparisons of the 1901 census with the Registrar General's Annual Report for the same year shows that the number of children aged 14 and under in a metropolitan borough can be predicted fairly accurately on the basis of the crude birth rate, the ratio between the first and the second generally being between 10:1 and 11:1 since the census gives the number of those in each age-group for every London borough, while crude birth rates are available for the smaller and more socially homogeneous registration sub-districts, the birth rate of each of my 81 areas has been assumed to be the same as that for the registration sub-district in which it is placed, and the proportion of the population aged under 14 has been taken as that for the borough with the birth rate most nearly the same; where a sub-district has a higher birth rate than any borough the proportion has been multiplied by 9.55, the ratio between the two highest borough proportions, and where it has a lower rate the proportion has been multiplied by 13.99, the ratio between the two lowest.

The list of churches and chapels within each parish has been taken from Booth's 'Religious Influence' series: the denominational range is comprehensive, but inevitably some churches will have escaped Booth's attention, while some of those listed by Booth were not included in the *Daily News* census.

Areas have been classified according to Booth's social map of London in 1900, also published in the 'Religious Influences' series. The areas chosen are those in which one colour is dominant: poor = blue or blue and purple; working class = purple; upper working class = pink; lower middle class = pink and red; middle class = red; wealthy = yellow or red and yellow. The greatest deficiency of Booth's system is that although he is aware of the important status distinction between clerks and artisans, both tend to live in streets marked pink on his map, red being reserved for those with one or more servant.

Table 11   Adult attendances at Church of England services in 1902–3 as a percentage of estimated adult population in 8 areas.

Poor

1. Rotherhithe	6.9	8. Waterloo	4.6	15. Hackney Wick	3.2
2. St. Georges	6.7	9. B.G., South	4.2	16. Deptford Crk	3.1
3. Borough	6.0	10. Battersea Park	4.0	17. Bromley	2.9
4. Lisson Grove	5.5	11. Vauxhall	3.9	18. Kensal N.T.	2.8
5. City Road	5.5	12. Walworth	3.8	19. Kings Cross	2.4
6. Peckham N.T.	5.3	13. Clerkenwell	3.6	20. Somers Town	1.6
7. B.G., West	5.2	14. B.G., S.E.	3.5		

Working Class

1. Soho	9.4	5. Plumstead	5.4	9. Bermondsey	4.4
2. N. Camberwell	8.9	6. Isle of Dogs	5.3	10. Camden Town	4.2
3. Nine Elms	7.5	7. Peckham N.	5.1	11. Stepney	3.9
4. Kentish Town	5.6	8. Clapham Jnct	5.1	12. Barnsbury	2.9

Upper Working Class

1. Kentish T. N.E.	8.7	6. Peckham Rye	6.8	11. Deptford	4.4
2. Plumstead Cmn	8.5	7. Holloway	6.6	12. DeBeauvoir Twn	4.1
3. Lavender Hill	7.6	8. Queens Park	6.1	13. S. Bermondsey	3.2
4. Stockwell	7.4	9. Dalston	6.0		
5. S.N., South	7.2	10. Fulham	5.3		

Lower Middle Class

1. Lewisham	21.7	5. W. Hampstead	9.2	9. Camden Town W.	6.3
2. W. Kensington	12.0	6. Catford	8.1	10. E. Dulwich	5.9
3. Camden N.T.	10.2	7. Shepherds B.	6.6		
4. S. Battersea	10.2	8. Bow	6.3		

Middle Class

1. Kilburn	19.3	4. Brockley	10.9	7. Wandsworth	9.6
2. Clapham	12.3	5. Balham	10.9	8. U. Holloway	9.2
3. W. Hackney	11.2	6. Brixton	10.1	9. S. Hackney	6.1

Wealthy – Suburban

1. Blackheath & Lee	27.6	3. Eltham	23.2	5. Highbury	17.0
2. Sydenham	24.4	4. Dulwich & Herne Hill	17.5	6. Hampstead	15.4
				7. St. John's Wood	10.9

Wealthy – West End

1. S. Kensington	34.5	5. Upper Chelsea	22.1	8. Earls Court	17.6
2. Belgravia	28.9	6. Knightsbridge	20.0	9. W. Brompton	16.6
3. Kensington	26.2	7. Bayswater	18.8	10. Mayfair	15.3
4. Marylebone	23.5				

Table 12   Adult attendances at Nonconformist chapels in 1902–3
as percentage of estimated adult population in 81
areas

Poor

1. Deptford Creek	14.5	8. Borough	6.4	15. Hackney Wick	2.6
2. B.G., W.	12.0	9. Walworth	5.0	16. City Road	2.0
3. Waterloo	10.6	10. Bsea Park	4.1	17. Somers Tn	2.0
4. Clerkenwell	8.3	11. St. Georges	3.6	18. Bethnal Grn S.	1.4
5. Lisson Grove	7.3	12. Kensal N.T.	3.5	19. Rotherhithe	1.2
6. Peckham N.T.	7.0	13. Bromley	3.4	20. Bethnal Grn S.E.	1.0
7. Kings X.	6.6	14. Vauxhall	3.3		

Working Class

1. Kentish Tn	9.9	5. Bermondsey	6.6	9. Soho	3.5
2. Nine Elms	8.8	6. Camden Town	5.6	10. Clapham J.	2.7
3. Plumstead	8.2	7. Isle of Dogs	5.1	11. Stepney	2.1
4. Peckham N.	8.1	8. Barnsbury	4.6	12. Camberwell N.	0.7

Upper Working Class

1. Peckham Rye	14.6	6. Lavender H.	7.8	10. Dalston	6.6
2. Stoke		7. Plumstead C.	7.8	11. Stockwell	6.6
Newington, S.	14.5	8. Queens Park	7.7	12. Deptford	3.4
3. L. Holloway	9.7	9. Kentish Town	7.1	13. Fulham	2.5
4. S. Bermondsey	9.5	N.E.			
5. DeBeauvoir Town	8.6				

Lower Middle Class

1. Lewisham	17.8	5. Catford	9.8	8. Shepherds B.	4.6
2. Bow	12.7	6. Camden Tn W.	6.4	9. W. Kensington	4.3
3. S. Battersea	12.1	7. W. Hampstead	4.8	10. Camden N.T.	1.2
4. E. Dulwich	11.3				

Middle Class

1. W. Hackney	13.2	4. U. Holloway	10.2	7. Brockley	7.8
2. Wandsworth	12.2	5. S. Hackney	9.7	8. Kilburn	6.4
3. Clapham	11.4	6. Balham	8.8	9. Brixton	5.8

Wealthy Suburban

1. Highbury	16.5	4. Hampstead	12.4	6. St. John's Wood	10.4
2. Eltham	15.3	5. Sydenham	11.1	7. Dulwich and	
3. Blackheath and				Herne Hill	7.2
Lee	12.8				

Wealth — West End

1. Kensington	9.7	5. S. Kensington	3.1	8. W. Brompton	1.4
2. U. Chelsea	9.5	6. Bayswater	2.6	9. Knightsbridge	–
3. Belgravia	4.9	7. Earls Court	2.1	10. Mayfair	–
4. Marylebone	3.7				

Table 13   Women as a percentage of those aged fifteen and over
                    counted by the *Daily News* in 1902–3 at services of
                    various denominations in Inner London.

Church of England	65.67%
Roman Catholic	64.20
Baptist	59.80
Presbyterian	59.19
Brethren	58.53
Utd. Methodist F.C.	57.33
Congregationalist	56.98
Wesleyan	56.97
Salvation Army	56.84
COUNTY OF LONDON*	53.88
Primitive Methodist	51.59

*Percentage of females in the population aged fifteen and over in the County of
London at the decennial census, 1901.

Table 14   Occupations of men married in Bethnal Green classified by type of ceremony used.

	Church of England, 1888		Registry Office, 1913	
Gentleman	1	0.2%	1	0.7%
Forces	–	–	–	–
Professional	1	0.2	–	–
Employers and managers	10	2.0	4	2.8
'Junior' professional	8	1.6	–	–
Clerical	27	5.3	15	10.6
Retail	43	8.5	8	5.7
Skilled	167	33.0	51	36.2
Semi-skilled	68	13.4	20	14.2
Unskilled	155	30.6	32	22.7
Service	25	4.9	8	5.7
Forces	1	0.2	2	1.4
	506		141	

Nonconformist, 1880–1901

	Baptist		Congl.		Wesleyan		Combined	
Gentleman	–	–	–	–	–	–	–	–
Forces	–	–	–	–	–	–	–	–
Professional	5	2.4%	4	2.5%	4	5.5%	13	2.9%**
Employers and managers	13	6.3	11	6.8	6	8.2	30	6.8 **
'Junior' professional	3	1.4	5	3.1	4	5.5	12	2.7
Clerical	50	24.0	56	34.6†	15	20.5	121	27.3 **
Retail	22	10.6	23	14.2	6	8.2	51	11.5
Skilled	78	37.5	47	29.0	23	31.5	148	33.4
Semi-skilled	22	10.6	14	8.6	10	13.7	46	10.4 **
Unskilled	10	4.8	–	– ††	4	5.5	14	3.1 **
Service	4	1.9	2.	1.2	–	–	6	1.4 **
Forces	1	0.5	–	–	1	1.4	2	0.5
	208		162		73		443	

**Difference from Church of England percentage significant at the 1% level using the Standard Error.
†Difference from Baptist percentage significant at 5% level.
††Significant at 1% level.
Source: Marriage registers in Bethnal Green and Bow district register office.

Table 15 Occupations of men married in Lewisham classified by type of ceremony used.

Church of England

	1898–1901		1913		Combined	
Gentlemen	5	1.3%	1	0.3%	6	0.8%
Forces	4	1.0	3	0.8	7	0.9
Professional	21	5.3	16	4.0	37	4.7
Employers and managers	23	5.8	32	8.1	55	6.9
'Junior' professional	18	4.5	12	3.0	30	3.7
Clerical	76	19.2	118	29.8	194	24.5
Retail	43	10.9	21	5.3	64	8.1
Others	–	–	–	–	–	–
Skilled	103	26.0%	94	23.7%	197	24.8
Semi-skilled	28	7.1	32	8.1	50	7.6
Unskilled	54	13.6	33	8.3	87	11.0
Service	16	4.0	24	6.1	40	5.1
Forces	5	1.3	10	2.5	15	1.9
	396		396		792	

Registry Office

	1899	1913	Combined	
Gentleman	–	2	3	0.8%
Forces	1	2	3	1.3
Professional	1	2	3	1.3
Employers and managers	4	5	9	3.7
'Junior' professional	1	3	4	1.6
Clerical	14	18	32	13.1
Retail	3	7	10	4.1
Skilled	35	32	67	27.5
Semi-skilled	21	13	34	13.9
Unskilled	33	28	61	25.0
Service	8	6	14	5.7
Forces	1	4	5	2.0
	122	122	244	

Nonconformist, 1899–1914

	Baptist		Congl.		Wesleyan		Other Meth.		Combined	
Gentleman	1	1.3%	–	–	1	0.3%	–	–	2	0.3%
Forces	–	–	–	–	1	0.3	–	–	1	0.2
Professional	1	1.3	20	9.6%††	13	4.5	2	3.5%	36	5.7
Employers and managers	2	2.6	19	9.1	23	8.0	6	10.5	50	7.9
'Junior' professional	5	6.6	13	6.2	9	3.1	4	7.0	31	4.9
Clerical	27	35.5	65	31.1	92	32.1	21	36.8	205	32.6**
Retail	8	10.5	15	7.2	33	11.5	6	10.5	62	9.9
Skilled	15	19.7	40	19.1	66	23.0	13	22.8	134	21.3
Semi-skilled	9	11.8	8	3.8	22	7.7	–	–	39	6.2
Unskilled	5	6.6	18	8.6	19	6.6	3	5.3	45	7.2**
Service	3	3.9	9	4.3	5	1.7	2	3.5	19	3.0
Forces	–	–	2	1.0	3	1.0	–	–	5	0.8
	76		209		287		57		629	

Presbyterian, 1899–1914

Gentleman	–	–
Forces	–	–
Professional	4	11.4%
Employers and managers	7	20.0
'Junior' professional	4	11.4
Clerical	7	20.0
Retail	3	8.6
Skilled	6	17.1
Semi-skilled	1	2.9
Unskilled	1	2.9
Service	2	5.7
	35	

**Difference from percentage for marriages in Anglican Churches significant at 1% level using Standard Error.
††Differences from percentage for other Nonconformist denominations significant at 1% level using Standard Error.
Source: Marriage registers in Lewisham district register office.

Table 16 Occupations of husbands at all *Quaker* weddings at meetings in Inner London.

	1885–1895		1905–13	
Gentleman	2	1.6%	–	–
Professional	10	7.8	13	9.8
Employers and managers	37	28.9	37	27.8
'Junior' professional	10	7.5	14	10.5
Clerical	23	18.0	35	26.3
Retail	15	11.7	8	6.0
Retired	–	–	1	0.7
Skilled	22	17.2	14	10.5
Semi-skilled	6	4.7	4	3.0
Unskilled	2	1.6	4	3.0
Service	1	0.8	3	2.3
	128		133	

1885–95. Manual Workers: 24.3%
1905–13. Manual Workers: 18.8%

Source: Registers at Library in Friends' House, Euston Road, N.W.1.

Table 17 Church attendances in Bethnal Green at the *British Weekly* and *Daily News* censuses as a percentage of all those living in the borough.

	1886–7	1902–3
C. of E.	6.0	6.1
R. C.	–	0.6
Baptist	3.6	2.8
Congregationalist	3.1	2.8
Wesleyan	1.7	1.8
Others	1.9	1.8
Total	16.3	15.9

Table 18 Church attendances in Lewisham as a percentage of the population of the borough.
(The unit used in 1886–7 is the area of the future borough.)

	1886–7	1903
C.of E.	28.5	15.7
R. C.	0.5	1.2
Congregationalist	6.1	3.9
Baptist	2.5	2.7
Wesleyan	4.1	2.7
Other Methodist	1.8	1.1
Others	2.0	3.2
Total	45.5	30.5

Table 19 Church attendances by adults in 1903 as a percentage of the adult population of the district.

	Catford	Lee, Blackheath and Eltham
Estimated Adult Population	18,924	16,943
C.of E.	8.1	27.6
R. C.	–	2.8
Congregationalist	1.4	4.7
Baptist	2.0	4.4
Wesleyan	5.6	0.4
Other Methodist	0.7	0.3
Others	0.4	3.3
Total	18.2	43.5

Table 20   Church Attendances in Inner London, 1886—7 and
              1902—3

| | 1886—7 | | 1902—3 | |
	Total	% of pop	Total	% of pop
Church of England	548,848	13.52	429,822	9.43
Roman Catholic	111,894	2.76	93,572	2.05
Baptist	120,630	2.99	108,455	2.38
Congregationalist	116,949	2.88	105,535	2.31
Wesleyan	80,463	1.98	78,139	1.72
Presbyterian	30,387	0.75	24,778	0.54
Salvation Army	29,395	0.72	22,402	0.49
Jews	4,330	0.11	26,612	0.58
Others	114,593	2.81	113,046	2.48
Total	1,157,489	28.52	1,003,361	21.98
Estimated Population	4,058,735		4,557,386	

Source: British Weekly, 5.11.1886—17.12.1886, 13—20.1.1888; Mudie-Smith, op. cit.

Table 21   London Church Attendances 1902—3: Changeover From
              1886—7 share of Population. The boroughs are placed
              according to the number of domestic indoor servants
              per 100 families in 1901. Thus Hampstead (1) has 81.4
              per 100 and Shoreditch (28) has 5.7

1.	Hampstead	−38.9%	15.	Hackney	−25.8%
2.	Kensington	−41.6	16.	St. Pancras	−30.7
3.	Westminster	−22.3	17.	Islington	−22.2
4.	Chelsea	− 9.3	18	Deptford	−30.6
5.	St. Marylebone	− 9.7	19.	Camberwell	− 8.2
6.	Paddington	−38.9	20.	Woolwich	−12.5
7.	Lewisham	−33.0	21.	Battersea	−27.7
8.	Wandsworth	−49.4	22.	Stepney	− 8.8
9.	S. Newington	−37.8	23.	Finsbury	+ 4.2
10.	Greenwich	− 9.8	24.	Poplar	−17.3
11.	Holborn	−16.2	25.	Southwark	−23.3
12.	Hammersmith	−29.4	26.	Bermondsey	+12.2
13.	Fulham	−18.4	27.	Bethnal Green	− 2.5
14.	Lambeth	−27.5	28.	Shoreditch	−12.8

LONDON −23.2

Table 22   Birthplaces of those enumerated in metropolitan boroughs and suburban districts with large middle- and upper-class populations.

Using Spearman's Rank Correlation coefficient, church attendance (see Table IX) is negatively related to the proportion of the population born in the County of London at a low level of significance. $R = -0.40$; $t = 1.82$ with 17 degrees of freedom; $p < 0.10$.

There is no statistically significant relationship between the proportion born 'elsewhere' and church attendance. $R = 0.02$.

	Female domestic indoor servants per 100 households	Birthplaces 1911		
		County of London	Outer London	Elsewhere
Hampstead	73.7	50.5%	3.5%	46.0%
Kensington	70.7	51.5	2.3	46.2
Westminster	54.5	46.5	1.6	51.9
Chelsea	54.4	55.4	1.4	43.2
St Marylebone	48.3	54.4	1.8	43.8
Paddington	40.8	54.5	3.8	41.7
Ealing	40.3	26.5	23.8	49.7
Wimbledon	35.8	31.5	25.2	43.7
Hornsey	33.5	39.7	22.1	38.2
Wandsworth	24.6	61.7	2.6	35.7
Lewisham	24.5	64.2	2.8	33.0
Croydon	24.1	27.0	35.8	37.2
Stoke Newington	20.6	69.7	4.1	26.2
Acton	19.2	33.1	26.6	40.3
Greenwich	18.7	69.1	1.9	29.0
Holborn	18.6	56.6	1.7	41.7
Willesden	17.1	38.9	26.6	34.5
Ilford	15.9	33.8	31.1	35.1
Enfield	15.2	22.4	42.6	35.0

Source: Birthplaces taken from 1911 census, numbers of domestic servants per 100 households from *London Statistics*, 1914–15, p.52.

Note: The category 'Outer London' includes only those born in the 14 suburban districts for which separate census figures are available: others born in Outer London will be counted as born 'elsewhere'.

Table 23   Birthplaces of those enumerated in metropolitan boroughs and suburban districts with predominantly working-class populations.

Using Spearman's Rank Correlation coefficient, church attendance is negatively related to the proportion of the population born in the County of London at a low level of significance. $R = -0.35$; $t = 1.73$ with 21 degrees of freedom; $p < 0.10$.

The relationship between church attendance and the proportion of the population born 'elsewhere' is not statistically significant. $R = 0.20$; $t = 0.95$ with 21 degrees of freedom.

	Female domestic indoor servants per 100 households, 1911	Birthplaces 1911		
		County of London	Outer London	Elsewhere
Fulham	13.8	65.6%	1.9%	32.5%
Hammersmith	13.4	60.4	3.0	36.6
Lambeth	13.0	69.2	1.7	29.1
Hackney	12.8	76.8	3.7	19.5
Woolwich	12.6	61.8	2.8	35.4
St Pancras	12.3	67.0	1.6	31.4
Camberwell	11.7	76.8	1.6	21.6
Deptford	11.4	76.7	1.5	21.8
Leyton	10.6	37.4	37.1	25.5
Battersea	10.6	70.2	1.7	28.1
Islington	10.0	73.3	2.6	24.1
Edmonton	8.2	36.9	38.8	24.3
Walthamstow	7.2	43.8	29.5	22.7
Tottenham	7.2	43.0	32.2	24.8
West Ham	7.0	31.6	46.2	22.2
East Ham	6.9	38.2	35.0	26.8
Stepney	6.4	68.0	1.5	30.5
Poplar	5.4	79.5	3.9	16.6
Southwark	5.1	79.3	1.2	19.5
Finsbury	5.0	79.8	1.5	18.7
Bermondsey	4.2	83.5	1.0	15.5
Shoreditch	3.9	85.7	1.9	12.4
Bethnal Green	3.5	83.4	1.7	14.9

Table 24   Large-scale industry in the industrial districts of London.

	Average number of employees per factory or workshop, 1907	Percentage of occupied males working in industries characterised by large-scale production, 1911
Greenwich	34	26.7%
Woolwich	69	25.9
West Ham	*	22.0
Enfield	*	21.0
Poplar	37	19.9
Deptford	22	18.9
Bermondsey	38	18.0
Edmonton	*	15.3
East Ham	*	15.0
Acton	*	14.0
Battersea	21	13.5
Finsbury	27	13.0
Southwark	24	12.3
Camberwell	18	12.1
Walthamstow	*	12.0
Islington	15	11.0
Shoreditch	20	10.9
Hammersmith	20	10.9
Willesden	*	10.8
Tottenham	*	10.8
Fulham	22	10.7
Hackney	15	10.2
Stepney	17	9.9
Lambeth	18	9.5
Bethnal Green	13	8.6
St Pancras	20	7.9

*No figures available.
Sources: 1911 census; 1907 factory and workshop census, as summarised in *London Statistics,* 1911–12, pp 73–88.
Notes: According to the figures in London Statistics, 1911–12, pp. 84–8, the average number of employees per factory or workshop in Greater London in 1907 was 20.1. The average was over 30 in the categories 'Metals,

machinery, etc.', 'Chemicals' and 'Gas and electricity', and in the following sub-categories: Hats and caps, Shirts and linen collars, Bookbinding, Cardboard boxes, Paper, Cocoa and chocolate, Fruit preserves, Brewing and distilling, Beer bottling, Tobacco, Tanning, China and earthenware, India rubber, Explosives.

Because not all of these appear separately in the census occupational statistics, the following categories of worker have been defined as working in industries 'characterised by large-scale production': All workers in 'Metals, machines, implements and conveyances', and workers in Explosives; Oil, grease, etc.; Skins; Bookbinding; Other food; Tobacco; Spirituous drinks; Gas, water, electricity.

Table 25   Population of Greater London, 1801–1911

	Inner London	Outer London	Total
1801	959,310	155,334	1,114,644
1851	2,363,341	317,594	2,680,935
1881	3,830,297	936,364	4,766,661
1891	4,227,954	1,405,852	5,633,806
1901	4,536,267	2,045,135	6,581,402
1911	4,521,685	2,729,673	7,251,358

Source: London Statistics, 1911–12, p. 52.

Note: Inner London is defined as the area that formed the County of London in 1889; Greater London is equivalent to the Metropolitan Police District as it existed in 1911.

Map 1: Metropolitan Boroughs
Female domestic indoor servants per 100 households in 1901

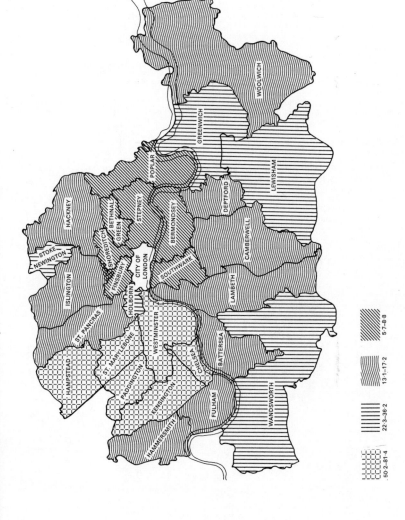

Map 2: London 1900

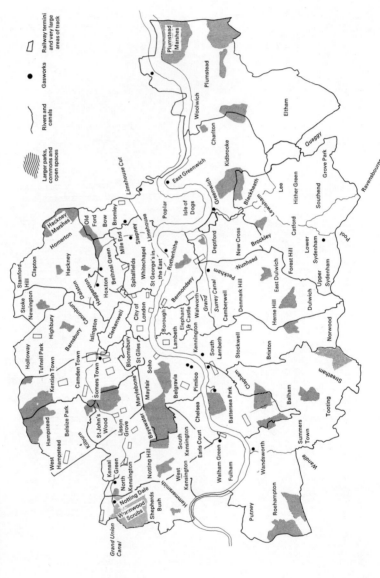

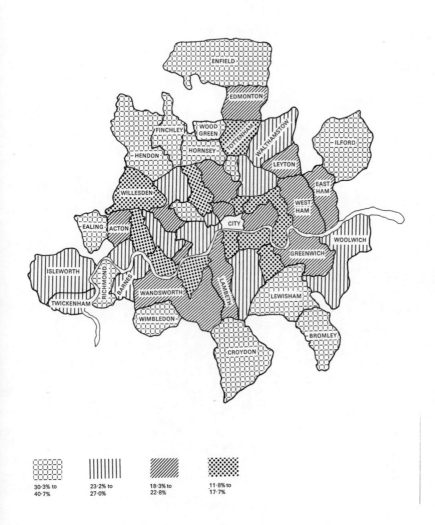

Map 3: Church attendance in Greater London, 1902-3

Map 4: 81 areas of London

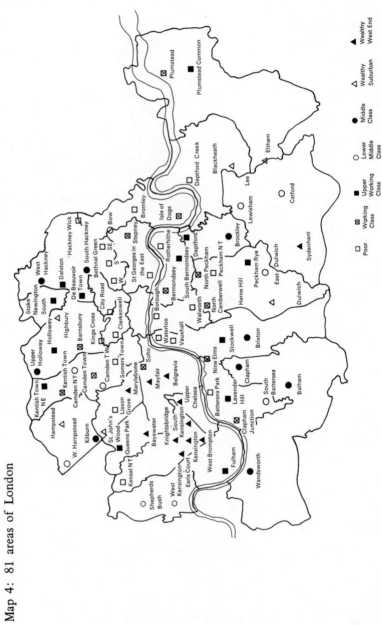

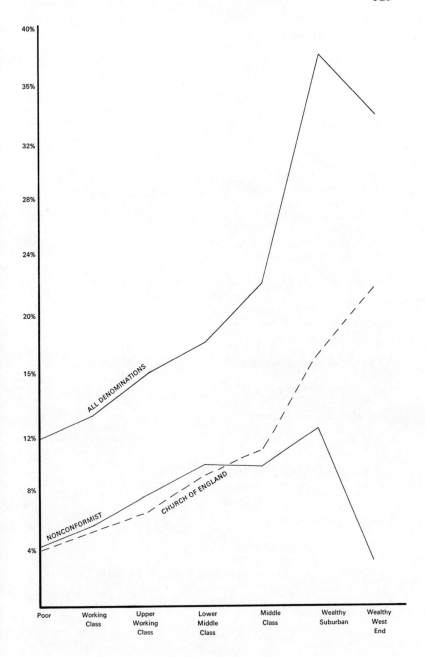

Diagram 1: Adult Church attendance in London, 1902-3

BIBLIOGRAPHY

I Primary Sources

(i) *Unpublished*
(1)Notebooks and private papers.
(2)Diocesan denominational and other central church records.
(3)Local records.
(4)Marriage registers.

(ii)*Newspapers and Periodicals*
(1)Church Magazines.
(2)Special series.
(3)Papers used more extensively.

(iii) *Official Publications*
(1)Parliamentary Papers.
(2)Others.

(iv) *Collections of Cuttings*

(v)*Church Histories*

(vi)*Memoirs and Biography*

(vii)*Fiction*

(viii)*Other Primary Sources*

II Secondary Sources

(i) *Works mainly about London*

(ii)*Other works mainly about nineteenth- and twentieth-century England*

(iii)*Other Works*

III Year Books and Works of Reference

I Primary Sources

(i) *Unpublished*
(1) Notebooks and Private Papers,
Booth Collection, British Library of Economic and Political Science, London School of Economics, Houghton Street, W.C.2.
Harrison Collection.
> British Library of Economic and Political Science.
J. M. Thompson Collection (Diary of 1902 and letters, largely from 1911-12). Bodleian Library, Oxford.
Diary of Rev. J. Woodroffe, 1887-92.
> St. Matthew's Church, Bethnal Green, E.2.
Typescript autobiography by Rev. R. J. Evans.
> Greater London Record Office, County Hall, S.E.1.
Diary of James Oppenheimer, City Missionary.
> St Giles in the Fields Church, W.C.1.
(2) Diocesan, Denominational and other Central Church Records
London Visitation Returns, 1858, 1862, 1883, 1900.
> Fulham Papers, Lambeth Palace, S.E.1.
Rochester Visitation Returns, 1881, 1885, 1889, 1894, 1899, 1903. G.L.R.O.
Southwark Visitation Returns 1907, 1915, 1919. G.L.R.O.
Ecclesiastical Commissioners Files for St James the Great, Bethnal Green (12033); Christ Church, Hampstead (18163), All Souls, Hampstead (28867), St Stephen, Hstd (45267), St Mary, Primrose Hill (46277); St Margaret, Lee (25637), Holy Trinity, Lee (25728), Good Shepherd, Lee, (62957), St Augustine, Grove Park, (67208); St Mark, Lewisham (44375), St John, Southend (50975, 85529), St Swithun, Hither Green (64910), St Andrew, Catford (78444), Holy Trinity, Sydenham (28691), St Michael, Sydenham (29243), St Philip, Sydenham (38610), All Saints, Sydenham (82295). Ecclesiastical Commissioners, Millbank, S.W.1.
Frederick Temple Collection, (Highgate and Spitalfields Boxes).
> Fulham Papers, Lambeth Palace.
(3) Local Records
Bethnal Green
Bethnal Green Road, Independent Chapel, Minutes 1854-89.
> Tower Hamlets Library, Bancroft Rd, E.1.
St Jude's, Bethnal Green, Vestry Minutes 1894-1914.
> Tower Hamlets Library.
St James the Less, Bethnal Green, Miscellaneous papers
> At the Church.
Oxford House, Annual Reports,
> Oxford House Derbyshire St., E.2.
Hackney
Southgate Road, Brotherhood Church, Council Minutes 1926-39, Trust Deeds, Notes by a former member.
> Islington Library, Holloway Road, N.7.

Hampstead
Lyndhurst Road, Congregational Church, Minutes 1880-1925, Church Manuals.   At the Church.
West Hampstead Congregational Church, Minutes 1894-1913.
G.L.R.O.
Rosslyn Hill Unitarian Church, Minutes and Annual Reports, 1862-1932.   Dr. Williams' Library, Gordon Square, W.C.1.
St Cuthbert's, West Hampstead, Vestry Minutes 1891-1916.
G.L.R.O.
St. Saviour's South Hampstead, Transcript of Minutes of Organising Committee 1846-8.
Swiss Cottage Library, Finchley Road, N.W.3.
Islington
Caledonian Rd. Wesleyan Church, Trustees' Minutes, 1894-1917.
Methodist Central Archives, City Road, E.C.2.
Islington Wesleyan Circuit, Minutes, 1883-99.
Methodist Central Archives.
Lewisham
Burnt Ash Congregational Church, Minutes, 1884-1910.
At the Church.
St Cyprian's, Brockley, Minutes of Church Committee, 1910-15.
Lewisham Library, Old Road, S.E.13.
Penge
Anerley Road Congregational Church, Minutes of Mission and of Church Guild, 1884-99.   G.L.R.O.
Poplar
St Stephen's, North Bow, Vestry Minutes 1885-1914.
Tower Hamlets Library.
St Marylebone
Greville Place Congregational Church, Minutes 1858-1924 (including occupational list of members).   G.L.R.O.
Shoreditch
New Tabernacle, Old St., Minutes 1911-27, Trust Deeds, List of Members, 1918.   G.L.R.O.
Stepney
Toynbee Hall Collection.   G.L.R.O.
St Anne's, Spitalfields (Roman Catholic) Miscellaneous Papers (including personal details of men joining confraternity 1858-60).
At the Church.

Westminster
St Patrick's, Soho, (Roman Catholic).
Annual Reports.
Archives of the Archbishop of Westminster, Westminster Cathedral, S.W.1.
(4)Marriage Registers
Records of all weddings since 1837 are kept in district Register Offices, and I have consulted the registers for Bethnal Green (Bow Register Office, Bow Road, E.3.), Hampstead (Old Town

Hall, Haverstock Hill, N.W.3), Lewisham (Lewisham Register Office, Lewisham High Street, S.E.13) and St Marylebone (Old Town Hall, Marylebone Road, N.W.1). Access to these is restricted, but duplicate registers from many churches are held at the churches themselves or at the Greater London Record Office.

I have seen the following registers in places other than the district Register Office:

St Andrew's, Bethnal Green; St James the Great, Bethnal Green; St Matthew's, Bethnal Green; St John's, Paddington; St Clement's, Notting Hill; St Mary's, Lewisham.   G.L.R.O.
St Stephen's, Lewisham; St Cyprian's, Brockely. Lewisham Library.
New Tabernacle, Old Street.   G.L.R.O.
Quaker Register (recording all weddings at Quaker Meetings in Britain since 1837).   Friends' House, Euston Road, N.W.1.

(ii)*Newspapers and Periodicals*
(1)Church Magazines

Oxford House Magazine, Oxford House Chronicle.	Oxford House.
St Andrew's, Bethnal Green.	Tower Hamlets Library.
St Jude's, Bethnal Green.	Tower Hamlets Library.
Trinity, Finchley Road.	Swiss Cottage Library.
Rosslyn Hill, Unitarian.	Swiss Cottage Library.
St Mary's, Lewisham.	Lewisham Library.
St Stephen's, Lewisham.	Lewisham Library.
St Peter's, London Docks.	At the Church.

St Stephen's, Rochester Row.
    Westminster Library, Buckingham Palace Rd., S.W.1.

(2)Special Series in Newspapers and Periodicals

'How to spend a pleasant Sunday', *Punch*, 13 June 1877.
'Agnosticism and Women', in *Nineteenth Century*, April-May 1880.
'The Agnostic at Church', in *Nineteenth Century*, Jan-April 1882.
'Religious Census of London', *British Weekly*, 5 November 1886-17 December 1886 and 13 January 1888-20 February 1888.
'The Down-Grade', a series of articles by R. Shindler and C. H. Spurgeon in the *Sword and Trowel*, March-April 1887, August 1887-February 1888.
'Religion at Oxford' and 'Religion at Cambridge', two articles in the *Church Quarterly Review*, October 1902 and October 1904.
'Religion and Science', a weekly series in the *Clarion*, 13 February 1903-28 October 1904.
Symposium on the results of the *Daily News* Religious Census, *Daily News*, 9 July 1903, 16 July 1903.
'The English Sunday', correspondence and reports in the *Daily Telegraph*, 28 September 1905-14 October 1905. Reports on the 'Woolwich Crusade' in the *Woolwich Gazette and Plumstead News*, 4-25 September 1917, and in the *Woolwich Herald, Eltham and District News, Pioneer and Labour Journal* and *Church*

Times, 4-28 September 1917.
(3)Newspapers and Periodicals Used More Extensively.
Hampstead and Highgate Express
East End News
East London Observer
Bethnal Green News
Lewisham Courier
Lewisham Gazette (subsequently *Lewisham and Lee Gazette* and *Borough of Lewisham Gazette.*)
Lewisham Independent (subsequently *Borough News*, and then *Lewisham Borough News*)
Lewisham Journal
Official Report of the Church Congress (published annually)

(iii) *Official Publications*
(1)Parliamentary Papers
1852-3, LXXXIX, Religious Worship (England and Wales).
1857-8, IX, S.C. of the House of Lords apppointed to inquire into the Deficiency of means of spiritual instruction and places of Divine Worship in the Metropolis and other populous districts . . .
1884-5, XXX, R.C. on the Housing of the Working Classes.
1886, XXV; 1887, XXIX, XXX; 1888, XXXVI, XXXVII, R.C. on the Working of the Elementary Education Acts.
1887, LXXI, Condition of the Working Classes.
1905, XXX; 1906, XL, R.C. on the Means of Locomotion and Transport in London.
1906, XXXIII, XXXIV, R.C. on Ecclesiastical Discipline.
Census Reports, 1881, 1891, 1901, 1911.
(2)Others
London County Council, Minutes of Proceedings (copies at Greater London Record Office.)

(iv)*Collections of Cuttings*
Cuttings relating to Bethnal Green churches.
Tower Hamlets Library.
Cuttings relating to I ewisham churches.   Lewisham Library.
Cuttings relating to Hampstead elections. Swiss Cottage Library.
Miscellaneous items relating to Hampstead churches.
Swiss Cottage Library.
Scrapbook containing cuttings relating to Approach Road Congregational Church, Victoria Park.   Tower Hamlets Library.

(v)*Church Histories*
Bethnal Green
Roberts, C. E. T., *St Peter's, Bethnal Green*, (1884) (In Spitalfields Box, in the Temple Collection).
Deptford
Remembering the Way, (a history of Lewisham High Road Congregational Church, 1954).

Hampstead
Buffard, F., *Heath Street Baptist Church* (1961).
Chesnutt-Chesney, F. C. *All Souls', Hampstead* (1929).
Fall, T., *Trinity Church* (n.d.).
Sadler, T., Squire, E., Sharpe, H., *Rosslyn Hill* (n.d.), *St. James Jubilee Book* (1937).
(All of these are in Swiss Cottage Library.)
Lambeth
Spedding, R. K., *Resurgam* (a history of Effra Road Unitarian Church, 1941).
(In Dr. Williams Library.)
Lewisham
Lemmy, R., *Hither Green Congregational Church* (1949).
Peters, G., *The Vanished Village* (a history of Trinity Congregational Church, Catford, 1954).
Catford Hill Baptist Church (1953).
(All of these are in Dr. Williams' Library.)
Stepney
Darby, M., *The First Hundred years at St Peter's, London Docks* (n.d.).
(At the Church).
Stoke Newington
Thorncroft, M., *Trust in Freedom* (a history of Newington Green Unitarian Church) (n.d.).
(In Dr. Williams' Library.)
Westminster
Kaye, E., *History of the King's Weigh House Church* (1968).
(In Dr. Williams' Library)

(vi)*Memoirs and Biography*

The subjects of these books lived all or part of their life in London, except for Barclay, Davies and Edwards.

Acorn, G., *One of the Multitude*, Macmillan, London, 1911.
Aglionby, F. K., *Life of Edward Henry Bickersteth*, Longmans, London, 1907.
Aldington, R., *Life for Life's Sake*, Cassell, London, 1968 (first published 1941).
Aldred, G., *No Traitor's Gait!*, Strickland Press, Glasgow, 1955-7.
Amis, K., *What Became of Jane Austen?*, Constable, London, 1970.
Annan, N., *Leslie Stephen*, MacGibbon and Kee, London, 1951.
Asquith, C., *Haply I May Remember*, Barrie, London, 1950.
Barclay, T., *Memoirs and Medleys, The Autobiography of a Bottle-Washer*, Backus, Leicester, 1934.
Barnes, G.N., *From Workshop to War Cabinet*, Jenkins, London, 1924.
Barnett, H., *Canon Barnett, His Life, Work and Friends*, 2

vols., Murray, London, 1918.

Bell, G. K. A., *Randall Davidson*, 2 vols., OUP, London, 1934.

Bettany, F. G., *Stewart Headlam*, Murray, London, 1926.

Birrell, A., *Things Past Redress*, Faber, London, 1937.

Bligh, E., *Tooting Corner*, Secker and Warburg, London, 1946.

Booth, M., *Charles Booth, A Memoir*, Macmillan, London, 1918.

Bradley, W. L., *P. T. Forsyth*, Independent Press, London, 1952.

Brill, K., *John Groser, East London Priest*, Lutterworth, London, 1971.

Brockway, F., *Inside the Left*, Allen and Unwin, London, 1942.

Brockway, F., *Bermondsey Story*, Allen and Unwin, London, 1949.

Carlile, J. C., *C. H. Spurgeon*, Kingsgate Press, London, 1933.

Carlyle, J., *Jane Walsh Carlyle, A Selection of Her Letters*, Gollancz, London, 1949.

Carpenter, J. C., *Charles Gore, A Study in Liberal Catholicism*, Faith Press, London, 1960.

Carpenter, S. C., *Winnington-Ingram*, Hodder and Stoughton, London, 1949.

Church, R., *Over the Bridge*, Heinemann, London, 1955.

Collier, E. C. F., *A Victorian Diarist, 1873-95*, Murray, London, 1944.

Collier, E. C. F., *A Victorian Diarist, 1895-1909*, Murray, London, 1946.

Cooper, D., *The Rainbow Comes and Goes*, Hart-Davies, London, 1958.

Cuff, W., *Fifty Years' Ministry*, Baptist Union, London, 1915.

Dash, J., *Good Morning Brothers!*, Lawrence and Wishart, London, 1969.

Davies, C. S., *North Country Bred*, Routledge, London, 1963.

Eastwood, G. C., *George Isaacs*, Oldhams Press, London, n.d.

Edwards, W. J., *From the Valley I Came*, Angus and Robertson, London, 1956.

Ervine, St. J., *God's Soldier: General William Booth*, 2 vols., Heinemann, London, 1934.

Ferguson, R., *We Were Amused*, Cape, London, 1958.

Flint, E., *Hot Bread and Chips*, Museum Press, London, 1963.

Flint, E., *Kipper Stew*, Museum Press, London, 1964.

Garnett, D., *The Golden Echo*, Chatto and Windus, London, 1953.

Gill, E., *Autobiography*, Cape, London, 1940.

Goldman, W., *East End My Cradle*, Faber, London, 1940.

Gosse, E., *Father and Son*, Heinemann, London, 1907.

Gowing, E. N., *John Edwin Watts-Ditchfield*, Hodder and Stoughton, London, n.d.

Haight, G., *George Eliot*, OUP, London, 1958.

Hammerton, H. J., *This Turbulent Priest*, [Charles Jenkinson], Lutterworth, London, 1952.

Hardy, V., *As It Was*, Johnson, London, 1958.

Harrison, A., *Frederic Harrison*, Heinemann, London, 1926.

Harrison, F., *The Creed of a Layman*, Macmillan, London, 1907.

Haw, G., *From Workhouse to Westminster, The Life Story of Will Crooks*, Cassell, London, 1911.

Henson, H. H., *The Retrospect of an Unimportant Life*, 3 vols., OUP, London, 1942-6.

Hill, B., *Boss of Britain's Underworld*, Naldrett, London, 1955.

Holland, B., *Life of Spencer Compton, Eighth Duke of Devonshire*, 2 vols., Longmans, London, 1911.

Holloway, J., *A London Childhood*, Routledge, London, 1966.

Holroyd, M., *Lytton Strachey*, 2 vols., Heinemann, London, 1967-8.

Hughes, D., *Life of Hugh Price Hughes*, Hodder and Stoughton, London, 1904.

Hughes, M. V., *A London Child of the Seventies*, OUP, London, 1934.

Hughes, M. V., *A London Girl of the Eighties*, OUP, London, 1936.

Hughes, M. V., *A London Home in the Nineties*, OUP, London, 1937.

Jackson, T., *Solo Trumpet*, Lawrence and Wishart, London, 1953.

Jasper, A. S., *A Hoxton Childhood*, Barrie and Rockliff, London, 1969.

Jenkins, R., *Sir Charles Dilke*, Collins, London, 1958.

Kellett, E. E., *As I Remember*, Gollancz, London, 1936.

Kent, W., *The Testament of a Victorian Youth*, Heath Granton, London, 1938.

Kent, W., *John Burns: Labour's Lost Leader*, Williams and Norgate, London, 1950.

Kenward, J., *The Suburban Child*, CUP, Cambridge, 1955.

Keppel, S., *Edwardian Daughter*, Hamilton, London, 1958.

Kirk, F. J., *Reminiscences of an Oblate of St. Charles*, London, 1905.

Lansbury, G., *My Life*, Constable, London, 1928.

Lax, W. H., *Lax of Poplar*, Sharp, London, 1927.

Leventhal, F., *Respectable Radical*, [George Howell], Routledge, London, 1971.

Liddell, A. G. C., *Notes From the Life of an Ordinary Mortal*, Murray, London, 1911.

Lidgett, J. S., *Reminiscences*, Epworth, London, 1928.

Lockhart, J. G., *Cosmo Gordon Lang*, Hodder and Stoughton, London, 1949.

McCabe, J., *Twelve Years in a Monastery*, Watts, London, 1930 (first published 1897).

Magnus, P., *Edward the Seventh*, Murray, London, 1964.

Mann, T., *Memoirs*, Labour Publishing Company, London, 1923.

Marchant, J., *Dr. John Clifford*, Cassell, London, 1924.

Margrie, W., *My Heart's Right There*, London, 1947.

Martin, B., *An Impossible Parson*, Allen and Unwin, London, 1935.

Martin, K., *Father Figures*, Hutchinson, London, 1966.

Masterman, L., *C. F. G. Masterman*, Nicholson and Watson, London, 1939.

Menzies, L., *Father Wainright*, Longmanns, London, 1947.

Micklem, N., *The Box and the Puppets*, Bles, London, 1957.

Miles, S., *Portrait of a Parson*, [W. C. Roberts], Allen and Unwin, London, 1955.

Morrison, H., *Herbert Morrison*, Odhams Press, London, 1960.

Mosley, O., *My Life*, Nelson, London, 1968.

Nevinson, H. W., *Changes and Chances*, Nisbet, London, 1923.

Okey, T., *A Basketful of Memories*, Dent, London, 1930.

Osborne, C. E., *Life of Father Dolling*, Arnold, London, 1903.

Paget, S., *Henry Scott Holland*, Murray, London, 1921.

Peel, A., and Marriott, J. A. R., *Robert Forman Horton*, Allen and Unwin, London, 1937.

Pike, G., *Life and Work of Archibald G. Brown*, Passmore and Alabaster, London, 1894.

Prestige, G. L., *Life of Charles Gore*, Heinemann, London, 1935.

Reeves, J., *Recollections of a School Attendance Officer*, London, 1914.

Russell, B., *Autobiography*, 3 vols., Allen and Unwin, 1967-9.

Russel, B. and P., *The Amberley Papers*, Allen and Unwin, London, 1937.

Simey, T. S., and M. B., *Charles Booth, Social Scientist*, OUP, London, 1960.

Sitwell, O., *Left Hand, Right Hand!*, 5 vols., Macmillan, London, 1945-50.

Smith, B. A., *Dean Church*, OUP, London, 1958.

Snell, H., *Men, Movements and Myself*, Dent, London, 1936.

Soutter, F. W., *Recollections of a Labour Pioneer*, Fisher

Unwin, London, 1923.

Albert Spicer, A Man of His Time, by One of His Family, 1938.

Stevens, T. P., *Father Adderley*, Werner Laurie, London, 1943.

Sutherland, D., *The Yellow Earl*, [Fifth Earl of Lonsdale], London, 1965.

Thompson, A. M., *Here I Lie*, Routledge, London, 1937.

Thompson, L., *Robert Blatchford*, Gollancz, London, 1951.

Thorne, G., *The Great Acceptance, The Life Story of F. N. Charrington*, Hodder and Stoughton, London, 1912.

Thorne, W., *My Life's Battles*, Newnes, London, 1925.

Tillett, B., *Memoirs and Reflections*, Long, London, 1931.

Titterton, D. V. R., *The World is so Full*, London, 1961.

Trevelyan, J. P., *Life of Mrs. Humphry Ward*, Murray, London, 1923.

Tweedsmuir, S., *The Lilac and the Rose*, Duckworth, London, 1952.

Vine, E. C. H., *Charles Henry Vine of Ilford*, Allenson, London, 1933.

Warwick, F., *Afterthoughts*, Cassell, London, 1931.

Webb, B., *My Apprenticeship*, Allen and Unwin, London, 1926.

Webb, B., *Our Partnership*, Allen and Unwin, London, 1948.

Wells, H. G., *An Experiment in Autobiography*, 2 vols., Gollancz, London, 1934.

Wilcox, J. C., and Kensit, J. A., *Contending for the Faith*, [John Kensit], London, n.d.

Willey, B., *Spots of Time*, Chatto and Windus, London, 1964.

Williamson, J., *Father Joe*, Hodder and Stoughton, London, 1963.

Willis, F., *101 Jubilee Road*, Phoenix, London, 1949.

Willis, F., *Peace and Dripping Toast*, Phoenix, London, 1950.

Willis, T., *Whatever Happened to Tom Mix?*, Cassell, London, 1970.

Woolf, L., *Sowing*, Hogarth Press, 1970.

(vii) *Fiction*

Aldington, R., *Death of a Hero*, Sphere, London, 1965 (first published 1929).

Bullen F., *The Apostles of the South-East*, Hodder and Stoughton, London, 1901.

Bullock, S., *Robert Thorne, The Story of a London Clerk*, London, 1907.

Galsworthy, J., *The Man of Property*, Penguin, Harmondsworth, 1951 (first published, 1906).

Gissing, G., *New Grub Street*, Modern Library, New York, 1926 (first published, 1891).

Gissing, G., *In the Year of the Jubilee*, Watergate, London, 1947, (first published 1892).

Gissing, G., *Born in Exile*, Gollancz, London, 1970, (first published 1892).

Grossmith, G. and W., *The Diary of a Nobody*, Penguin, Harmondsworth, 1945, (first published 1892).

Howard, K., *The Smiths of Surbiton*, Chapman and Hall, London, 1906.

Margrie, W., *Roses and Kippers*, Watts, London, 1930.

Morrison, A., *Tales of Mean Streets*, Methuen, London, 1894.

Morrison, A., *A Child of the Jago*, Methuen, London, 1896.

Tressell, R., *The Ragged Trousered Philanthropists*, Panther, London, 1965, (first published 1914).

Trollope, A., *Can You Forgive Her?*, OUP, London, 1948 (first published 1864-5).

Trollope, A., *The Way We Live Now*, OUP, London, 1941 (first published 1874-5).

Ward, Mrs. H., *Robert Elsmere*, Nelson, London, 1952 (first published 1888).

Wells, H. G., *Ann Veronica*, Fisher Unwin, London, 1909.

Wells, *Ann Veronica*, Fisher Unwin, London, 1909.

[White, W. H.,] Mark Rutherford, *The Autobiography*, Trubner, London, 1881.

[White, W. H.,] Mark Rutherford, *The Revolution in Tanner's Lane*, Trubner, London, 1887.

(viii)*Other Primary Sources*

Allen, G., 'The New Hedonism', *Fortnightly Review*, New Series, cccxxvii, March 1, 1894, pp.377-92.

Arnold, M., *Culture and Anarchy*, Smith Elder, London, 1869.

Arnold, M., *God and the Bible*, Smith Elder, London, 1874.

Arnold, M., *St. Paul and Protestantism*, Smith Elder, London, 1875.

Arnold, M., *Literature and Dogma*, Smith Elder, London, 1876.

Aristocracy, A Member of the, *Manners and Rules of Good Society*, Warne, London, (1888 ed.)

Atlay, J. B., (ed.) *Trial of the Stauntons*, Hodge, Edinburgh, 1911.

Barrett, G. S., 'The Secularization of the Pulpit', address printed in *Congregational Year Book*, 1895.

Barrett, G. S., 'The Secularization of the Church', address printed in *Congregational Year Book*, 1895.

Besant, W., *South London*, Chatto and Windus, London, 1899.

Blatchford, R., *God and My Neighbour*, Clarion Press, London, 1903.

Booth, C., *Life and Labour of the People in London*, 17

vols., Macmillan, London, 1902-3.

Booth, W., *Darkest England and the Way Out*, Salvation Army, London, n.d..

Bray, R., *Labour and the Churches*, Constable, London, 1912.

Cairns, D., (ed.), *The Army of Religion*, Macmillan, London, 1919.

[Courtney, L. H.], *The Diary of a Church-Goer*, Macmillan, London, 1904.

Courtney, W. L., (ed.), *Do We Believe?*, Hodder and Stoughton, London, 1905.

Darwin, C., *On the Origin of Species*, Harvard UP, Cambridge Mass., 1964 (first published 1859).

Davies, C. M., *Orthodox London*, 2 vols., London 1874-5.

Escott, T. H. S., *England: Its People, Policy and Pursuits*, 2 vols., Cassell, London, 1879.

[Escott, T. H. S.] *Society in London*, Chatto and Windus, London, 1885.

Escott, T. H. S., *Social Transformations of the Victorian Age*, London, 1897.

Esquiros, A., *Religious Life in England*, London, 1867.

Gavin, H., *Sanitary Ramblings*, London, 1848.

Goblet d'Alviella, Comte, 'Une Visite aux Eglises Rationalistes de Londres', *Revue des Deux Mondes*, septembre-octobre, 1875.

Haw, G., *Christianity and the Working Classes*, Macmillan, London, 1906.

Horne, C. S., *Nonconformity in the XIXth Century*, Free Church Council, London, 1905.

Horne, C. S., *The Brotherhood Movement, A New Protestantism*, London, 1913.

Hueffer, F. M., *The Spirit of the People*, Alston Rivers, London, 1907.

Jackson, H., *The Eighteen Nineties*, Cape, London, 1931 (first published 1913).

Jackson, J., *A Charge Delivered to the Clergy of the Diocese of London*, Skeffington, London, 1884.

Jones, H., *East and West London*, Smith Elder, London, 1875.

Le Play, F., *Les Ouvriers Européens*, Tours, 1877 (first published 1855).

Llewellyn Smith, H., *The New Survey of London Life and Labour* 9 vols., Macmillan, London, 1930-5.

Loane, M., *The Queen's Poor*, Arnold, London, 1905.

Loane, M., *From Their Point of View*, Arnold, London, 1908.

Lowther-Clarke, W. K., *Facing the Facts: an Englishman's Religion*, Nisbet, London, 1911.

McCabe, J., *The Decay of the Church of Rome*, Methuen,

London, 1909.

Masterman, C. F. G., and others, *The Heart of the Empire*, Fisher Unwin, London, 1901.

Masterman, C. F. G., *From the Abyss*, Brimley Johnson, London, 1902.

Masterman, C. F. G., *The Condition of England*, Methuen, London, 1909.

Mayhew, H., *London Labour and the London Poor*, London, 1861-2.

Mudie-Smith, (ed.), *The Religious Life of London*, Hodder and Stoughton, London, 1904.

Paine, T., 'The Age of Reason', *The Complete Writings of Thomas Paine*, 2 vols., Citadel Press, New York, 1945.

Ritchie, J. E., *The Religious Life of London*, London, 1870.

Rossiter, W., 'Artisan Atheism', *Nineteenth Century* vol. XXI, February 1887, and vol.XXII, July 1887.

Rowntree, B. S., *Betting and Gambling, A National Evil*, Macmillan, London, 1905.

Russell, C., *The Catholics of London and Public Life*, London, 1907.

Russell, G. W. E., *An Onlookers Notebook*, London, 1902.

Shaw, G. B., 'The Quintessence of Ibsenism', *Complete Works of Bernard Shaw*, Constable, London, 1930.

Sherwell, A., *Life in West London*, London, 1897.

Taine, H., *Notes on England*, English Translation, Thames and Hudson, London, 1957.

Talbot, N. S., and others, *Foundations*, Macmillan, London, 1911.

Trevelyan, W. B., *Sunday*, Longmans, London, 1902.

Winnington-Ingram, A. F., *A Charge Delivered to the Clergy and Churchwardens of London*, Wells Gardner, London, 1905.

Winnington-Ingram, A. F., *A Charge Delivered to the Clergy and Churchwardens of London*, Wells Gardner, London, 1911.

Wright, T., *Some Habits and Customs of the Working Classes*, London, 1867.

Young, F., (ed.), *The Trial of Harley Harvey Crippen*, Hodge, Edinburgh, 1920.

Young, F., (ed.), *The Trial of the Seddons*, Hodge, Edinburgh, 1914.

III Secondary Sources

(i)   *Works substantially about London*
Barratt, T. J., *The Annals of Hampstead*, 3 vols., Black, London, 1911.
Bédarida, F., 'Londres au Milieu du XIXe Siècle', *Annales*, vol.XXIII, no.2, mars-avril 1968.
Byrne, S., *The Changing Face of Lewisham*, Lewisham Public Libraries, London, 1965.
Chesney, K., *The Victorian Underworld*, Penguin, Harmondsworth, 1972.
Clayton, R., (ed.), *The Geography of Greater London*, Philip, London, 1964.
Coleman, B. I., 'Church Extension Movement in London, c. 1800-1860', University of Cambridge, Ph.D. thesis, 1968.
Coppock, J. T., and Prince, H. C., (eds.), *Greater London*, Faber, London, 1964.
Daniel, M., 'London Clergymen', University of London, M. Phil. Thesis, 1965.
Dyos, H. J., 'The Suburban Development of Greater London South of the Thames, 1836-1914', University of London Ph.D. thesis, 1952.
Dyos, H. J., *Victorian Suburb*, Leicester UP, 1961.
Dyos, H. J., 'The Slums of Victorian London', *Victorian Studies*, vol.XI, no.1, September 1967.
Dyos, H. J., 'The Speculative Builders and Developers of Victorian London', *Victorian Studies*, vol.XI, no.4, Summer 1968.
Fagan, D., and Burgess, E., *Men of the Tideway*, Hale, London, 1966.
Gartner, L. P., *The Jewish Immigrant in England, 1870-1914*, Allen and Unwin, London, 1960.
Gilley, S. W., 'Evangelical and Roman Catholic Missions to the Irish in London, 1830-70', University of Cambridge Ph.D. Thesis, 1971.
Gilley, S. W., 'The Roman Catholic Mission to the Irish in London', *Recusant History*, vol.X, no.3, October 1969.
Gilley, S. W., 'Heretic London, Holy Poverty and the Irish Poor', *Downside Review*, vol.LXXXIX, no.294, January 1971.
Gilley, S. W., 'English Catholic Charity and the Irish Poor in London', *Recusant History*, vol.XI, nos.4-5, Jan-April 1972.
Gilley, S. W., 'The Catholic Faith of the Irish Slums,' H. J. Dyos and M. Wolff (eds.), *The Victorian City*, 2 vols., Routledge, London, 1973.
Hall, P. G., *The Industries of Greater London*, Hutchinson, London, 1962.
Hall, P. G., 'The East London Footwear Industry', *East London Papers*, vol.V, no.1, April 1962.

Harrison, B., 'The Sunday Trading Riots of 1855', *Historical Journal*, vol.VIII, no.2, June 1965.

Harrison, J. F. C., *History of the Working Men's College*, Routledge, London, 1954.

Hobsbawm, E. J., 'The London Labour Market in the Nineteenth Century', Glass, R., (ed.), *London, Aspects of Change*, Macgibbon and Kee, London, 1964.

Jackson, J. A., *The Irish in Britain*, Routledge, London, 1963.

Kellett, J. R., *The Impact of Railways on Victorian Cities*, Routledge, London, 1969.

Lees, L. H., 'Social Change and Social Stability among the London Irish, 1830-70', Harvard University Ph.D. thesis, 1969.

Lees, L. H., 'Irish Slum Communities in Nineteenth Century London', Thernstrom, S., and Sennett, R. (eds.), *Nineteenth Century Cities*, Yale UP, New Haven, 1969.

Lovell, J. C., *Dockers and Stevedores*, Macmillan, London, 1969.

Martin, J. E., *Greater London, An Industrial Geography*, Bell, London, 1966.

Mass Observation, *Puzzled People*, Gollancz, London, 1947.

McDonnell, K. G. T., 'Roman Catholics in London, 1850-1865'.

Hollander, A. E. J., and Kellaway, W., (eds.), *Studies in London History*, Hodder and Stoughton, London, 1969.

McLeod, D. H., 'Membership and Influence of the Churches in Metropolitan London 1885-1914', University of Cambridge Ph.D. Thesis, 1971.

The Oxford House in Bethnal Green, London, 1948.

Pasquet, D., *Les Ouvriers de Londres*, Paris, 1914.

Pelling, H., *Social Geography of British Elections, 1885-1910*, Macmillan, London, 1967.

Pevsner, N., *London, Except the Cities of London and Westminster*, Penguin, Harmondsworth, 1952.

Pike, E. R., *Human Documents of the Age of the Forsytes*, Allen and Unwin, London, 1969.

Pimlott, J. A. R., *Toynbee Hall*, Dent, London, 1935.

Pollins, H., 'Transport Lines and Social Divisions', Glass, R. (ed.), *London, Aspects of Change*, Macgibbon and Kee, London, 1964.

Quigley, H., and Goldie, I., *Housing and Slum Clearance in London*, Methuen, London, 1934.

Rasmussen, S. E., *London, The Unique City*, Penguin, Harmondsworth, 1960, (first published, 1934).

Reeder, D. A., 'Some Patterns of Development in West London, 1801-1911', Dyos, H. J. (ed.), *The Study of Urban History*, Arnold, London, 1968.

Rose, M., *The East End of London*, Cresset Press, London,

1951.

Rubinstein, D., *School Attendance in London, 1870-1914*, University of Hull, 1968.

Samuel, R., 'Comers and Goers', Dyos, H. J., and Wolff, M., (eds.), *The Victorian City*, 2 vols., Routledge, London, 1973.

Sheppard, F., *London, 1808-70; The Infernal Wen*, Secker and Warburg, London, 1971.

Shipley, S., *Club Life and Socialism in Mid-Victorian London*, History Workshop, Oxford, 1971.

Smith, W. S., *The London Heretics*, Constable, London, 1967.

Smyth, C., *Church and Parish*, SPCK, London, 1955.

Stedman Jones, G., *Outcast London*, OUP, London, 1971.

Taylor, J. H., 'London Congregational Churches since 1850', *Transactions of the Congregational Historical Society*, vol.XX, no.1, May 1965.

Thompson, P., *Socialists, Liberals and Labour, The Struggle for London, 1885-1914*, Routledge, London, 1967.

Tobias, J. J., *Crime and Industrial Society in the 19th Century*, Penguin, Harmondsworth, 1972.

Whitting, P. (ed.), *History of Fulham*, London, 1970.

Willmott, P., and Young, M., *Family and Kinship in East London*, Penguin, Harmondsworth, 1962.

Willmott, P., and Young, M., *Family and Class in a London Suburb*, New English Library, London, 1967.

Wohl, A. S., 'The Housing of the Working Classes in London, 1815-1914', Chapman, S. D. (ed.), *The History of Working Class Housing*, David and Charles, Newton Abbot, 1971.

(ii) *Other works substantially about nineteenth- and twentieth-century England*

Anderson, M., *Family Structure in Nineteenth Century Lancashire*, CUP, Cambridge, 1971.

Armytage, W., *Heavens Below!*, Routledge, London, 1961.

Banks, J. A., *Prosperity and Parenthood*, Routledge, London, 1954.

Banks, J. A., and O., *Feminism and Family Planning in Victorian England*, Liverpool UP, 1964.

Banks, J. A., and O., 'The Bradlaugh-Besant Trial and the English Newspapers', *Population Studies*, vol.VIII, no.1, July, 1954.

Beck, G. A., (ed.), *The English Catholics, 1850-1950*, Burnes and Oates, London, 1950.

Binfield, C., 'Nonconformity in the Eastern Counties, 1840-85', University of Cambridge, Ph.D. thesis, 1965.

Binfield, C., 'The Thread of Disruption', *Transactions of the*

Congregational Historical Society, vol.XX, no.5, May 1967.

Binfield, C., 'Chapels in Crisis', *Transactions of the Congregational Historical Society*, vol.XX, no.8, October 1968.

Blewett, N., *The Peers, the Parties and the People*, Macmillan, London, 1972.

Bowen, D., *The Idea of the Victorian Church*, Montreal, 1968.

Briggs, A., *Victorian Cities*, Penguin, Harmondsworth, 1968.

Budd, S., 'The British Humanist Movement, c. 1860-1966', University of Oxford, Ph.D. thesis, 1969.

Budd, S., 'The Loss of Faith', *Past and Present*, no.36, April 1967.

Calley, M., *God's People*, OUP, London, 1966.

Campbell, F., 'Birth Control and the Christian Churches', *Population Studies*, vol.XIV, November 1960.

Chadwick, O., *The Victorian Church*, 2 vols, A. and C. Black, London, 1966-70.

Clarke, P. F., *Lancashire and the New Liberalism*, CUP, 1971.

Coale, A. J., 'The Decline of Fertility in Europe from the French Revolution to World War II', Behrman, S. J. (ed.), *Fertility and Family Planning, A World View*, Michigan UP, Ann Arbor, 1969.

Coleman, T., *The Railway Navvies*, Penguin, Harmondsworth, 1968.

Cominos, P., 'The Late Victorian Revolt, 1859-95', University of Oxford, Ph.D. Thesis, 1958.

Cominos, P., 'Late Victorian Respectability and the Social System', *International Review of Social History*, vol.VIII, 1963, (published in two parts).

Coxon, A. P. M., 'A Sociological Study of the Recruitment, Selection and Professional Socialisation of Anglican Ordinands', University of Leeds, Ph.D. thesis, 1965.

Cruikshank, M., *Church and State in English Education*, Macmillan, London, 1963.

Currie, R., *Methodism Divided*, Faber, London, 1968.

Davies, D. H., *Worship and Theology in England, 1850-1900*, Princeton UP, 1962.

Faulkner, H. U., *Chartism and the Churches*, Columbia University, New York, 1916.

Foster, J. O., 'Capitalism and Class Consciousness in Earlier Nineteenth Century Oldham', University of Cambridge Ph.D. thesis, 1967.

Foster, J. O., 'Nineteenth Century Towns – A Class Dimension', Dyos, H. J. (ed.), *The Study of Urban History*, Arnold, London, 1968.

Glass, D. V., and Eversley, D. E. C., *Population in History*, Arnold, London, 1965.

Glass, D. V., and Revelle, R., *Population and Social Change*,

Arnold, London, 1972.

Goodridge, R. M., 'Nineteenth Century Urbanisation and Religion: Bristol and Marseilles, 1830-80', Martin, D. (ed.), *A Sociological Yearbook of Religion in Britain, 2*, SCM Press, London, 1968.

Goodridge, R. M., 'Religion and the City, With Reference to Bristol and Marseilles,' 1830-80', University of London M.Phil. thesis, 1969.

Gorer, G., *Exploring English Character*, Cresset Press, London, 1955.

Grant, J. W., *Free Churchmanship in England, 1870-1940* Independent Press, London, n.d..

Harrison, B., 'Underneath the Victorians', *Victorian Studies*, vol.X, no.3, March 1967.

Harrison, B., 'Religion and Recreation in Nineteenth Century England', *Past and Present*, no.38, December 1967.

Harrison, B., *Drink and the Victorians*, Faber, London, 1971.

Harrison, B., and Trinder, B., 'Drink and Sobriety in an Early Victorian Country Town: Banbury, 1830-60', *English Historical Review*, Special Supplement, no.4.

Harrison, J. F. C., *Learning and Living*, Routledge, London, 1961.

Hennell, M., 'Evangelicalism and Worldliness, 1770-1870', Cuming, G. J., and Baker, D. (eds.), *Studies in Church History*, 8, CUP, 1972.

Hobsbawm, E. J., *Labouring Men*, Weidenfeld and Nicolson, London, 1964.

Hobsbawm, E. J., *Primitive Rebels*, 2nd ed., Manchester UP, 1971.

Hollingsworth, T. J., *Historical Demography*, Hodder and Stoughton, London, 1969.

Inglis, K. S., 'The Labour Churches', *International Review of Social History*, vol.III, 1958.

Inglis, K. S., 'The Religious Census of 1851', *Journal of Ecclesiastical History*, vol.XI, no.1, April 1960.

Inglis, K. S, *Churches and the Working Classes in Victorian England*, Routledge, London, 1963.

Irvine, W., *Apes, Angels, and Victorians*, Weidenfeld and Nicolson, London, 1955.

Isichei, E., *Victorian Quakers*, OUP, London, 1970.

Jaeger, M., *Before Victoria*, Chatto and Windus, London, 1956.

Jones, P. d'A., *The Christian Socialist Revival in England, 1877-1914*, Princeton UP, 1968.

Jones, R. Tudur, *Congregationalism in England, 1662-1962*, Independent Press, London, 1962.

Kent, J., *From Darwin to Blatchford*, Dr. Williams' Library, London, 1966.

Kent, J., 'Hugh Price Hughes and the Nonconformist Conscience', Bennett, G. V., and Walsh, J., (eds.), *Essays in Modern English Church History*, A. and C. Black, London, 1966.

Kent, J., 'American Revivalism and England in the Nineteenth century', Papers Presented to the Past and Present Conference on Popular Religion, 7 July 1966.

Kent, J., 'The Victorian Resistance: Comments on Religious Life and Culture, 1840-80', *Victorian Studies*, vol.XII, no.2, December 1968.

Kent, J., 'The Role of Religion in the Cultural Structure of the Later Victorian City', *Transactions of the Royal Historical Society*, 5th Series, vol.XXIII, 1973.

Kiernan, V., 'Evangelicalism and the French Revolution', *Past and Present*, no.1, 1952.

Kitson Clark, G., *Churchmen and the Condition of England, 1832-85*, Methuen, London, 1973.

Lockwood, D., *The Blackcoated Worker*, Allen and Unwin, London, 1958.

Martin, D. A., 'Some Utopian Aspects of the Concept of Secularisation', *International Yearbook of the Sociology of Religion*, 1966.

Martin, D. A., *A Sociology of English Religion*, SCM Press, London, 1967.

Martin, D. A., *The Religious and the Secular*, Routledge, London, 1969.

Mayor, S., *The Churches and the Labour Movement*, Independent Press, London, 1967.

McLeod, H., 'Class, Community and Region: The Religious Geography of Nineteenth Century England', Hill, M., (ed.), *A Sociological Yearbook of Religion in Britain*, 6, SCM Press, London, 1973.

Mews, S. P., 'The Effect of the First World War on English Religious Life and Thought', University of Leeds M.A. thesis, 1967.

Mews, S. P., 'Liberalism and Liberality in the Church of England', Hulsean Prize Essay, University of Cambridge, 1968.

Mews, S. P., 'Reason and Emotion in Working Class Crusade of 1911', Cuming, G. J., and Baker, D. *Studies in Church History*, 8, CUP; 1972.

Mews, S. P., 'Reasons and Emotion in Working Class Religion', Baker, D. (ed.), *Studies in Church History*, 9, CUP, 1972.

Moore, R., 'The Political Effects of Village Methodism', Hill, M., (ed.), *A Sociological Yearbook of Religion in Britain*, 6, SCM Press, London, 1973.

Moser, C. A., and Scott, W., *British Towns, A Statistical Study of their Social and Economic Differences*, Oliver and Boyd, Edinburgh, 1961.

Neale, R. S., *Class and Ideology in the Nineteenth Century*, Routledge, London, 1972.

Norman, E. R., *Anti-Catholicism in Victorian England*, Allen and Unwin, London, 1967.

Obelkevich, J., 'Religion and Rural Society in South Lindsey, 1825-75', University of Columbia Ph.D. thesis, 1971.

Oliver, J., *The Church and the Social Order*, Mowbray, London, 1968.

Payne, E. A., *The Baptist Union*, Kingsgate Press, London, 1959.

Payne, E. A., 'The Down-Grade Controversy', an unpublished essay at Baptist Church House.

Peckham, M., 'Darwinism and Darwinisticism', *Victorian Studies*, vol.III, no.1, September 1959.

Peel, J., 'The Manufacture and Retailing of Contraceptives in England', *Population Studies*, vol.XVII, no.1, July 1963.

Pelling, H., *Origins of the Labour Party, 1880-1900*, 2nd ed., OUP, London, 1966.

Pelling, H., *Popular Politics and Society in Late Victorian England*, Macmillan, London, 1968.

Perkin, H., *The Origins of Modern English Society, 1780-1880*, Routledge, London, 1969.

Pickering, W. S. F., 'The 1851 Census – A Useless Experiment?', *British Journal of Sociology*, vol.XVIII, no.4, December 1967.

Pickering, W. S. F., 'Abraham Hume, A Forgotten Pioneer in Religious Sociology',
Archives de Sociologie des Religions, no.33, 1972.

Quinlan, M., *Victorian Prelude*, Columbia UP, New York, 1941.

Reader, W. J., *Professional Men. The Rise of the Professional Classes in Nineteenth Century England*, Weidenfeld and Nicolson, London. 1966.

Reckitt, M., (ed.), *For Christ and the People*, SPCK, London, 1968.

Rex, J., and Moore, R., *Race, Community and Conflict*, second ed., OUP, London, 1969.

Robertson, R., 'The Salvation Army: The Persistence of Sectarianism,' Wilson, B. R., (ed.), *Patterns of Sectarianism*, Heinemann, London, 1967.

Rowell, D. G., *Hell and the Victorians: A Study of the Nineteenth Century Theological Controversies concerning Eternal Punishment and the Future Life*, Clarendon Press, Oxford, 1974.

Rowell, D. G., 'The Origin and History of Universalist Societies in Britain, 1750-1850', *Journal of Ecclesiastical History*, vol.XXII, no.1, January 1971.

Royle, E., *Victorian Infidels. The Origins of the British*

Secularist Movement, 1791-1866, Manchester UP, 1974.

Royle, E., *Radical Politics, 1790-1900: Religion and Unbelief*, Longmans, London, 1971.

Rule, J., 'The Labouring Miner in Cornwall, c. 1740-1860' University of Warwick, Ph.D. Thesis, 1971.

Scott, P. G., 'Cricket and the Religious World in the Victorian Period', *Church Quarterly*, vol.III, no.1, July 1970.

Simon, B., *Education and the Labour Movement*, Lawrence and Wishart, London, 1965.

Spencer, A. E. C. W., 'The Demography and Sociography of the Roman Catholic Community in England and Wales', Bright, L., and Clements, S., (eds.), *The Committed Church*, London, 1966.

Symondson, A., (ed.), *The Victorian Crisis of Faith*, SPCK, London, 1970.

Tholfsen, T. R., 'The Artisan and the Culture of Early Victorian Birmingham', *University of Birmingham Historical Journal*, vol.IX, no.2, 1954.

Tholfsen, T. R., 'The Intellectual Origins of Mid-Victorian Stability', *Political Science Quarterly*, vol.LXXXVI, no.1, March, 1971.

Thompson, D. M., 'The 1851 Census, Problems and Possibilities' *Victorian Studies*, vol.XI, no.1, September 1967.

Thompson, D. M., 'The Churches and Society in Leicestershire, 1851—81', University of Cambridge Ph.D. thesis, 1969.

Thompson, E. P., ' "Rough Music": Le Charivari anglais', *Annales*, vol.XXVII, no.2, mars-avril 1972.

Thompson, F. M. L., *English Landed Society in the Nineteenth Century*, Routledge, London, 1963.

Voll, D., *Catholic Evangelicalism*, English Translation, Faith Press, London, 1963.

Walker, R. B., 'Religious Changes in Nineteenth Century Liverpool', *Journal of Ecclesiastical History*, vol.XIX, no.3, October 1968.

Ward, W. R., *Religion and Society in England, 1790-1850*, Batsford, London, 1972.

Wickham, E. R., *Church and People in an Industrial City*, Lutterworth, London, 1957.

Willey, B., *Nineteenth Century Studies*, Chatto and Windus, London, 1949.

Willey, B., *More Nineteenth Century Studies*, Chatto and Windus, London, 1956.

Wilson, B. R., *Religion in Secular Society*, Watts, London, 1966.

Yeo, S., 'Religion in Society: A View from a Provincial Town in the late Nineteenth and early Twentieth Centuries', University of Sussex, Ph.D. Thesis, 1971.

Yeo, S., 'A Contextual View of Religious Organization', Hill, M., (ed.), *A Sociological Yearbook of Religion in Britain*, 6, SCM Press, London, 1973.

(iii) *Other works* (chiefly those dealing with similar themes in other countries or in earlier periods)

Abell, A. I., *The Urban Impact of American Protestantism*, Harvard, UP, Cambridge, Mass., 1942.

Acquaviva, S. S., *L'Eclipse du Sacré dans la Civilisation Indusrtielle*, French Translation, Paris, 1967.

Agulhon, M., *La République au Village*, Paris, 1970.

Ahlstrom, S., 'Theology and the Present-Day Revival', *Annals of the American Academy of Political and Social Science*, vol.CCCXXXII, November 1960.

Ahlstrom, S., 'The Radical Turn in Theology and Ethics: Why it occurred in the 1960s', *Annals of the American Academy of Political and Social Science*, vol.CCCLXXXVII, January 1970.

Andersen, J. O., *Survey of the History of the Church in Denmark*, Copenhagen, 1930.

Berger, P., *The Social Reality of Religion*, Penguin, Harmondsworth, 1973.

Boulard, F., and Rémy, J., *Pratique Religieuse Urbaine et Régions Culturelles*, Editions Ouvrières, Paris, 1968.

Bourdeaux, M., *Opium of the People*, Faber, London, 1965.

Connell, K. H., *Irish Peasant Society*, OUP, London, 1968.

Cross, R. D., *The Church and the City*, Bobbs-Merrill, New York, 1967.

Cross, W., *The Burned Over District*, Cornell UP, Ithaca, 1950.

Davies, E. T., *Religion in the Industrial Revolution in South Wales*, University of Wales Press, Cardiff, 1965.

Desroche, H., 'Athéisme et socialisme dans le marxisme classique', *Archives de Sociologie des Religions*, no.10, juillet-décembre 1960.

Drummond, A. L., *German Protestantism since Luther*, Epworth Press, London, 1951.

Freytag, J., and Ozaki, K., *Nominal Christianity: Studies of Church and People in Hamburg*, English Translation, Lutterworth, London, 1970.

Glock, C., and Stark, R., *Religion and Society in Tension*, Rand McNally, Chicago, 1965.

Glock, C., and Stark, R., *American Piety: The Nature of Religious Commitment*, University of California Press, Berkeley and Los Angeles, 1968.

Gustafsson, B., *Kyrkoliv och Samhallsklass i Sverige omkring 1880*, Lund, 1950 [includes summary in English].

Hadden, J., *The Gathering Storm in the Churches*, Garden

City, 1968.

Herberg, W., *Protestant, Catholic, Jew*, 2nd ed., Doubleday, New York, 1960.

Hickey, J., *Urban Catholics*, Chapman, London, 1967.

Hill, C., *The World Turned Upside. Down*, Temple Smith, London, 1972.

Houtart, F., *L'Eglise et la Pastorale des Grandes Villes*, Etudes Religieuses, Bruxelles, 1955.

Howe, D. W., 'The Decline of Calvinism', *Comparative Studies in Society and History*, vol.XIV, no.3, June 1972.

Hudson, W. S., *Religion in America*, Scribner, New York, 1965.

Isambert, F.-A., *Christianisme et Classe Ouvrière*, Casterman, Tournai, 1961.

Jenkins, D., *The Agricultural Community of South-West Wales at the Turn of the Twentieth Century*, University of Wales Press, 1971.

Latourette, K. S., *Christianity in a Revolutionary Age*, vol.IV, Eyre and Spottiswoode, London, 1962.

Lenski, G., *The Religious Factor*, 2nd ed., Anchor, New York, 1963.

Lidtke, V., 'August Bebel and German Social Democracy's Relation to the Christian Churches', *Journal of the History of Ideas*, vol.XXVII, April-June 1966.

Luckmann, T., *The Invisible Religion*, English translation, Macmillan, London, 1967.

Maclaren, A. A., 'Religion and Social Class in Mid-Nineteenth Century Aberdeen', University of Aberdeen Ph.D. thesis, 1971.

Marcilhacy, C., *Le Diocèse d'Orléans sous l'Episcopat de Mgr Dunlanloup*, Plon, Paris, 1963.

Marcilhacy, C., *Le Diocèse d'Orléans au Milieu du XIXe Siècle*, Sirey, Paris, 1964.

May, H. F., *Protestant Churches and Industrial America*, Harper, New York, 1949.

Molland, E., *Church Life in Norway*, English Translation, Minneapolis, Augsburg Publishing House, 1957.

Moroney, M. J., *Facts from Figures*, 2nd ed., Penguin, Harmondsworth, 1956.

Niebuhr, H. R., *The Social Sources of Denominationalism*, New York, 1929.

Pin, E., 'Hypothèses rélatives a la Désaffection religieuse dans les Classes inférieures', *Social Compass*, vol.IX, no.5-6, 1962.

Pope, L., *Millhands and Preachers*, Yale UP, New Haven, 1942.

Poulat, E., 'Socialisme et anti-cléricalisme', *Archives de Sociologie des Religions*, no.10, juillet-décembre 1960.

Robertson, D., 'The Relationship between Church and Social Class in Scotland', University of Edinburgh Ph.D. thesis, 1966.

Shanahan, W. O., *German Protestants face the Social Question: The Conservative Phase, 1815-1871,* University of Notre Dame Press. Notre Dame, 1954.

Stromberg, R., *Religious Liberalism in Eighteenth Century England*, OUP, London, 1954.

Thomas, K., 'The Double Standard', *Journal of the History of Ideas*, vol.XX, 1959.

Thomas, K., *Religion and the Decline of Magic,* Weidenfeld and Nicolson.

Tomasson, R. F., *Sweden, Prototype of a Modern Society*, Random, New York, 1970.

Vrcan, S., 'Implications of the Religiosity as a Mass Phenomenon in a contemporary Socialist Society', *International Yearbook for the Sociology of Religion*, vol.VII, 1971.

Walker, D. P., *The Decline of Hell*, Routledge, London, 1964.

Walker, W. M., 'Irish Immigrants in Scotland: Their Priests, Politics and Social Life', *Historical Journal*, vol.XV, no.4, December 1972.

III   *Year Books and Works of Reference*
The Official Yearbook of the Church of England
The Catholic Directory
Minutes of the Wesleyan Methodist Conference
Minutes of the Annual Conference of the Primitive Methodist Church
Baptish Handbook
Congregational Year Book
London Statistics
Statistical Abstract for London
General Register Office, *The Classifications of Occupations,* 1966 edition

Index

Districts of London and London churches are classified by boroughs.